W9-DEV-076

Is Tibet Forgotten . . .

Is Tibet Forgotten . . .

We Hope Not

Tibetan Aid Project

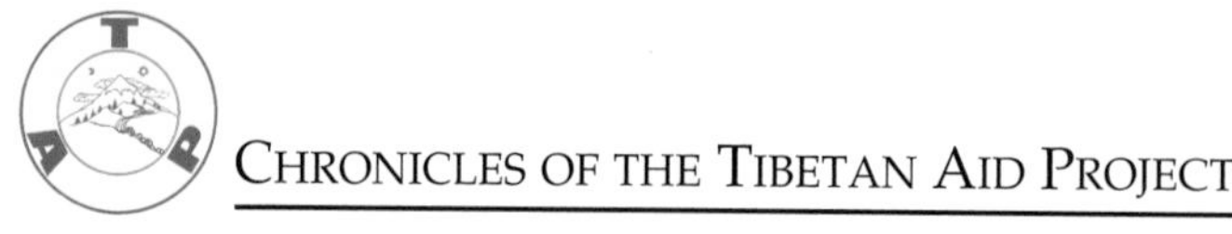

CHRONICLES OF THE TIBETAN AID PROJECT

From the Roof of the World
Your Friends, the Tibetan Refugees
Is Tibet Forgotten

The Tibetan Aid Project is an operation of the Tibetan Nyingma Relief Foundation Tax I.D. #23-743-3901. All contributions are tax-deductible.

Photographic credits: photos on pages 33–41, 299–303, 305 courtesy of Marilyn Silverstone/Magnum Photo Agency. All other photographs are from the archives of the Tibetan Aid Project and/or the Tibetan Nyingma Meditation Center and are used by permission.

Published by Dharma Publishing on behalf of the Tibetan Aid Project. Typeset in Palatino and Avant Garde Gothic. Printed and bound in the United States of America by Dharma Mangalam Press.

ISBN 0-89800-395-4
ISBN 978-0-89800-395-6
Library of Congress Control Number: 2005937300

9 8 7 6 5 4 3 2 1

Dedication

To the lineage of Buddha, Dharma, and Sangha,
and to the land of the Great Arhats.

May the Dharma strengthen;
May the Tibetan refugees flourish;
May the seeds now scattered in the four directions
spread wisdom throughout the world,
transforming the tragedy of Tibet
into a catalyst for peace
and harmony.

Contents

For the past four decades, Tibetan civilization has faced the risk of total destruction, and that remains true today. While monasteries in Tibet are now reopening, and it is no longer dangerous to admit to being a practicing Buddhist, it may be too late. I deeply fear that the vitality of Tibetan culture may have been drained and the spirit of the people broken beyond repair. Whether the tradition of Dharma in Tibet can continue in succeeding generations remains an open question.

For this reason I consider it essential to do what I can to preserve and pass on the Dharma as my own people practiced it. Unless those of us who still remember Tibet as it once existed work to preserve its treasures, the tradition of knowledge that has guided my people for more than a millennium will be lost. Great works of philosophy and spiritual insight, superb guides to meditative realization, profound insights into the nature of reality and the place of human beings in the cosmos: All will disappear from the face of the earth.

Even though I have no special gift or power, I have learned that I cannot let my own lack of skill or qualifications stop me. I have the deep wish to act for the preservation of this knowledge, and that is enough.

—Tarthang Tulku, Founder
Tibetan Aid Project

Thirty-Six Years of Working for Tibet

Through the 1970s and most of the 1980s, TAP focused on the immediate humanitarian needs of Tibetan refugees in India and Nepal. At a time when knowledge of Tibet was still very new in the West, it supported as best it could the efforts of refugee lamas to re-establish their culture in exile and demonstrate the self-reliance, patience, and courage that has always characterized the Tibetan spirit. Incorporated as TNRF, the Tibetan Nyingma Relief Foundation, TAP raised funds to help build monasteries that traditionally served as the heart of Tibetan culture as well as educational and religious centers, then offered support for education and ceremonies. In tandem with the Tibetan Nyingma Meditation Center, it also helped sponsor visits by the leaders of the four major Buddhist schools of Tibet, helping to connect the traditions with the interest in Buddhism that was growing at that time in the West.

Now, forty-six years after Tibetans sought refuge in India, Ladakh, Nepal, and Bhutan, and nearly four decades since they began entering Europe and America, centers for the study and practice of Tibetan Buddhism have been established throughout much of the world. Some of these centers have resident teachers who give lectures and seminars and host the visits of masters who travel among them giving teachings and initiations. Some of them have also established publishing houses that produce books on the Dharma and translations of Tibetan texts.

Inside Tibet, the story is different. Externally, from a tourist perspective, Buddhism would seem to be supported. The major monasteries have undergone cosmetic improvements: the temple and stupas of bSam-yas have been rebuilt, for example, and the soaring Potala and the temples and monuments of Lhasa inspire the visitor with wonder and awe. Restrictions have been eased in some areas, and monks can be seen tending the temples. But from a political viewpoint, little has changed in the past forty-six years. Tibet, long an independent country with its own language and institutions, has seen its traditional government replaced by the Chinese system, and Chinese have moved to Tibet in large numbers. Settling mostly in central and eastern Tibet, they have significantly changed the size and appearance of Tibetan cities. Tibetan houses have been largely replaced by Chinese-style apartments, and Chinese shops and open stalls line widened streets paved for car and truck traffic and illuminated by street lights and traffic signals.

Although the old monasteries outside of Lhasa have been restored to look much the same as before, their peaceful, remote settings are now crisscrossed with dusty roads and obscured by airborne pollution. The landscape bears the scars of heavy vehicles; communication towers rise from the plains and among the hills, and the vistas are not as spacious and uplifting as they were in the recent past. Religious practice has also changed significantly. Monasteries near villages and cities maintain very few of their traditional practices and Dharma studies, although the more remote monasteries may observe them more actively.

While education in Tibet today tends to focus on grammar, poetry, and calligraphy, in the old days, when I was a student about fifteen or sixteen years of age, the monasteries emphasized philosophy, meditation, and devotional practices, and the students had opportunities to develop understanding in the course of long retreats. With little to distract or disturb them, students were free to devote their full time and energy to study and practice. Even the diet was simple—there was not much variety, but no one went hungry. There were religious ceremonies in the monasteries and ceremonies for village families to mark significant events. For family as well as monastic life, it was a healthy system that fostered contentment while serving both practical purposes and spiritual accomplishments. Now it is not the same way.

Fifty to sixty years ago, most Nyingma and Kagyu monasteries had numerous branches. Many of these branches were small retreat huts and caves spread out from the parent monastery in a radius of a hundred miles or so, set in remote places where students could live in relative solitude to engage in the five preliminary practices and be taught individually by great teachers. Unfortunately, those days are almost gone. Now it is necessary to find out what restrictions are in place and what is needed to travel in the more remote places. The sense of reverence and devotion that seemed to permeate the atmosphere and fill the heart with faith is all very different from what it was before.

I have been back to Tibet three times between 1983 and 1993 and have seen for myself the changes that have affected the quality of every aspect of life. The Tibetan people seemed more cheerful in previous decades and had more facilities for practice. Life was more simple and stable, focused on human values that had changed little over the centuries. I lived in Tibet for my first twenty-five years studying, traveling, and working in various parts of the country, so I had the full taste of that experience and am familiar with its quality and flavor. Perhaps other Tibetans have similar memories.

In happier times, Tibetan masters were renowned for spiritual attainments that surpassed the accomplishments of India's greatest yogis, and unusual manifestations bore witness to a lama's spiritual power. There is a saying that the test of a real lama was the same as the test for real gold—you find out the truth when you burn it. This saying refers to the relics that were found in a lama's ashes after cremation—exquisite crystal statues and images, too small and too perfectly formed to have been carved by human hands. I remember seeing, for example, a perfect crystalline image of the eleven-headed, thousand-armed Avalokiteshvara only a quarter of an inch high. It is said that one lama's body was found to be completely impermeated with such relics, which were all that remained from his cremation.

Among the greatest of these yogis were Padmasambhava and his disciples. For eleven hundred years, great masters and healers followed in their footsteps and perfected very powerful practices. There were also scholars such as Blo-gros mTha'-yas, known as Bodong, who devoted his whole life to the Dharma and communicated its meanings in depth. His writings filled a hundred volumes, a truly vast achievement. I hope there are still a few living masters like them, although it is not easy to find them today.

In recent decades, due to the communist takeover of Tibet and the years spent in exile, we have lost many great masters, both inside and outside of Tibet. Inside Tibet, the hardships suffered by Tibetans during the Cultural Revolution fell heaviest on the most venerated lamas, who, like the larger landowners, were perceived as elite and brutally humiliated. While most of them have now passed away, the blessings of their lineages still remain in Tibet, and some lamas are quietly continuing these traditions. Many of the lamas who escaped to India also died, for they were among the oldest of the exiles and more susceptible to diseases unknown in their homeland. A new generation has arisen, largely educated outside of Tibet, and younger ones are just beginning their training.

While the education of young lamas in exile today may not be as completely traditional as it was sixty years ago in Tibet, it is substantial. I believe that it will produce students with similar values and knowledge, good people able to continue the traditions for a while longer. Their paths may be difficult, for the influence of samsara is growing in Tibet as it is also throughout the world. Inside or outside of Tibet, there is less emphasis on a full lifetime of renunciation. As a result, the qualities manifested by Dharma practitioners are changing. There are not as many practitioners as there were in earlier times, and very few of them have obvious results.

The knowledge transmitted through the lineages is urgently needed today, perhaps more than at any other time in the past two thousand years. As the Buddha foretold, the kaliyuga is upon us and is rapidly overshadowing the world. Communism is one of its manifestations, but there are other forces also that are destructive to the spiritual path. Some are overtly anti-Dharma or against all religions in general. The humanities and other subjects related to history and culture may become secondary to science and materialism, which may not value or support religious views and values. Religion may come to be seen as inadequate, not scientific enough to be valued equally with the improvements that science has brought to the physical aspects of our existence.

At the same time, our sense of ourselves is changing: Without a strong grounding in spiritual practice, we are losing sight of what is important to human life. Our choices reflect our confusion; conflicts are increasing globally, and individuals are suffering more as cycles of change come ever more rapidly. Time is speeding up, changing the ways we live, driving our lives, sapping our creativity, and taking away our freedom. Many people now realize we cannot control our time or even our way of life.

In these darkening times, we can take encouragement from the scriptures—the words of the Buddha and the writings of the great masters of the enlightened lineages. In the hands of those who have not forgotten, the scriptures can be brought to life and transmitted even now. This thought has sustained our work for thirty-six years, and it continues to inspire us today.

Working for Tibet in America

Forty-five years ago, circumstances beyond my control separated me from Tibet and brought me to India as a refugee. Thirty-six years ago, my wish to do more for the Dharma and my people led me in turn to America, where I founded the Tibetan Nyingma Meditation Center (TNMC) in 1969 and began the activities that developed into the Tibetan Aid Project (TAP). As the public responded, showing interest in Tibet and in Buddhism, I established the Nyingma Institute in 1973 and incorporated Dharma Publishing and Dharma Press in 1975. That same year we began construction of Odiyan, envisioned as a home for the Dharma and a country retreat center. From 1978 through 1981, I worked with Dharma Publishing and Dharma Press to produce *The Nyingma Edition of the sDe-dge bKa'-'gyur and bsTan-'gyur,* up to then a distant, almost impossible dream, and established the Yeshe De Text Project in 1983 to continue collecting and reproducing sacred texts. The Yeshe De Project has now developed into a major team effort dedicated to printing and distributing Tibetan texts and art. It is supported by Dharmacakra Press and Dharma Mangalam Press, created on the grounds of Ratna Ling, a new community center near Odiyan. From our centers in Berkeley and Odiyan, I have continued to work for Tibet in my own way. Our work has expanded over the years, and the results of our efforts have now reached most parts of the world.

Through TAP and TNMC, with the support of Dharma Publishing, the staff of the Yeshe De Project, and Nyingma Institute students who volunteer to help prepare the books for shipment, we have done what we could to preserve what remains of the scriptures and all that supports their realization. We work to preserve sacred texts, together with the mandalas and sacred art necessary for practices to transform body, speech, and mind, and we raise funds to distribute them free of charge to individual practitioners and to the libraries of monasteries and retreat centers.

Sixteen years ago, I founded the annual World Peace Ceremony at Bodh Gaya, where up to ten thousand practitioners continue to gather to pray for the longevity of the Dharma, for peace and harmony in the world, and for all who suffer from aggression and separation. When these ceremonies began, we started making a few books to distribute to participants. As the need for these texts became more apparent, we increased our efforts to offer larger quantities of books. Over 1.5 million of our books are now in three thousand libraries in India, Tibet, Ladakh, Nepal, Bhutan, and Sikkim. Six to eight thousand copies of each of the fifty or more volumes we produce every year continue to be distributed to monasteries and participants in the ceremony. As of January, 2006, a person attending every ceremony since 1989 will have his own library of 330 different volumes. If these could some day be translated into Western languages, that would be a truly astonishing achievement.

We do the best we can to preserve the Dharma in high-quality books, designed with care and respect, printed with paper and ink that will last a long time. There are countless details that need attention, but my time is limited, and there are no Tibetan scholars here to help with this work. For many tasks I have to rely on my Western students and volunteers who are motivated to work with us for a few months or years. Only a few of them can read Tibetan, and none are truly fluent; they have their own way of understanding Dharma, so directions may be misunderstood or misinterpreted. There are lapses, and mistakes happen, yet they work with an open heart, sensing that there is beauty and blessing in these teachings.

From time to time, when I see signs that this work has strengthened their connection to the Dharma and awakened compassion for Tibet and the Tibetan people, I am encouraged that Western students can receive the Dharma in a meaningful way. So I stay here in America, and we work together. Financially, we have very little, but we have faith, and I trust we will be able to go on.

The Tibetan Aid Project: Origins and Vision

When I first came to America, lamas I knew in India wrote asking for support, and I did my best to connect them with pen friends. As some of my older lama friends may remember, the conditions then were very different from today. There were many details and obstacles involved in getting funds to refugees in remote areas of India, where access to banks was difficult and it was hard to keep up with changing fund transfer procedures. While we did our best to address these issues and bridge the gaps in communication, not all pen friend relationships were successful. The cultural and language differences were great; there were expectations on both sides, and these were not always fulfilled. Still, more than two thousand Western pen friends sustained their support for the refugees during a critical decade of transition, and some relationships blossomed into long-standing friendships. In all, it was an unusual, rewarding, and yet painful experience—the need was so great, and there was only so much we could do.

Now, thirty-six years later, I still treasure the photographs of my friends and all those we sought to help, and publish some of them here to honor their memory. Many have now passed away, and those who remain might not wish to dwell on these sad and difficult times or recall their experiences as refugees. But whether sad or heartwarming, they are part of our history; some good must come of these tragic times, and it seems important that we not forget.

Looking back on these years, I see the connections between Tibetan and Western pen friends as seeds for a deeper understanding that has had far-reaching effects—for the transition of Tibetans into new cultures worldwide, for the transmission of the Dharma to the West, and for the revitalization of the Dharma in traditional Buddhist lands. Understanding has continued to develop, both within our domestic and international Nyingma organizations and also more widely, wherever former pen friends may be active. Some early Western pen friends became TAP's donor base and contributed to our efforts throughout the 1980s and beyond; others became students or volunteered to help as their circumstances permitted. For most, participating in TAP's projects has developed knowledge and respect for Tibetan culture. For some, this connection has led to pilgrimages to Buddhist holy places and awakened a serious interest in Buddhist teachings.

Since 1993, TAP has greatly expanded its circle of supporters, some of whom make great efforts to support projects that now encompass education, ceremonies and retreats, fundraising events, and the shipping of books and art to the annual World Peace Ceremony. TAP has also funded books—including this volume—that document the Tibetan experience and keep alive the memory of Tibet's spiritual vitality and remarkable contributions to the world's treasury of knowledge. TAP's publications are intended both to inform the West and remind Tibetans coming of age in a new environment of their priceless heritage. *Letters of Hope*, a collection of letters from refugees received by TNMC and TAP, was TAP's gift to this new generation. Like this present volume, it is offered with prayers that the experiences of the refugees be not forgotten, but live on as reminders of the value of the Dharma and the human dignity, courage, and beauty that enriches the enduring legacy of Tibet.

Sharing Observations and Experiences

In the first part of this volume, and here and there throughout it, are some of the thoughts that have been accumulating in the back of my mind. Although I cannot lay claim to great spiritual accomplishments, I have been blessed with many opportunities to observe and to learn, first from great masters in Tibet and then through working and living in India and America. Through the compassion of my Gurus, I have had a wide range of teachings and experiences, and in the course of my work I have studied, at least to some degree, several thousand books. I have traveled to many countries and worked with a wide range of people in different walks of life.

Now that I have some knowledge of how things work, it seems time to express what I think, what I've felt, and what I have done. This year, I dictated some of my thoughts to Elizabeth Cook, a long-time TNMC student and Dharma Publishing editor, and worked with her to compile and edit this updated account of our activities on behalf of the Dharma and Tibet. Coming from such a varied background, my thoughts tend to manifest in various ways, some related more to Dharma, and some to samsara; others are grounded in philosophy, and still others express my own opinions and experiences over the past forty years. These comments are not meant to be judgmental or critical of anyone or anything specific, they simply reflect my own observations, a way of thinking things through to clarify my own understanding. I offer them here in the hopes that they may be helpful to others in some way.

Why We Work For Tibet

In contrast to traditional Tibet, our Nyingma organizations in America, Europe, and Brazil cannot rely on a broad base of support, but have to find ways to support their own living expenses. This makes the time available for Dharma work even more precious. Although we continue to build our country center, maintain our educational institute, and publish books in Western languages, we are acutely aware that people have been suffering in Tibet for forty to fifty years, and people everywhere are fearful, pressured by aggression and other powerful negative forces. Whether this karma has its roots in ignorance, the ego of strong individuals, or the polarity of religious dissension, or whether it is an expression of the kaliyuga's apocryphal darkness and turmoil, it is clear that suffering is widespread and there are many obstacles to meritorious action.

Life passes as quickly as one night's dream, and the minds and hearts of individuals are not always cheerful. If we do not appreciate the preciousness of time and use our time well, life tends to lose its meaning. In this light, I do everything I can to support the work of the Tibetan Aid Project by assessing the needs of monasteries in Tibet and India and by sponsoring schools and retreats for Nyingma lamas in Nepal and Tibet. Although faith is hard to explain to people who may not understand, I believe that prayer has great power and devotional practices generate merit. So we sponsor prayers and ceremonies to relieve the negative karma that afflicts our world and offer a hundred thousand butter lamps each day for world harmony and peace, for the longevity of the Dharma, and for a better life for the Tibetan people.

Since 1974, TAP and TNMC have also sponsored ceremonies every year within the Sarma schools—Gelug, Kagyu, and Sakya. In Tibet, every monastery was self-sufficient; each was mindful of its associated branches, but this kind of widespread support was rarely, if ever, offered by one school to another. But in conditions we faced in exile, help was needed to keep all our traditional practices alive. I had faith that the benefits of these practices would reflect widely throughout our communities and beyond, and I am grateful for the opportunity to support all our traditions in this way. Sometimes, I wonder if any other organization has been inspired to do the same thing.

When I first came to America, there were very few lamas in this country, so I invited high lamas of all schools to visit our centers and introduced them to our students and activities. They gave talks and made some videos of their visit, but later, their recollections of these contacts seem to have largely faded from mind. For support in carrying out our projects, and for the results we have accomplished, I thank my Western students and volunteers who stayed with me and persevered. For thirty-six years, funds generated by their efforts have enabled TAP to carry out its mission to help preserve the culture of Tibet. TAP's representatives have led pilgrimages to India and Tibet, stimulating interest in revitalizing sacred sites. TAP is now supporting restoration projects in bSam-yas and other places that still resonate with the blessings of Tibet's spiritual heritage.

While I continue to advise TAP and direct the Yeshe De Text Preservation Project, I am also involved in construction projects and daily activities at Odiyan. Our work is varied and complex. It requires an array of sophisticated skills that take time to develop, and we have to rely mostly on volunteers who require training. Yet most of our volunteers can commit to working for only six months to a year, and they may lack the patience to comprehend why we work as we do or the dedication to move beyond the limits of their self-interest. They have their own interests and motivations, and these sometimes conflict with our needs.

Because we always have at least four or five major projects in progress at the same time, each day brings new challenges. Each individual has his or her own character and personality; some of them are new to our community, and our longer-term workers may not share their knowledge skillfully or provide good examples of caring and leadership. To keep the work flowing smoothly, I need to encourage students and volunteers and deal with their issues and concerns in a friendly way, which is not always easy. At any one time, some of them will be confused or distracted by emotionality or personality conflicts. Directions may seem to be understood, but communication—with me and among themselves—may not be clear and complete. Since their understanding of traditional responsibilities and attitudes is not yet fully developed, mistakes are made that cost time and materials. It seems we are working harder each year, although our results come more slowly than I would like.

Directing all of our projects also involves keeping track of many details and making certain they all come together to meet our goals in a timely way. Since we must minimize expenses, we do not hire professionals or workers outside our community. I rely on our production staff to keep equipment in good repair and participate in monitoring the electrical, plumbing, and watering systems of Odiyan, controlling the vegetation, changing the gardens each season, repairing the fences and irrigation systems, and other such tasks, but these tasks are easily overlooked in the course of meeting production deadlines. As a result, much of my time is spent watching for lapses and reminding our staff to make certain that everything gets done. Since it is hard for one person to oversee everything and keep the work flowing without getting desperate, it might seem to an observer like I'm a watchdog barking all the time. Sometimes, when I think of monasteries blessed with hundreds of students to take care of these kinds of details, I wish there were something they could do to help us out. On the other hand, I am thankful that we have been able to accomplish so much with so few people and such limited resources.

In recent years, I have delegated responsibility to our directors for TAP and some of our other organizations, but I am not certain that their skills and knowledge are necessarily better than mine or that they are dedicated to this work in the same way. I realize that our directors, like many people today, have conflicting obligations that take time and energy, but I beg them to work hard every day and give TAP their best effort. It takes hard work and dedication to sustain TAP's commitment, and TAP has recently increased this commitment by contributing to Yeshe De's book production. I deeply appreciate the effort TAP's staff has made to sustain the shipping of books year after year. Theirs is an outstanding contribution and a welcome support for our efforts on behalf of Tibet. .

I also thank the Yeshe De staff, which has worked intensively on protecting, preserving, and promoting the Tibetan heritage for more than twenty years. Each year, ten to fifteen TNMC students typeset, print, and collate books for shipment and distribution to Tibetans in Asia. Their production spans the range of sacred texts, including Sutras, shastras, Tantra, and the works of the great masters of India and Tibet. They also reproduce valuable collections of sacred art, including rare images essential for continuing traditional Nyingma practices. Still others work full time on printing mantras and assembling them into tens of thousands of prayer wheels.

Traditionally, this work has been done in countries where Buddhism is well-established, by scholars and craftsmen thoroughly trained in its purpose and value. But today the Sanghas of traditional Buddhist lands are focused on their own survival, so our community has come forward to support them in these ways. Having experienced this work from both sides, east and west, for thirty-six years, I am proud of the members of our community who work for Dharma Publishing, TAP, the Nyingma Institute, and the Yeshe De Project.

These thirty-six years have been a long journey. Our work is constant and often difficult; we have had setbacks, mistakes, and disappointments, and we have struggled with personal limitations and shortages of materials. We do not have rich sponsors or support from foundations. Funds usually come to us in small amounts, and only recently have we been able to stabilize TAP's receipts through benefit dinners and pledges from loyal supporters. At the same time, we have done our best to maximize our efforts while minimizing expenses; our staff is supported by other areas of our organization, so donations can be applied responsibly in ways that benefit Tibetans and generate merit for our donors. Our organization is efficient, yet it remains small. It is worthy of the help and good will of all who read this message. With more funding, much more could be accomplished.

From a larger perspective, it is clear that our results are significant, and somehow, all aspects of our work continue to expand. I cannot view these accomplishments as my personal success, for this work is necessary for Buddhism to survive. The texts must be produced and distributed widely so individuals can understand their meanings and the depth and vastness of the knowledge they express. Such a purpose can only succeed with the blessings of Guru Rinpoche and the masters of the enlightened lineage

I come from the land of snows—my motherland, the place where I studied the Dharma and the symbols and images that open the heart to realization, and learned how to create prayer wheels, prayer flags, and other implements of our culture. My masters taught me that life is impermanent and needs to be invested in a worthy cause. Throughout my years in the West, I have drawn strength from their guidance, their examples, and the teachings that prepared me for this work. Remembering their dedication to the Dharma, and their great kindness and compassion, I have always felt that I owe it to them to do something worthwhile.

This work—all that we have had the good fortune to accomplish through TAP, TNMC, Dharma Publishing, the Nyingma Institute, and the Yeshe De Project—is my gesture on behalf of the Tibetan people. I am grateful for this opportunity to share the results of our productivity by giving the books and art we produce to all schools free of charge. I firmly believe that this kind of service has no parallel today. I pray that the Tibetan Aid Project will continue far into the future, and that whoever directs it will carry it further, for the welfare of the Tibetan people, for all that they can offer the Western world, and for the longevity of the Dharma.

Sarvam Mangalam

Tarthang Tulku
Odiyan, September 2005

In Commemoration

According to the teachings of the enlightened Buddha, each individual sets in motion his or her own karma and eventually reaps the rewards of all actions accumulated over time. The principle of cause and effect is said to apply to whole peoples as well; thus kingdoms and cultures are subject to what is called collective karma. From this point of view Tibet, like all nations, is responsible for the rise and fall of its fortunes throughout history.

Spiritually oriented people have always found a way to learn from karma, and the past decades of personal tragedy for myself and so many other Tibetans have brought many lessons in the true meaning of impermanence, the message of the Buddha's First Noble Truth. This realization turns the mind toward the ultimately reliable refuge, our only real home, the way of enlightenment.

After suffering for so many years, we have realized that remaining in the darkness of mourning and clinging to the pain of the past does not lead anywhere. When I saw my mother again for the first time in many decades and asked her about the nightmarish events of the 1960s in Tibet, she told me, "My dear son, it is not worth remembering, it will only spoil your sleep. Better let go of the experiences of the past."

Those of us with faith in the Dharma can contemplate the real cause of all harm as the three poisons of ignorance, hatred, and attachment. Those who bring about harm are not aware that they are intoxicated by these poisons. They may not realize how much grief they have brought to others. Over-confident in their own view, blindly intent on their own ideals, they do not see the falsity of their goals or the consequences of their actions, which eventually will thrust them into realms of unimaginable suffering.

Understanding this lets us defuse the force of resentment and blame so that it cannot possess the heart and prolong unhappiness. By finding ways to use difficult circumstances to strengthen the practice of nonattachment, forgiveness, and compassion, we can contribute to the transformation of the dark emotions that dictate human actions.

—Tarthang Tulku, Introduction, *Letters of Hope*

Part One

Remembering

Chapter One

Foundation of Dharma

According to the teachings of the Buddha, our world has an important role to play in the universe. Here on this earth many enlightened Buddhas have appeared in the past and will continue to appear in the future. In our present kalpa, known as Bhadra, the fortunate aeon, the Buddhas Krakucchanda, Kanakamuni, and Kashyapa have already come and gone. The most recent is the World-Honored One, Shakyamuni, the Buddha of our time, born more than twenty-five centuries ago.

The Sutras relate that the Enlightened One, out of boundless compassion for living beings, descended from Tushita Heaven to take birth as a prince of the Shakya clan and demonstrate the twelve great acts of a Buddha. Born in the garden of Lumbini, the Bodhisattva took seven steps in each of the four directions and announced the intention to put an end to suffering. Seven days later, his mother Maya passed away, and he was raised by his aunt, Prajapati.

The Bodhisattva was known in his youth as Siddhartha, he who accomplishes his purpose, and later as Gautama, after his family's lineage of descent. In his father's palace in Kapilavastu, he lived a life of luxurious ease, his every desire anticipated and instantaneously fulfilled.

At the age of twenty-nine, seeing that wealth, pleasure, and beauty could not conceal the reality that life was limited and afflicted with suffering, the Bodhisattva resolved to discover how

The Yambu Lhakang ('Om-bu bla-khang, built 3rd century B.C.E.), where signs of the Dharma appeared at the time of King lHa-tho-tho-ri.

beings could set themselves free. His search led far beyond the palace gates to the greatest teachers of his time, then to the banks of the Nairañjana River, where he practiced hardships for six years. Having demonstrated that none of these teachings—even the path of the rishis, the powerful sages of ancient India—led to complete and lasting liberation, he made his way to the Bodhi Tree.

Taking his place on the Vajrasana, the unshakable seat of enlightenment, the Bodhisattva vanquished Mara, Lord of Illusion. As the Great Being demonstrated the unparalleled awakening of a Buddha, light radiating from his body streamed through the universe, enabling beings everywhere to conceive the thought of enlightenment. His body manifested the thirty-two major and eighty subsidiary marks of Nirmanakaya, the physical signs of a fully Enlightened One, and he became the Buddha Shakyamuni.

For forty-five years, as the Buddha transmitted the 84,000 aspects of the Dharma, individuals with different orientations understood the view, meditation, and conduct that would liberate them from ignorance, relieving them from the burden of karma and klesha.

At Sarnath and at many places thereafter, Shravakas heard the Buddha's First Turning teachings as directions for drying up the flow of the kleshas that stimulate actions (karma) and sustain samsaric cycles of birth and death, leading to the nirodha of the Arhat. At Vulture Peak, the Bodhisattvas dedicated to the liberation of all beings received the teachings of Prajnaparamita, known as the Second Turning, and at Mt. Malaya, Vaishali, Shravasti, and various other locations, Bodhisattvas rejoiced upon hearing the Tathagathagarbha teachings of the Third Turning. Profound and vast, the Second and Third Turning teachings enable Bodhisattvas to transform the very nature of karma and klesha, cultivate compassion that responds effectively to the sufferings of others, and develop the skillful means that liberate all beings from samsara.

Manifesting in various forms, in Oddiyana, Mount Meru, and in other realms, the Tathagata transmitted the sublime Tantras, teachings that can lead to liberation within a single lifetime.

Gathered in the Vinaya, Sutra, and Abhidharma, the Buddha's teachings supported the development of shila, samadhi, and prajna, the three trainings of moral perfection, meditation, and wisdom. These teachings and practices sustained the Sangha as monks carried the Dharma throughout India and beyond, to Sri Lanka, Myanmar, Kashmir, Central Asia, and China. Monasteries were built and schools established to intensify insight into the teachings. Wherever the Dharma took hold, it awakened the love of knowledge and beauty, nurturing the growth of philosophy, art, and literature.

Centuries of meditation and analysis inspired the rise of four major philosophical schools and a wealth of shastras, treatises that probed the workings of the human mind and the structure of reality. Vajrasana, Nalanda, Vikramashila, and other monasteries developed into major centers of learning, endowed with great treasuries of sacred texts and art. The texts gave access to the direct speech of the Buddha, while the art, encoded with symbols that convey subtle levels of meaning, manifested the inner and outer qualities of the fully Awakened One.

Nalanda, birthplace of Shariputra and renowned for its comprehensive collections of Sutras and Abhidharma teachings, developed into a major educational center, where Mahayana masters sought to unfold the full significance of the view, path, and result of the Buddha's Second and Third Turning teachings. Here the great master Nagarjuna, disciple of Saraha, focused on understanding the Prajnaparamita teachings and explicating the profound view of shunyata. Emphasizing twenty-seven topics and using a fourfold method of analysis, he demonstrated how one avoids the extremes of nihilism and eternalism. Nagarjuna's commentaries, explicated and extended by his disciple Aryadeva, became known as Madhyamaka, the Middle Way. It inspired two major streams of explication: Prasangika, formulated by Buddhapalita and Candrakirti, and Svatantrika, propounded by Bhavaviveka.

A second stream of commentaries was inspired by the Bodhisattva Lord Maitreya, who responded to the prayers of Asanga by transmitting the Abhisamayalamkara, a precious teaching that reveals the architecture of the path to enlightenment embedded within the longer Prajnaparamita Sutras. Asanga also received teachings from Maitreya on the vastness and beauty of Buddha nature, the teachings of Tathagatagarbha, the threefold nature, the graduated path to enlightenment, and other aspects of the Dharma set forth in the Third Turning Sutras. Commentaries on these works by Asanga and his brother Vasubandhu, together with the shastras of masters in their lineage, inspired the streams of Cittamatra, Yogacara, and Vijnanavada. For the inestimable value of their contributions, Nagarjuna and Asanga are known as the Two Great Ornaments of the Mahayana.

Foremost among the many great masters who continued to unfold the Bodhisattva view and path were Candrakirti, proponent of the Prasangika view; the lay scholar Candragomin, explicator of vijnana in the tradition of Asanga; and Shantideva, famed for his compelling presentation of the six perfections and the way to enlightenment. As the streams of Mahayana philosophy branched and flourished, they were supported by the proofs of valid knowledge established by Dignaga and Dharmakirti, India's foremost logicians and masters of pramana, the science of knowledge.

In the eighth century, the great paṇḍita and abbot Shantarakshita received all the major lineages of Mahayana philosophy and logic and merged them in a brilliant synthesis of the traditions of Nagarjuna and Asanga. His work prepared the way for the broad-based philosophical studies that took root and thrived in Tibet.

Chapter Two

Tibet: Land of Dharma

Tibet, aptly known as the Roof of the World, is the highest point on our planet. Framed by the Himalayas, it rises like a great spire radiating the light of awakening. This light has been shining for more than two millenia, first in India and for the past 1,300 years in Tibet.

According to the Mani bKa'-'bum, our culture has been closely connected to the Dharma from its very beginnings when "monkey-like" tribes—most likely aboriginal beings blessed with abundant body hair—were guided to the fully human state by the Great Bodhisattva of Compassion, Avalokiteshvara. The rGyal-rabs-gsal-ba'i-me-long goes on to explain how, inspired by the Great Bodhisattva, these monkey-like beings learned to plant barley, lentils, and wheat. Over the generations, as their diet improved and they cooperated to raise their crops, their behavior and physical appearance gradually changed. As their bodies became less hairy, they began to protect them with leaves and tree bark. As their social interactions became more complex, language developed and customs took form.

In this ancient era ten different groups of nonhumans (mi-ma-yin) held sway over the land, each dominant for a period of time. The nonhumans were eventually supplanted by human tribes who inhabited twelve or more territories known as rgyal-phran, or "little kingdoms." Old records describe four great tribes and six other tribes, and relate that for centuries, power was divided among them. No

Tibet: The land at the Roof of the World.

ruler commanded enough strength or respect to unite the tribes and protect the land. As a result, the people were impoverished and undirected, unable to progress beyond the level of survival.

In the third century B.C.E., a stranger descended from the mountains and was met by a group of Tibetans representing the various tribes who had congregated in that area. According to the ancient Bon-po tradition, he had descended from heaven, while Buddhist traditions hold that he was related to the Shakyas or Licchavis of northern India. Marveling that such a remarkable being had miraculously appeared at this auspicious time and impressed by his noble appearance and bearing, they made him their king and carried him on their shoulders to his new home. Known as gNya'-khri bTsan-po, the "neck-borne king," he became the first king of the

Yarlung dynasty. He and his forty-two successors ruled Tibet for the next twelve centuries.

The last thirteen kings of the dynasty are known as the Happy Generations, for they ruled during the golden age that dawned as the light of the Dharma reached the Land of Snow and great Bodhisattvas took birth as Dharma Kings to guide the transmission of the Lord Buddha's teachings.

Dharma Kings and Bodhisattvas

In the fourth century, lHa-tho Tho-ri (374–494 C.E.), an emanation of the Bodhisattva Samantabhadra, became Tibet's twenty-eighth king. During his reign, a casket containing Buddhist Sutras, dharanis, and mantras and a golden stupa mysteriously appeared at the royal palace. Although no one could read these texts, the king respected their significance. He had them preserved for the future, when their meaning would become known.

During the seventh century, Srong-btsan sGam-po (569–650 C.E.), manifestation of the Bodhisattva Avalokiteshvara and the thirty-third king of Tibet, prepared the foundation for Dharma transmission. Greatly extending the empire founded by his father, he established a new constitution, instituted a code of sixteen moral rules, and built the capital city of Lhasa. To enrich Tibetan culture, he invited scholars and craftsmen from surrounding lands to Tibet. Respected yet feared by his neighbors, Srong-btsan sGam-po was rumored to command a magical army, for no other way could his neighbors account for the king's ability to control a domain that reached into China on the east, north and west across Central Asia, east along the Hindu Kush mountains, and southeast into Nepal and India.

Early in his reign, Srong-btsan sGam-po commissioned his minister Thon-mi Sambhota to create a written language suitable for translating Dharma texts and sent him to India to learn Sanskrit. Upon his return, Thon-mi prepared the first Tibetan grammar. The king translated the first Dharma text into Tibetan and composed the Mani bKa'-'bum, a work instructing how to comprehend the Dharma together with historical and cultural narratives.

Through marriage alliances with Khri-btsun, daughter of Amshuvarman, king of Nepal, and Kong-jo, princess of T'ang dynasty China, Srong-bstan sGam-po connected Tibet with two strongly Buddhist cultures. Each of his queens brought a priceless rupa (image) of the Buddha that embodied the blessings of the Enlightened One and ensured the success of the Dharma in Tibet. From Nepal, Khri-btsun, a manifestation of Green Tara, brought the Jo-bo chung-ba, the image of Mi-bskyod rDo-rje (Akshobhyavajra) carved at Bodh Gaya in India, and from China Kong-jo, an emanation of White Tara, carried the Jo-bo Rinpoche. Presented to a Chinese emperor centuries earlier by an Indian king, the Jo-bo Rinpoche had been created in Magadha by the artist Vishvakarman and was said to have been blessed by the Buddha himself.

Before temples could be built to enshrine these images, it was necessary to pacify the land. For this purpose Srong-bstan sGam-po erected fourteen temples in places Kong-jo identified through divination. Then Khri-btsun built the temple of Ra-sa-'phrul-snang to house the Jo-bo-chung-ba and Kong-jo erected the temple of Ra-mo-che for the Jo-bo-chen-po. After the king died, the Jo-bo-chung-ba was moved to the Ra-mo-che temple and the Jo-bo-chen-po was placed in the gTsug-lag-khang.

Early in the next century, Khri-lde-gTsug-btsan, also known as Meg-ag-tsoms, became Tibet's thirty-seventh king. Supported by his Chinese wife Kim-sheng, he invited Buddhist monks from Khotan and built seven monasteries for monks arriving from other regions of Central Asia. He then sent envoys to India and China to collect texts and dispatched a messenger to invite the great masters Buddhaguhya and Buddhashanti to Tibet. Although they remained

Mountain cave retreat in the Yamalung region, Central Tibet.

at their hermitage on Mount Kailasha, they prepared written teachings on Sutra, Kriyayoga, and Upayoga that the messengers delivered to the king. But when smallpox broke out, the king's ministers of state blamed the disease on the activities of the Buddhists; Kimsheng died, and the king was forced to ask the monks to leave Tibet.

Dharma transmission began in earnest during the reign of Meg-ag-tsoms' son, Khri-srong lDe'u-btsan (742–797 C.E.), who became Tibet's thirty-eighth king. Revered as an emanation of Manjushri, Khri-srong lDe'u-btsan invited Shantarakshita, who had been born nine hundred years earlier in fulfillment of his ancient vow to work with the king to establish the Dharma in the Land of Snow. This vow came to full fruition when the king invited Padmasambhava, the Great Guru of Oddiyana, to Tibet to pacify forces opposing

Dharma transmission. When this was accomplished, the king, abbot, and guru—the mkhan-slob-chos-gsum—worked together to build bSam-yas, Tibet's first monastery.

Shantarakshita, the great master who embodied the major streams of the Sutrayana lineages, ordained the first monks in the Vinaya lineage of the Buddha's son Rahula and taught the fundamental doctrines of the Sutrayana. Padmasambhava and the Kashmiri paṇḍita Vimalamitra transmitted the Mantrayana, and the twenty-five disciples of Padmasambhava mastered the tantric teachings and activated them in the land of snows. Among these disciples were King Khri-srong lDe'u-btsan, Pa-sgor Vairotsana, and Ye-shes mTsho-rgyal, each of whom achieved levels of realization equal to their masters.

Translation and Transmission

At bSam-yas, a hundred Tibetan lotsawas, among them Vairotsana, rMa Rin-chen-mchog, sKa-ba dPal-brtsegs, gNubs-chen Sangs-rgyas Ye-shes, and Cog-ro Klu'i rGyal-mtshan, worked with Shantarakshita, Vimalamitra, and a hundred other panditas from India and Kashmir to translate the sacred texts and transmit the Sutrayana and Mantrayana lineages to their disciples. At the beginning of the ninth century, as recorded in the lDan-dkar-ma dkar-chag, translations of nearly five hundred Sutras and shastras had been completed and placed in the royal palace. The Inner Tantras of Maha, Anu, and Ati had also been translated into Tibetan and their lineages solidly rooted in Tibetan soil. Two generations later, King Ral-pa-can (806–836 C.E.), emanation of the Bodhisattva Vajrapani, further consolidated the Dharma in the Land of Snows. He appointed a commission headed by dPal-brtsegs to standardize translation practices and revise the written language used for translating Dharma texts. Under his patronage, Jinamitra, Danashila, Ye-shes sDe, and scores of other Indian paṇḍitas and Tibetan lotsawas vigorously continued the work of translation. This eighth and ninth-century transmission took place during a most fortunate era when the Dharma was at its height in India, so that the full array of the Buddha's teachings was transplanted to Tibet.

At the end of the reign of Ral-pa-can, the Dharma transmission was interrupted for seventy years, but the lineages of the Vinaya were safely transferred to eastern Tibet where they were preserved and transmitted to ten disciples. The lineages of the Mantrayana were protected by gNubs-chen Sangs-rgyas Ye-shes and other members of the White Sangha, who continued to transmit and practice the teachings quietly in remote retreat centers throughout the land. As soon as Buddhist teachings could be openly practiced again, these two unbroken streams of Sutrayana and Mantrayana were reunited in central Tibet, and the Dharma once again flourished.

In this era the Indian master Smritishrijnana made his way from India to Tibet. The Tibetan masters Rin-chen bZang-po, Mar-pa Lo-tsa-ba, and 'Brog-mi Lo-tsa-ba traveled to India, while Dipamkara Atisha arrived from India and blessed Tibet with his presence. Tantras newly obtained from India were translated and teaching lineages established. The lineages of these teachings were called gSar-ma or new traditions, while the lineages brought earlier to Tibet became known as sNga-'gyur rNying-ma, the ancient transmission.

The transmission of the Dharma that flowed into Tibet between the seventh and thirteenth centuries was the most comprehensive in Buddhist history. By the time the teachings of the Buddha declined in their homeland, the land of snows had become a vital home of the Dharma. Schools based on the Eight Great Enlightened Practitioner Lineages were successfully established, time and again producing masters whose accomplishments matched those of the realized ones of India.

With the inspiration of living examples of the Arya Sangha, spiritual practice became the very heart of Tibetan civilization. A deep respect for the Three Jewels pervaded the whole society, orienting the way of life toward peacefulness, generosity, and the development of compassion and wisdom.

A Precious Continuity

When I reflect on the history of Buddhism in Tibet since the building of bSam-yas in the eighth century, I see the history of the lineages unfolding through the writings of such great masters as Rong-zom Mahapandita and Klong-chen-pa; Atisha, Brom-ston, and the masters of the bKa'-gdams tradition; Rin-chen bzang-po and Blo-ldan Shes-rab; 'Khon dKon-mchog-rgyal-po and the five great lords of the Sa-skya family; Mar-pa lo-tsa and Mi-la-res-pa, founders of the bKa'-brgyud tradition, and the great masters of the bKa'-brgyud lineages of 'Brug-pa and sTag-lung-pa.

From the fourteenth century onward, U-rgyan gTer-bdag Gling pa, 'Jigs-med Gling pa, Bu-ston, Dol-po-pa, Bo-dong Rinpoche, Taranatha, Tsong-kha-pa and his disciples, and the Fifth Dalai Lama continued the gSar-ma lineages and established monasteries and schools. Within the Nyingma tradition, the great monasteries of Kah-thog, sMin-gro-gling, rDo-rje brag, dPal-yul, rDzogs-chen, and Zhe-chen each developed between five hundred and a thousand branches that extended the lineage widely in eastern and central Tibet. Although many of these branches were small retreat centers, they were well-suited for the solitude and intensive practices that bring the Mantrayana teachings to fruition. History records that they were very successful for fifty to a hundred years, then experienced different levels of activity as conditions changed.

When I look through the vast collections of Dharma history and literature, this success is not so difficult to understand. Vairotsana alone had an incredible wealth of knowledge and translated hundreds of texts; Mar-pa also was a great master and prolific translator. In more recent times, Klong-chen-pa worked with great energy and devotion to produce profound and beautiful texts. The knowledge transmitted through the masters of the enlightened lineage extended throughout all parts of Tibet and across its borders into China, Mongolia, and Nepal. Now aspects of this knowledge have reached all parts of the world, inspiring practitioners in Europe and the Americas as well.

Some of the Buddhist traditions were more oriented toward the practice of shila and the paramitas, principal teachings of the Bodhisattvayana, but Tibet was a land of great practitioners, and each school can point to its highly accomplished practitioners in both monastic and yogic traditions. The Buddhist teachings are deeply ingrained, not only among monks, but also in the general population. Householders have a deep sense of the importance of their position; they have faith in the Buddhist teachings and an understanding of karma that supports a serious approach to fulfilling their responsibilities. As a result, their lives and work have a quality of goodness. Even in exile, Tibetans still manifest these aspects of our culture.

Although some would claim that Tibet before 1960 was uncivilized and medieval, populated by nomads, Tibet has a beautiful language, an enlightened religion, and a distinguished culture and history. Its extensive artistic and literary traditions are supported by an array of works on the forms of art and its related technologies; architecture; aesthetics and the literary arts; science, a sophisticated medical system, ritual arts, astrology, and geomancy. Tibet sustained highly developed scholastic traditions, and the scholars fully educated within these traditions were truly impressive.

The richness of our ancient traditions could match those in any land. Even people in the most technologically advanced nations of the world know that Tibetans have good hearts and heads, not necessarily in the Western-style sense of scientific accomplishment, but in the fully human meaning, genuine, sincere, and kind.

Chapter Three

The Tibet I Remember

The Tibet I remember was a beautiful land, not a frozen and barren desert as it is sometimes depicted, but a land of majestic snow mountains and valleys green with grass and willows that merge into the jungles of southeastern Tibet. Much of Tibet is about 15,000 feet above sea level, with rivers flowing through valleys defined by mountains and hills. In the valleys of the east, snow lasts only four months of the year. As the snow melts, flowers carpet the valley floors, painting the landscape with delicate yet vibrant colors, and clear streams sustain the animals that range freely over the meadows. The land always seemed fresh and the air vibrant with energy, which made travel an interesting and revitalizing experience. People generally traveled on horseback, in a group of ten to twenty, and everywhere you looked you could see empty space with huge expansive vistas. Having traveled widely in central and eastern Tibet, I became very familiar with Tibet's mountains and valleys and their seasonal changes.

Tibet has a special environment, not in the exaggerated sense that Westerners associate with myths of Shangri-la, but in the significant and interesting atmosphere of some of its remote and sparsely populated valleys, permeated with a sense of dynamic presence. Since monasteries did not allow hunting or fishing in their environs, in valley after valley wild animals roamed freely, without fear of harm by human beings.

Bang-so dmar-po, the tomb of King Srong-btsan sGam-po located in the Yar-lung valley, is the most sacred of the 26 burial mounds in this area. *(2005)*

Having had the opportunity to travel in Kham, Amdo, and central Tibet, I know much of Tibet's geography, including its valleys and vegetation. Because the land of Tibet is so rugged, it is easy to imagine that life there is full of great physical hardship, making each day a struggle to survive, but this is not so. The people of Tibet love their land deeply and consider it the most beautiful place on earth. Although winters in most of Tibet were long and severe, life in the sheltered river valleys offered all the basic necessities. In some areas there was an abundance of fruits such as apricots, peaches, pears, small apples, raspberries and walnuts, and almost every area had its own regional delicacies.

With no sources of pollution, the air was fragrant and clear. A multitude of stars shone brilliantly in the thin and clear night air;

the plants exuded fragrances unknown elsewhere, giving the flowing wind a nourishing quality that one could almost taste. Deeply healing, these elements effortlessly dissipated whatever agitation might arise in the mind, supporting a sense of lightness and joy. Meditation came naturally; thoughts were easy to direct and the senses were softer and more relaxed, more inwardly communicative with mind.

Perhaps because there was very little agitation to disturb the mind, Tibetans, especially monks and nuns, tended to have a natural bright, outgoing quality, and the great lamas I knew were extraordinarily cheerful and light-hearted. In the West we call that happiness, but in Tibet I simply thought it was normal. I now know that there are not many people in the West that enjoy that sense of joyful contentment.

Memories of Tibet

My family lived in a country in the eastern part of Great Tibet known as 'Gu-log, which, according to the genealogies of the legendary spirits, was continuously governed by its own rulers descended from those spirits. We lived near the Yellow River, where many cranes came to nest each summer, and I remember the swans, some yellow and some white, that made beautiful sounds as they flew over the river. My home region, like certain other parts of Tibet, had lakes that varied in hue from yellow to blue or reddish, taking their color from the rocks in and around them.

From childhood, I remember the summertime as especially beautiful, with birds and little animals everywhere. Although fish were plentiful, and spring floods would leave more fish stranded on the banks of the river than the birds could eat, the people of our village would not take them. In our village, calling someone a fish-eater was a teasing or possibly insulting act, for they, like most Tibetans, did not eat fish, pork, or chicken.

The staple foods for all Tibetans were barley and tsampa made from barley flour, supplemented by some kinds of vegetables when these were available. Since barley grows at a high altitude, it is very nutritious and tasty when roasted, ground, and mixed with yak butter. Tibet had many sheep and yaks, so dairy products and meat were plentiful. The milk of yaks is thick with cream and can be churned easily; after it is boiled, the rich reddish crust that forms on its top can support the weight of small rocks. The thick cream below the crust is used to make yogurt and cheese, all of which are abundant, especially in summer.

Villagers use different kinds of flour to make noodle soup in the evenings; they also make a very thick cake with butter and small yams. Small but very sweet and nutritious, Tibetan yams grow naturally without special cultivation, and huge quantities of them can be easily collected from the fields.

Villagers in eastern Tibet would sometimes travel to China or to other places to obtain various supplies, but basically they lived very simply, conserving resources. The whole lifestyle was simple, with few dishes to wash or household articles to clean. The air was cool and dry, and the fields were very large. Any garbage generated was eaten by the birds or dogs, and waste disposal was simple and naturally sanitary. There was rarely any kind of litter, not even the paper that one sees everywhere in the West. Paper was precious, as was ink. Both were developed in Tibet centuries ago in order to print sacred texts. We used it all, so there was no waste.

The Tibetan Way of Life

Some of the village people were quite wealthy, having as many as 50,000 sheep and 500 yaks. Wool and animal products made in the villages were traded widely and were a major support for Tibet's largely barter economy. Renown for its quality, Tibetan wool was often woven into beautiful yet durable thin cloth, pressed into felt or tightly woven into robes that were very strong and water-resistant, such as the outer robes worn by lamas. Meat was made into many different kinds of sausages and dried for jerky, much of which was given to the monasteries. Tibetan houses were simply furnished. Fire for heating and cooking was fueled by willow-wood and dried yak dung, so it was virtually smoke-free.

Householders lived simple lives, caring for their families, tending their land and their animals, and observing marriages, anniversaries, and other traditional rituals of lay life. The people were simple in a way; they had little education but they were very respectful of the monks and lamas, many of whom were their sons or other members of their family. They supported the monks with offerings and essential supplies such as tea, butter, tsampa, and meat, a simple diet but very delicious when one is accustomed to it. Lamas who lived in the villages served lay families as healers and took care of their medical and spiritual needs, while monks who lived in the monasteries went out to the villages each year, performing marriage, anniversary, and funeral ceremonies and receiving alms in the form of food and supplies sufficient to last for a year.

I have memories of beautiful monasteries, retreat places, and celebrations in mountains, when people would dress up and travel to different mountain sites for holiday-like celebrations. Sometimes villages sponsored ceremonies that lasted five to ten days, inviting lamas to carry out the rituals. This kind of support relieved the monks from many tasks related to basic survival, allowing them more time to devote to their practice.

Each village carried on its own traditions. Members of the community took care of each other, cooperating and sharing good times and misfortunes in a true community spirit, and supporting one another in times of need. An entire village would often mourn for a whole year as a gesture of respect for one family's loss. Every

Tibetan respects the traditions of his or her community and participates fully in all aspects of its life.

Monasteries, Heart of Tibetan Culture

Tibetans have always supported men and women who chose to follow a religious path, whether they adhere to the vows of the monk or nun or become householders or wandering yogins. They respect all who dedicate themselves to the Buddhadharma without discriminating among members of various schools. When lamas and monks passed through a village on a pilgrimage to seek teachings or visit a sacred shrine, the villagers would greet them warmly and offer them food and shelter. At times, ten or fifteen lamas might gather together in this way and lead a hundred or so villagers in reciting prayers and performing ceremonies.

Materially, the Tibetan way of life was simple, but intellectually, it was rich and strong, maintained and upheld by highly educated lamas and scholars. The monasteries were the major centers of cultural transmission, training centers for the lineages of wise masters and the arts and sciences of Tibet.

In my youth, there were over six thousand monasteries and nunneries in Tibet, with many smaller retreat centers for sustained meditation practice. Each area, from Kham and Golok in the east to U and Tsang in the center, and to Ladakh in the west, had its own dialect, style, customs, rituals, and politics. The four major schools of Tibetan Buddhism are found in various strengths in these different areas. Kham had large monasteries that belonged to all schools—Nyingma, Sakya, and Kagyu, as well as some Gelugpa monasteries. The region south of Kham, in Khyerlo, around Litang, was predominantly Gelugpa, while Gyarong and Golog were mostly Nyingma. The region around Lhasa, while predominantly Gelugpa, also had a number of small Nyingma monasteries, including some historically important retreat centers that date from the seventh through ninth centuries.

Each monastery had a unique character, with its own special deities and Dharmapalas. The monasteries had beautiful offerings—gold and the finest materials from many lands, including brocades from the East, and even Italian cloth—and their temples, rich in art, were truly impressive. Ceremonies were held on the tenth and twenty-fifth of the lunar month, on new and full moon days, and at other times as well, up to fifty to sixty times annually. Some monasteries observed major ceremonies that continued as long as forty days.

Life in the Monasteries

There was always a vibrant dynamic of religious practices and scholastic studies. At any one time, monks might be practicing many different sadhanas along with their associated visualizations and devotional exercises, or participating in the chanting of ten times one hundred million mantras, or taking refuge and performing their preliminary practices. Students trained to be good monks and students by studying Vinaya, Abhidharma, and Madhyamaka. It would take students several years of concentration and discipline to master each text completely. Students prepared for the complex Vajrayana initiations by studying these classical subjects for four to five years, exercising humility and respect and becoming a positive influence within the Sangha.

Monasteries encompassed a wide and diverse range of scholastic and religious functions. Some monasteries became repositories of specific teachings, while larger monasteries became major educational centers with specialized colleges for study of the Sutras, commentaries, and Tantras. Some monasteries focused on philosophy, ritual studies, or the arts of sculpture, painting, ritual arts, calligraphy, or dance, while others were more devoted to meditation.

Among them were centers renowned for the performance of rituals and transmission of advanced practices for the attainment of higher states of consciousness. Following curriculums modeled on the educational programs of Nalanda, Vikramashila, and Odantapuri, the great Buddhist universities of India, major Tibetan monasteries continued to unfold the profound meanings of the Buddha's teaching through philosophical dialectic, logic, and metaphysics, and through practices that penetrated the most subtle obstacles to enlightenment.

Through the centuries, some centers became well known for their specialized studies in grammar, poetry, or medicine. Some prepared boys for becoming lamas, while others, especially in Lhasa, prepared future householders and laypersons for secular life. This diversity makes it difficult to generalize about Tibetan Buddhism, the specific emphases of each tradition, and the richness of the cultural traditions preserved in the monastic centers. To gain an accurate overview of how they operate, one would have to travel to a number of different monasteries in each of the traditions and observe them first-hand.

In the small monasteries, monks did not talk much, but focused on study or practice, or gathered for rituals. Some teachers were very strict, and their students may have had a more difficult time, but otherwise life was naturally light, in contrast to the heavy quality I have often noticed in the West. The monastic way of life was generally simple and easy. One lama could live four to five months on one bag of tsampa, and tea was always available. Lamas owned two or three bowls, and there were few pots and pans to clean.

In the monasteries, as in the villages, we had to prepare for winter mindfully and store up food in advance for both people and animals. Some places were so cold in winter that even when wearing warm clothing, travelers could freeze their faces and feet. I have seen their faces so frozen that they had moustaches of ice, and their skin so tight and drawn up that they appeared to be laughing.

In other respects, winter was a tranquil time—a time to enjoy being quiet and alone. There were fewer people, so there were fewer interactions and less potential for confusion. There was some aggression from time to time, or an occasional anxiety or upset, but we did not have the same kind of worries that plague so many in the West. Our livelihood was simple, and we did not have big expectations. With little to do outside of food preparation, life could seem like an ongoing retreat. Undisturbed by noise or pollution, mind could become crystal clear.

A Culture Lost?

For twenty-five years I lived in this blessed Dharma realm, studying and practicing in my own limited way, trying to take the best advantage of an extraordinary opportunity. My Dharma education commenced with my parents whose deeply religious orientation permeated my childhood. It continued with formal studies at renowned monasteries. There I met the rarest of masters, whose qualities were impossible to comprehend with the ordinary mind.

Then in the late 1950s the dark winds of destruction swept over my homeland with hurricane force, severely damaging the civilization of the Roof of the World. My personal destiny played out so that I became one of those fortunate to escape. But I also count myself unfortunate for I was not able to remain with my dearest teachers, friends, and family, and share their experiences.

For those of us who became refugees, those times in Tibet are past, and our lives have radically changed. We suffered on the long and dangerous journey to India and adapted slowly to an environment that was nearly the opposite of what we knew in Tibet—many people, speaking many different languages, with different customs, food, and ways of interacting. The past and all we knew and loved was closed to us, while the future seemed completely uncertain.

Over the next ten years, our heads became crowded, almost numb, with many more stimulations and pressures, and we began to lose touch with the tranquil spirit of Tibet. Having no place of our own, all we could do was try to preserve what we cherished in our hearts and minds, doing our best to keep alive the light of our civilization and share it with whomever might be interested.

Have we forgotten Tibet? While the Tibetan people continue to respect their religious and cultural traditions, and the monasteries and educated lamas who exemplify and maintain them, the culture itself is suffering greatly. The traditional elements unique to our way of life are more difficult to find today. There is a sense of loss, not only in my experience, but also for other Tibetans who have established themselves in Europe and India and elsewhere. They may have difficulty remembering that special sense of being alive that growing up in Tibet imprints on body, senses, and mind.

Now when I return to Tibet from time to time, I can see the differences reflected in all elements of the environment—in the water, air, sky, mountains, the simple life, and nourishing food. I am again reminded that the simple food I enjoyed at home and in the monasteries was more satisfying than the offerings of the finest restaurants I have known since in my travels in Europe, Asia, and America. In every way, from the simplest, most common aspects of daily life to the feel of the elements and the sense of time and space, Tibet and the West are as different as night and day.

Chapter Four

Opening the Eye of Dharma

Since the time of the Buddha, enlightened masters have demonstrated the power of the Dharma to open mind and senses to truth that underlies the physical realm of appearances. Tibetans have long respected the benefits of "seeing with Dharma eyes," and have made great sacrifices to obtain and protect that knowledge, embodied today by holders of the eight great lineages of transmission. For centuries, the Dharma shaped the culture of Tibet, and the culture of Tibet in turn held open doors to the Dharma. Now the Dharma has faded in Tibet, and the culture and environment that sustained it has been seriously disrupted. Access to the blessings of the Dharma now rests with the lineages in exile, with those masters who have the knowledge and the skillful means to open the eyes of others to the enlightened view. If the gates to enlightenment are to remain open, it is essential that the lineages continue, and that there be students willing and able to receive their teachings.

This is especially critical within the Nyingma tradition, where transmission depends upon the ability of the teacher and the receptivity of the student. Nyingma texts do not present knowledge in the classical way, but use a symbolic language rich in technical terms to point out subtleties essential for developing the enlightened view. A hundred or more of these terms may be unique to Nyingma and unfamiliar to practitioners of the Sarma traditions. The meanings of these terms are not accessible through concepts alone, but must be realized experientially through meditation.

To understand what insights these terms express, practitioners learn the theory and study the concepts intellectually, then deepen their understanding through meditation. Over time, meditation transforms the practitioner's view, giving access to the deeper currents of mind and illuminating the profound and subtle meanings of such familiar Dharma terms as carya, phala, bhumi, and marga. Seen from within this experiential perspective, scriptural terms convey meanings that transcend conceptual understanding.

The Lineages: Keys to Understanding

Scripture is a map to realization, but meditation is necessary to understand how this map operates on the deeper levels of consciousness. A master who has attained this comprehensive understanding can accurately transmit Dharma knowledge, but Western students face specific obstacles in benefiting from a master's guidance. However they might wish to extend their knowledge, by themselves, they lack access to the subtleties of the symbolic language used in the root texts. Their education does not prepare them for understanding the limitations of dualistic concepts, and they may not find a teacher who can provide the proper instructions for transcending them. If students cannot free their minds from a dualistic orientation, how can they comprehend the significance of terms such as Dharmadhatu or prajna, or understand what is meant by enlightenment?

While it is possible to describe advanced practices on the conceptual level, concepts alone cannot give access to paramartha (ultimate truth). No matter how far we extend the ladder of concepts, it will never reach all the way to the ultimate meaning of such terms as prajnaparamita. Students need a better way to bridge the gap between concepts accessible to the rational mind and knowledge that is realized through direct experience. The gap between the conceptual level and paramartha may be much shorter than it appears, for in the universal embrace of the Triple Gem, they are seamlessly interconnected. What allows us to cross over from one to the other is the shift in view made possible through upaya, the application of skillful means.

Students may not realize how closely prajna is intertwined with upaya, or appreciate that upaya is essential to transcending the limitations of conceptual thought and attaining the enlightened view. Qualified masters can explain this interconnection to students who sincerely wish to understand, but qualified masters are not easy to find and conditions for realization are not as favorable now as they were in the past. Even if such a master can be found, the question becomes, can the student develop the attitudes and openness that ensure a successful outcome? How does the student learn to appreciate the lineage and respect the teachings? Western educational systems do not develop the kind of mutual trust and respect necessary for a student to benefit from the guidance of a spiritual teacher.

Since the foundation for Dharma studies is not well established in the West, students tend to read Buddhist texts without understanding where each kind of teaching fits into the enormous body of Dharma teachings. But attempting to understand the Dharma without an overview of its historical and philosophical development is much like trying to assemble a thousand-piece jigsaw puzzle without reference to the finished picture. Mixing different traditions, styles, and levels of the teachings, unaware of how the traditions and schools developed in different times and places, they may find Buddhist concepts interesting, but be confused by teachings that appear contradictory. When students follow their own interest, learning about the Dharma through the filters of their individual psychology and assumptions, their understanding is likely to be fragmented and the picture they assemble may not be coherent. If so, it is not likely that they will advance toward liberation, and what they do learn may not be helpful to others.

Western students also encounter more subtle obstacles. The Western mind is trained to be skeptical, to challenge knowledge and come to conclusions based on its own individual way of reasoning. Such a mind does not necessarily believe that the scriptures are the authentic words of the Buddha, or that the teachings as they have been traditionally transmitted are relevant to Westerners in the same way. Influenced by their own notions and logic, Western students are quick to come to their own conclusions and interpret the Dharma in a way that sounds good to them. Convinced by their own thoughts and feelings, they tend to adopt styles of expression that feel more familiar and 'right,' or perhaps seem more interesting and dynamic than traditional approaches. From this perspective, central Dharma teachings—such as the ten bhumis, the five paths, the importance of discerning clearly between positive and negative, and understanding the relationship between cause and effect—may no longer seem essential or even relevant to their situation.

Intellectualizing the Dharma and allowing the skeptical mind full sway tends to strip out the subtle pointers to enlightenment embedded within the teachings. Those who take this approach can only communicate what their minds can understand on the conceptual level and what accords with their own emotions and rational sensibilities. Although this approach creates confusion that obscures the way to liberation, it is familiar and widely accepted in the West. When the Dharma is taught in this way, and the student in turn applies this approach and passes it on, confusion solidifies with each cycle, effectively sealing off access to the Dharma.

There are different approaches that express truth more directly and protect the power of the Dharma to lead to enlightenment. The Buddhist traditions have systematic programs of study that develop clear understanding and open doors to transformation. The Theravadin way focuses on the path of the Arhat, who attains nirodha (cessation) by completely burning out the roots of karma and klesha, eliminating all possibilities of return to samsara. The Mahayana, the way of the Bodhisattva, goes further. The Bodhisattva's purpose is not to retire permanently from samsara, but to become enlightened for the benefit of others. The difference between the Hinayana and Mahayana way of understanding the goal of the spiritual path is explained in detail in the Lankavatara and Saddharmapundarika Sutras.

In my experience, Western students tend to lack a genuine sincerity of purpose that would encourage them to prepare themselves properly and demonstrate respect for the Dharma and the lineage. Their motivations seem more rooted in curiosity than inspired by the teachings; they just want to know what Buddhism is about, and they feel that this is a good enough reason to seek out a teacher. But curiosity is a worldly attitude oriented to the self and its interests. dPal-sprul Rinpoche compares such students to hunters who stalk a deer to get its musk. Attitudes based on self-discipline and respect for the value of the Dharma are more likely to lead to knowledge.

The Dharma has much to offer us today. Approached with a willing heart and an open mind, the teachings are so relevant to our lives that they seem to be speaking to us directly, and their truths are humbling in their purity and compassion. They show us how to become more confident, how to develop positive attitudes, how to go beyond our problems and understand them, how to treat emotions nicely so they will not lead us into the hell realms, where misery builds upon misery.

Although problems and frustrations could stimulate us to develop more positive attitudes, it is very difficult to benefit from these experiences. Confusion accumulates and produces ignorance; ignorance invites the kleshas, emotionality that torments body and mind and produce suffering for ourselves and others. Once this kind of suffering takes hold, we cannot stop it—mind clings to it and will not let it go. The memories live like shadows in our mind, ready at any moment to re-awaken painful thoughts and feelings. In this way, mind becomes the generator of more suffering; it manufactures its own karma and keeps us bound to samsara. As long as our minds are enmeshed in samsara, there is no way out.

Seeing with Dharma Eyes

If we can see with Dharma eyes, we can learn how to free our minds from emotional turmoil and end these cycles of negativity. The way lies through devotion, contemplation, prayer, and ritual, supported by analysis that points out the arrogance of mind and the scriptures that inspire us to correct it. Teachings such as Prajnaparamita reveal that our problems arise from ignorance rooted in an incorrect view of self (svabhava). They also provide the antidote: knowledge of nihsvabhava (no svabhava), prajna, and shunyata. When the meanings of these terms are thoroughly understood, we can transcend pride and ego and deprive the kleshas of their power.

To develop this depth of knowledge, we begin on the conceptual level, using the tools of language to analyze and reflect on the meanings of essential terms. Then we need to go further, bringing the meaning of these concepts alive through contemplation, prayer, and visualization until they merge with the whole of our being and activate enlightened understanding. A teacher who has this kind of experience can guide students from the conceptual level to the awakened level of shunyata. If the student studies well, respecting the Dharma, the guide, and the lineage, results will come. Once students experience this process, they will never again doubt the true value of the Dharma.

Prajna refers to the wisdom that transcends conceptual understanding, while upaya is the skillful means that free us from the limitations of ordinary understanding. Activated by karuna (Bodhisattva compassion), upaya leads us step by step to the highest understanding of shunyata, and shunyata opens the Dharma eye of prajna parampara, wisdom completely gone beyond—beyond self, beyond concepts, beyond even the thought of enlightenment. As the great master Nagarjuna explains, prajna (wisdom) and upaya (skillful means) are two separate concepts, but when they are activated through realization, they become inseparable, just as sweet is inseparable from sweetness, and water is inseparable from wetness. When one attains that level of understanding, the ordinary conceptual way of thinking and analyzing merges into the all-pervasive view, where prajna and upaya, karuna and shunyata are ultimately inseparable.

Ordinary concepts cannot contain the true meaning of prajna and karuna, wisdom and compassion. Neither can words convey the power of the Bodhisattva's practice and the beauty of the Bodhisattva's realization. Beyond all the words and expressions, beyond all the blessings, beyond all the discipline, meanings, and transformation, theirs is the ultimate realization, the only universal and irrevocable truth. I wish all students could be inspired by their example to have faith in the Dharma and confidence in their ability to follow the path to enlightenment.

The Dharma clarifies how illusion becomes our identity and how this identity—this self-orientation—becomes our reality. The self-orientation carries over from perception to perception, from thought to thought, sustaining a sense of continuity and maintaining the illusion that things are the way that they appear to be. To be free, we need to question, investigate respectfully and humbly, penetrating deeper and deeper into the meanings until a higher wisdom shines through and we see how we get caught in this illusion. Then we can wake up and see with Dharma eyes. We can practice karuna and upaya, compassion and skillful means, and embody them through knowledge, so that they become one with our being. Once we touch this level of knowledge, we will have no wish to return to samsara.

On a relative level, samsara is rife with misery and disappointment, and nirvana is far away. But ultimately, from the perspective of awakened understanding, nirvana is not so distant, and samsara is a repository of treasures, the essential catalyst for awakening, the source of the frustration and discontent that motivates us to turn to the Dharma. Knowing samsara, seeing clearly the true nature of suffering, we realize that the Dharma is truly our precious opportunity: the way to be truly human, the way to be truly free.

Opportunity for Awakening

The joy of awakening could be much closer than we might realize. In Nyingma there is a saying, if you practice in the morning, you could become enlightened in the evening; if you practice in the evening, you could be enlightened in the nighttime. So great are the Buddhas, so powerful is the Dharma, and so strong is the lineage, that each time we practice with devotion and faith, we may be blessed with deeper understanding.

We are fortunate that the Buddha demonstrated the way to enlightenment, that he turned the Wheel of the Dharma, and that his teachings are available to us today. We are fortunate that the Buddha's blessings remain with us, that there is still truth we can pursue, and that we can live and work within the Dharma. When we open our eyes to the sufferings of others caught up in less fortunate circumstances, we may realize how blessed we are and how great are the opportunities to do something positive. Here, in the midst of samsara's confusion, frustration, and pain, the light of the Dharma still shines, keeping open the possibility for enlightenment.

Thus we are offered a great opportunity to free ourselves from karma and klesha and all that separates us from the bliss of enlightenment. The opportunity to liberate our minds from loneliness and frustration, and from all that feeds discontent and creates pain for ourselves and others is within our reach—we have only to awaken faith in the Buddha, Dharma, and Sangha. Where there is faith, there is also love that transcends self-concern and connects us with all beings. Love empowered by faith warms the heart and inspires action that benefits others.

Even when we lack perfect understanding of prajna or karuna, we can do our best to dedicate our hearts and heads to the Dharma. We can have confidence, and rely on our own understanding to lead us closer to truth. As the light of discriminating awareness develops, it will become more clear what has lasting value and what does not, and it will be easier to sustain faith and loyalty to the Dharma. Faith and loyalty empower dedication, and dedication leads to knowledge that finds expression in the actions of body, speech, and mind. Realized and manifested through enlightened action, Dharma knowledge may become unassailable, a way of being that could become humanity's greatest treasure. We need this knowledge to guide our human destiny.

As long as the scriptures remain and the enlightened lineages continue, we have a precious opportunity to engage a new vision of human freedom and manifest its blessings—a mind free of desire and grasping, free of attachment, frustration, and discontent. In liberating the mind, we liberate the whole of our being. Life becomes meaningful, a field of beauty, open to manifold possibilities.

Part Two

Regenerating

CHAPTER FIVE

To Preserve a Tradition

The Tibetan Aid Project grew out of my experience as a refugee and my wish to help ease the sufferings of my people, who had been uprooted from all that sustained their identity and livelihood. When I and so many other Tibetans arrived in India more than forty years ago, we lacked even the rudiments for survival in a land so very different from our own, where we did not know the language or the culture. Estimates vary, but there may have been about sixty thousand refugees in all who arrived in Nepal and India in 1959. Of these, there were little more than seven thousand monks and only a few hundred tulkus to sustain the entire range of Tibetan Buddhist schools and lineages in India. In the years that followed, Tibetans continued to make their way over the dangerous mountain passes. Although many died or were turned back before reaching the border, the number of refugees eventually increased to a hundred thousand or more.

Many of the older lamas had suffered greatly from their journey over the Himalayas, and the Indian heat and humidity gave them no respite. The Indian diet—what food the refugees were able to obtain—did not agree well with Tibetans already weakened from their difficult transition from the cool clear air of the northern plateau, 11,000 feet above sea level, to the heat and humidity of near sea-level India. Lack of water in many of the early refugee camps compounded the problems by inhibiting agriculture, limiting the diet to mostly lentils and rice. Before long, many refugees were ill or dying,

The golden temple of bSam-yas monastery was established in the eighth century C.E. Destroyed during the Cultural Revolution, it has been rebuilt.

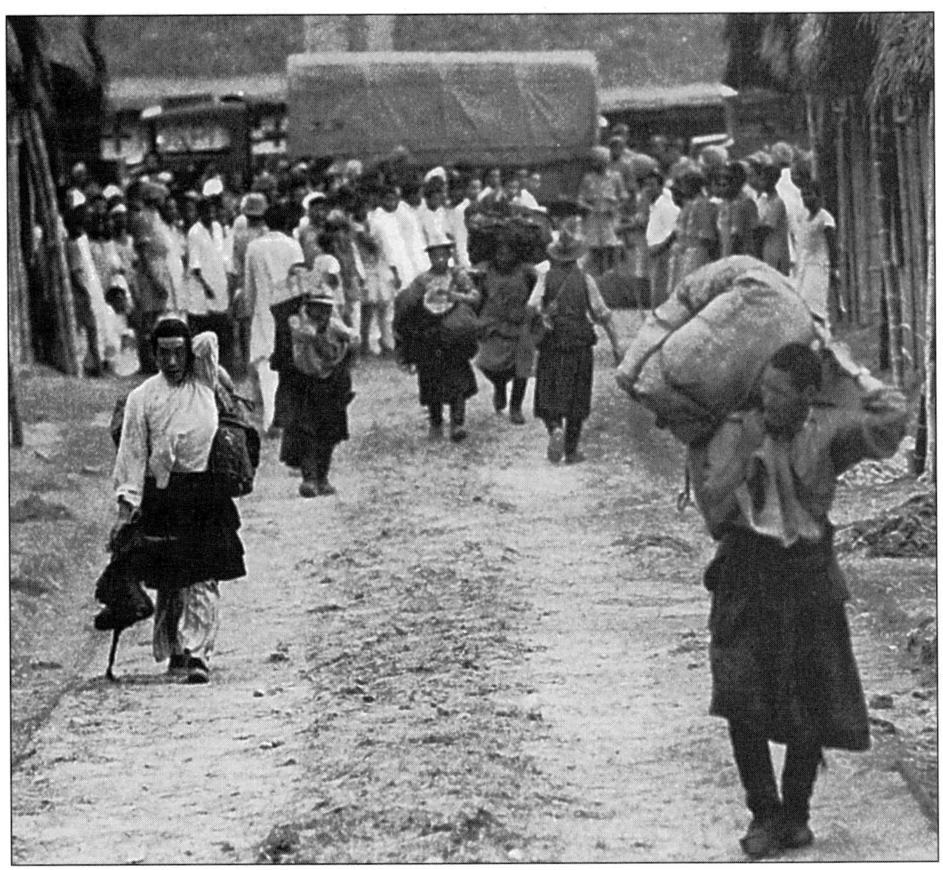

Watched by curious villagers, refugees arrive in Missamari, near Tezpur, one of two refugee camps established in the spring of 1959.

unable to adjust to India's radically different environment and living conditions, and vulnerable to serious diseases for which they had no immunity.

Even worse was the anguish of separation from families, parents, friends, teachers, and monasteries. Even those who were well-educated, good people, from stable homes and monastic situations suffered tremendous emotional and psychological trauma. Tibetans had long regarded the Chinese as allies, but now that situation had radically changed, and no one knew what to expect. What would happen now under Chinese domination? Would Tibet's culture and civilization survive? Would the Tibetan language continue? And if not, would the future of the Dharma traditions rest with a few thousand refugee lamas and monks? Physically, psychologically, emo-

Exhausted from crossing the Himalayas, refugees make their way through the subtropical forests of northern India toward an uncertain future.

tionally, and spiritually, conditions were difficult beyond belief. There were no Buddhist temples in which to pray and no monasteries where we could come together for practice and mutual support. The sense of isolation was enervating. Days and nights merged into a long nightmare that left many of us paralyzed for months. Hundreds—lamas, monks, nuns, and laypersons, perhaps one out of every ten refugees—died within the first few years.

From time to time, when I think of those times, I recall that most of my fellow refugees were strong and healthy men in the early thirties, and it comes as a sad surprise to realize that there are now very few of them left alive. Even after all these years, these events still call forth strong reflections. The tragic feeling we felt then is a bond that still shadows our lives.

The refugees crossed the Himalayas mostly on foot; some had mules or horses to carry them or their few belongings. Above, those who cannot walk further are transported to the settlement camps in wagons.

Top: Refugees find their way amongst the hastily-constructed bamboo shacks of Missamari that will be their home in exile. Below, many lie down at the first opportunity, too ill, confused, or exhausted to take the next step.

Young and old, monk and laypersons, Khampa ladies from Eastern Tibet—all share alike in the disruptions of lives uprooted from all that is familiar.

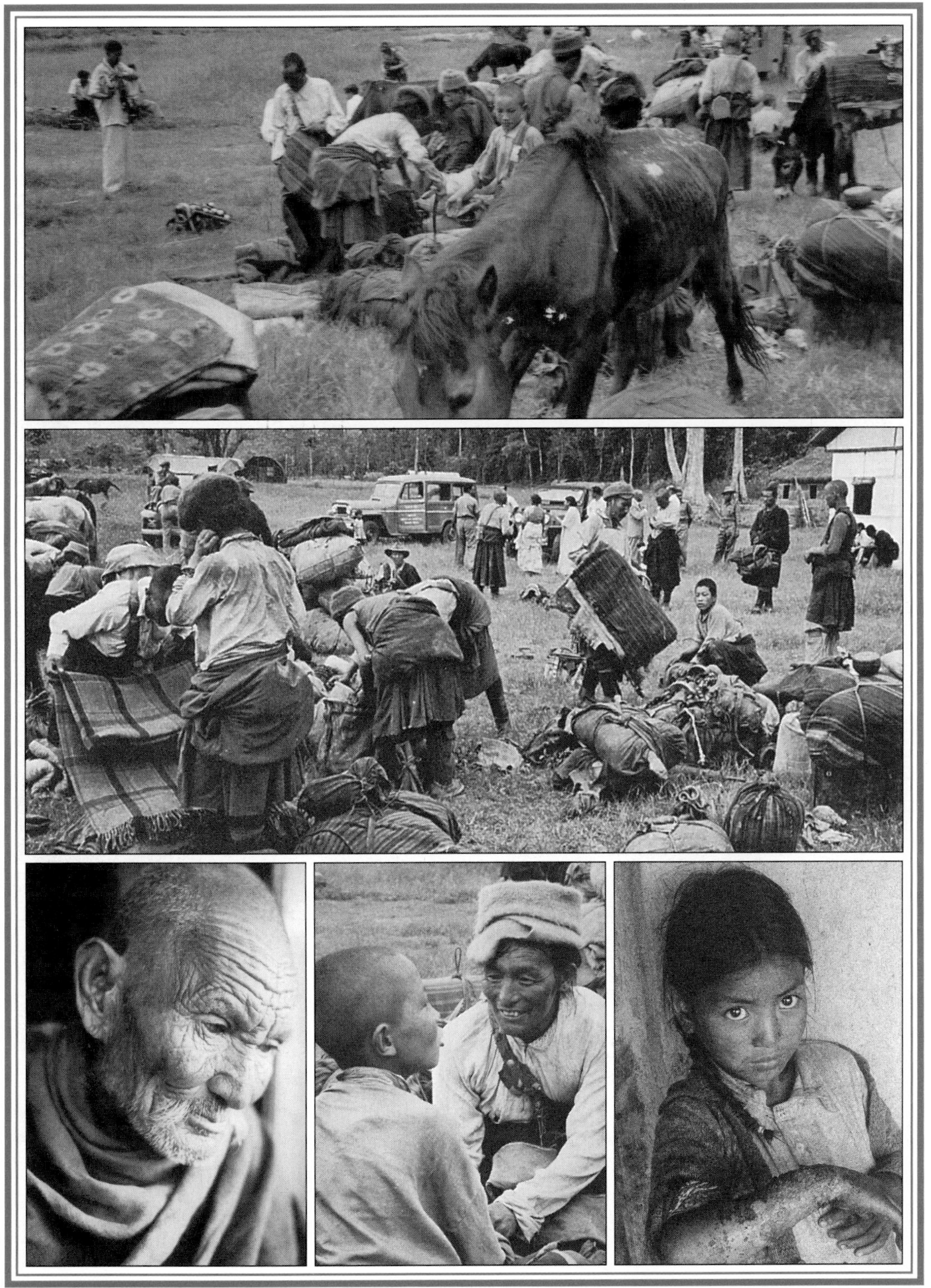

The journey is especially hard on the aged and the very young. Vulnerable to tuberculosis in the hot low altitudes of India, many do not survive.

Numb with shock, many dream of a quick return to Tibet. Others set about learning how to live in a new environment. Education of the young is a high priority.

Striving to Survive

Survival was the focus of those early years in exile. For the refugees fortunate enough to have good health and energy, requirements for survival began to penetrate the shock of dislocation, and they started to create a basis for surviving, for learning new skills and the local language, and considering how to begin educating their children. Gradually, land was obtained for permanent settlements in the more environmentally hospitable regions of Kalimpong, Darjeeling, Dharamsala, Dalhousie and other Himalayan regions and hill stations, and the Dalai Lama and other private groups began organizing and encouraging the refugees. In the 1960s and 1970s, settlements were established in forty or fifty places in northern and southern India, Nepal, Bhutan, Sikkim, and Ladakh. As the refugees worked industriously to grow their own food and develop cottage industries, the settlements took hold and, slowly, began to flourish. Sustained by their determination to be self-reliant, the refugees began to lift themselves from the isolation of abject poverty to create viable communities.

From the outset, high lamas did what they could to publish texts and re-establish the foundations of our culture. In 1963, at the request of Dudjom Rinpoche, I accepted a post at Sanskrit University in Banaras. While living in Banaras, I set up a press to print texts I had brought with me from Tibet and sought to honor the memory of my parents and teachers by supporting the ceremonies that are central to the Sangha's vitality.

During the early 1960s, there had been considerable sympathy in Western lands for the plight of the Tibetan refugees, and Western nations had helped with basic needs as the refugees sought to establish a basis for survival and reestablish their religious and cultural traditions. But the flow of aid diminished sharply in the late 1960s, and the situation in India became critical Many of the refugees were still living in harsh and difficult conditions, and the older lamas continued to weaken and pass away at a frightening rate. If the knowledge held by the learned lamas could not be transmitted to a new generation, ***the lineages preserved unbroken for more than two thousand years could be lost within one or two decades.***

In 1968, with these thoughts weighing heavily on my mind, I came to America. In 1969 I settled in Berkeley and began offering classes and seminars in the area. A short time later, when students attending classes and ceremonies began to express interest in a long-term commitment to study and practice, I met with them to establish the Tibetan Nyingma Meditation Center (TNMC). At this meeting, I described my vision of what we would need: a permanent home, where students who wished to do so could live and work together; a printing press, to reprint texts I had brought with me from Tibet; an educational institute, and a country center, where Tibetans could come and Western students could complete their studies by undertaking a traditional three-year retreat. TNMC was formally established as a California nonprofit corporation sole on October 6, 1969.

About this time, I started collecting discarded shoes, boots, shirts, and other useful items to send to the refugee settlements in India. As students and acquaintances helped in this effort, I described the hardships the refugees had endured and encouraged them in their wish to help. When they heard that even five to fifteen dollars a month could make a great difference for the refugee lamas, my students gladly pledged small monthly amounts to be sent to India. This was the beginning of the Pen Friend Program, which connected Tibetan refugees with Western individuals willing to communicate and send aid directly to them.

As lamas sent us names of their friends and students in need, I established the Tibetan Aid Project (TAP) and sought to provide humanitarian aid to the refugees in any form possible. To help fund TAP's early projects, I dedicated to it a portion of the pledges paid

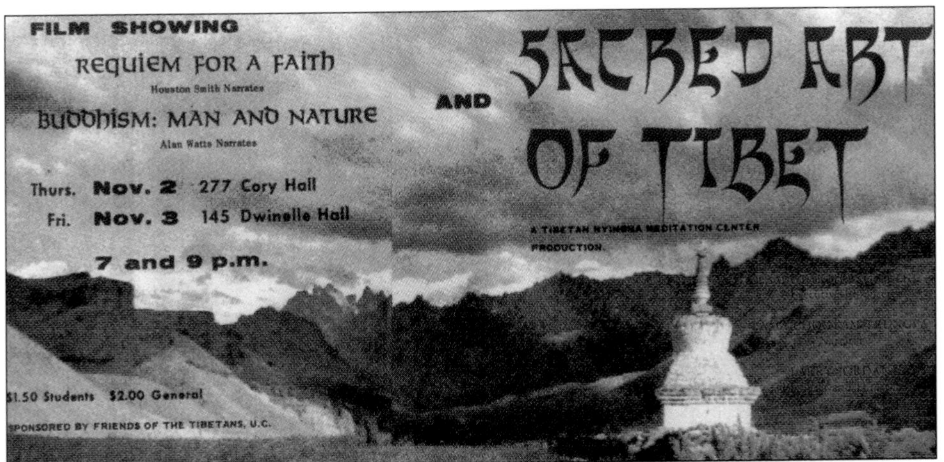

An early brochure announcing TNMC's Sacred Art Exhibit and the showings of films on Tibet.

by members of TNMC. At that time, TAP consisted of myself and a few students who helped with correspondence.

Finding Ways to Help

From 1969 through the early 1970s, we sought to inform the public and help the Tibetans in India by every means possible. We organized exhibits of Tibetan sacred art that featured screenings of films on Tibet, including *Requiem for a Faith*, a moving presentation of Tibetan Buddhism with scenes of Tibet before 1959. We also obtained films from the Indian consulate that documented how desperate the situation was for Tibetan refugees in India.

In 1972, soon after we moved into Padma Ling, a former fraternity house that became the permanent home of TNMC, I set up an office for TAP and encouraged the volunteer staff to reach out to a larger public through regular mailings. Already our activities were beginning to form a mandala of support for the work ahead. A few students had learned the rudiments of printing, an activity that led to the creation of Dharma Press and Dharma Publishing and enabled us to distribute information. Since my classes were expanding and attracting a wider range of people, I developed plans for the Nyingma Institute and incorporated it in 1972. When the Nyingma

Institute moved into its permanent home in 1973, we made use of its facilities for hosting benefit dinners, film showings, exhibits, and seminars. Each event offered fresh opportunities to communicate TAP's mission and encourage public participation.

We continued to collect old clothes, shoes, and vitamins and sent them to India, and organized rummage and flea market sales that raised funds to assist with the construction of Penor Rinpoche's monastery being established in southern India. At one point, one of my students even arranged to have tons of survival biscuits shipped to India from Civil Defense bomb shelters in Los Angeles. This project presented a tremendous task of coordination and communication for such a small group, but the final result was disappointing, for the food did not keep well in the Indian heat.

As more people learned of the efforts that Tibetans were making to rebuild their culture, the number of pen friends continued to grow. Some became more deeply involved in the Tibetan cause, traveling to visit the refugees and offering their services. At the same time, TAP sought support from the federal government for bringing sixty Nyingma lamas and their families to the United States. Although these efforts continued over several years, they were ultimately unsuccessful.

Medical Care in Nepal

Tibetan refugees continued to suffer terribly from an array of serious diseases unknown in Tibet. Lamas and laypersons alike, weakened by malnutrition and stress, were vulnerable to tuberculosis, cholera, dysentery, and hepatitis, and the older ones especially were dying in alarming numbers. Medicines were in short supply; traditional Tibetan doctors had no experience with these diseases, and there was rarely any other medical care available in the refugee settlements.

In 1972, my wife Nazli went to Nepal on behalf of the Tibetan Aid Project. The plan was to set up a temporary medical clinic, while assessing what could be done to cope with the problem on a long-term basis. The clinic was established in Bodhnath, on the outskirts of Kathmandu, where many of the refugees had congregated. Although its resources were limited, it could offer antibiotics, skin ointments, multiple vitamins, first aid kits, and bandages. Clinic staff also distributed clothing and dehydrated food.

The Nepal clinic served the refugees for six months. For many of its patients, the care it provided was the first they had received since they arrived. Property was bought in the hopes of establishing and staffing a permanent clinic, but not enough funds could be raised to accomplish this. The doctors who had volunteered with TAP returned home, but two of them later traveled to India on their own and donated their services to a Tibetan settlement for a year. The land was placed in the care of Jampal Lodoe, a Tibetan lama living in Nepal. Jampal Lodoe later made it available to H. H. Dilgo Khyentse, who developed it.

Communicating the Need: Gesar News

In 1973, I encouraged a few students to produce *Gesar News* as a way of informing the public of our teachings and activities. Since most of *Gesar*'s readers were TAP supporters eager for news of the refugees and their living conditions, TAP encouraged students and friends to visit the refugees and write of their experiences. A letter from a student who had stayed with Khenpo Palden Sherab, a Tibetan lama in Sarnath, described the Nyingma community in Sarnath and their efforts to build a monastery and library on land purchased with the help of TNMC and TAP:

> One of the major problems that the Nyingmapas have is lack of facilities. They are housed in a long, dilapidated house which surrounds a courtyard. The rooms are small

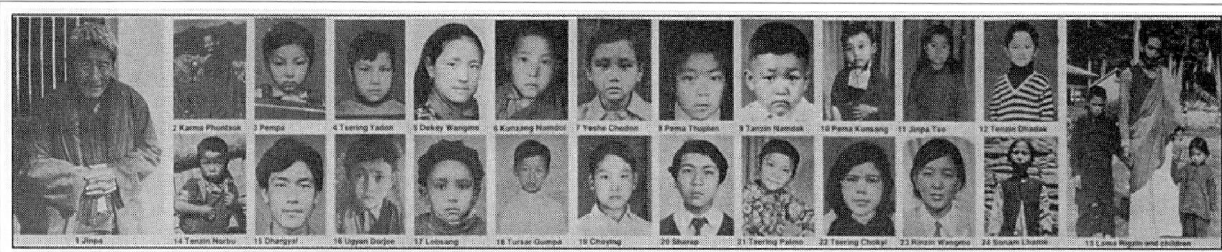

Children napping in an orphanage

How Can I Help a Tibetan?

Having a Tibetan pen friend is one of the best ways of helping and knowing the Tibetan people and learning their culture. The program bypasses bureaucratic middlemen and offers direct personal assistance. We have many Tibetans of all ages and backgrounds on our waiting list: lamas, monks, students, orphans, aged men and women, and families. We urge you to correspond with a Tibetan and send him or her $10–15 or whatever amount circumstances permit each month. This amount can enable an aged lama to continue his religious practice, a young monk to receive teachings before the older generation passes away, a student to go to school or enable parents to support their children.

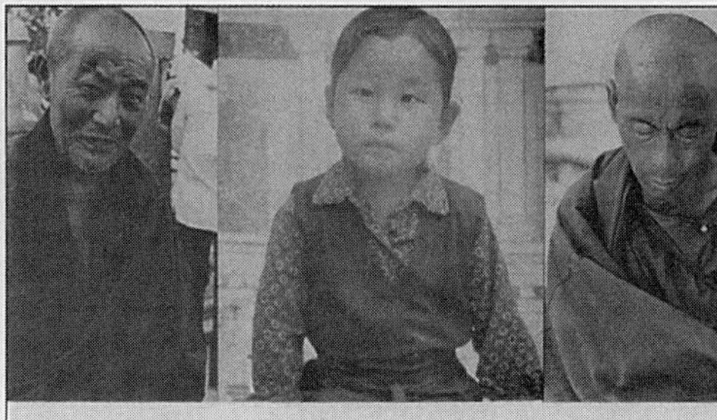

effective in promoting the Pen Friend program. TAP and Dharma Publishing co-sponsored the publication of Jataka tales for children: biographical stories of the Buddha. TAP supplied half of the initial printing costs and is now receiving good dividends.

What is the Pen Friend Program?

The Pen Friend Program began with the idea that when an American and a Tibetan correspond with each other, they can help each other and mutually share their lives. Since Tarthang Tulku's initial suggestion that each of his students correspond with a Tibetan pen pal, and possibly send him $10–15 a month, more than 1000 Tibetans have found American pen friends through our Pen Friend Program.

Although posters and benefits stimulate sup-

gram grows more effectively by word of mouth. Funds are equally distributed to all Tibetan refugees, schools, orphanages, and camps, primarily by way of international money order. A Tibetan wrote to his American pen pal:

> I have just finished my annual examinations, and I have done perfectly well. Due to the rains and my hard efforts in studies, I am now afflicted with T.B. Should it be convenient to you, I shall be very much thankful if you could send me some

What is the Heritage of Tibet?

When Mahayana Buddhism was in danger of virtual extinction in its birthplace, India, Tibetans journeyed on foot across the Himalayas and managed to bring to Tibet most of the vital texts and oral transmissions from the few great Buddhist teachers then still living in India. Thanks to their hard work and foresight, by the time of the Muslim conquest of India in the 8th Century, Mahayana Buddhism in its most complete possible form was safely at home in Tibet.

For the next thirteen centuries (right up to 1950) Tibetans not only preserved the Mahayana Buddhist tradition but successfully made it their way of life. While other peoples began to increasingly busy themselves in an endless conquest of the external world, Tibetans tuned their lives to the spirit of the Dharma—to peace and compassion.

Have Tibetans Been Able to Adapt to New Lands?

Now uprooted from their homeland they find themselves not only in a strange world but also in a strange century. Moving from the roof of the world to the tropical plains of India, Tibetan refugees have become susceptible to diseases unheard of in their native land. Despite hardship and poverty, they have maintained their dignity as a cultured people even in exile. They have struggled hard and with good cheer for the past seventeen years to preserve their unique heritage and carry on the Tibetan Buddhist tradition under most difficult circumstances. But it is doubtful if they can carry on any further without outside help. The task of preserving their culture remains more urgent than ever before. One of mankind's greatest spiritual legacies is endangered and the labors of countless lamas of the past thirteen centuries will be erased if the profound and sophisticated psychological techniques inherent in the teachings are not communicated thoroughly to the West.

What Can I Do to Help TAP?

If you're thinking about putting this away and doing something later, don't. It has been over 20 years since Tibetans left their country. They need your help now, or it will be too late to ensure that the younger generation grows strong and able to carry on their cultural tradition. Please take out a pen now and fill out the form on the next page.

Children's lives, old people's dignity and the very fabric of an entire culture are now hanging by a thread for survival. There are people to save all over the world, but there are few endangered cultures with a comparable depth of psychological and spiritual teachings. This industrious nation of people would not ask for your aid if they could prevent it. Won't you help?

Tibetan children drin

Brochures and posters prepared by TAP volunteers informed the public of the importance of providing aid to the refugees and introduced the Pen Friend Program.

and impractical, and can be used only for sleeping. There are no extra rooms, no library, and no temple. Last year a small piece of land was bought for a small gompa and library. . .

Tibetans have great difficulties as refugees. The Nyingma Center tries to help as much as possible by sending money to refugee camps and monasteries and coordinating the Pen Friend Program. Interested people can ask for the name of a Tibetan lama who needs help. The students at Sarnath have all requested pen friends, but not all have one as yet. For as little as ten dollars a month all the basic necessities can be purchased in India; more is a great help. Many warm friendships have arisen in the past four years between Tibetans and Americans.

We can also arrange support for refugee children, many of whom live in orphanages because they have lost their families or their parents must work on roads or construction sites far away to survive. . . . To help, please contact the Center and we will give you the name of a Tibetan needing support and explain the best ways to send money.

Gesar's first issue included an announcement of plans for establishing a Nyingma country center in California on land with a stable, healthy environment where Tibetans could form a self-sufficient agricultural community.

With its fourth issue, *Gesar* became a quarterly magazine and the principal vehicle for TAP's annual financial reports to its donors. Reports on TAP activities appeared in almost every issue, along with periodic features on the progress Tibetans were making in constructing monasteries and re-establishing their traditions.

The Tibetan Aid Project offers assistance to all four schools of the Tibetan tradition. Each month several hundred dollars are sent to various lamas and refugee groups throughout India. In addition, during October, TAP was able to contribute

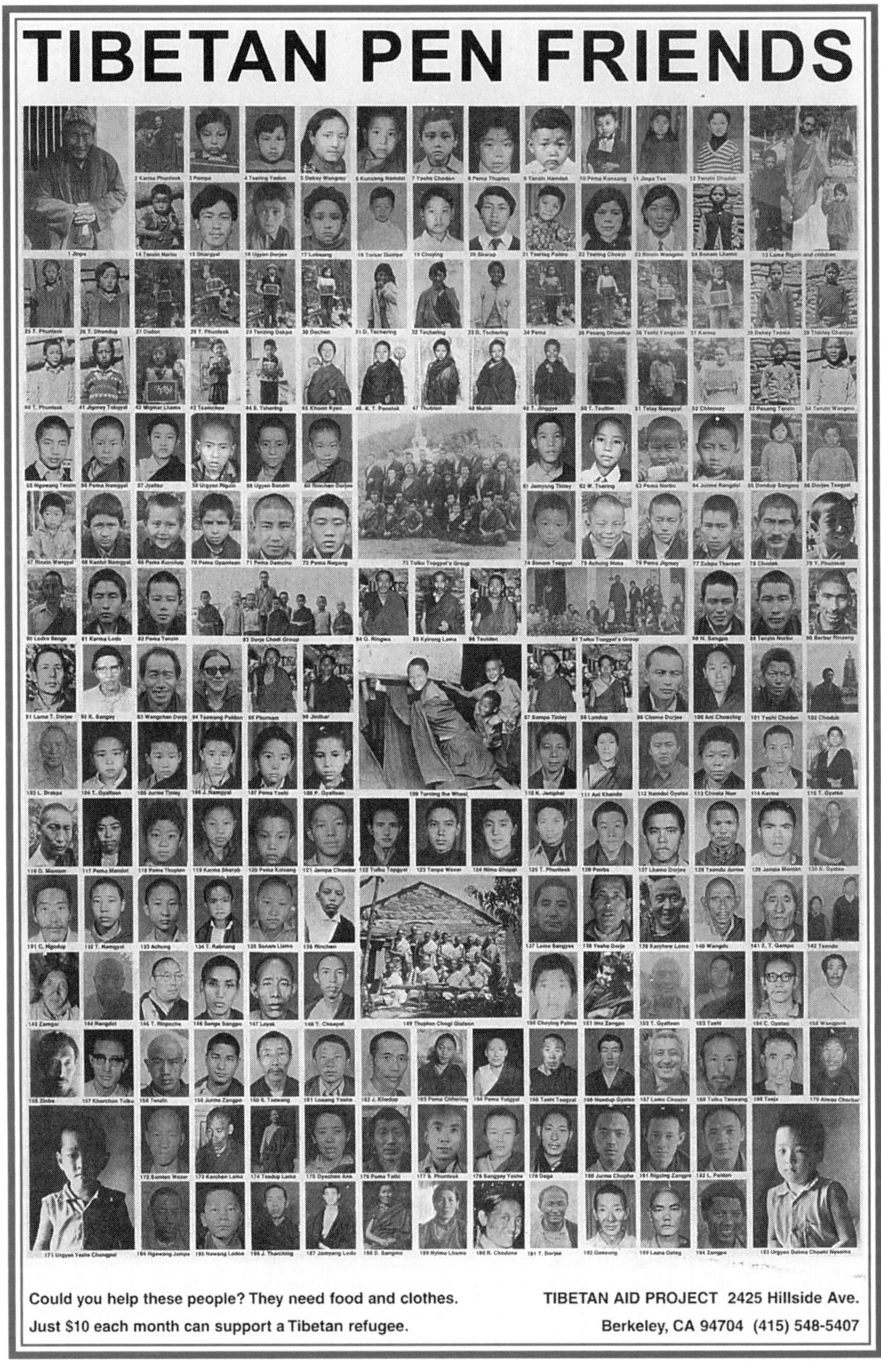

This poster, one of three produced by the Tibetan Aid Project, helped put a human face on a desperate situation. The posters were widely distributed.

> $1,000 to the Catholic Relief Fund for food distribution to the Tibetans. Much support has also been given to help bring lamas to the West. The Tibetan Nyingma Meditation Center donated $4,000 to His Holiness Karmapa and the eleven lamas accompanying him during his recent visit.
>
> —*Gesar* 2:2 1974

For Western readers who found it hard to believe how far even a little support would go, TAP emphasized often that a small monthly donation—even as little as $10 or $15—could provide all the basic needs for a monk, a nun, or a small child for a month.

> We always like to add a little note in *Gesar* asking for help in supporting Tibetan refugees in India. The economic conditions in this area are really difficult, and for Tibetans, especially those trying to continue their studies, life is very hard. Therefore, since the Center's inception, we have been arranging for Americans to correspond with and support individual Tibetans. Because the cost of living in India is considerably less than in the West, only $15–$20 a month will supply most of the essentials of life for these people. If any of our readers are interested in developing a relationship with a Tibetan refugee, please write to TNMC. We would also be happy to forward small donations or arrange for larger grants to specific groups or centers in India.
>
> —*Gesar* 1:4, spring 1974

Gesar continued to feature news of eminent lamas and the centers they were establishing. Since there were few other sources for this kind of information, TAP supporters followed these articles with great interest, taking to heart the hardships the lamas had to deal with, and encouraged by their progress. Unfortunately, the news often included sad reminders of the passing or serious illness of outstanding masters.

Each month, more letters arrived from India requesting Pen Friends.

Pen Friend Program

The most successful of TAP's early efforts was the Pen Friend Program, which provided Western individuals a way to assist Tibetans at a time of critical need. Over the next ten years, TAP received requests for pen friends from around three thousand Tibetans and heard from a nearly equal number of Westerners wishing to help.

Dharma Press printed brochures explaining the Pen Friend Program as well as three large posters featuring pictures of Tibetans

TAP volunteers worked diligently to match requests with Pen Friends.

who were asking for Pen Friends. TAP distributed them throughout the United States, inspiring several hundred more people to participate in the program.

In 1977, TAP reported, "Although posters and benefits stimulate support for the Tibetan plight, TAP grows most effectively by word of mouth through the joy experienced and expressed in helping someone in need." By 1977, TAP had connected more than a thousand Western individuals with Tibetan pen friends. Two years later, the number of Western pen friends had increased to two thousand.

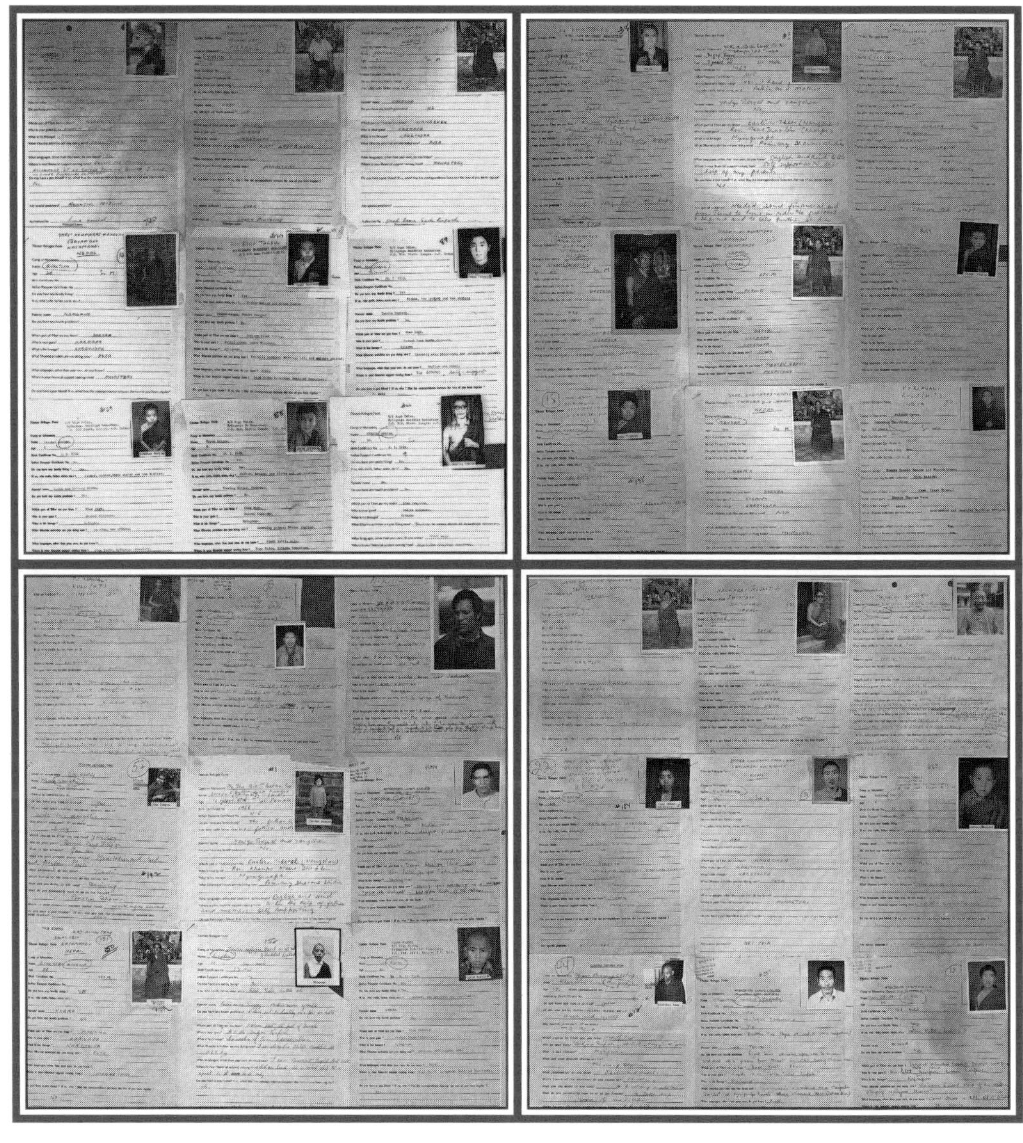

Refugees could relocate often, and with little advance notice. TAP went to great lengths to keep records current.

Many participants continued this support monthly for two to three years, and some continued much longer. While there were some difficulties in communication, and Americans and Tibetans did not always understand each others' expectations, some connections made through this program evolved into mutually beneficial friendships that were still strong ten or more years later.

The Pen Friend Program expanded at startling speed. Tibetans requesting pen friends ranged from orphaned children to the elderly, from tulkus and lamas to monks, nuns, and even whole families. TAP requested photographs so Western pen friends could see the person they were sponsoring.

"Please don't forget me.
I am a Tibetan refugee living in India and
we need your support to live."

Photographs of Tibetans requesting Pen Friends were made into posters and placed at schools, in busses, and in community centers throughout Berkeley and Oakland. Often TNMC students and other Pen Friends sent them to friends in other parts of the country for them to post also.

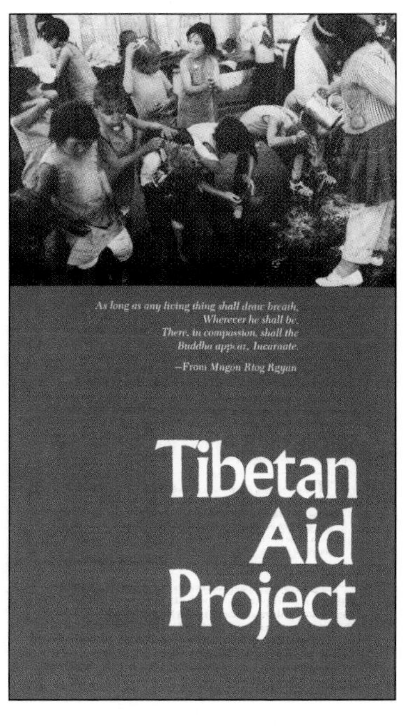

As long as any living thing shall draw breath,
Wherever he shall be,
There, in compassion, shall the
Buddha appear, Incarnate.
—From Mngon Rtog Rgyan
Tibetan
Aid
Project

It has now been many years since the Chinese took control of Tibet and began what would become a systematic demolition of Tibet's ancient culture. Within ten years, nearly all of Tibet's six thousand monasteries were destroyed. Where there were once 600,000 monks and nuns, only a few thousand monks, nuns, and tulkus remain in Tibet today. In the 1980s and 1990s, the Chinese government has relaxed restrictions on building religious sites, and the restoration of some monasteries is underway. But the thoroughness of the destruction and the disruption of Tibetan culture makes the prospect of genuine restoration tenuous at best.

The brochure illustrated above, and reproduced in full on the following pages, was published in 1974. For a public largely unaware of Tibet, its history, or its culture, this brochure put a human face on the plight of the Tibetan refugees. It clarified the desperate sense of urgency that underscores TAP's mission and made it possible for Tarthang Tulku's Western students to comprehend why Tibetan culture must be preserved.

"Ironically, the preservation of the Tibetan heritage lies with those refugees who are least able to cope with the constant battle for survival in modern India. These are the great scholars and meditators. They are not worldly men and they are often the aged. The most complete collection of Buddhist texts exists only in the Tibetan language and it is important that they be preserved. But these texts will be useless without men who have the living knowledge of the unbroken and rich spiritual and psychological nuances. It is absolutely essential that the Lamas and their students live together in communities, so that the teachings can be passed on to the next generation. If these small, struggling communities are broken up, the teachings will perish forever. It will all be decided in this generation. Will Tibetan civilization survive, or will it disappear forever from the living memory of man?"

The Background

The cultural heritage of Tibet is unique and important to this modern world. Over a thousand years ago, in the eighth century A.D., the full range of the Buddha's teachings were brought to Tibet by the great Indian scholar and saint, Padma Sambhava. These teachings were subsequently destroyed in India by foreign invasions, but due to the natural isolation of Tibet, they survived in a living, unbroken oral and written lineage that was passed on from teacher to disciple. That lineage continues to this day, and Tibetan (Vajrayana) Buddhism is a living link in man's cultural heritage. Yet the teachings contain profound and sophisticated psychological techniques which are highly useful and meaningful to modern man.

> *"There are about 20 people who live in caves and eat only lentils. But with the price of food becoming more and more exorbitant, they are finding it difficult to get even the most basic foods. Even if a little money could be sent to the Lama there, it would help. He is a lovely person. He looks after all the people there and gives them teachings. . .'*
>
> A letter requesting aid

In 1959, a foreign invasion struck Tibet with tragic and devastating force. The great monasteries, universities, and libraries were destroyed. The religious and intellectual leaders were either killed, imprisoned, or forced to give up monastic life. Yet nearly 100,000 people managed to escape from Tibet (including 10,000 monks and Lamas). Carrying a few precious books and religious treasures, these refugees made their way, with great hardship, across the Himalayas to safety—in the hot, hungry plains of India.

> *"Thank you very much for your help. Here I am, better than before, so you don't worried about me, because I hope I will not die in this time. However my right liver is very paining and also chest pain and both my legs are yellow due to water. Later on I will send you a Lama's bowl made of Tibetan wood. It is very old one. I hope you like it because it belongs to me. . ."*
>
> Letter from a pen friend

The government of India has done its best to help, but we all know that India is a very poor country with vast and innumerable problems. There is little to share, and they have not been able to give any aid at all for the last four years. A tiny handful of model villages and farms have been developed through donations from New Zealand, Switzerland and Canada, but most of the Tibetan refugees live in small camps, in extreme poverty, on dry, marginal land. There is little employment except in small craft cooperatives. The unfamiliar climate, real hunger, and diseases such as tuberculosis, dysentery, cholera, and hepatitis (all aggravated by malnutrition), are constant problems. Despite constant hardships, these people have not sunk into apathy. Instead, they tax their strength to the utmost by attempting to build schools, monasteries and temples to preserve and transmit their priceless tradition. Their main concern is not their own survival or prosperity, but the survival of their culture. But they cannot continue without outside help.

> *"Here we are, trying to build a nice monastery, but it is very difficult for us to finish it, as the cement is very scarcity and expensive. The farmers are in a very deserted situation as the fields are drying due to scarcity of rains. For one solid month here, we didn't get rain. . ."*
>
> Letter from a pen friend

Khenbo Marwa with his students living in a cave, practicing Dharma in Northern India

The world is changing so fast, and so much is being lost, so rapidly. The mystery religions of ancient Greece and Egypt, or Europe's own medieval religious heritage are now only dusty museum relics. We bravely put our time and money into attempts to save the whales or the flood-ravaged museums of Florence and Venice. And there is so much misery in the world that we soon become hardened. Will there be time to save the cultural heritage of Tibet?

> *"I have just finished my annual examinations, and I have done perfectly well. Due to the rains and my hard efforts in studies, I am now afflicted with T.B. Should it be convenient to you, I shall be very much thankful if you could send me some T.B. medicines and vitamins. . ."*
>
> Letter from a 21 year old pen friend

Ironically, the preservation of the Tibetan heritage lies with those refugees who are least able to cope with the constant battle for survival in modern India. These are the great scholars and meditators. They are not worldly men and they are often the aged. The most complete collection of Buddhist texts exists only in the Tibetan language and it is important that they be preserved. But these texts will be useless without men who have the living knowledge of the unbroken tradition of oral teachings, with its profound and rich spiritual and psychological nuances. It is absolutely essential that the Lamas and their students live together in communities, so that the teachings can be passed onto the next generation. If these small, struggling communities are broken up, the teachings will perish forever. It will all be decided in this generation. Will the magnificent civilization of Tibet survive, or will it disappear forever from the living memory of man?

> *"I am a young girl of 17. My father is a poor old man with T. B., and a very large family to support. I am quite good in studies. Last year I stood first in all sections of my class. But my father cannot afford the expenses of my schooling. If I do not receive aid, soon, I will have to leave school and help the family. . ."*
>
> Letter requesting a pen friend

How You Can Help

The Tibetan Aid Project supports all sects of Tibetan Buddhism without favoritism. We invite you to:

1. Join the pen-pal program, by corresponding directly with a Tibetan monk or student. We ask each pen pal to send $5.00 or $10.00 (or more) per month to his Tibetan friend. This money can provide food and lodging for a student, or help support a family. Your friend will write to

Pen Friend Program Aid to Tibetans

Since Pen Friends sent funds directly to their correspondents, TAP could only estimate the actual amounts reaching Tibetans in any one year. Based on the number of Pen Friends and the amounts pledged, TAP estimates that Pen Friend aid averaged $36,000 yearly from 1969 through 1979 and $9,000 in 1980, a total of $405,000. During 1974–75, the first full year after TAP was incorporated as TNRF,

you and tell you how he is doing. This is a direct, person-to-person means of assistance, and avoids all administrative and governmental red-tape, or possible misuse of funds. Every penny will be used to help people, and you will have the satisfaction of knowing that you are doing something personally, to help the world food situation.

2. Donate to the general fund of the Tibetan Aid Project. These contributions will be used to provide food and health services. Either a single gift or monthly pledge would be of great help.

3. Contribute directly to a monastery or school in India. Construction has been halted in many places for lack of funds. Clinics and dispensaries often lack the most basic drugs and medications.

4. Help bring Tibetan teachers to America. The Tibetan Nyingma Meditation Center is working to establish a rural community where

TAP offered $2,869 to supplement individual aid. In 1976, TAP disbursed $11,883, followed by $7,984 in 1977 and $8,100 in 1978. At that point, TAP's contributions to ceremonies were increasing; support for Pen Friends declined to $774 in 1979 and $1,463 in 1980. The total disbursed directly by TAP for the Pen Friend program between 1974 and 1980 came to $33,073. Combined with the estimate of funds being sent to Tibetans by individual pen priends, the total support was likely close to $438,073.

Tibetan language, art, music, philosophy and religion can be taught. We hope this will help to preserve the Tibetan heritage for the benefit of mankind. You can sponsor the immigration of an individual Lama, or contribute to the general immigration fund.

5. Help us spread the word. Speak to your friends and associates, and try to enlist their aid. Persuade your church group, club, office, school, etc. to adopt a pen-friend or monastery. Help us distribute literature, or donate your talents for a benefit. If you belong to another meditation or Yoga group, start your own refugee aid project.

If you would like to write directly to any of these Dharma leaders, for further information about their Dharma groups, please write to:

His Holiness the Dalai Lama
Head of the Gelugpa Sect
Gangchen Kyishong
Dharamsala Dist. Kangra
Himachal Pradesh India

His Holiness Gyalwa Karmapa
Head of the Kargyudpa Sect
Dharma-Chakra-Center
Rumtek Monastery
Gangtok, Sikkim India

His Holiness Sakyapa Tenzin
Head of the Sakyapa Sect
Sakya Centre
187 Rajpur Road
P. O. Rajpur
Dehra Dun (UP) India

His Holiness Dudjom Rinpoche
Head of the Nyingmapas
Madhave Nikunj
P. O. Kalimpong
Dist. Darjeeling, W. B.
India

H. H. Mindoling Tichen—Head of the Nyingmapas
Sando Pelri Monastery P. O. Kalimpong Dist. Darjeeling India

Brochures, posters, and mailings were crucial to raising awareness of the urgent need to support the refugees' efforts to survive and re-establish the foundations of their culture in very different environments. TAP relied heavily on the good will of local individuals who volunteered their services.

Funds Distributed to Tibetan Refugees by Tibetan Nyingma Relief Foundation and Tibetan Nyingma Meditation Center
January 1969–March 1980

Year	Ceremonies	Immigration/ Visitation	Relief	Penfriend Support thru Office	Penfriend Support Sent Independently*	Yearly Total Dollars	Yearly Total Rupees**
1969	—	—	—	—	36,000	36,000	288,000
1970	—	—	—	—	36,000	36,000	288,000
1971	—	—	530	—	36,000	36,530	292,240
1972	—	10,226	782	—	36,000	47,008	376,064
1973	—	7,748	1,268	—	36,000	45,016	360,128
1974–5	—	3,000	6,316	2,869	72,000	84,185	673,480
1976	5,100	13,236	10,357	11,883	36,000	76,576	612,608
1977	12,770	—	207	7,984	36,000	56,961	455,688
1978	8,300	1,251	238	8,100	36,000	53,889	431,112
1979	13,860	10,953	266	774	36,000	61,853	494,824
1980	26,687	800	5,937	1,463	9,000	43,887	351,096
Totals	$66,717	47,214	25,901	33,073	405,000	$577,905	4,623,240

Two thousand penfriends have been requested by Westerners over the past 10 years. Of these 2000 a few hundred have sent their funds through the TAP-TNRF offices. We estimate 200 people send $15/mo each year minimum for the funds sent independently to Tibetans.
***This total is calculated on a conversion rate of 8 rupees per $1. At many times over the years, the rate may have been higher.*

Pen Friends in Monastic Centers

After 1980, as the needs for basic survival became less pressing, TAP began to join with TNMC in sponsoring ceremonies and supporting reconstruction and education so that the traditional monastic way of life could continue in exile. TAP ceased coordinating the Pen Friend Program and no longer served as an intermediary between Western and Tibetan pen friends. For a time, the program came to an end, although some individuals continued their relationship with their pen friends on their own.

In 1988, however, when I decided to help establish a Nyingma shedra (school for philosophic studies) in Nepal, the program was revived. The new Pen Friend program was designed to support students at this school as well as students at other monasteries and

Donations made through the Pen Friend Program 1989–1995 (last year of Program)

1989	
Individuals	$280
Total	$280

1990	
Dechen Dorjee, Sikkim	$120
Individuals	$108
Total	$228

1991	
Dechen Dorjee, Sikkim	$500
Ka Nying Shedrup Ling	$420
Nyingma Mahabuddha Vihara	$500
Rigo Tulku, Bir	$500
Individuals	$1,275
Total	$3,195

1992	
Ka Nying Shedrup Ling	$900
Nyingma Mahabuddha Vihara	$3,200
Rigo Tulku, Bir	$4,200
Independents	$100
Individuals	$2,754
Total	$11,154

1993	
Dechen Dorjee, Sikkim	$5,400
Ka-Nying Shedrup Ling	$600
Nagi Gonpa Nunnery	$1,200
Nyingma Mahabuddha Vihara	$3,100
Rigo Tulku, Bir	$3,800
Taklung Tsetrul	$3,620
Individuals	$3,683
Total	$21,403

1994	
Dechen Dorjee, Sikkim	$2,200
Nagi Gonpa Nunnery	$3,500
Nyingma Mahabuddha Vihara	$1,100
Rigo Tulku, Bir	$2,300
Taklung Tsetrul	$1,200
Individuals	$3,683
Total	$10,300

1995	
Nagi Gompa Nunnery	$490
Independents	$8,995
Total	$9,485
Grand Total	$56,045
Total including Nyingma Institute of Nepal	$128,757

nunneries through monthly donations of $20. By now Tibetan culture and teachings and the situation of the Tibetan refugees were far better known in the West, and the new Pen Friend Program attracted strong support. Hundreds of new donors enrolled.

In a change from previous practice, all funds contributed by pen friends now came directly to TAP, which forwarded them on a regular basis to the monastic centers and schools in Tibetan exile communities. In turn, someone designated by each center or school passed the funds on to specific individuals. This approach allowed for keeping accurate records of how moneys were distributed and greatly improved the chances that funds would arrive with minimum delay and confusion.

By 1993, TAP was sending funds to over twenty monastic centers and shedras. As letters and snapshots arrived at the TAP offices in Berkeley in a steady stream, individuals were assigned donors based on interests and specific needs. New friendships were soon flourishing, and Westerners again had the satisfaction of knowing the modest monthly sums they sent were contributing to the preservation of a culture with much to offer the world.

Between 1989 and early 1993, support from 425 individual donors from eight countries—United States, Brazil, Holland, Germany, Japan, Austria, Switzerland, and Hong Kong—was distributed to more than four hundred students and nuns. In all, from 1969 to 1992, a total of 2,425 Westerners participated in the Pen Friend program. Their support, given at such a critical juncture, made a difference far greater than is obvious in the financial reports alone.

After operating successfully for several years, the Pen Friend Program was discontinued in 1995. Under the system that replaced it, the monasteries, nunneries, and schools themselves took full responsibility for distributing funds among practitioners and students, based on their own evaluations of the needs and circumstances of the individuals for whom they were responsible.

TIBETAN NYINGMA RELIEF FOUNDATION: FINANCIAL ACTIVITY
November 1, 1974–May 31, 1977

	Total To Date	*Nov. 1976– May 1977*	*1975– 1976*	*1974– 1975*
Receipts				
Donations	$50,005.76	$ 8,553.20	$21,280.46	$20,172.10
Pen Friends	17,398.78	6,570.28	9,467.00	1,361.50
Special Projects (net)	5,473.02	-0-	2,735.00	2,738.02
Jataka Tales	565.28	565.28	-0-	-0-
Interest	1,910.59	350.76	899.88	659.95
Total Receipts	75,353.43	16,039.52	34,382.34	24,931.57
Disbursements				
Relief Support	46,336.59	11,173.00	25,184.00	9,979.59
Pen Friend Distribution	18,755.44	6,099.70	11,698.24	957.50
Register letters/postage	2,183.28	282.62	957.90	942.76
Office—Int'l Money Orders	2,338.10	35.02	546.37	1,756.71
Nepal Dispensary	3,994.11	-0-	2,000.00	1,994.11
Promotion:				
Brochures & posters	1,728.48	360.65	452.76	915.07
Gifts to donors	732.02	-0-	-0-	732.02
Transportation	373.73	-0-	-0-	373.73
Other	540.19	-0-	256.00	284.19
Food shipment to India	471.87	-0-	-0-	471.87
Total Disbursements	77,453.81	17,950.99	41,095,27	18,407.55
Net Excess (Deficit)	$(2,100.38)	$(1, 911.47)	$(6,712.93)	$ 6,524.02

In addition to the above funds disbursed through TNRF in the first two years of operation, TNMC donated over $25,000 to maintain and sponsor traditional Buddhist ceremonies in the four major schools in Nepal, India, and Sikkim; to promote general assistance to the Dharamasala Clinic and other worthy projects; and to sponsor the visits of Tibetan lamas. Together, TAP and TNMC disbursed over $100,000 between November 1974 and May 1977. These figures are in addition to the offerings of Western pen friends, who sent their contributions directly to the refugees.

As described in *Your Friends the Tibetan Refugees,* "For some donors, this new approach lacked the sense of personal contact that had been so meaningful in the past, but the new approach had major advantages. In the past, there had been concerns about unequal treatment of individuals based on factors over which the Tibetan pen friends had no control. Now such problems no longer arose. At the same time, the new program helped donors appreciate more fully that their contributions were vital in helping to shape a larger vision: the preservation of Tibetan culture as a whole.

Educational support **TAP Penfriend Shedra Support 1988–1993**

Sikkim Shedra	$6,020
Ka-Nying Shedrup Ling	1,920
Nagi Gonpa	1,200
Rigo Tulku, Bir	8,500
Khocchen Tulku, Dehra Dun	6,800
Taklung Tsetrul, Simla	3,620
Tarthang Nyingma Institute, Nepal	47,237
Independents	7,800
sMin-grol-gling, Tibet	1,400
Other Monasteries in Tibet	1,200
TOTAL	$85,697

Direct Aid: Tibetan Nyingma Relief Foundation

Since TAP was not authorized by law to collect and send money directly, a few students helped coordinate aid, informing participants of the best ways to send funds, medicines, and other supplies to India. Coordination turned out to require more effort than expected: banking procedures shifted often, Tibetans had to move unexpectedly, the refugee camps were often distant from cities, and Tibetans had difficulties traveling to banks to receive their funds.

Over the years, TAP devised various methods for transferring funds and getting essential supplies to the refugees.

Travelers Carry Supplies and Funds

In the early years, eager to get desperately needed medicines and funds to the refugees, TAP asked travelers to carry supplies and donations to the camps directly. Some of these travelers sent back pictures of the refugees and letters describing their impressions of the conditions Tibetans were coping with, in their struggle to survive. TAP published a number of these communications in *Gesar Magazine* to clarify the need for assistance and encourage participation in the Pen Friend program. The response was heartwarming, but as participation increased and TAP received more requests for aid, it became difficult to keep up with the flow of correspondence, cope with difficulties in communication and mail delivery in India, and maintain the necessary records.

To help resolve these difficulties and enable TAP to serve Tibetans more efficiently, I incorporated TAP as the Tibetan Nyingma Relief Foundation (TNRF). It was founded on November 6, 1974 as a California charitable nonprofit organization, corporation number 725771. Now able to receive and distribute funds directly, TAP's directors initated a series of six fundraising benefits held between 1974 and 1976. Among them was a series of well-attended concerts held at Stanford University and "The Tibetan Approach to Emotional Balance," a seminar sponsored by TAP at the University of Southern California and led by mental health professionals who donated their time. More than three hundred psychologists, counselors, teachers, and students attended this weekend of workshops and lectures describing Tibetan and Western views and approaches to psychological health. The seminar was recorded on tape and distributed by TAP as a fundraising project.

TNRF's primary stated purpose was to distribute funds for the welfare of the Tibetan people in exile and to preserve the Tibetan

Buddhist tradition. Once the corporation was established, TNRF's directors expanded the scope of aid to provide funds for irrigation, wells, and crop cultivation, as well as food distribution and other general relief activities. They also began documenting the experiences of Tibetan refugees and generated funding for a program to support the visits of physicians, nurses, and paramedics to refugee settlements, where emergency care and the teaching of preventive medicine could help save many hundreds of lives.

Working Against Time

Among TAP's first disbursements after incorporation were funds for emergency assistance to 250 lamas at Venerable Penor Rinpoche's Nyingma Monastery in Byalakuppe, South India, which was then under construction. In the mid-1970s, when India experienced food shortages, TAP organized a large food shipment to Tibetan refugees and continued to support an ongoing medical program. Through articles in *Gesar Magazine* and direct mailings, TAP's staff continued to make known the needs of the refugees and the urgent need to support their efforts to re-establish their culture in India.

> "Without sufficient aid, the teachings that have been passed on for generations may be lost. But with our concerted efforts, the delicate thread of this heritage can be preserved from the thieves of time and ignorance . . . .
>
> "The Nyingmapas in particular have many serious difficulties. Their important monasteries were mainly located in eastern Tibet, with a few scattered elsewhere. This meant that they had to travel great distances to escape the Chinese invasion, and very few leaders survived this ordeal. Those leaders who were able to make it out are growing old. As the Nyingmapas traditionally have remained uninvolved in politics, and have devoted their energies to practicing the Dharma, they have no strong central organization behind

them and are especially threatened. The knowledge they have preserved over the centuries is particularly valuable, as many Buddhist scholars have now recognized."

—*Gesar*, spring 1976

A letter from a young Tulku, Thupten Tharje, a student at the Nyingma Lama's College in Clement Town, India, illustrates the conditions faced by many young lamas responsible for continuing the lineages:

". . . . I was born at Bodh Gaya, where the Lord Buddha attained his Enlightenment. I am 13 years old now. My parents migrated from Tibet to India during the Chinese invasion of our country in 1960. I joined this college in 1970.

"In our college, we have 63 monks plus staff—in all about 100 people. We have two classes, one is upper and the other is lower. I am in the lower class. When I go to the upper class, I shall be taught art, meditation, science, math, culture, and rituals. Our classes are in Tibetan and we don't learn English, but we have a manager who knows English and helps us in our correspondence.

"Our college is constructing a huge monastery of three stories of 85′ by 80′ by 90′. The outer walls of two stories have been completed, but due to lack of funds, our work had to be stopped. Our institution does not get aid from any country, group, or society. We solely depend on support from people like your good self. We have our Litho press here, where we print religious books.

"We have eight acres of land on high ground. The monks have dug a well 30′ deep so far. Now we have to requisition the services of expert people to dig further in order to get water for irrigation of the land.

"In college, we get everything free—books, stationery, lodging, clothing, and medicines. Most of the monks are poor and parentless.

"Yes, friend, you are the only pen friend I have. We have many friendless monks here who also need financial help. The sum of $10 sent regularly each month is enough for me. In case you could help more, kindly write to our Guru who would suggest other monks' names for sponsorship. Our college needs more financial help to complete projects at hand.

"All the best and good wishes and blessings to you."

—*Gesar,* spring 1976

Chapter Six
Preserving a Threatened Heritage

In 1974, the Tibetan Nyingma Relief Foundation and the Tibetan Nyingma Meditation Center began to supplement the TAP Pen Friend program by sending our books and thanka reproductions to refugee communities with travelers visiting their pen friends in India, sponsoring ceremonies by lamas and monks of the four major schools, and hosting visits to the United States. Many lamas and monks were working tirelessly to reestablish their culture and traditions in exile. Although the need was great and our staff and resources were very limited, knowing the hardships they had to endure and the scope of what they were seeking to accomplish, we sought to support as many of them as best we could.

The photographs included in these pages commemorate some of the great lamas who provided leadership for monastics and laypersons alike, inspiring their communities with examples of dedication, energy, and wisdom. These are only a few of the refugee lamas and teachers who worked for the Dharma during this difficult period of resettlement, but they are representative of the spirit that enabled the refugees to survive the anguish of these times and reconstruct their lives and their traditions. When I look through our old photographs today, I recognize many of the boys and young men who were then in their teens, and am surprised to realize that they are now in their fifties and sixties. Many of them are now eminent lamas or accomplished practitioners, while others have lived out their days and are no longer with us. Seeing them, I am reminded of how quickly time passes, and how precious are opportunities to support Dharma transmission in these troubled times. Knowing that even our small contributions have made a difference for many of these young lamas, I am encouraged to continue our efforts to educate the young and do our best to preserve the culture.

Nearly all of the older masters have now passed away, but the monasteries they founded and the teachings they upheld created the potential for their traditions to continue. It is my hope that new generations of Tibetans will continue to uphold the heritage of these great ones and take inspiration from the power of their love and compassion.

Throughout the 1970s and well into the 1980s, TAP/TNRF received and responded to a wide variety of specific requests for aid. Some were requests for support for individuals, for vitamins and medical treatments, and for education and training in the traditional arts. Other requests were more traditional, involving sponsorship of prayer ceremonies, pilgrimages, butter-lamp offerings, one-year and three-year retreats, and support for traditional enthronement ceremonies for high lamas. Whenever possible, TAP also responded to requests for help with projects related to temple construction, repairs, and improvements. The following letter was one of many requests that TAP received during these years.

> "You have seen the land of our college where we wanted to cultivate food, but it could not be done due to lack of water. We can dig the earth and make a well for irrigation, but financial difficulties tie our hands. There is no canal in this area, nor can the refugee colony provide us drinking water for irrigation purposes as they themselves are experiencing difficulties.
>
> "The college would remain ever grateful for your help if you could do something for irrigation of our land so that we

(continued on page 79)

In Memory of Great Masters Now Passed On

Above, left: Khenpo Tsondru, a Nyingma lama from 'Gu-log and a great master of the Dzogchen Nyingthig lineage, was a great scholar and meditation practitioner, master of the Sutras and shastras and accomplished in poetry, grammar, and medicine. He was in the same lineage as Bodpa Tulku, a lineage continued today by only a few. Many of his disciples have worked to continue their tradition outside of Tibet.

Above, central picture, left: Minyag Khenpo Rapgyay held the Palyul lineage and the lineages of Chogtrul Rinpoche. He was a courageous and dedicated lama who escaped from the Chinese on several occasions. He went first to Kalimpong, where he organized many young lamas. He was sent next to Rewalsar, the first Nyingma monastery in India, and then to Dehra Dun, where he worked with Jampal Lodoe Rinpoche. He also founded Palyul Chokor Ling in Kangra. A visionary of great energy, integrity, and faith, he served as spiritual father to numerous students.

Above, right: Lopon Sonam Zangpo trained in both the Drukpa Kagyu and Nyingma traditions. His teacher was Togden Shakya Shri, student of Adzom Drugpa. A highly realized master, artist, and meditator, he built several temples and repaired the Svayambhu Stupa. He and Tarthang Tulku received important teachings from Jamyang Khyentse Chokyi Lodro in Sikkim in 1959, then went to India on pilgrimage to the sacred places.

Above, front center: Khenpo Thupten Mewa was originally from Mewa monastery in Kham, an important center with 1,000 students. He and Tarthang Tulku studied together at Changma Ritro in 1955, and again as students of Bodpa Tulku. In India, he founded a retreat center at Pangaon caves, a site sacred to Padmasambhava.

Above, left: Khorlo Lama worked closely with Minyag Khenpo Rapgyay on behalf of the Dharma and the Nyingma lineage. He resided at Rewalsar, but passed away at an early age.

Above, right: Ngagchen Sherab Lama, a disciple of Dudjom Rinpoche and an important Nyingma master, with his wife Pema Lhazom.

Above left, Dapsang Tulku, a Kagyu lama who founded a monastery in Kathmandu. Center, Chusang Lama, from Dorje Drag in Tibet, was head of the monastery at Rewalsar and teacher of Ngawang Zabtrang Namgyal. He was originally from Minyak in Kham. He and Tarthang Tulku were close friends. Right, Thopgay Lama, a lama of the Nyingma school.

Opposite page: Lama Karam Singh (left), was a student of Khenpo Tubga, one of the most renowned scholars in Dzachuka.

Venerable Urgyen Tulku (center), a descendant of Chokyur Dechen Lingpa, assisted H. H. the Karmapa in Nepal for many years, working at a temple that is now under the direction of the Zhwamarpa. He founded Ka-Nying Shedrup Ling in Kathmandu, a large monastery now under the direction of his son Chokyi Nyima Rinpoche. Widely respected as a teacher, he also founded and supervised Nagi Gompa, a major nunnery. A number of his teachings have been published in English in recent years, giving Western students the benefits of his compassion and wisdom.

Sai Yung Sang Dechen (right, the wife of Urgyen Tulku and mother of Chokyi Nyima Rinpoche and Chokling Rinpoche, was an active helpmeet in her husband's work. In the 1990s, together with her husband, she built a large temple at Asura Cave in Nepal, where the Great Guru Padmasambhava practiced the Vajrakila and Heruka sadhanas. TAP contributed funds for the temple's large gold spire.

> may yield some crops from our precious field to feed the students and teachers."
>
> —Ven. D. G. Khochen Tulku Rinpoche
> Nyingma Lama's College

Appeals for help made it clear that as late as 1977, there were an estimated 4,000 Tibetan refugees still without permanent shelter.

> There are widows with young children to support, there are orphans. There are also those who are too old and sick to work:
>
> ". . . we are childless in our old age and have no one to look after us. We are facing difficulties of immense burden. My brother is a t.b. patient and is incapable of doing anything. I, likewise, am a t.b. patient and have no work whatsoever. We all live on the small earnings of my wife who is employed in a carpet factory . . . full of prayers, I implore that this may reach the heart of a benevolent person. . ."
>
> —*Gesar*, fall 1977

Communicating the Need More Widely

Throughout the 1970s, TAP continued to raise awareness of the various types of aid that were needed: medical supplies and vitamins, tuberculosis treatment kits, ointment for boils and sores, bandages

Relying on their own resources, refugee lamas build the Nyingma Lama's College in Dehra Dun. TAP and TNMC support their efforts through Pen Friends and direct assistance.

and first aid kits, and suitable second-hand clothing; warehouse space and trucks in California and overseas for storing and transporting supplies; physicians and medical personnel to volunteer service at especially needy refugee camps in Nepal and India; equipment for irrigation, well-digging, and crop cultivation, together with agricultural experts experienced in the difficulties of growing crops in arid desert and mountanous terrain.

The call for help went further, appealing to volunteers with free time and ideas or talents in the arts, music, or handicrafts, or experience and skills in organizing and presenting fund-raising projects such as crafts fairs, lectures, seminars, film showings, or concerts. TAP's staff was small but motivated and energetic; it pursued every avenue that seemed even remotely possible.

While TAP worked to convey the scope and urgency of the aid needed, Tibetans in India and Nepal continued to make good use of whatever opportunities and assistance came their way. Although they suffered greatly from separation from their families and home monasteries, and had little training for the kinds of work available to them, the refugees worked hard to establish communities, schools, and printing presses. The building of monasteries, representing the very heart of the Tibetan people, was a high priority.

As reported in the *Annals of the Nyingma Lineage in America* (volume II, 1977),

> In spite of their hardships, the Tibetan people maintain their dignity as a cultured people and continue to meet worldly obstacles with cheerful hearts. Though they have confronted their plight as refugees, they have not accepted the assumption that they must live in impoverished conditions. They have built schools, homes, and temples entirely out of the rock, mud, and clay of the earth, when there were no other materials available. In addition, the Tibetans have dedicated themselves to creating a more human environment with

their own ingenuity. Even the poorest refugee takes time to improve his home, while many others work together to build craft centers and encourage industrious activity.

To support these efforts, in 1974 TAP appealed to foundations and applied for grants for direct aid. Two foundations responded: the Lily Endowment and the Irwin Sweeney Miller Foundation made small one-time grants, but it became clear that ultimately, TAP and TNMC, like the refugees, would have to rely on their own resourcefulness and hard work, offering whatever they could to support the long-range survival of the lineages, preserve the treasures of Tibetan culture, and manifest the meaning and value of the Dharma within Western lands. To accomplish this, it would be necessary to cultivate bonds of mutual trust and appreciation beween the lineages and Western students. It was my hope that TAP could, in its small way, serve as a bridge to this kind of understanding.

Connecting East and West

Especially in the early years, TAP helped fund visits to America of prominent lamas who gave blessings at Padma Ling, Odiyan, and the Nyingma Institute. The presence and dedication of these venerable masters helped Western students appreciate the importance of lineage and deepen their understanding of the nature of Dharma transmission. In the first decade of Nyingma in the West, Rinpoche invited the heads of the four major schools.

H. H. the Dalai Lama was welcomed at the Nyingma Institute on October 1, 1979. After receiving students, he delivered a public address from the Institute's porch to an audience of about five hundred gathered in the street below. Upon leaving the Institute, he visited Padma Ling and blessed the preparation of *The Nyingma Edition of the bKa'-'gyur and bsTan-'gyur.*

Tarthang Rinpoche welcomes leaders of the four major schools of Tibetan Buddhism to the Nyingma Institute. Left, H. H. the Dalai Lama, 1979; right, H. H. Gyalwa Karmapa, 1974.

H. H. Dudjom Rinpoche, head of the Nyingma tradition in exile, visited TNMC in 1972 and again in 1976. In 1976, he blessed the Institute and gave a public talk attended by two hundred people. He also visited Odiyan, where he blessed the land and presided over purification ceremonies.

H. H. Sakya Trizin, head of the Sakya school, accompanied by Kunga Lama, abbot of Ngor Ewam Choden, gave blessings at the Nyingma Institute in August 1974 and encouraged students in their study of Dharma.

H. H. Gyalwa Karmapa, leader of the Karma Kagyu tradition, accompanied by numerous attendants, presided over the Black Hat ceremony in the temple of Padma Ling and gave blessings at the Nyingma Institute and Dharma Press in October 1974.

H. H. Dilgo Khyentse, accompanied by the young tulku Zhechen Rabjam, visited the Nyingma Institute and Dharma Press and conducted ceremonies at Padma Ling and Odiyan in 1976.

TAP sponsors visits of leaders of the four schools, who give blessings to students at the Nyingma Institute and Padma Ling. Left, H. H. Sakya Trizin visits the Nyingma Institute, 1974. Right, H. H. Dudjom Rinpoche visits in 1972. Returning in 1976, he gives blessings to TNMC students at Padma Ling, the Nyingma Institute, and Odiyan.

TAP and TNMC have continued to sponsor the visits of other Tibetan teachers and lamas who have blessed the Nyingma centers with their presence. Chogyam Trunpa, Khenpo Thupten, Khenpo Palden Sherab, Khenpo Tsewang Dongyal, Tulku Thondup, and Dodrup Chen Rinpoche, who visited the Nyingma centers in the 1970s; Lama Jigste Golok, Gyatul Domang, Thinley Norbu, and Dzongsar Khyentse, who visited in the 1980s; Thubten Nyima and Chokyi Nyima, who came in the 1990s; and Nyichang Rinpoche, who came in the 1990s and 2000s.

Some of these distinguished visitors have participated actively in sculpture and calligraphy projects, supported the Nyingma Institute's educational programs, and contributed to the Yeshe De Project's ability to produce typeset editions of Tibetan texts. In the 1980s, Khyentse Sangyumma, widow of 'Jam-dbyangs mKhyen-

H. H. Dilgo Khyentse, accompanied by the young Zhechen Rabjams, visits the Nyingma organizations in 1976 and leads ceremonies in Berkeley and Odiyan. Dzongsar Khyentse, incarnation of Tarthang Rinpoche's teacher, 'Jam-dbyangs mKhyen-brtse Chos-kyi Blo-gros, meets with students at Padma Ling and the Nyingma Institute in 1986.

brtse Chos-kyi Blo-gros and members of her family also honored the Nyingma centers with their presence.

Ten Years of Service

Each year, TAP published an account of its activities and a full financial disclosure in *Gesar Magazine*. Friends of TNMC who traveled to India and Nepal often visited the refugee communities carrying vitamins and medical supplies, and some wrote articles describing the refugees' living situations and their progress in reestablishing their culture, monastic communities, and educational systems. To broaden this base of support, TAP generated publicity for the refugees' situation, preparing posters and brochures and giving interviews to interested reporters. Administrative expenses were cut to the bone so that TNRF could distribute 98% of funds received to refugees expressing need.

By 1979, ten years after TAP's founding, thousands of dollars in cash assistance had been sent to the refugees through the coordinated efforts of TNMC and TNRF, and TAP's Pen Friend Program had generated thousands of dollars more by connecting more than two thousand Westerners to Tibetan monks, lamas, lay people, school children, and the aged. In addition, TNMC's support for ceremonies and traditional religious practices (described below in greater detail) had been ongoing. Among the major contributions were more than $6,500 in 1978–79 to sponsor prayers for the longevity of the Dalai Lama and $25,000 offered to Tibetan Dharma communities for religious ceremonies in 1980, an especially important year in the Tibetan calendar.

In 1979, two decades after Tibetans had sought refuge in India and other Himalayan lands and one decade after the founding of TAP, the majority of Tibetans had learned new skills and had become reasonably self-sufficient. Though some still had difficulty providing funds for educating their children, their ingenuity and self-reliance had enabled them to obtain sufficient food, shelter, and clothing, and to build monasteries and community facilities. Most of the refugees were living in good settlements with medical and educational facilities nearby.

The Need to Persevere

The courage of the refugees, supported by the power of their faith and the strength of their culture, enabled them to survive in exile and establish themselves in unfamiliar climates and cultures in many parts of the world. While their needs for basic survival were becoming less pressing, the urgency of preserving and transmitting their culture was increasing. TAP's focus began to shift from primarily humanitarian support to support for revitalizing Tibet's culture and institutions. In an environment where Tibetan cultural and religious traditions were not widely known, it became important to convey the value of preserving them. TNMC's exhibits of sacred art had been a start. *Gesar Magazine* took up the effort by featuring articles on Tibetan culture as well as TAP's humanitarian activities.

Clarifying the Issues: A Voice from Tibet

By the late 1970s, a few young Tibetans had graduated from universities in India and were studying in America and Europe. Among them was Dawa Norbu. While living in Berkeley, he addressed a question on the minds of long-time TAP contributors: Do Tibetans still need our contributions?

Noting that it was now seventeen years since the Tibetans fled their country, he pointed out that Tibetans were fast becoming forgotten in the waves of new refugees from Vietnam, Biafra, Bangladesh, and other cultures in crisis. In the 1960s, international agencies had responded generously to the plight of refugees from Tibet. As a child, he himself had benefited from this support, which enabled some young Tibetans to attend private schools and qualify for programs of higher education. "But now all of the sympathy seems to have evaporated and most of the aid has dried up. It is now almost impossible for the Tibetan children born in exile to get an opportunity like mine." He went on to explain,

> Change is in a way inevitable. There may indeed be needs greater than the Tibetans' elsewhere. But there are certain vital aspects of Tibetan rehabilitation which have been neglected, if not ignored, by relief agencies in the past. Most of the agencies involved in the Tibetan rehabilitation were non-Buddhist; they were not concerned with the cultural aspect of the rehabilitation. Specifically, they were concerned with building houses and reclaiming land. This is not intended to belittle the great effort of various agencies, it is only to point

to a simple fact which usually does not reach the public: that cultural rehabilitation and cultural preservation were declared not within the scope of the voluntary agencies . . .

What Tibetans Need: The Task Ahead

Continuing, Dawa Norbu clarifies what is necessary for Tibetans to survive in exile:

> ***Tibetans cannot really live without their religion,*** and that was one of the main reasons they fled their own country. Tibetan life revolves around a Gompa (temple or little monastery), and without that, it is almost inconceivable that Tibetans can feel at home or be considered as rehabilitated. Apart from being the pivot of their life, monastic centers also act as the repository of Tibetan culture. In this respect, Tibetan lamas in exile have a historical responsibility to preserve the Tibetan culture, which faces the danger of extinction. It is also an unfortunate fact that among the various classes of refugees it is the lamas who have suffered the most. For they were the least prepared for the unprecedented difficulties that have beset Tibetan life since 1959 . . .
>
> Just as science is not a panacea for human happiness, religion is not either, by the same token. But even my limited stay in this most different society seems to convince me that the modern man has much to gain from the Tibetan Buddhist tradition. Professor Soskin has written that the 'input of Tibetan knowledge could over the next quarter-century revolutionize Western psychological thought, and, in the process, make major contributions to Western religious and philosophical thought as well.'
>
> Although the Tibetan refugees have been rehabilitated in an elementary sense during the last fifteen years or so, the

> important task of preserving Tibetan culture has been largely neglected. But the Tibetans in exile are determined to do their best in preserving and saving whatever remains of the Tibetan civilization. For this they need your help.
>
> —*Gesar* 4:4:43–46

A similar point was expressed in this summary of the refugees' progress published in *Annals of the Nyingma Lineage in America 4 (1995)*:75–76:

> In the 1960s and 70s, settlements were established in forty or fifty places in northern and southern India, Nepal, Bhutan, Sikkim, and Ladakh. The Tibetans worked industriously to grow their own food and establish self-sufficient enterprises so they did not need to rely on outside support.
>
> This determination to be self-reliant carried the refugees from the isolation of abject poverty to the creation of entire communities working together. Schools were starting, printing presses founded. Over the years, the Tibetans have established over 200 monasteries and nunneries outside of Tibet.
>
> During the past thirty years, the Tibetan refugees have accomplished far more than seems humanly possible. Persevering through one challenge after another, working with courage and devotion, they have made strenuous efforts to preserve their heritage and way of life.
>
> But the ancient way of life is still in danger. Though there are success stories, most of these monasteries are barely surviving, for they no longer have the consistent community support they had in Tibet. The abbots bear the burden of providing basic necessities for monks and nuns who have dedicated themselves to religious pursuits.
>
> ***The situation in Tibet is far worse than that of the exiles.*** The Communist government has deliberately tried to remove the

'old ways' and eradicate the influence of the Dharma. Not only have temples, monasteries, libraries, and statues been destroyed but the hearts and minds of the people have been deeply wounded. The ever-present ruins of the old way of life are constant reminders of loss and destruction, yet people can scarcely bear to remember the past. Within one generation, there may be no one left in Tibet who can recollect that the ancient way of wisdom was once cherished in the Land of Snows.

Reassessing Priorities

By 1979, it seemed the time had come to focus more strongly on preserving the cultural heritage of Tibet. The resources of TNMC and Dharma Publishing were already deeply committed to the publication of the *Nyingma Edition of the bKa'-'gyur and bsTan-'gyur*, and the work of building a country center, envisioned as a sanctuary for Tibetan culture and a home for the Dharma in America, was entering a critical phase. Although funds were limited, it was still possible to continue some support for the refugee communities through TAP's general funds.

During the 1980s, TAP's efforts continued on a more limited scale. While TAP continued to administer the Penfriend Program and to respond to survival-oriented needs, TNMC now took the lead, founding the Yeshe De Text Preservation Project, assessing possibilities for reconstruction in Tibet, increasing contributions for traditional ceremonies in the four major Tibetan Buddhist schools, and supporting research that would soon lead to much more extensive text preservation efforts. Guided by a long-range vision, TNMC drew upon all resources at its command to develop skills, materials, and funds for supporting education, construction, and revitalization of the Tibetan Dharma traditions. As TNMC has opened new fields of opportunity for preserving and revitalizing all that relates to Dharma study and practice, TAP has sought ways to help these efforts flourish. Since 1989, TAP has supported TNMC by helping to fund the building of stupas, the restoration of statues, and the creation of paintings and other ritual materials such as the printing and sewing of hundreds of prayer flags.

Commemorating a Heritage of Beauty and Peace

The Tibetan Aid Project is dedicated to encouraging the progress of the Tibetans living in Tibet and in exile. We take this time to remember the recent sacrifices and hardships which the Tibetan people have endured. Our efforts are offered to the Tibetan people and their friends in the West. May older Tibetans continue to draw inspiration from the rich beauty of the Tibetan civilization and may young Tibetans learn to appreciate their heritage more deeply. May the precious knowledge traditions that have sustained the people of the Land of Snows endure and flourish in the future.

—TAP Brochure, 1991

Part Three

Revitalizing

Scenes of recovery: Tibetans strive to re-create their culture.

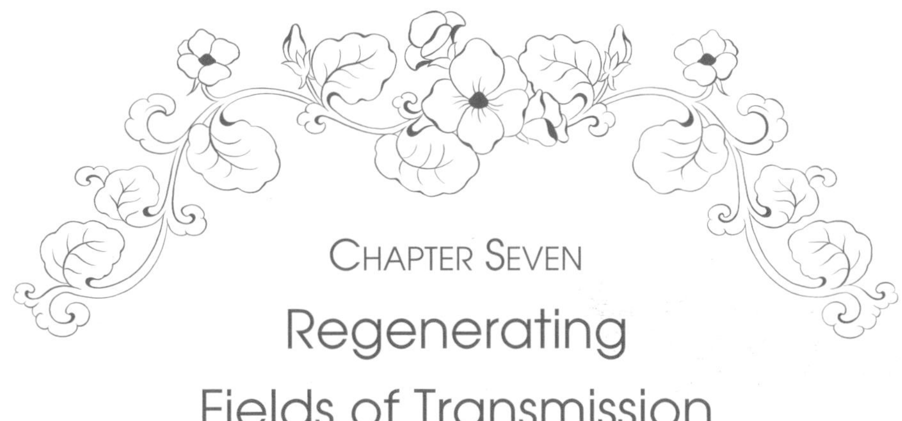

Chapter Seven

Regenerating Fields of Transmission

Ceremonies are skillful means for relaxing the hold of self and personality and entering the inner sanctuaries of heart and mind. Here, in the expansive field of being, free of samsaric concerns, the self-oriented, dualistic mind melts away and yields to a more universal understanding. Carried out by large assemblies of accomplished practitioners, ceremonies deepen the experience of teachings too subtle and profound to be communicated in any other way. Within this concentration of blessings and spiritual power, teachings and lineages can be transmitted purely, as if pouring the contents of one vessel into another.

From a student's perspective, ceremonies are opportunities to learn the prayers that invite blessings, the visualizations that dissolve the barriers between the sacred and mundane, and the meditations that penetrate illusion and reveal truth directly. For their elders, ceremonies are opportunities to focus their accumulated merit and spiritual power to dispel confusion, aggression, and greed from the minds of people everywhere and invite the blessings of harmony and peace. Ceremonies are thus the very life-blood of spiritual life. Essential for the survival of the lineages, they preserve the vitality of the Dharma, sustain knowledge and skills in the ritual arts, and benefit all of humanity.

For Tibetans living in exile, separated from family and familiar sources of support, ceremonies have additional significance, for the tragedy of their loss is part of the pattern of our times. Along with

Ceremonies require extensive preparation and may last two weeks or even more. Above, musicians practice their roles in a ceremony.

progress, almost unnoticed in the rapid flow of change, is our darker heritage of aggression, conflict, invasion, and general confusion as to the nature of human needs. The pain of those caught up in these turmoils reflects widely, influencing our lives, our societies, and our environment. In these times, when all other means have failed to provide solutions, ceremonies that integrate prayer, faith, and devotion have great power to heal and reconnect humanity with sources of meaning and value. During years of dislocation and devastating loss, ceremonies provided occasions for the Sangha to come together, take strength from their faith, and offer the transforming blessings of compassion to people everywhere.

Preparing for ceremonies is itself a practice. Monks spend days or even weeks preparing the temple, cleaning ritual implements, creating and ornamenting traditional offerings, practicing musical instruments, studying texts, and intensifying their meditation practice. During the ceremonies, participants chant prayers and read aloud from the sacred texts for days or even weeks at a time. Sponsors support the monks by providing funds for food, tea, offerings,

Jampal Lodoe, head of the Nyingma Lama's College near Dehra Dun, leads a ceremony outside the newly built monastery.

and incidental needs for the duration of the ceremony. In addition, TNMC and TAP have often taken these opportunities to share the products of our Dharma work in America with the Tibetan Sanghas by providing ceremony participants with thankas and books produced by Dharma Publishing.

Ceremonies that involve a hundred thousand repetitions of specific prayers—or multiples of a hundred thousand—are especially auspicious. One hundred thousand signifies universality, indicating that these prayers are being offered on behalf of beings throughout the cosmos and beyond. The concentration of experienced practitioners, focused on the benefit of others, activates the power of blessings, calms negativity and agitation, and generates merit. At the close of the ceremony, participants dedicate this merit to beings everywhere, to brighten their lives and advance them on the path to enlightenment. Those who sponsor ceremonies share in this merit and can generally dedicate it to any worthy purpose. Opportunities to support the Dharma traditions in this way have traditionally been viewed as a great blessing.

Top, lamas perform a traditional ritual dance. Lower, monks and students prepare tormas (ritual offerings) from barley flour and butter.

Top, Kagyu monks participate in a Gyalwa Kanjur reading. Lower, an assembly of Gelug monks perform a Kanjur reading at Sera University.

The deep reverberations of large drums accompany the formal offerings and mark significant points in the ceremony.

Early Support for Ceremonies

Soon after TNMC was founded in 1969, I began offering funds as possible to sponsor recitations of traditional prayers by lamas working to reconstruct monasteries and reestablish their traditions. Every year since 1972, TNMC and TAP have sponsored ceremonies in the centers of the four major Tibetan schools in India and the Himalayas, with each school performing ceremonies as appropriate for their tradition. In 1976, the first year shown in our records, TNMC and TAP offered $5,100 for ceremonies; in 1977, $12,770, and in 1978, $8,300. Since then, funding has steadily increased, from $13,600 in 1979 to $26,687. From 1976 through 1980, a total of $66,717 was distributed to a total of eighty-one centers and lamas: thirty-two in the Gelugpa tradition, thirteen Kagyu, five Sakya, and thirty-one Nyingma.

Ceremony Support: TNMC and TAP 1971–2000

Ceremony	Times requested
rGyal-wa bKa'-'gyur Rinpoche Recitations	316
Guru Rinpoche Prayers and Sadhanas	90
Vajrakila Phurpa Sadhana	149
100,000 Tara Prayers	311
Medicine Buddha Sutra Puja	18
Heart Sutra	140
Amitayus Sutra and Dharanis	29
Ye Dharma Mantras	20
Hayagriva Sadhanas	33
Sitatapatra Prayers	185
Additional ceremonies requested	211
Total	**1,502**

*These figures do not include contributions for the World Peace Ceremonies of the Four Schools.

The emphasis on ceremonies strengthened in 1981, when TAP and TNMC worked in tandem on projects related to education and actively promoted the revitalization of Tibet's religious and cultural heritage. At that time, TAP's small staff was also involved in producing *The Nyingma Edition of the bKa'-'gyur and bsTan-'gyur* and preparing major collections of bKa'-'ma and gTer-ma texts for a much larger compilation that became *Great Treasures of Ancient Teachings.* Although the level of TAP's outreach and income declined in the 1980s, offerings for ceremonies and construction projects continued under the direction of TNMC, and the number of ceremonies funded by TNMC continued to increase. According to TAP reports, by the summer of 1990, TNMC and TAP together had contributed a total of $504,420 for ceremonies.

CEREMONY FUNDING: TNMC AND TAP 1976–1985

Gelugpa	
H.H. the Dalai Lama	$600
Thekchen Choeling	200
for 15 centers	4,500
Ling Rinpoche, Bodh Gaya	3,275
Drepung Monastery	1,665
Dzongkar Chode Datsang	400
Gaden Choepel Ling	200
Gaden Jam Ghon	200
Gaden Tharpa Choeling	400
Gaden Thubten Choeling	200
Gaden Jantse Datsang	325
Gaden Monastery	1,565
Gelugpa Students Committee	890
Gomang Datsang College	1,240
Gyuto Tantric College	1,865
Gyudmed Tantric College	2,415
Loling Datsang	1,240
Sera Monastery	1,015
Serjey Monastery	980
Sermey Datsang	990
Shartse Norling Datsang	1,040
Others	1,100
Total	$26,745

Kagyupa	
H.H. Gyalwa Karmapa	$830
Khamtrul Rinpoche	1,850
Dhazang Tulku	1,015
Dorzong Rinpoche, Tashi Jong	1,755
Ven. Ontul Rinpoche	755
Thupten Sangag Choeling	8,010
Kagyud Student Committee	640
Lama Wangdor	2,630
Thrangu Rinpoche	965
Others	875
Total	$19,325

Sakyapa	
H.H. Sakya Trizin	$3,155
Khenpo Appey, Sakya College	1,930
Sakya Students Union	890
Khenpo Sangye Tenzin	765
Tharig Tulku	952
Others	750
Total	$8,442

Nyingmapa	
H.H. Penor Rinpoche	$300
H.H. Dilgo Khentse	21,665
Khenpo Dazer	2,655
Khenpo Dechen Dorje	2,235
Dodrup Chen Rinpoche	1,685
Golok Tulku	1,115
Jedrung Rinpoche	815
Dzongsar Khyentse Rinpoche	3,785
Khyentse Sangyum	660
Khenpo Thubten Mewa	2,855
Shaptrul Sangye Dorje	2,165
Khetsun Zangpo	1,280
Nyingma Monastery Rewalsar	3,305
Ka-Nying Shedrup Ling	4,600
Nyingma Students Committee	1,440
Nyingmapa Mahabuddha Vihara, Dehra Dun	4,390
Pema Norbu Rinpoche	6,200
Tulku Pema Wangyal	740
Rigo Tulku	3,365
Ripa Tulku/Dorje Namgyal	2,030
Thuprig Dorje	825
Trushig Rinpoche	1,230
Taklung Tsetrul Rinpoche	1,280
Zangdok Palri Monastery	765
Others	1,430
Total	$74,115

GRAND TOTAL 1976–1985 **$128,627**

Ceremonies Sponsored: TNMC and TAP. 1974–1986

Ceremony	Total	Nyingma	Sakya	Kagyu	Gelug
bKa'-'gyur Rinpoche	88	31	6	14	37
bsTan-'gyur Reading	1	-	-	-	1
100,000 Tara Prayers	200	90	26	41	43
Heart Sutra	113	43	19	24	1
Vajrakila Prayers	47	33	8	5	1
Amitayus longevity	29	13	7	7	2
Prajnaparamita	13	6	5	1	1
Guru Rinpoche and Dakini Puja	17	6	6	4	-
Ye Dharma Mantra	18	11	3	4	-
Dharmapala Mantras	4	4	-	-	-
Hayagriva Mantras	29	20	2	5	2
Longchenpa Puja	20	17	-	3	-
100,000 Medicine Buddha Prayers	14	-	1	-	13
10,000 Sitatapatra	10	1	-	-	1
Sixteen Arhat Prayers	3	2	-	-	1
Prayer Flags	3	-	-	-	1
100,000 Butterlamp Offerings	3	1	-	-	2
100,000 Manjushri Namasamgiti	5	1	-	-	4
100,000 Mani Prayers	3	-	-	2	1
Stupa Paintings and Statues	4	1	-	3	-
Sampa Lhundrup	3	3	-	-	-

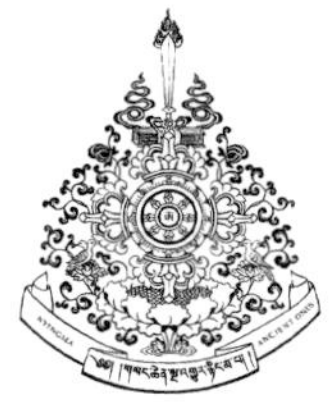

Serving the Four Schools
Summary of Activity, TNMC/TAP 1988–1996

1988

100,000 Tara prayers at ten monasteries in Nepal	$75,446
Taru Monastery	
Zhechen Tennyi Dargye Ling	
Dapzag Monastery	
Thrangu Tashi Choling	
Maitreya Mandir	
Shelkar Chode Gaden Lepshad Ling	
Nyingmapa Wishfulfilling Center for Study and Practice	
Neman Pao Rinpoche Monastery	
Samtenling Tibetan Monastery	
Urgyen Tulku's Monastery (500,000 recitations)	

1990

Ceremonies	$26,086
Tamang Buddhist Association, Darjeeling	
Zhechen Tennyi Dargye Ling, Nepal	
Ka-Nying Shedrup Ling, Nepal	
Asura Caves, Nepal	
Nyingma Shedra, Nepal; others	
Monastery support	$118,195

1991

Preservation of Nyingma linages and philosophical studies in eight monasteries, nunneries, shedras, and retreat centers in east Tibet	$28,034

Traling Gonpa (branch of Kathog)
Tenpo Gonpa (branch of Tarthang)
Se Gonpa (Jonangpa Tradition)
Lungkar gonpa (Gelug-pa)
Yag Go Gonpa (branch of Tarthang)
Dongzong Gonpa (hermitage of Do Khyentse)
Tumpo Gonpa, specializing in Payul and Nyingthig traditions
Do Gonpa, specializing in Nyingthig

1993

Central Tibet and Nepal $121,689

TIBET

Samye Funds for monthly ceremonies (248 days of Pujas attended by fifty to one hundred lamas); funds for reconstruction of Pehar temple.

Dorje Drag Three years support for eighty-two days of ceremonies annually and for maintenance of forty monks.

Mindroling Funds for repairs to the roof; support for monks, ceremonies, and offerings for three years. Gold for creating statues of Guru Padmsambhava, King Trisong Detsen, and Abbot Shantarakshita.

Tsering Jong Three years support for nuns; funds for monthly ceremony offerings; funds to repair the temple roof; shelves to hold the Kanjur.

Shugseb Nunnery Support for ceremonies and living expenses for nuns for three years.

Palri Offerings and three years' support for monthly ceremonies.

Nyepur Shugseb Support for ceremonies and living expenses for three years; sponsorship of paintings of the Dzogchen lineage.

NEPAL

Ka-Nying Shedrup Ling One year of support for sixty students enrolled at the shedra.

NEPAL (*continued*)

Asura and Maratika Caves: one year of support for retreatants at Asura caves; funds for rebuilding the retreat center at Maratika Caves.

1995

Nepal and Tibet $123,190

NEPAL

Pharping Monastery

Nagi Gompa Nunnery

Trulshik Rinpoche's Monastery

Pharping Stupa Foundation (Sakyapa)

Ka-Nying Shedrup Ling (Losar Ceremonies)

Nyingma Institute of Nepal

Maratika Caves

TIBET

Tsongsen Gompa Pagse

Dorje Drag

Shugseb Nunnery

Deldre Monastery

Dregong Shedra

Dergun Wenre Monastery

Lhasa Jokhang

Mindroling Monastery

Samye Monastery

Uru Shaye Lhakhang

Tarthang Monastery Shedra

Extensive charts of ceremonies sponsored 1994–2005 are given at the end of this volume.

1996

India, Nepal, and Tibet $106,753

NORTHERN INDIA
Mindroling
Sakya College
Sakya Moanstery
Pema Awam Choegar Geumay Ling
Ngagyur Samten Choekhor Ling
Rigo Tulku's Monastery
Urgyen Thundup's Monastery
Dzongsar Khyentse's Shedra
Nyingma Monastery
Kangtrul Kagyud Monastery
other monasteries and centers

NEPAL
Choling Rinpoche
Tenga Rinpoche
Yantse Rinpoche
Dechen Rinpoche
Chokyi Nyima Rinpoche
Urgyen Tulku Memorial
Rabjam Tulku
Taru Rinpoche
Ka-Nying Shedrup Ling
(retreat support for ten monks for three years at Parphing)

TIBET
Offerings for Dorje Drag given at Bodh Gaya

Total Offerings for Ceremonies for the Four Schools 1988–1996 $450,282.

rGyal-wa bKa'-'gyur Rinpoche Beginning in 1976, TNMC/TAP has sponsored annual observances of this highly meritorious ceremony by the monks of the five major Gelug monasteries in India: Drepung and Gaden at Mundgod; Gyudmed Tantric University, Gurupura; Gyuto Tantric University, Bomdila; and Sera Monastic University, Bylakuppe. At least 31 of these ceremonies have also been sponsored for Nyingma monasteries, 14 for Kagyu, and 5 for Sakya. This ceremony, which centers on reciting the entire 108 volumes of the bKa'-'gyur, the words of the Buddha, is a highly symbolic act that has great significance for the Sangha as a whole. In essence, it replicates the early councils of the Sangha, convened after the Buddha's Parinirvana to affirm the truth of the teachings and the Sangha's resolve to uphold them and manifest their blessings.

Generally performed by a large assembly of the monastic Sangha, this recitation generates great merit and invites blessings on beings of the ten directions. For the Sangha separated from its homeland, for those growing up with no memory of Tibet, and for the longevity of the Buddhadharma itself, it was especially important to keep the spirit of this ceremony alive. In the early years, TNMC offered lamas presiding over the bKa'-'gyur Rinpoche recitations $500 for each ceremony. Since 1996, this amount has increased to $1,000 for each rGyal-wa bKa'-'gyur ceremony sponsored. Additional funds have been offered for exceptionally large gatherings.

Tara and Sitatapatra Prayers These ceremonies, important in the development of Bodhicitta, include 100,000 repetitions of the mantras of Tara, mother of compassion, or Sitatapatra, bearer of the white umbrella of protection. TAP/TNMC have sponsored these prayers for monasteries and nunneries of all Tibetan traditions.

Prajnaparamita Heart Sutra Central to all Mahayana traditions, the Heart Sutra expresses the essence of Prajnaparamita. A hundred thousand repetitions of this teaching, or of the mantra it contains, opens mind and heart to the meaning of shunyata.

Vajrakila These ceremonies are generally observed within the Nyingma and Sakya schools, traditions that continue this lineage most strongly. TAP/TNMC have sponsored this ceremony on numerous occasions for Nyingma monasteries in India and Nepal and also for Sakya monasteries.

Guru Rinpoche This ceremony includes multiples of 100,000 recitations of the Vajra Guru mantra and other prayers that invoke the blessings of the Great Guru. TAP and TNMC have sponsored this ceremony most often for Nyingma, Kagyu, and Sakya monasteries.

Additional ceremonies sponsored include multiple recitations of the Manjushri-namasamgiti, the Bhadracarya-pranidhana, and the Ye Dharma mantra; recitation of texts and prayers related to the Medicine Buddha and the Sixteen Arhats; sadhanas to yi-dams specific to each tradition; and ceremonies with special significance for the Nyingma school.

Monlam Chenmo In 1989, TNMC organized the first Ngagyur Nyingma Monlam Chenmo, the World Peace Ceremony at Bodh Gaya. Inspired by large gatherings for major ceremonies once held by the Dalai Lamas in Tibet, this was the first ceremony in exile to invite participants from all Nyingma monasteries. The World Peace ceremonies are described in greater detail in chapter nine.

Kagyu and Sakya Monlams Initiated and sponsored by TNMC between 1993 and 1995, World Peace Ceremonies have been observed each year by both the Kagyu and Sakya traditions. In 1995, TNMC funded foundations to support the continuation of these ceremonies in perpetuity. Since 1996, TAP and TNMC have continued to contribute $3,000 for each Monlam.

As of December 31, 2004, TNMC and TAP had sponsored a total of 1,503 ceremonies (not counting the World Peace Ceremonies), including seven observances of the Tongdrub Vajra Guru described below and 324 recitations of the rGyal-wa bKa'-'gyur Rinpoche.

Blessings of a Hundred Million Mantras

In the late 1980s, I was inspired by the thought of revitalizing the Tongdrub Vajra Guru Ceremony, a traditional Nyingma practice in which hundreds of monks gather to recite the Vajra Guru mantra one hundred million times. Even in pre-1959 Tibet, it had been difficult to assemble the large gathering of lamas and monks necessary to perform this powerful ceremony, which requires the leadership of highly qualified lamas and the participation of at least two hundred practitioners for a period of ten days to two weeks. In the 1990s, in response to the increasing instability and suffering in the world, I began to encourage some of my lama friends to organize and lead this ceremony. Between 1998 and 2003, TAP and TNMC jointly sponsored seven of these ceremonies, offering $12,000 for each ceremony for a total cost of $96,000. Since these ceremonies counteract the imbalances and catastrophes that characterize the deepening of the kaliyuga, they have a special relevance to our times, and we plan to continue sponsoring them in the future.

Trulzhig Rinpoche, 2001

Thubten Mewa, Rewalsar, 1999

Taklung Tsetrul, Dorje Drag Monastery, 2000

Sakya Trizin, Kathmandu Valley, Nepal, 2001

Sakya Trizin, Dehra Dun, 2002

Khochen Tulku, Nyingma Lama's College, 2003

Trulzhig Rinpoche, 2003 and 2004

Compassion for All Beings

In recent years, TNMC has sponsored a ceremonial demonstration of compassion for all beings, symbolized by the ritual release of many thousands of fish in holy places. Shatrul Rinpoche, abbot of Rigzin Drubje Ghatsal Monastery in Pharping, Nepal, has presided over at least three of these observances.

Enlarging the Field of Merit

Starting in 1989, most of the funds for ceremonies were redirected into major efforts to support prayers at holy places for the four schools of Tibetan Buddhism and revitalize certain ceremonies of special importance for preserving rare lineages. In addition to sponsoring ceremonies at monasteries widely dispersed in India, I sought also to gather support for larger, more centralized ceremonies at Bodh Gaya, site of the Buddha's enlightenment. Although TNMC continued to sponsor ceremonies at individual monasteries, this new effort gathered momentum over the next few years and became the central focus of major text preservation efforts as well.

As TNMC's revitalization activities intensified, TAP resumed an active role in cultural preservation. In recent years, TAP's involvement in important projects has continued to steadily expand, and its role for the future has become more clearly defined. TNMC continues to provide the vision for revitalization, assess the needs, and generate sacred texts, art, prayer wheels and prayer flags, and other ritual materials through the Yeshe De Text Preservation Project, while TAP arranges for and funds the distribution of these essential materials. Since 2002, TAP has also raised funds to support the production of sacred texts, the restoration of monastic libraries, and the giving of major collections of books to individual practitioners.

TAP now supports construction of monasteries and nunneries, sponsors ceremonies in India and Nepal, and contributes to TNMC's efforts to fund the building of stupas, restore statues, and produce prayer flags and prayer wheels. To support these projects, the international Nyingma centers in Holland, Germany, and Brazil, officially authorized in the early 1990s, established TAP offices and began to sponsor fundraising events.

Chapter Eight

Preserving through Publication Sacred Texts and Art

When I came to America in 1968, I hoped to find a way to continue the work of Dharma Mudranalaya, the press I had established in Sarnath. A few months after settling in Berkeley, I acquired a small hand-press and showed my students how to print leaflets and study materials for their classes. Among the first leaflets produced was an announcement of the founding of Dharma Press that described our intention to print the Tibetan texts I had brought with me. Although two of these texts were printed the following year, it became necessary to focus first on developing the capacities of Dharma Press and establishing our organizations on a more solid foundation. For the next ten years, as students developed the necessary skills and Dharma Press added essential equipment for typesetting, printing, and binding, the wish to preserve the Dharma teachings continued to guide our efforts.

During the early 1970s, we worked to research availability and to acquire sacred texts, including several editions of the bKa'-'gyur and bsTan-'gyur, the traditional compilation of the teachings of the Buddha, together with commentaries and related texts by Buddhist masters translated mostly from Sanskrit between the eighth and fourteenth centuries C.E. It soon became clear that there were very few sets of this comprehensive collection outside of Tibet, and most of them were either generally unavailable or not clear enough to reproduce well. These findings convinced me that, while the obstacles were formidable and our resources might not be sufficient, the continued existence of these precious texts was in jeopardy, and we had to make the effort. In the course of our research, we drew upon the resources of university libraries to obtain clearer copies of folios missing or illegible in our editions.

Creating The Nyingma Edition of the Tibetan Buddhist Canon

In 1979, after nine years of planning and preparation, Dharma Publishing and Dharma Press began production of *The Nyingma Edition of the bKa'-'gyur and bsTan-'gyur*. From January 1979 through September 1981 I met daily with artists and Dharma Publishing editors involved in research to review their results, assess what was needed to take the next step, and initiate the gathering of additional information. Fortunately, I was able to locate historically important Tibetan catalogs and lineage records, while the editors collected whatever catalogs, indexes, and bibliographies were available in Western languages. Many hours were spent on educating the staff on the importance of this work and providing background information on panditas and lo-tsa-bas.

After much deliberation, I decided to supplement the 4,502 texts of the sDe-dge edition with 593 works included in other canonical editions, a recent Tibetan translation of the Dhammapada, and nine texts preserved only in Chinese (seven early Abhidharma texts, the Mahavibhasha, a massive compendium of Abhidharma, and the Mahaprajnaparamita-shastra, attributed to Nagarjuna.) As described in *Creation for the Future: The Nyingma Lineage in the West,*

> Printing of the texts, initiated late in 1979, was completed on July 22, 1980, the anniversary of the birth of Guru Padmasambhava. The remaining elements making up *The Nyingma Edition* came together during the following year, as we developed ways to present research information in the preliminary pages of each volume: comparative charts listing texts

Volumes of The Nyingma Edition, *together with displays of its sacred art and maps were shown to the public in Berkeley in 1983.*

in all major editions; charts giving specific information on each text; and a series of 120 maps (one for each volume) presenting historical information on Dharma transmission. Title pages were prepared for each text, giving the Tibetan and Sanskrit names in original scripts as well as roman letters and the calligraphy for whatever corresponding Chinese translations existed in the Chinese Tripiṭaka.

Together with the texts, we published 231 Tibetan thanka reproductions (two in most volumes) gathered from museums and private collections around the world, together with a series of 262 line drawings that included a complete traditional set of iconographic images. Over the course of a year, I researched numerous publications and traditional texts to develop designs for the dedication pages, tables of contents, section openings, and ends of sections, while an artist prepared line drawings of famous stupas, Buddhist symbols, and artistic elements to incorporate into these designs. Late in 1980, it was decided to use Lantsa script for the section titles as a traditional gesture of respect and blessing, and to end each volume with drawings of Dharmapalas and stupas. In shaping and developing all these details, we made every effort to convey the beauty and preciousness of the teachings.

Completion of the Nyingma Edition

The entire 120-volume collection was printed on acid-free paper, edge-gilded, gold-stamped, and bound with the highest quality of materials. Each phase of the project presented new challenges. In the middle of printing it became necessary to relocate our press and all the materials printed up to that time. When binding began, the commercial wing of our press, our main source of income, had to shut down to focus on the enormous amount of hand-work involved. For a time, it seemed our resources would not hold up, but day after day, we managed to continue.

For each volume we prepared a 'Golden Key', a detailed bookmark listing the texts and relevant information in each volume. Designed to last for at least three hundred years, *The Nyingma Edition* preserves 5,109 texts, a total of 192,000 Tibetan folios. Since its release in 1981, *The Nyingma Edition* has been distributed to libraries worldwide. Sets of *The Nyingma Edition*, currently valued at $50,000, were donated to H. H. the Dalai Lama, Dharamsala; H. H. Penor Rinpoche, Byalakuppe; H. H. Sakya Trizen in Dehra Dun, India; the Center of Buddhist Studies in Domkhar, Bhutan; the Central Institute of Higher Tibetan Studies in Sarnath; Ka-Nying Shedrup Ling, in Kathmandu, Nepal; and Tarthang Monastery (two sets) and Khra-gling Monastery, both in Tibet. Distribution was planned to ensure that the sacred texts survive natural disasters, wars, and forced relocations, which have seriously affected the Dharma in the past and also in recent history.

The preface to *The Nyingma Edition* describes our wish to present the texts in a way that honors their origin and value:

> *The Nyingma Edition* is an offering to the Dharma, designed to evoke in the reader the sense of respect and gratitude with which students of Buddhism traditionally approach the teachings. It is as perfect as our limited capacity and knowledge allow. . . . As our skills and insights have grown, we have slowly learned to coordinate publishing, printing, financial, artistic, and scholarly considerations. With 120 volumes to prepare, every change or addition has been a major project in itself, and only unusual care, flexibility, and ingenuity have made it possible to operate in the face of limited funds and the lack of appropriate equipment. Often, I have recalled with wonder the achievements of the masters who secured and translated the canonical works, kept alive the lineage of transmission, and preserved and compiled the texts. Our efforts and difficulties seem insignificant compared with their monumental accomplishments.
>
> In preparing *The Nyingma Edition,* I have taken responsibility for supervising the various elements of research, design, and production, making many complex decisions that affected the presentation of the Canon. I hope that I have chosen wisely, for in these difficult times the light of the Dharma can bring great blessings. Though others will be able to improve on our work, I truly believe that access to the teachings can be of incalculable value for the modern world.
>
> —Tarthang Tulku

The publication of *The Nyingma Edition* was covered by the international press. Various sources called it "a milestone in Buddhist history," " a major breakthrough in text preservation," and "a tour de force of the printer's art." But to those who worked on this complex project, its success was due to the blessings of the lineage and to the power of the Dharma itself, for it was nothing short of miraculous that a publication of this size and quality could have been produced by our small staff, especially with such limited resources.

Compiling a Nyingma Canon

Compiled, copied, and transmitted as a single collection since the fourteenth century, the texts of the bKa'-'gyur and bsTan-'gyur, the scriptural foundation for all Tibetan Buddhist traditions, had survived intact to the present day. But there were many thousands of additional texts transmitted within the Nyingma tradition that had never been assembled and preserved in this way. Each of the major monasteries specialized in specific teachings and practices, and students wishing to study them would have to travel to those locations. Although some collections of bKa'-'ma and gTer-ma texts, as well as gSung-'bums (collected works) of great masters had been compiled, copies of these collections were few and widely dispersed. With the disruption of Tibetan culture in the 1960s, these texts were even more rare than those in the bKa'-'gyur and bsTan-'gyur.

For many years I had dreamed of collecting all the works of the Nyingma tradition and compiling them into a single coherent publication. When planning the volumes of *The Nyingma Edition,* I had in fact asked that eleven volumes be reserved for an edition of the rNying-ma rGyud-'bum, the hundred thousand Tantras brought to Tibet in the eighth century and not included in the bKa'-'gyur and bsTan-'gyur. In 1983, after completing *The Nyingma Edition,* I established the Yeshe De Project as a way to continue the work of preserving the sacred texts.

In 1983, and again in 1986, I had the opportunity to travel in eastern Tibet. Wherever I went, seeing the devastation of the monasteries, schools, and libraries convinced me of the urgent need to continue our work and do everything possible to preserve all the texts that sustained the Nyingma lineages. Although I was not qualified to undertake such a monumental task, and there were no learned scholars who might assist me, through the kindness of my teachers, great masters rich in wisdom and compassion, I had some familiarity with the teachings and a basic foundation in language and philosophy. Considering how few copies of these texts existed, how close they had come to being lost completely, and the printing capacities we had developed in printing *The Nyingma Edition,* I felt obligated to make the effort to compile them and publish them in a form that could last for hundreds of years.

While in eastern Tibet, I was able to commission the first complete printing since 1936 of the sDe-dge edition of the rNying-ma rGyud-'bum. This alone was a great blessing: difficulties arose during the printing, and for a time I feared that the printers would not continue. Although the printing was completed, it is not likely that this edition will be reprinted again in my lifetime. There were further blessings as well, for each volume, shipped by mail from eastern Tibet, across China, and overseas to America, arrived safely in Berkeley several months later. Now that we had four different editions of this rare collection as well as major compilations of bKa'-ma (texts transmitted continuously) and gTer-ma (texts concealed by Padmasambhava for later recovery), I decided to publish them all in the same durable, high-quality, hardbound format as the volumes of *The Nyingma Edition.*

Although production began in 1986, further research convinced me of the importance of including whole collections of the works of Nyingma masters and possibly the works of Indian and other Tibetan masters as well. I encouraged the Yeshe De staff to research the holdings of libraries and museums in Japan, China, and India as well as libraries in Europe and the private collections of lamas in India, Sikkim, Bhutan, Nepal, and Tibet.

In the course of this research, and during my own journeys to Asia, we located texts of more than 150 Nyingma authors and collected film for research purposes from numerous libraries. The texts acquired in this way included works in Tibetan as well as Sutras and Tantras in Sanskrit, the Shel-dkar, lHa-sa, and sNar-thang editions of the bKa'-'gyur, a large number of gSung-'bum (collected texts) of as many as four hundred Tibetan masters, and a major collection of South Asian art.

Although I did not intend to expand the scope of this project so greatly, one set of texts led to the next, with each one so precious or rare that it was not possible to exclude it. As the collection expanded, I named it *Great Treasures of Ancient Teachings.* To produce this collection, I established Dharmacakra Press, an entirely new printing facility dedicated to preserving Tibetan texts. Since it began operations at Odiyan in 1987, Dharmacakra Press has produced Tibetan texts day and night with very few interruptions.

Unexpected Discoveries

Over the next ten years, under my direction and editorial review, the Yeshe De staff worked intensively to collect and produce the texts that are now part of *Great Treasures.* Even when research showed where the texts were located, persistent efforts and expense were often required to obtain a copy of the texts that we could reproduce. There were also unexpected blessings, as when priceless teachings that I had thought were lost long ago came to us almost miraculously, or we located works by major lineage holders that were previously unknown.

Eventually we also added texts on the literary arts, medicine, ritual arts and technology, biographies, general histories of the Dharma in India and Tibet, histories and comprehensive lineage records of both Nyingma and Sarma schools, and other subjects common to all Tibetan traditions. Although the collection grew twice as large as I

When completed, sets of Great Treasures of Ancient Teachings *will help restore the libraries lost when thousands of Tibetan monasteries were damaged or destroyed during the Cultural Revolution.*

had originally anticipated, we have yet to locate and include a number of important texts that are likely to exist in private collections.

The production of *Great Treasures of Ancient Teachings* continued intensively from 1988 through 1995; ten more volumes were compiled and printed by the year 2000, and sixteen more were completed in 2001. The works of more than four hundred authors—about two thousand traditional Tibetan volumes—have now been compiled and preserved in 625 atlas-size western-style

Ten Sections of Great Treasures of Ancient Teachings

rNying-ma-rgyud-'bum Editions Four editions of the ancient Tantras of the Nyingma School; a manuscript edition and part of another. 70 Western volumes, 2,198 major texts.

Inner Tantra sDe-gsum-kha-skong Works by early Nyingma masters, including rDzogs-chen rGyud-bcu-bdun, Klong-chen-mdzod-bdun, sNying-thig-ya-bzhi, dGongs-pa-zang-thal, others. 17 Western volumes, 493 major texts.

The bKa'-ma-rgyas-pa Tantric texts and practices compiled by 17th-century masters, with additional works collected by Dudjom Rinpoche and Tarthang Rinpoche. 24 Western volumes, 358 major texts.

Rin-chen-gter-mdzod Treasure texts recovered by 230 masters, compiled by the 19th-century masters Kong-sprul Blo-gros mTha'-yas and 'Jams-dbyangs mKhyen-brtse dBang-po. 43 Western volumes, 3,210 major texts.

Works of Nyingma Masters Collected works by 150 masters on subjects ranging from philosophy and meditation to poetry and medicine. 314 Western volumes, twenty thousand major texts.

Commentaries in the Shastra Tradition Commentaries, systems of study, explications, and other works by Indian and Tibetan masters on Prajnaparamita, Madhyamaka, Cittamatra, Abhidharma, Logic, and Vinaya. 44 Western volumes, 456 major texts.

General Instructions on Sutra and Tantra Works by Nyingma and major Sarma masters on teachings, meditation practices, prayers, and ritual. 33 Western volumes, 815 major texts.

Biography and History Jatakas, Avadanas, biographies, monastic and lineage records, Dharma histories, and pilgrimage guides. 27 Western volumes, 175 major texts.

Arts and Sciences Medicine, biology, chemistry, and earth sciences; astrology, mathematics, and cosmology; literary studies, sacred art. 31 Western volumes, 379 major texts.

Volumes in Progress and Volumes Not Yet Located

bound books. Three times as extensive as the bKa'-'gyur and bsTan-'gyur, with over 30,000 major texts holding about 84,000 teachings, *Great Treasures* can appropriately be viewed as a Nyingma Canon.

A hundred more Tibetan volumes are in various stages of production, and still more texts are on hand awaiting review. To the best of my knowledge, we have now compiled about seventy-five percent of the Nyingma texts that have survived to the present day. Until we are certain that the collection is complete, the search for additional texts will continue. Our hope is that this enormous collection, when completed, will help restore the libraries lost in the widespread destruction of Tibetan monasteries during the 1960s.

Generating Libraries: New Typeset Editions

While the *Great Treasures* collection was essential for preservation, distribution of such a large collection would necessarily be limited, and teachers and students needed books they could carry and study with greater ease. On my travels to India and Nepal in the early 1990s, I became acutely aware that students in the Nyingma shedras did not have the books they needed to comprehend the distinctive views and emphases of our tradition. Unless these books could be provided quickly, valuable aspects of our tradition could be lost within a single generation.

A few years earlier, I had worked with Khenpo Thupten, a visiting lama, to design a type font in the sDe-dge woodblock style, with graceful shapes and elegant proportions. Several students transferred the drawings for each character into a computer to make a digital font. This font, which was later expanded to include more than 1,140 glyphs, is unusually flexible: It can reproduce Tibetan transcriptions of Sanskrit letters as well as special symbols and expressions found in some Tibetan texts. The Yeshe De staff began using this font in 1987, when they input Klong-chen-pa's Seven Treasures and other important Nyingma texts. In 1989, I began to select additional texts from *Great Treasures* to offer directly to the Sangha attending the World Peace Ceremony in Bodh Gaya. The Yeshe De staff has continued to typeset more texts every year since.

In 1991, I offered a few volumes of the Seven Treasures to participants at the second World Peace Ceremony at Bodh Gaya. Each year, for all but one of the World Peace ceremonies since 1991, we have worked ever harder to provide the Nyingma Sangha with texts essential to their tradition, and have distributed thousands of books to individuals and monasteries of the Sarma traditions as well. The entire Yeshe De staff, along with two fully-equipped press facilities, is now fully dedicated to what has become a long-range project: to endow at least three thousand libraries throughout the Himalayas with major collections of Buddhist texts. For this project, the *Great Treasures* collection has been an invaluable resource, a true treasury of knowledge we can draw upon to brighten the light of the Buddhadharma throughout Himalayan lands and inspire a new generation of students to engage in research and translation.

Providing the Foundation for Dharma Studies

Although the order of production evolved over time, beginning with texts considered most rare and essential, looking back, I can see that it fell into a logical progression. It began with essential works of the Maha, Anu, and Atiyoga teachings, known as the Inner Tantras—the rarest and most valuable teachings transmitted within the Nyingma tradition. Distribution from 1996 to 1998 focused on works of the greatest Nyingma masters, including rare practice texts never before published, biographies of Guru Padmasambhava, and an early history of Dharma transmission to Tibet.

In 1998, with more schools for higher Buddhist studies in operation and their enrollments increasing, the focus shifted to typesetting and printing major collections of shastras from the bsTan-'gyur, together with extensive commentaries by such vener-

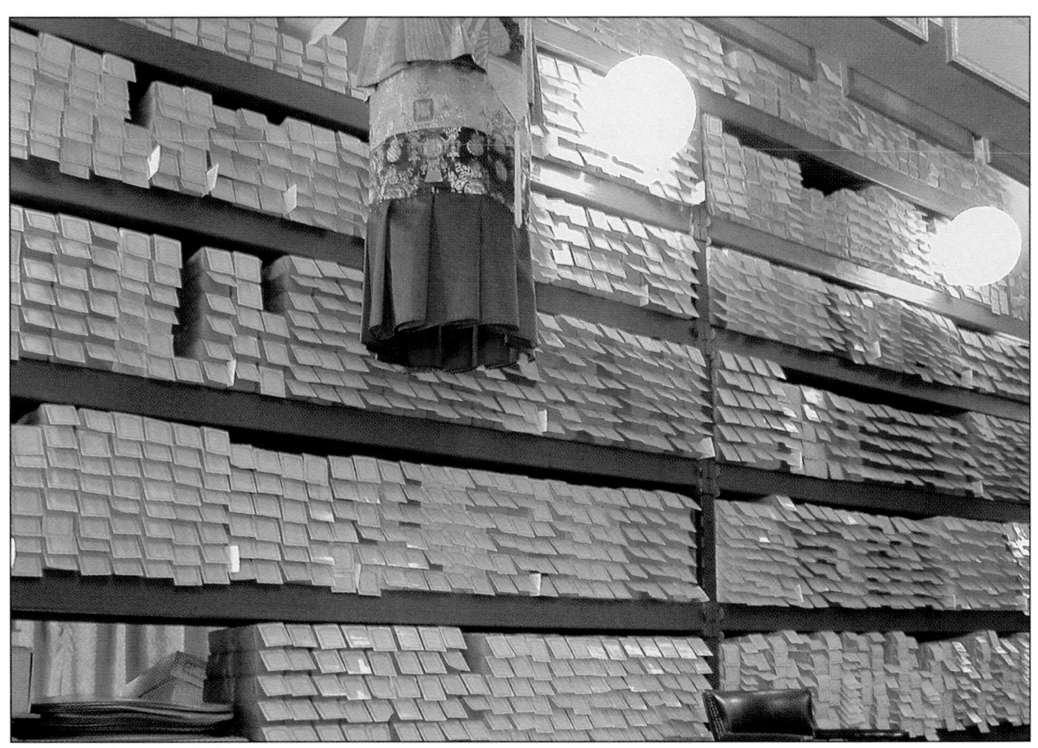

A complete set of typeset Tibetan texts constitutes an extensive library of Sutras, Tantras, commentaries, and other works by the great Indian and Tibetan masters, as well as teachings on practicing the Bodhisattva path.

ated Tibetan masters as Lama Mipham and Paltrul Rinpoche. The shastras are the basis for the study of Vinaya, Prajnaparamita, and Abhidharma, subjects that develop shila (moral perfection), samadhi (meditative realization), and prajna (discerning wisdom)—the Three Trainings that open the gates to enlightenment. The central importance of Prajnaparamita inspired the greatest masters to write shastras that bring out the significance of its most profound teachings on the Bodhisattva view and path. The works of these masters inspired two major streams of Mahayana philosophy: Madhyamaka, based on the shastras of Nagarjuna, and Cittamatra-Yogacara, inspired by the teachings of the Bodhisattva Maitreya and the commentaries of Asanga and Vasubandhu. Works by the great logicians Dignaga and Dharmakirti, important in maintaining guidelines for valid knowledge, were also included in this series.

Taught at Nalanda, Odantapuri, and Vikramashila, and preserved in the bsTan-'gyur, the shastras became the foundation of a Dharma education accepted by all schools of Tibetan Buddhism. Through our publications and distribution at the World Peace Ceremonies and other occasions, I have sought to make this body of knowledge available to students of all Tibetan traditions, together with works that support spiritual practices, including canonical commentaries on the Manjushri-namasamgiti and five large volumes of Dharanis.

For Nyingma students, we typeset and printed thirteen major shastras that included the commentary of mKhan-po gZhan-dga', a nineteenth-century Nyingma master renowned for his balanced approach to the works of the great Indian masters. Although his commentaries have been the foundation for education within the Nyingma school for more than a century, they were not generally available in India. When I realized that young Tibetans were growing up unaware of the depth of scholarship transmitted within their tradition, I gave the commentaries of gZhan-dga' a high priority for production and distribution.

In 2001, when we considered printing the six-volume Ratnakuta Sutra, I decided to create a new, larger design appropriate for the words of the Buddha, and asked the Yeshe De staff to use this design also in preparing the entire Prajnaparamita Sutra in 100,000 lines. At twenty-seven Tibetan volumes in length, this Sutra is the most extensive of the Prajnaparamita teachings. Although we had already printed and distributed the 25,000-line and 8,000-line Prajnaparamita teachings, since the 100,000-line teaching carries special merit and blessings needed in our times, it seemed important to distribute it also to practitioners of all Tibetan traditions.

Having come this far, in 2002, I decided to systematically produce most of the 108 volumes of the bKa'-'gyur in this format, including the entire Avatamsaka Sutra, the Vinaya, a series of Nges-don Sutras, more than 250 additional Sutras, and the Sarma

Tantras. Profound and comprehensive, these texts represent authentic true knowledge, the highest wisdom of the Enlightened Ones. For those who can read and understand them, they are the most precious of treasures. That same year, TAP established the Light of Wisdom Campaign, a three-year fundraising program to sponsor production of 100,000 books of Sutras and the cost of shipping them to Bodh Gaya for distribution at the World Peace Ceremonies.

As of December 2004, the Yeshe De staff has typeset and printed over 200 volumes containing 1,336 titles by 182 authors. TNMC and TAP have distributed, completely free of charge, over 1,500,000 books to lamas, monks, and nuns at the annual World Peace Ceremony at Bodh Gaya and other places as well. These books include the esoteric Maha, Anu, and Atiyoga teachings, accounts of the Buddha and his past lives, important Sutras and shastras of the Indian and Tibetan traditions, works by the great Nyingma masters and some important texts by the great masters of other schools. As a result of these efforts, members of more than 3,000 Nyingma monasteries, libraries, refugee settlements, and retreat centers in India, Nepal, Sikkim, Ladakh, Bhutan, and Tibet have received an extensive collection of essential texts in the traditional Tibetan format. Three hundred larger Nyingma monasteries and shedras have received hundreds of additional sets of books.

The books produced by the Yeshe De Project span the entire range of the Dharma, providing students a comprehensive education. Building upon a sound foundation of Sutras and shastras, they enable students to progress to the higher teachings that lead to the most complete and perfect experience of enlightenment. When this project is completed, for the first time in history, as many as six thousand Tibetan practitioners will have their own libraries of essential Sutras and shastras to sustain their studies and practices.

At present this work is essential to preserve these texts and provide lamas with materials for educating their students, so they can continue and extend the living tradition for many more generations.

It also increases possibilities that in the future these teachings can be translated into Western languages. Westerners may also learn to read the original works, and through them connect more closely with the incarnation lineages of the great masters and Bodhisattvas.

I hope that some day more Westerners will be able to read these books as Tibetan masters and lotsawas expressed them, freed from the need to rely on translations into languages that have not yet developed concepts that convey their true meaning. Students seeking a thorough mastery of these teachings must prepare well by learning Tibetan, studying the Dharma terms, and performing the sNgon-'gro practices. Then understanding can unfold in a steady progression, supported by study of the shastras that relate to the Sutras and systematize their teachings. The works of mKhan-po gZang-dga', who focused on thirteen great shastras as subjects for intensive study, are especially important for Western students seeking a comprehensive foundation.

Blessings of Preservation

It is now three decades since I began training students in ways to produce books that convey Dharma qualities, using strong, durable materials and beauty of design to indicate the lasting value of the teachings they contain. Students now know how to typeset Tibetan as well as English, how to incorporate balanced and symbolic designs, and how to print with attention to quality while avoiding waste that is considered inevitable in most printing operations today. These skills are not used for commercial purposes; they are dedicated exclusively to producing books that support the Dharma.

The magnitude of the work we have undertaken—perhaps unprecedented in history—seems almost impossible, considering our limited resources and knowledge. Even the individual-sized books involve a total of 130 stages of production and distribution, and all these stages are carried out by fifteen individuals that constitute the

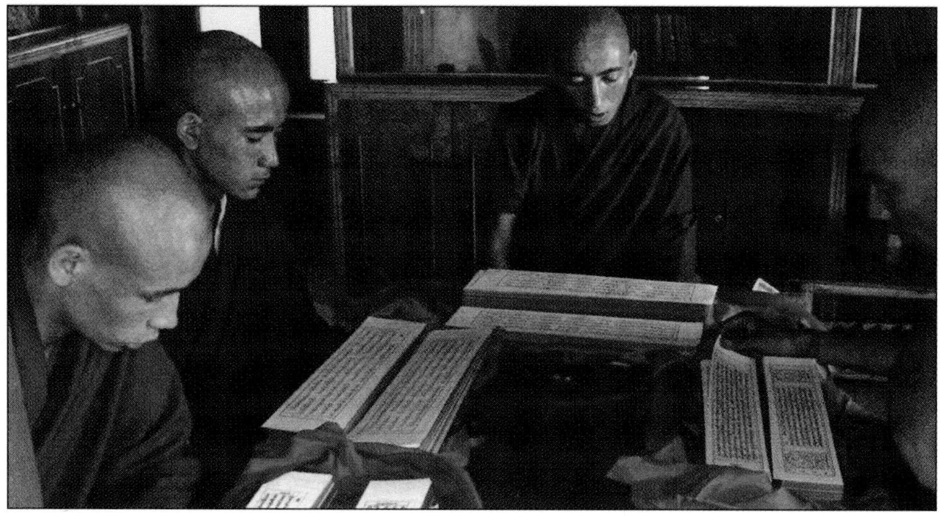

The sacred texts are highly venerated, stored on high shelves, and treated with the greatest respect. These monks in Ladakh are reading Yeshe De's loose-leaf pothi style volumes in the traditional way, in a clean, orderly environment free of distractions.

Yeshe De staff, with assists from a small body of volunteers, especially at critical times of the year. Each year as we rush to reach our goals, we rarely stop to reflect on what we have accomplished, but when we look back over the past two decades, we can see the full extent of our labors. All of us have learned a great deal in working with these texts, each in his or her own way, and I am deeply gratified that we have the capacity to help Tibet and the Tibetan Dharma tradition at this troubled time.

The difficulties experienced with text production in the 1980s have become a distant memory; while the work has increased greatly in quantity, it has remained high in quality, and it also goes more smoothly. I can only attribute this development to the results of years of full-hearted engagement with the work and the blessings of the lineage. Supported by these blessings, we can continue our efforts, offering our time and energy to preserve the texts and commentaries that are the heritage of the great teachings of the Sutrayana and Mantrayana streams of Dharma transmission.

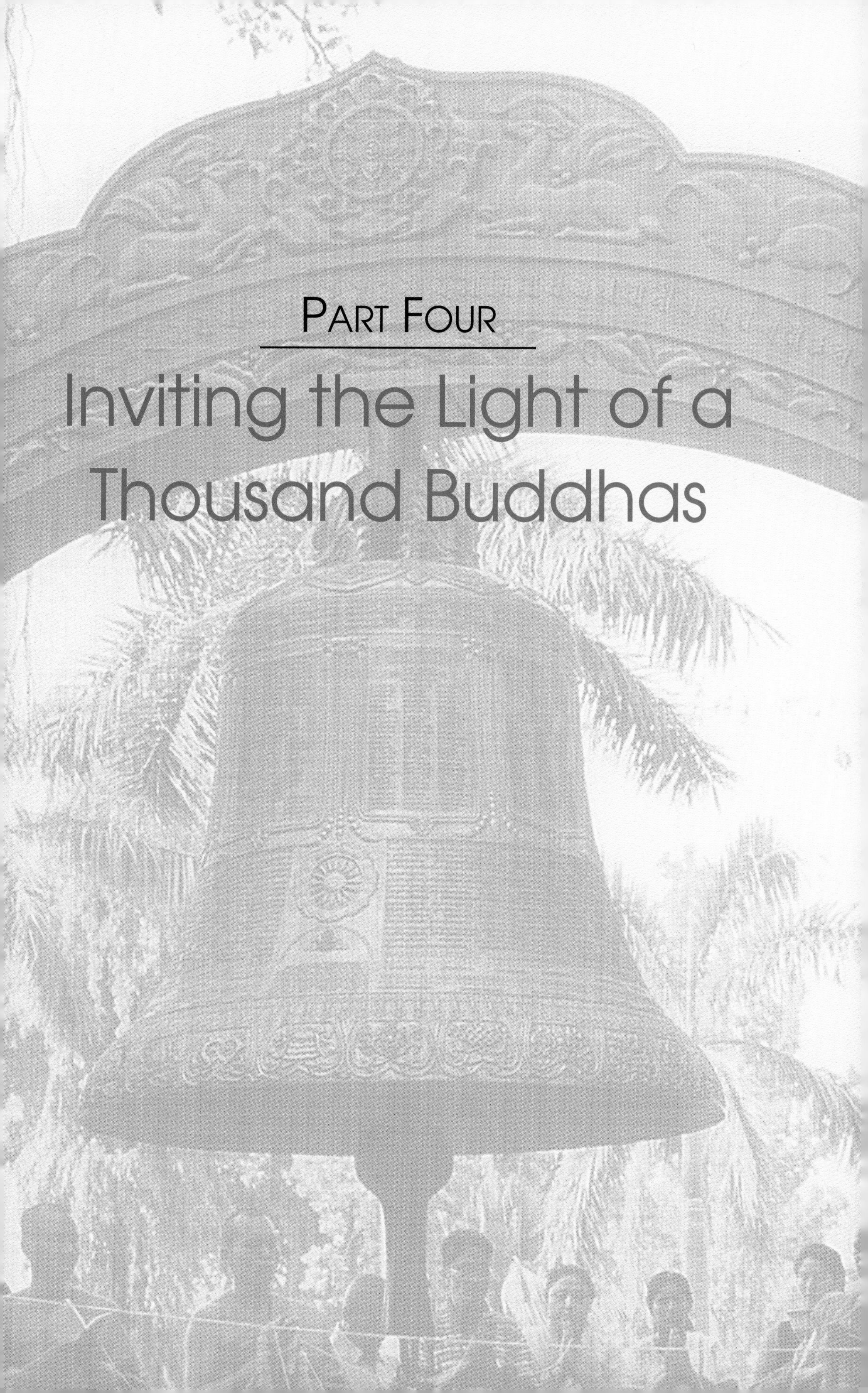

Part Four

Inviting the Light of a Thousand Buddhas

Chapter Nine

Revitalizing Holy Places: The World Peace Ceremonies

My teacher, 'Jam-dbyangs mKhyen-brtse Chos-kyi Blo-gros, one of the foremost masters of compassion and wisdom of this century, often performed sadhanas at Bodh Gaya, praying that the Dharma would once more emanate from Vajrasana to illuminate the ten directions of the cosmos. In 1962, three years after his passing, I came on pilgrimage to Bodh Gaya out of respect for my teacher's great kindness and my own deep concern for the survival of the Dharma in Tibet. I found this sacred site well maintained physically, but the compound, almost empty of practitioners, had a quiet, almost sleepy quality. Even so, I could sense its history as a living presence, the dynamic center of an invisible temple.

Recalling my teacher's vision, I thought of my friend lamas who had lost their monasteries in Tibet and the tens of thousands now struggling for survival. I prayed strongly, wishing the Dharma could come alive again through the power of the merit and virtue of such great masters, to bring peace to the world and relieve the sufferings of people everywhere.

For symbols of renewal and regeneration, it was natural to turn to Bodh Gaya, the root and central holy place for all Buddhist traditions. For centuries after the Buddha's Parinirvaṇa, great masters, teachers, and pilgrims continued to congregate at Bodh Gaya to renew their faith, remove obstacles, and strive to relieve suffering for all sentient beings. Among them were great Arhats, panditas,

The Mahabodhi Gandola, a temple topped by a fully-empowered stupa, marks the place where the Buddha brought the light of awakening into our world.

and siddhas; Nagarjuna and Atisha worshipped here, as did the Vidyadharas of the Vajrayana lineages. For all Tibetans, Bodh Gaya is the home of enlightenment, the point from which the teachings were disseminated in all directions and throughout the three realms. When this holy place fell into disrepair, the world went out of balance. The Dharma had declined in country after country, and now even Tibet was in chaos. The buildings and grounds of this sacred site had since been restored, but only devotion could reawaken its spiritual energy.

Generation of the Vision

While I strove to establish our organizations in America, the wish to support the Sangha in offering prayers at this holy place was never far from my mind. In the late 1970s, I began to contact lamas in a position to organize and lead traditional prayers at Bodh Gaya. In 1978, at my request, H.H. Dilgo Khyentse made arrangements for monks from Bhutan to travel to Bodh Gaya to offer prayers to the Thirty-five Buddhas of Forgiveness and perform a hundred thousand recitations of the Bhadracarya-pranidhana-raja, a prayer of aspiration for enlightenment recited within all Tibetan traditions.

In 1981, I again requested Ven. Dilgo Khyentse to lead an assembly of monks at Bodh Gaya in performing a hundred thousand recitations of the Manjushri-namasamgiti, a teaching the Buddha gave for the benefit of beings in all realms of existence, greatly revered by all Tibetan traditions. But obstacles arose and the ceremonies could not be completed. Later, with the assistance of Dodrup Chen Rinpoche and Ven. Khenpo Dechen Dorje, monks assembled at Bodh Gaya and performed 100,000 repetitions of both the Manjushri-namasamgiti and the Bhadracarya-pranidhana-raja.

Although TNMC was able to sponsor ceremonies for the four major schools throughout the 1980s, efforts to organize and sponsor large prayer assemblies of high lamas and monks at Bodh Gaya continued to meet with obstacles. In 1989, I decided to go to Bodh Gaya myself. After inviting leaders of the Nyingma Sangha to join me, I traveled to Bodh Gaya in December, 1989 to see what could be accomplished.

It was difficult to predict who would actually come to the ceremony or how it would develop. Our Nyingma Sangha was widely dispersed; travel was difficult for large groups of lamas and nuns, and most high lamas had pressing responsibilities within their own communities. Thus I was deeply moved that well over five hundred tulkus, lamas, monks and nuns from six countries made the effort to gather at Bodh Gaya and join me in prayers for world peace. This gathering, which continued for twenty-six days, became the first Ngagyur Nyingma Monlam Chenmo, the World Peace Ceremony. Although participants arrived at different times and not everyone could stay the entire time, about seven hundred lamas, monks, and nuns attended at least part of the ceremony. This was the first time in history that monks and lamas from so many Nyingma monasteries, representing all the lineages and traditions, had come together in a major convocation. This was especially significant in light of their separation from their home monasteries in Tibet. To extend the blessings further, TNMC also sponsored a hundred thousand recitations of the Manjushri-namasamgiti at five Gelug monasteries.

During the course of the ceremonies, brocade was brought from Varanasī and sewn into canopies, altar cloths, and ceremonial hangings for the Mahabodhi Temple. Toward the end of the ceremony, I distributed sacred texts prepared and printed under my direction by TNMC students in Berkeley: three Prajnaparamita Sutras, central teachings concerning shunyata and the nature of the Bodhisattva; the gSang-ba'i-snying-po (Guhyamulagarbha Tantra), an essential teaching; the sDud-pa-tshigs-su-bcad-pa, by the great fourteenth-century Nyingma master Klong-chen-pa, and the Bhadracarya-pranidhana-raja. In all, about eight hundred books were distributed to support education and practice. In a traditional gesture of

Each year, the Sangha assembles on the four sides of the Mahabodhi temple for the ten-day Monlam Chenmo, the World Peace Ceremony.

renewal and appreciation, one hundred and twenty new robes made by TNMC students were donated to the Sangha. The two thousand beggars outside the compound's gates each received gifts of new cloth and alms of two rupees per day.

The Vision Takes Hold

When my lama friends asked that this ceremony be repeated, I agreed to sponsor another ceremony the following year and support the lamas' travel expenses. Representatives from the six major Nyingma monasteries refounded in exile—Kah-thog, rDo-rje Brag, sMin-grol-gling, dPal-yul, rDzog-chen, and Zhe-chen—agreed to facilitate the necessary arrangements for the ceremony, which would now be observed for ten days.

Chanting begins in the early morning and continues until late afternoon. Western laypersons and pilgrims are seated behind the monks.

The prayers, offerings to the Sangha, and gestures of beautification of the Mahabodhi initiated in 1989–90 laid the foundation for the ceremonies that followed in 1991 and thereafter, as the World Peace Ceremony became an annual observance.

From *The World Peace Ceremony, Prayers at Holy Places 1994*:

> For the past five years, the Monlam Chenmo assembly has prayed for world peace. Special prayers have been offered for the healing of the Tibetan people who have suffered so greatly in recent times and for the restoration of the Dharma and the Sangha in Tibet. During these ceremonies, we have invited the blessings of the Lord Buddha, Guru Padmasambhava, Avalokiteshvara, Manjushri, Vajrapani, Samantabhadra, and Tara, together with Dakinis and Dharmapalas,

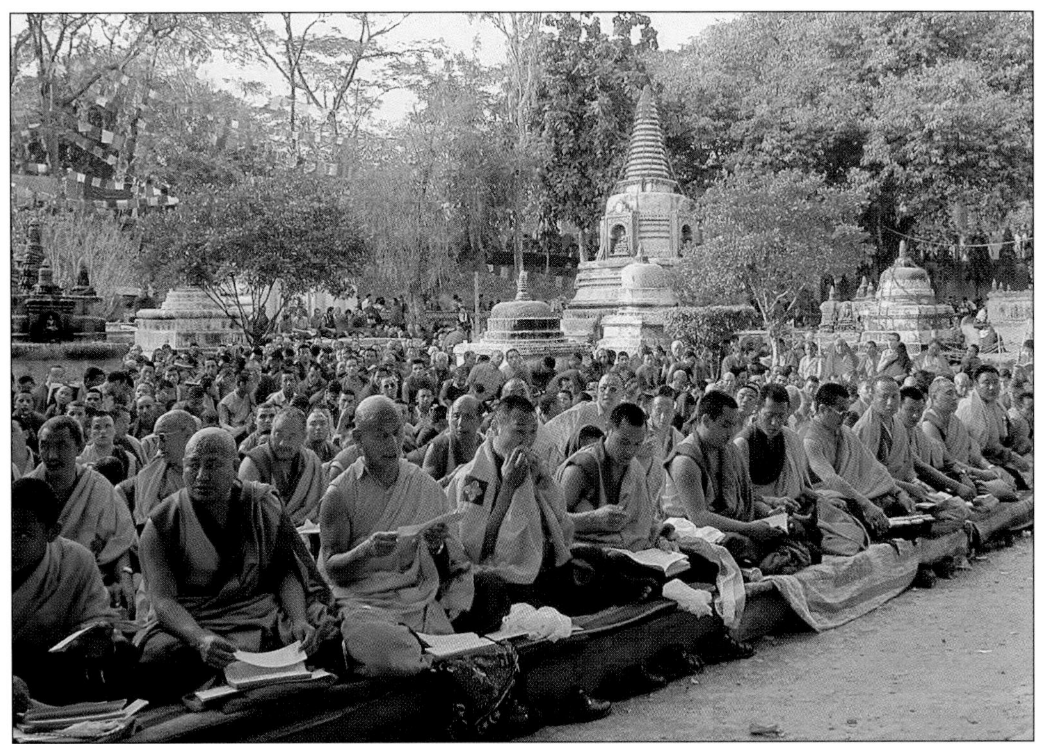

Every year, six to seven thousand monks and nuns and over ten thousand laypeople participate in the World Peace Ceremony at Bodh Gaya.

> to embrace the whole world. . . . The participants speak joyfully of their deepening appreciation for these acts of devotion. These seem signs that our motivation is good, that the results will be positive, and that the blessings of the Buddhas and Bodhisattvas are with us.
>
> May we continue to share in the great work of serving the Dharma by offering the Ceremonies for World Peace for the benefit of people everywhere. May the merit of our prayers promote the longevity of His Holiness the Dalai Lama, so that his enlightened guidance, which has promoted the success of all four schools in exile, continues forever.
>
> —Tarthang Tulku

The number of participants steadily increased, to two thousand in 1992, 3,700 in 1993, to the current average of 7,000 lamas, monks, and nuns and additional thousands of laypersons. Participants now

At high points in the ceremony, the sound of drums and the reverberating overtones of Tibetan horns stimulate the senses and awaken the mind.

travel to Bodh Gaya from as many as three thousand monasteries and retreat centers in India, Nepal, Tibet, Bhutan, and Sikkim.

Gathered at the very spot where Siddhartha Gautama was enlightened more than 2,500 years ago, the Sangha makes offerings of light, flowers, fruit, and incense, together with a hundred repetitions of the Pranidhanaraja and the Manjushri-namasamgiti. Many thousands of lay people travel to the state of Bihar to join the ceremonies, together with Buddhists from North and South America, Europe, and the Far East. Thanks to the graciousness of local and district government, the Bodh Gaya Temple Management Committee, and the Nyingma Monlam Chenmo Committee, the ceremonies have been successful year after year.

The annual celebrations have brought the Tibetan communities closer together, inspiring students to connect with their traditions and to experience directly the power of prayer at places blessed by

Dedication for the Four Schools Monlams

May the four schools of Tibetan Buddhadharma, embodiments of the three vehicles to realization, continue to hold open the doors to realization.

May the merit generated by these ceremonies ensure the longevity of His Holiness Tenzin Gyatso, the Fourteenth Dalai Lama, that his compassion and wisdom light the way to a free Tibet.

May the merit generated by the ceremonies for world peace heal the wound of aggressions, supporting peace in the world and happiness for all sentient beings.

May the Tibetan people once again be free to practice their faith in their homeland, and may Tibetans living in exile soon realize the joy of reunion.

May the leaders and teachers of all Dharma traditions live long and in happiness, that in teaching and guiding the Sangha they inspire many to bring forth enlightened wisdom and work for harmony and balance in the world.

May practitioners of the Dharma in East and West find ways to inspire one another with compassion and understanding, and may all Sanghas uphold the beauty of the Buddha's way, opening the hearts and minds of beings everywhere to a brighter vision of freedom.

Through the blessings of the Triple Gem, may the light of the Dharma radiate in all directions in time and space, diminishing the confusion and despair of these dark times and warming the hearts of all beings with compassion, love, and great joy.

—The World Peace Ceremony, Prayers at Holy Places, 1995

the Buddha's teachings. For Westerners who visit Bodh Gaya during the ceremonies, accounts of the Buddha and Sangha are no longer a myth, but have become a living presence in their lives.

For members and friends of the Nyingma organizations in the United States, Europe, Brazil, and Asia, the World Peace Ceremonies have provided opportunities to participate with the Sangha in places where the Buddha demonstrated the way to enlightenment. Many who have taken this opportunity to extend their travels have deepened their devotion and understanding by participating in pilgrimages to other holy places consecrated by the presence of the Buddha and the Sangha.

Monlams of the Four Schools

Several years after the Prayers for Peace began in Bodh Gaya, our thoughts turned toward Lumbini, Bodh Gaya, Sarnath, and Kushinagara, the four most important sites in the life of the Buddha. More than two thousand years ago, the Blessed One emphasized the importance of pilgrimage and prayer at these spiritually significant sites. For decades, I had cherished the thought that some day each of the four major Dharma traditions of Tibet could assemble in these holy places and revitalize them through their prayers. In 1992, after the benefits of the Monlam Chenmos in Bodh Gaya had become apparent, I approached lamas of the Sarma traditions with the idea of establishing annual Monlams in Lumbini, Sarnath, and Kushinagara as well.

In 1993 and 1994, TNMC was able to sponsor the World Peace Ceremony held by the Kagyu and Sakya schools at Lumbini and by the Gelug school at Sarnath. This support is a simple gesture of faith that prayer has value in the world, and that we can serve this value by supporting the great masters in offering humanity the blessings of their knowledge. To continue this support, I encouraged each school to establish foundations and offered $100,000 seed money to each foundation formed. In response, three new Monlam Foundations were established in 1994 to support the annual observance of the Monlam Chenmo within the major Sarma schools, with the understanding that the leaders of the Sarma traditions would shape their ceremonies as they saw best.

When established in 1994, the Sakya Foundation was headed by H.H. Sakya Trizin, the Kagyu Foundation by the Ven. Chokyi Nyima Rinpoche, and the Gelugpa Foundation by Ven. Samdhong Rinpoche. Operations of the Monlams after that time have been determined by the directors of each foundation.

Opening to Blessings

From the Introduction to *The World Peace Ceremony: Prayers at Holy Places 1995:*

> Since 1989, lamas, monks, and nuns of the Nyingma tradition have gathered each year at Bodh Gaya, India, the holiest place in all of Buddhism. For ten days, the assembly of the Sangha join in holy prayer dedicated to world peace. In recent years, thousands of laypeople have joined in these solemn ceremonies, nourished by the spiritual power that flows from the site of the Buddha's enlightenment. . . .
>
> As the World Peace Ceremonies have grown, the vision of what they might become has expanded as well. Few of us are able to devote our whole lives to intensive spiritual practice, but many people have the opportunity to take a few weeks to come together at this most holy of holy sites. The experience available through such practice, multiplied many times over through the special energy of the Vajrasana, can heal the pain

of samsara and renew the power of actions directed toward the liberation of all beings. . . .

If the members of Sanghas from Buddhist countries around the world could make their way to Bodh Gaya for the annual Monlam Chenmo, amazing transformations might become possible. Bodh Gaya may once more become the seed from which the shoots of love and wisdom grow. As the flowers of realization blossom, the fragrance of universal compassion can radiate throughout the world, bringing to all beings the blessings that are so sorely needed in these troubling times.

May those with faith in the Dharma heed the Buddha's injunction to visit the places where he acted for the sake of others. May they join in our efforts to renew Bodh Gaya as a center for spiritual growth and world peace. May the heavenly guardians of the Dharma guide us as we seek to bring about such transformation for the sake of future generations.

Chronicling the Monlam Chenmo

The development of the Monlam Chenmo has been recorded in a series of richly illustrated publications that were distributed to participants in the ceremony beginning in 1994. Intended to educate and inspire, each volume includes information on the precious heritage of the Buddha, Dharma, and Sangha, the importance of revitalizing the sacred sites, and prayers for the continued vitality of the lineages in exile. The first four volumes were produced in English:

World Peace Ceremony, Bodh Gaya (1993)
World Peace Ceremony, Bodh Gaya, 1994
Prayers at Holy Places, 1994
World Peace Ceremony, Prayers at Holy Places, 1995

A hundred monks assist the distribution team in organizing the rows of white boxes containing hundreds of thousands of sacred texts.

Since 1999, these commemorative publications have taken the form of an annual Deb-ther, published in Tibetan. The first Deb-ther included a catalog of the texts distributed in 1999 and a list of texts prepared for later publication, with selections from the scriptures on the value of offerings and the benefits of traditional practices. From 2000 on, the Deb-thers have included larger selections of scriptures and even entire texts of great value for Nyingma practitioners, often accompanied by major portfolios of sacred art, lists of texts distributed at the ceremony, and summaries of offerings.

For further details on the Monlam Chenmo 1989–1993, see *World Peace Ceremony, Bodh Gaya,* pp. 65ff. For 1994, consult *World Peace Ceremony 1994,* pp. 105ff, and for 1995, see *The World Peace Ceremony, Prayers at Holy Places, 1995,* pp 51ff. For accounts of the Monlams for all Four Schools, initiated in 1993, see *Prayers in Holy Places* (1994) and *The World Peace Ceremony, Prayers in Holy Places 1995.*

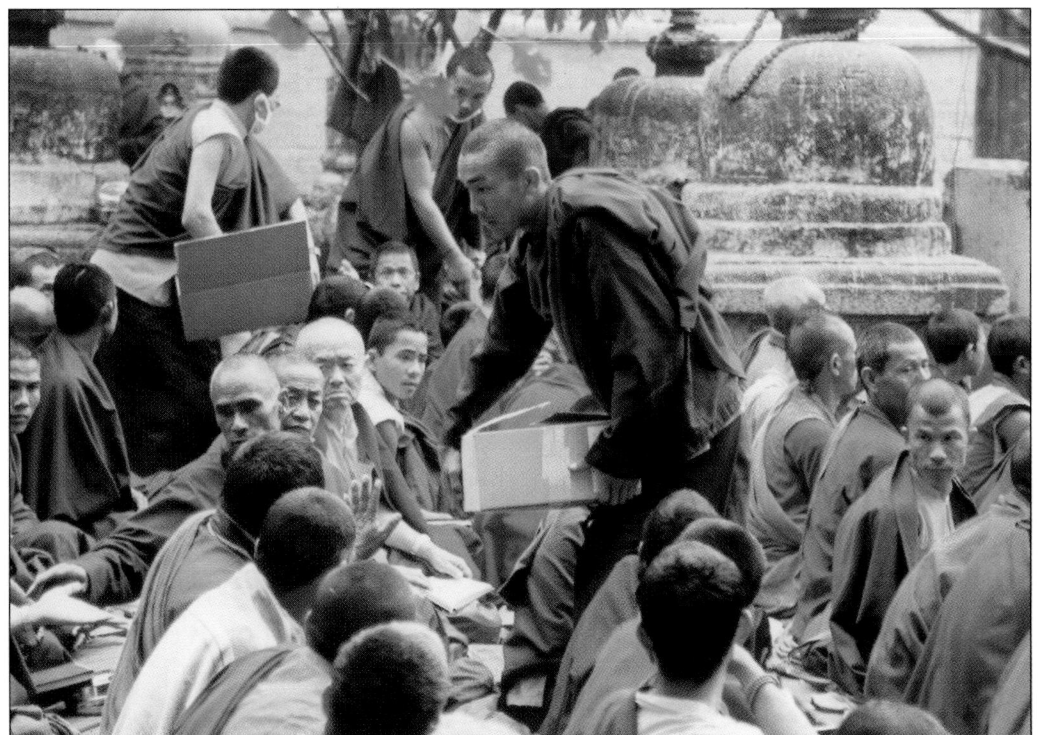

Monks distribute the texts during the ceremony. Hundreds of additional texts will also be distributed to centers in India, Nepal, Bhutan, and Tibet.

Offerings to the Sangha

At each annual ceremony, sacred texts and art produced by Dharma Publishing and the Yeshe De Project are offered as free gifts to the Sangha. Over the past fifteen years, more than 1.5 million books and over a million sacred art reproductions have been distributed to the four schools of Tibetan Buddhism to support traditional studies and practice. Over ninety thousand prayer wheels have been offered to practitioners, monks, nuns, and lay people alike. The ceremonies have helped revitalize the Dharma in its ancient homeland and have drawn attention to the long-forgotten majesty of Bodh Gaya, the most sacred site in Buddhism, where pilgrims and visitors from around the world now come in increasing numbers.

For the staff of the Yeshe De Project, the World Peace Ceremonies have become the focus for producing books that support a comprehensive Buddhist education. The publication program was designed to ensure that individuals as well as monasteries would have the texts they needed to continue the Nyingma lineages and comprehend the distinctive Nyingma interpretation of the works of the great Indian masters.

Sutras and shastras cherished by all Mahayana traditions have also been prepared and distributed to practitioners of the four schools. Members of three thousand Nyingma monasteries, retreats, and educational centers from India, Nepal, Sikkim, Bhutan, Ladakh, and Tibet have received individual copies, while additional sets of books have been offered to the larger Nyingma monasteries for their libraries and monastic colleges.

In recent years, the Yeshe De Project has focused on typesetting and printing greater numbers of Sutrayana texts and the essential commentaries (shastras) composed by Nagarjuna, Aryadeva, Asanga, Vasubandhu, and other great masters whose works form the foundation for Dharma studies for all schools of Tibetan Buddhism. While the number of volumes printed each year varies, about eight thousand copies of each volume are distributed at the World Peace Ceremony each year. The current goal is to provide Tibetan students and teachers with entire libraries of sacred texts that can serve as the foundation for a comprehensive education.

Offerings to Vajrasana

In the fall of 1993, TNMC students prepared 184 Buddhist flags sewn in strips of blue, yellow, red, white, and orange, colors with special meaning for the Buddhist Sangha. Blue is the color of the Dharmakaya, the Adibuddha, and the wrathful manifestations; red recalls the Sambhogakaya and the great masters of the Mahayana; yellow suggests the Nirmanakaya and Vinaya; white is traditional for the lay Sangha, and orange represents the Sangha of monks and nuns. Affixed to wires leading from the top of the Mahabodhi Temple out to the four directions, these flags celebrated the fundamental

The World Peace Bell, cast with sacred texts and images on both inside and outside, was offered to Vajrasana in 2002 and installed and dedicated during the World Peace Ceremony in 2003.

unity of the Buddhist traditions and brought to mind the comprehensive scope of the Buddha's teachings.

For the 1994 Monlam, TNMC produced a new series of prayer flags in fourteen different designs that had been printed during the eclipse of the sun in 1993 and four 36′ x 10′ banners, one for each side of the Mahabodhi Temple. Each of the huge banners bore an appliquéd image and a prayer lettered in gold in three languages in their traditional scripts. The east banner honored the Buddha's enlightenment, which brought the Dharma into the world. The banners on south, west, and north commemorated the mkhan-slob-chos-gsum: Shantaraksita, Guru Padmasambhava, and Khri-srong lDe'u-btsan, the Abbot, Guru, and King who worked together to transmit the Dharma to Tibet in the eighth century. Displayed at Bodh Gaya in 1994, the banners were taken to Sarnath for the

Each year, TNMC sponsors the lighting of hundreds of thousands of butter lamps during the ceremony. The light is a symbol of devotion and the potential of the mind to open to realization.

Longchen Varna Sadhana in 1995, where they were saved for display during future ceremonies.

In 1995, giant cylindrical victory banners were prepared to hang at the Mahabodhi Temple. Made of Oxford nylon and measuring thirty-five feet high by fifteen feet in circumference, the eight banners were sewn in five colors: red, blue, orange, yellow, and green. Although relatively simple in design, the sheer size of the banners made them a major project that took two full-time workers some two months to complete. The banners were later taken to Sarnath for the Longchen Varna Sadhana. During the ceremony, they were displayed on the sides of the Dhamekh Stupa, which is either the exact spot or close to the place where the Buddha turned the Wheel of the Dharma for the first time.

In December 1998, a banner bearing the text of the Padma dKarpo, or White Lotus teaching, was prepared for the tenth Monlam Chenmo. Prepared on vinyl using a plotter, the banner was mounted on the railings of the Mahabodhi Temple where it was read by the ceremony participants. Although I have not been able to attend the ceremonies in recent years, from 2000 to 2002, I shared my reflections with the Sangha in a series of plaques that the Yeshe De staff printed on large sheets of paper and mounted within the Mahabodhi compound.

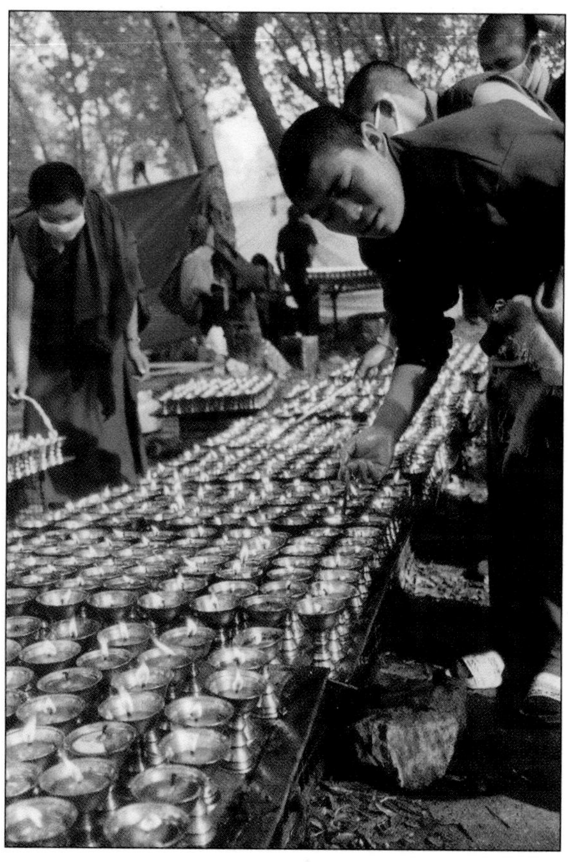

Nuns tend the butterlamp offerings set up outside of the Mahabodhi compound. Butterlamps are now housed in special structures sponsored by TNMC in 2003.

Butter Lamps: Calling Forth the Light of Dharma

At each of the Monlam Ceremonies, TNMC has sought to sponsor the lighting of a hundred thousand butter lamps each day, a total of a million in the course of a ten-day ceremony. In the early years of the Monlam, butter lamps were kept burning during the day along the circumambulation walkways, and candles were burned in the evening. In 1996, when the butter lamps used in these early years began to break and leak oil, TNMC sponsored the manufacture of 100,000 new butter lamps for use in the ceremonies that year and thereafter. Made of brass, these lamps were of higher quality, more durable, brighter, and more pleasing to the eye and hand. Yet inevitably, the burning of oil and candles generated smoke and left residues, raising environmental and preservation concerns.

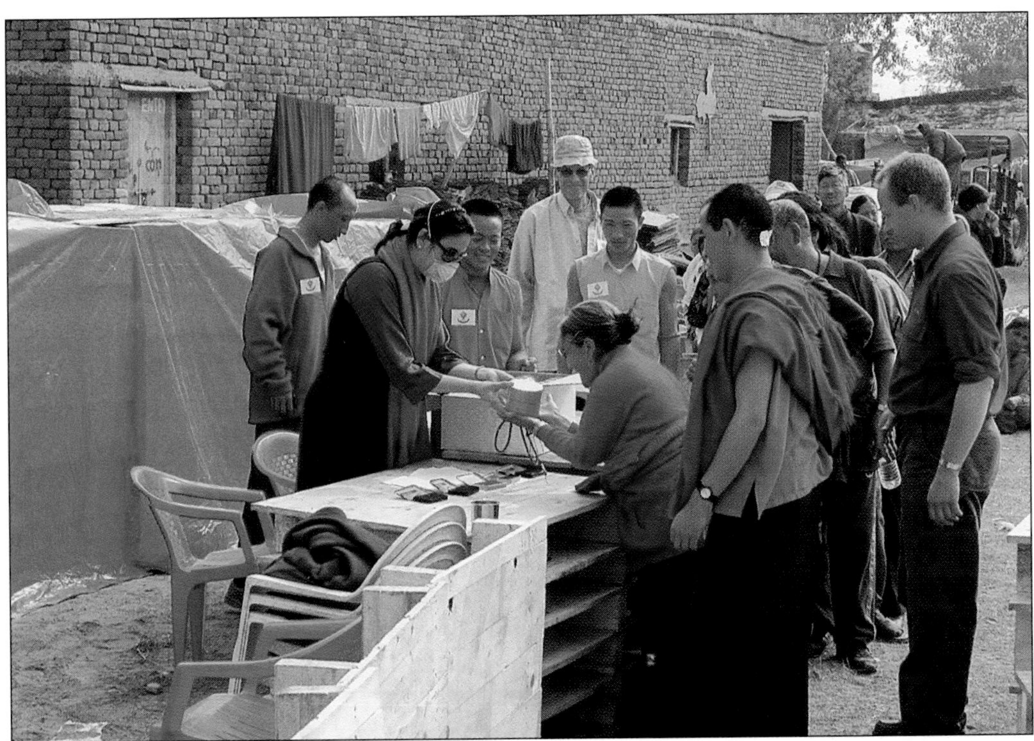

TNMC representatives offer prayer wheels to laypersons at a site designated by the Mahabodhi Temple Committee. From ten to twenty thousand prayer wheels are offered to participants each year.

In 2002, responding to these concerns and seeking to preserve the burning of butter lamps as a potent expression of keeping the light of the Dharma in our world, TNMC offered to sponsor the creation of eight butter-lamp houses within the Mahabodhi compound, and six have been created to date. The houses, made of reinforced concrete, are set in a park-like area south of the Mahabodhi Temple. Each house is about 43′ long, 25′ wide, and 13′ in height; each is equipped with its own independent purification system that filters the smoke and carbon particles for the eight thousand lamps inside. The houses are finished in a light brick color to match the Mahabodhi Temple and topped with a large golden lotus ornament. The butter-lamp houses were used for the first time during the Fourteenth World Peace Ceremony in 2003.

For the World Peace Ceremony in 2003, TNMC provided 10,000 new butter lamps, and has continued to sponsor the offering of

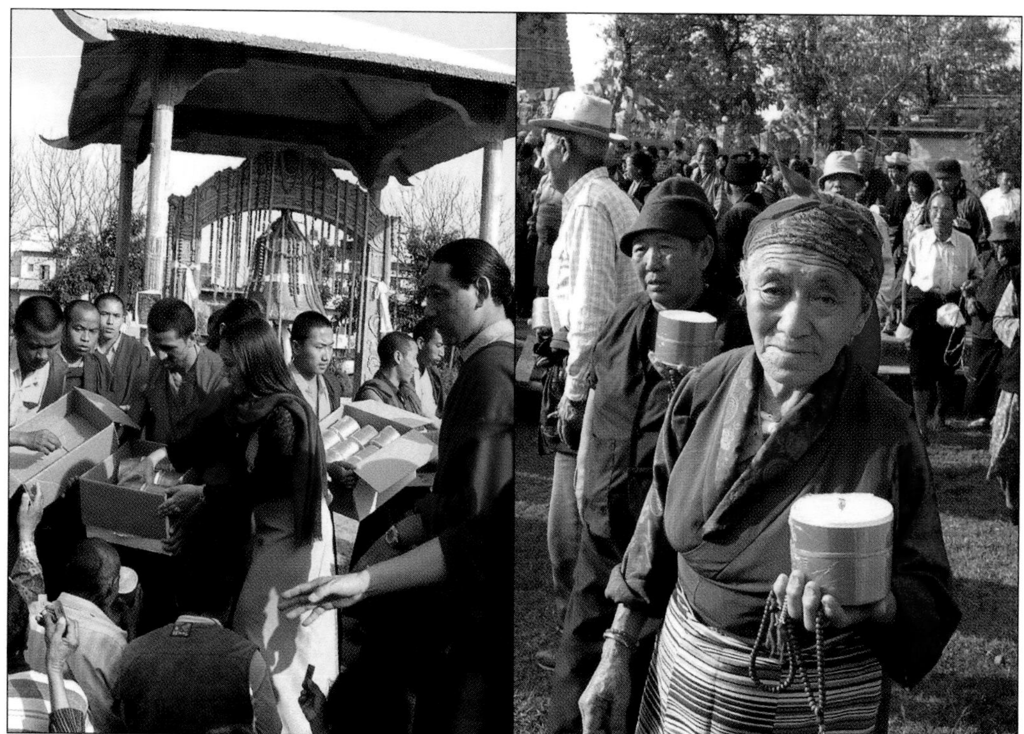

Prayer wheels enable everyone to share in the merit of spiritual practice. Since 1995, 94,000 prayer wheels have been distributed to monks, nuns, and laypersons attending the World Peace Ceremony.

three thousand lamps a day at a daily cost of 6,000 rupees, or 100,000 lamps per month for a total donation of Rs 180,000. An additional 150 rupees each day are provided to the eleven Tibetan monks and nuns responsible for performing the daily offerings. The total cost of sponsoring these offerings is Rs 229,500 per month.

Offering the Wheels of Dharma

Prayer Wheels, known to Tibetans as mani khorlo, 'Wheel of Jewels', are sacred instruments for accumulating merit, reflecting on the Buddha's teachings, and offering prayers for the happiness of all sentient beings. As a symbol of transmission, the Dharma wheel is often called a wish-fulfilling gem, since it contains mantras that activate the spiritual capacities of all beings. Through this invisible, silent way of praying, beings of all six realms of existence, on both macrocosmic and microcosmic levels, can become healthy in mind and body, activate their best qualities, and move closer to enlightenment.

The history of the wish-fulfilling gem teaches that prayer has the power to bring whatever you wish for into being. Whoever understands the power of prayer and has confidence in its outcome can experience this same result today. The Sutras say that prayer operates below the level of perception and conceptualization, so merit is accumulated even if a person has very little understanding. This is possible because mantra is wisdom in its purest form. Having emanated directly from enlightened being, mantra conveys benefits independently of ordinary language and concepts. Thus turning the wheels and pronouncing the mantras they contain can bring immeasurable benefit to self and others.

In 1994, to support this meritorious practice, TNMC produced the Dharma Wheel Cutting Karma specifically for participants in the World Peace Ceremonies. Although it can be turned by hand, it contains forty-two complete texts, including the entire Prajnaparamita Sutra in Eight Thousand Lines. In their original size, these texts fill more than twelve thousand folio-size pages, the equivalent of about fifteen Tibetan volumes.

While most of the prayer wheels distributed in the 1990s were given to the monastic community, wheels offered in 2000 were intended primarily for the thousands of Tibetan laypeople who annually make heroic efforts to attend the World Peace Ceremony and enrich it with their practice. Since laypeople, who lack the same access to the texts, practices, and rituals as monks and nuns, have traditionally depended on prayer wheels as a major focus of their practice, this gesture, repeated in following years, has been greatly appreciated. In all, a total of 53,686 Dharma Wheel Cutting Karma have been donated to Tibetans at Bodh Gaya.

In 2000, wishing to encourage this meritorious practice, I created a series of seven new prayer wheels. Since each wheel contains many tens of thousands of mantras, turning even one of these

Each night of the ceremony, offerings of light outline the ancient stupas and illuminate the entire Mahabodhi compound. Pilgrims continue to circumambulate the temple from early morning to late at night.

wheels for one minute generates at least a hundred million mantras. Starting in 2001, a different wheel has been distributed each year. As of January, 2005, TNMC representatives have distributed more than 94,000 prayer wheels free of charge to monks, nuns, and laypersons attending the World Peace Ceremony.

Offerings to the Less Fortunate

Bihar is a poor region, and there are many in the area surrounding Bodh Gaya who are destitute and homeless. As a small gesture, the Tibetan Nyingma Meditation Center has attempted to make certain that everyone in such circumstances receives donations at a ceremony held some distance from the temple. In 1995, for example, the amount distributed totalled $9,000 with as many as 10,000 individuals lining up each day to receive the offering. Our hope is that such a practice can activate positive forces that will improve the lot of the poor in the future.

World Peace Ceremonies, Bodh Gaya 1989–2005

See *TNMC Annals 5*, pp. 661–665 for more details of offerings and expenses related to the World Peace Ceremonies 1989–1997, and *Your Friends the Tibetan Refugees*, pp. 204–208 for the years 1989–2000. See also "Fifteen Years of World Peace Ceremonies," page 175.

World Peace Ceremony 1
December 22, 1989–January 15, 1990
Duration: twenty-five days

Participants: Seven hundred Nyingma lamas, monks, and nuns; laypeople, including four TNMC representatives

Principals:
H. H. Penor Rinpoche
H. H. Shatral Rinpoche
Ven. Rigo Tulku
Ven. Khenpo Dechen Dorje
Ven. Chogtrul Rinpoche
Ven. Sogtrul Rinpoche
Ven. Tsechu Rinpoche
Ven. Taklung Tsetrul Rinpoche
Ven. Khenpo Mewa Thupten Rinpoche
Ven. Khochen Rinpoche
Ven. Zankur Rinpoche
Ven. Tarthang Rinpoche

Monks, nuns, lamas from monasteries in southern and northern India, Nepal, Sikkim, and Tibet, headed by the lamas named above; additional delegations from the Central Institute of Higher Tibetan Studies and Nyingma Students Welfare Committee, Sarnath; Zhechen

Dargye Ling, Nepal; Ka-nying Shedrup Ling, Nepal; delegations of monks from Bhutan and nuns from Beru near Dehra Dun, India.

Recitations: 300,000 recitations of the Manjushri-namasamgiti

Other ceremonies sponsored 1989-90:

5 Gelugpa temples:

Sera, Gyudmed, Ganden, Tibetan Mahayana Buddhist University, and Drepung

Recitations (each temple)

100,000 Manjushri-namasamgiti recitations

World Peace Ceremony 2
January 1991
Duration: ten days

Participants: 1,500 Nyingma lamas, monks, nuns from monasteries in India, Nepal, Bhutan, Sikkim, Tibet; 1,000 laypeople, including six TNMC representatives

Principals:

H. H. Dilgo Khyentse
H. H. Shatral Rinpoche, leader
H. H. Penor Rinpoche
H. H. Minling Trichen Rinpoche
H. E. Rabjam Rinpoche
Ven. Rigo Tulku

Organization and administration:
Khenpo Rigdzin, Nyingma Institute of Nepal, Kathmandu

Recitations: Manjushri-namasamgiti, Bhadracarya-pranidhana-raja (at least a hundred thousand recitations of both of these texts have been offered at all subsequent ceremonies)

World Peace Ceremony 3
January 4–13, 1992.
Duration: ten days (established as an annual ten-day observance)

Participants: 2,500 Nyingma lamas, monks, and nuns from more than a hundred centers in India, Nepal, Tibet, Bhutan, and Sikkim. More than 2,000 laypeople, including 13 TNMC representatives.

Principals:

H. H. Penor Rinpoche
H. H. Minling Trichen Rinpoche
H. E. Rabjam Rinpoche
Ven. Taklung Tsetrul Rinpoche
Ven. Thubten Mewa
Ven. Tarthang Rinpoche

World Peace Ceremony 4
January 24–February 2, 1993

Participants: Six thousand Nyingma lamas, monks, and nuns, including 133 abbots and lineage holders and 2,500 laypeople, including fourteen TNMC representatives from Berkeley, Odiyan, Japan, Brazil, and Holland.

Principals:

H.H. Penor Rinpoche
H.H. Minling Trichen
H.E. Rabjam Rinpoche
Ven. Taklung Tsetrul Rinpoche
Ven. Tarthang Rinpoche

Organizers: Ven. Khochen Tulku and Ven. Rigo Tulku

Additional ceremonies:
Gelugpa monastery, Bodh Gaya
Theravadin monastery, Bodh Gaya

World Peace Ceremony 5
January 12–23, 1994

Participants: 4,500 Nyingma lamas, monks, and nuns, including 9 high lamas, 146 khenpos, six thousand laypeople, and a delegation of twenty-nine TNMC representatives from Berkeley, Odiyan, Brazil, Germany, and Holland.

Principals:

H.H. Penor Rinpoche
H.E. Rabjam Rinpoche
Ven Taklung Tsetrul Rinpoche
Ven. Kathog Situ Rinpoche
Ven. Tarthang Rinpoche
Ven. Khenpo Thupten Mewa
Ven. Situ Rinpoche
H.E. Dorje Lopon

Organizer: H. H. Penor Rinpoche

Additional offerings include

9,000 prayer wheels: Dharma Wheel Cutting Karma
1,440 Dharma Wheel Cutting Karma booklets
1,514 World Peace Ceremony books (1989–93)
3,000 btags-grol
100 prayer flags

Banners: 160 Buddhist flags; large ornamental hangings for the ceremony site; Bodh Gaya yolwas; 32 punz banners; Bodh Gaya streamers

World Peace Ceremony 6
February 1–10, 1995

Participants: 7,398 lamas, monks, and nuns from 300 centers; 30,000 laypeople, including 40 TNMC representatives from Berkeley, Odiyan, Brazil, Germany, and Holland.

Principals:

H. H. Penor Rinpoche
H. H. Minling Khenpo Tulku
H. H. Dzongsar Khyentse Rinpoche
H. H. Dudjom Rinpoche
H. E. Zhechen Rabjam
H. E. Dzogchen Rinpoche
H. E. Taklung Tsetrul Rinpoche
Ven. Kathog Situ Rinpoche

Ven Tarthang Rinpoche
Organizer: H.E. Zhechen Rabjam

World Peace Ceremony 7
January 20–29, 1996

Participants: 5,927 Nyingma abbots, tulkus, lamas, monks, and nuns from over 300 centers in India, Nepal, Sikkim, Bhutan, and Tibet; thousands of laypeople, including 22 TNMC representatives from Berkeley, Odiyan, Brazil, Germany, and Holland.
Organizer: Lamas from Sikkim

Additional offerings include:

10,000 Dharma Wheel Cutting Karma prayer wheel texts, rolled for insertion

Gold leaf

500 World Peace Ceremony 1995 books

World Peace Ceremony 8
January 10–19, 1997

Participants: 7,000 monks and nuns including 146 khenpos representing 256 monasteries
Organizer: H.E. Dzogchen Rinpoche

14,000 books prepared but not sent
(Rescheduled for shipment in 1998)

Ceremony Offerings and Expenses: See "Fifteen Years of World Peace Ceremonies," page 177.

World Peace Ceremony 9
January 28–February 6, 1998

Participants: More than 6,000 lamas, monks, and nuns from 300 centers; thousands of lay people, including seven TNMC representatives.

Organizer: H. H. Penor Rinpoche

World Peace Ceremony 10
January 17–26, 1999

Participants: 6,000+ lamas, monks, and nuns from 300 centers; thousands of lay people, including 18 TNMC representatives and 15 TAP pilgrims.

Organizers: H. E. Orgyan Topgyal, H. E. Rigo Tulku,
H. E. Khochen Tulku

Monlam Chenmo 11
January 6–15, 2000

Participants: More than 6,000 lamas, monks, and nuns from over 300 centers; thousands of laypersons, including 20 TNMC representatives.
Organizers: H. E. Taklung Tsetrul and H. H. Penor Rinpoche

World Peace Ceremony 12
January 25–February 3, 2001
Presiding
Kathog Gertse Rinpoche, on the east
Minling Khanchen Rinpoche, on the south
Penor Rinpoche, on the west
Ralu Rinpoche, on the north
Principals include Rabjam Rinpoche, Dzogchen Rinpoche,
Rigo Tulku
Participants: 6,000 lamas, monks, and nuns from over 300 centers, including 160 Khenpos and Tulkus

World Peace Ceremony 13
January 14–23, 2002

Presiding
Kathog Gertse Rinpoche, on the east
Minling Khanchen Rinpoche, on the south
Penor Rinpoche, on the west
Ralu Rinpoche, on the north
Principals

Monks and TAP representatives organize boxes of sacred texts at Bodh Gaya prior to distribution. A total of 418,000 books produced by the Yeshe De Project were offered to the Sangha in 2005.

Rabjam Rinpoche, Khyentse Yangtsi Rinpoche, Trulzhig Rinpoche, Sogyal Rinpoche, and Beru Khyentse Rinpoche; Participants: 10,000+ lamas, monks, and nuns, and at least 30,000 laypersons, including 12 TNMC representatives.

World Peace Ceremony 14
Date: February 2-11, 2003

Presiding

Kathog Gertse, on the east
Taklung Tsetul Rinpoche and Dzogchen Rinpoche, on the south
Penor Rinpoche, on the west
Ralu Rinpoche, on the north

Principals

Rigo Tulku, Kochen Rinpoche

Participants: 6,658 monks and nuns, including nine high lamas, 162 tulkus and khenpos
Organizers: Bhutanese managing group formed of representatives of major Bhutanese monasteries.

World Peace Ceremony 15
Date: February 2-11, 2004

Presiding:

Katog Gertse, on the east

Rabjam Rinpoche, Taklung Tsetrul, Minling Khanchen, and Trulzhig Rinpoche on the south, Penor Rinpoche, on the west, Lama Ralu, on the north

Participants: 6,100 participants, 150 Tulkus and Khenpos

Organizers: Ewam Chos sgar (Orgyan Tobgyal Rinpoche) and Zhechen Monastery (Rabjam Rinpoche)

World Peace Ceremony 16
Date: January 10th-19th, 2005

Presiding

Lama from Shugseb, on the east
Taklung Tsetrul, Minling Khanchen,
and Trulzhig Rinpoche on the south
Lama Ralu, on the north

Participants: 6800 monks and nuns, 185 Tulkus and Khenpos
Organizers: Namdroling (Penor Rinpoche) and Dzogchen Sri Singha (Dzogchen Rinpoche)

Nyingma Monlam Chenmo International Foundation

From 1989 through 1993, TNMC sponsored, organized, and managed the World Peace Ceremonies. In 1993, in cooperation with Penor Rinpoche and other prominent Nyingma lamas, I established the Nyingma Monlam Chenmo International Foundation to ensure the continuation of the World Peace Ceremony in perpetuity. Since 1994, leaders of the Nyingma Sangha in Asia, working through the Monlam Chenmo Foundation, have assumed responsibility for administration and coordination of the annual ceremony.

Bodh Gaya Trust

The Bodh Gaya Trust was established by the Head Lama on December 31, 1993 to support in perpetuity the World Peace Ceremony at Bodh Gaya. It is a nonprofit church auxiliary, exempt under IRC Sec. 501(c)(3), 501(a)(2) and 170(b)(1)(A)(ii), and under California Rev. and Taxation Code Sec. 23701(d). The Trust was funded on April 30, 1994; an amendment was written on April 7, 1997, and the Trust was granted tax-exempt status on August 14, 1997.

Longchen Varna, Sarnath and Bodh Gaya

In 1995, TNMC sponsored the first Longchen Varna Sadhana to commemorate the anniversary of the parinirvana of the great fourteenth-century Nyingma master, Kum-mkhyen Klong-chen Rab-'byams-pa (Longchenpa). Nyingma monasteries in Tibet had traditionally conducted this ceremony, which invokes the blessings of the enlightened lineage. Since 1959, when Tibetans were forced to seek refuge in other lands, this ceremony had only been observed in a limited way.

> "Thirty [now nearly forty] years ago, a few years after arriving in India, I resolved to observe this sacred time at Sarnath, and traveled there together with my Dharma brothers, Khenpo Thubten Mewa, Sangye Lama, Tsongdru, and the brother of my teacher Bod-pa Tulku. Together we pitched a small tent there and practiced for several days.

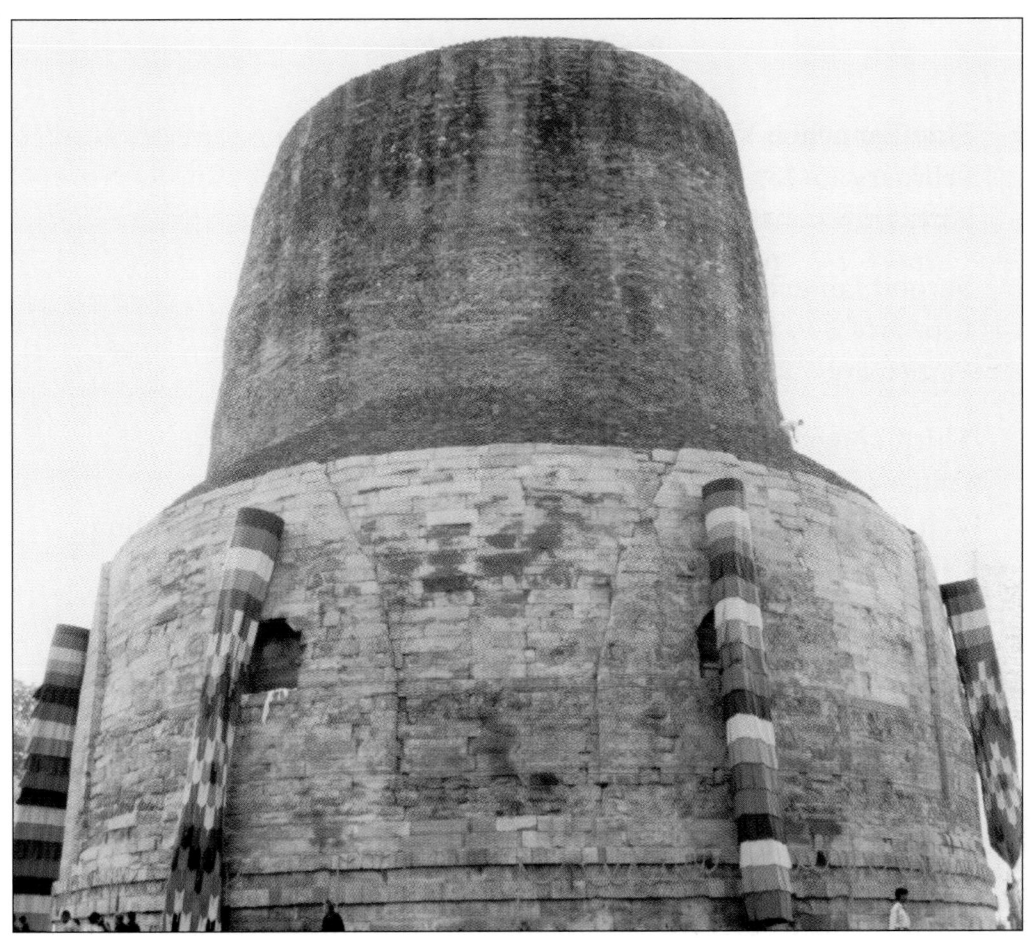

From 1995 through 2001, lamas, monks, and nuns gathered around the Dhamekh Stupa in Sarnath for the Longchen Varna ceremony. Since 2002, the Longchen Varna ceremony has been observed in Bodh Gaya. *(1995)*

"The memory of this experience inspired me to reestablish the Longchen Varna Sadhana in 1995. Since the anniversary of Klong-chen-pa's parinirvana falls in late January to mid-February, shortly after the World Peace Ceremony, participants in the Monlam Chenmo can travel directly from Bodh Gaya to this ceremony in Sarnath." — *TNMC Annals 5*, 1997

The Longchen Varna Sadhana was held in Sarnath from 1995 to 2001; since 2002, it has been observed in Bodh Gaya, shortly after the close of the World Peace Ceremony.

First Longchen Varna, Sarnath
February 15–18, 1995
Participants: 1,492 tulkus, monks, lamas, and nuns.

Second Longchen Varna, Sarnath
February 1–9, 1996
Participants: 1,500 tulkus, monks, lamas, and nuns.

Third Longchen Varna, Sarnath
January 22–26, 1997
Ven. Taklung Tsetrul and Ven. Khenpo Thubten Mewa presiding
Participants: 35 tulkus and 25 khenpos from India, Nepal, and Bhutan
2,600 monks, lamas, and nuns

Fourth Longchen Varna, Sarnath
1998
Ven. Kathog Gertse Rinpoche
and Thubten Mewa, presiding
Participants: 23 tulkus, including Tulku Gyurmed Dorje and Jamyang Chokyi Nyima; 11 khenpos, and 18 additional high lamas.

Fifth Longchen Varna, Sarnath
January 31–February 3, 1999
Organizer: Orgyan Topgyal
Ven. Khenpo Thubten Mewa
and Kathog Gertse presiding

Sixth Longchen Varna, Sarnath
January 21–23, 2000
Ven. Kathog Gertse Rinpoche presiding

Seventh Longchen Varna, Sarnath
February 8–11, 2001Kathog Gertse Rinpoche presiding.
1,000 monks and nuns
50 khenpos and tulkus

Eighth Longchen Varna, Bodh Gaya
January 29–31, 2002
Kathog Gertse Rinpoche presiding
Venerable guests: Trulshik Rinpoche
and Zhechen Rabjam Rinpoche
2,000 monks, nuns, and lamas

Ninth Longchen Varna, Bodh Gaya
February 16-19, 2003
Kathog Gertse Rinpoche and Nyichang Rinpoche presiding
Participants: 1,222 monks and nuns, 28 tulkus and khenpos, and 72 Theravadin monks simultaneously observing a pūja according to their tradition.

Tenth Longchenpa Ceremony 2004, Bodh Gaya
Ven. Kathog Situ Rinpoche presiding
Organized by TNMC
800 Participants
Total expenses 1995-2004 $395,502

Eleventh Longchenpa Ceremony 2005, Bodh Gaya
Drikung Kagyu and Orgyan Topgyal Rinpoche presiding
Organized by TNMC
800 participants

Horns and cymbals resound through the Mahabodhi compound at the close of the ceremony, stilling the mind and focusing the senses.

Longchen Varna Monlam Foundation

At the close of the first Longchen Varna ceremony in 1995, the lamas agreed that this important ceremony should be observed each year. In response, I established the Varna Longchen Monlam Foundation in 1995 to sponsor the ceremony on an annual basis. Looking ahead to the possibility of founding a permanent center, I offered funds that the Foundation used to purchase land in Sarnath. Ven. Khenpo Thupten Mewa and Ven. Orgyan Topgyal Tulku took responsibility for directing the foundation, assisted by its members, who included Khenpo Magpo Konchog, Thupten Gyatso, Donag Gyatso, and Tsultrim Angmo.

I feel it is a great blessing that the World Peace Ceremony at Bodh Gaya and the Longchen Varna Sadhana can be held each year to strengthen the Sangha and to offer the world the benefits of the Sangha's prayers and devotion. It is doubly beneficial that these ceremonies can be offered at two of the four great holy places, Bodh Gaya, where the Buddha first manifested enlightenment in the world, and at Sarnath, where the enlightenment of the first disciples brought the Sangha into being, establishing the foundation for the Three Jewels of Buddha, Dharma, and Sangha to continue long in our world.

Support for the Monlams: An Invitation

Tibetans traditionally make offerings and sponsor ceremonies as an act of devotion to Buddha, Dharma, and Sangha. Support for ceremonies conducted by the Sangha invites blessings on self and others and is intrinsically meritorious. We encourage anyone wishing to participate in this practice to contribute to any one of the Monlams. Funds are used for daily offerings to the monks or for sponsoring offerings of flowers and incense. Contributions may be made directly to TAP, which will take responsibility for them being used as the sponsor requests.

Tibetan Nyingma Relief Foundation
2910 San Pablo Avenue
Berkeley, CA 94702

Message for the Monlam

At the request of the Nyingma Monlam Chenmo International Foundation, Tarthang Tulku offered these thoughts for the announcement published in Hong Kong in 1999. Since the value of the Monlam Chenmo far transcends any single individual or school, we publish this excerpt from the message, wishing that the ceremony continue in perpetuity, and that the Sanghas of all Buddhist traditions join in restoring the light of the Dharma in its homeland.

FROM THE MESSAGE OF THE FOUNDER OF THE MONLAM CHENMO

Homage to Buddha, Dharma, and Sangha!

"Faith in the value and power of prayer led me to organize the first Monlam Chenmo at Bodh Gaya in 1989. At this most holy of the great Buddhist pilgrimage places, where the Buddha subjugated the obstacles to enlightenment, the power of practice is inconceivably multiplied. Surrounded by Dharma students whose practice is stable and strong, with the blessings of the Enlightened Lineage available, we can quickly overcome doubts and inner disharmony and develop our devotion.

"We human beings are fallible, and we may not always know how to act in ways that promote our own welfare and the well-being of others. At critical moments, we may discover that our power to change for the better is limited. Yet the knowledge and power of the Buddhas knows no such restrictions. As surely as actions have karmic consequences, so the power of merit accumulated by the Victorious Ones gives unerring access to the truth. When we seek the guidance of the lineage, we are calling on this truth. At this level, prayer, study, and practice are interconnected, for each makes available knowledge that can guide us in every action. Such knowledge transforms our innermost qualities, making us more effective agents of the Buddhas and Bodhisattvas as they work for the welfare of all sentient beings. As we dedicate our prayers to this purpose, our very being is transformed. The merit of our action grants us the power to accomplish our Bodhisattva vows.

"For hundreds of years Bodh Gaya was lost to humanity, but now it has been rediscovered. As we practice here, calling out in our need, we can truly hope that peace will prevail throughout Jambudvīpa. Knowing that science has limited power to protect us against war and natural disasters, against terrible accidents and willful acts of violence, what better way than to put our faith in the Dharma, dedicating our efforts at the Monlam Chenmo to the happiness of all? As we perform prostrations, offer butter lamps, and join in prayer, we can bring to mind the Buddhas and Bodhisattvas who have performed similar acts on this very spot, sharing in their merit by imagining that we are following in their footsteps. Chanting the awesome and deeply meaningful words of the Pranidhanaraja and the Manjushri-namasamgiti, we can activate the power of the lineage, so that the inconceivable becomes possible. Sitting quietly at the Bodhi tree, we can stabilize our minds, preparing for the transformation that comes with liberation. Prayer can work its magic, bringing peace to the restless heart, deepening our meditation, and strengthening our resolve. We know what to do and how to act, and can follow with perfect clarity the guidance offered by the Victorious One.

"For the past eleven years, I have done my best to support the Monlam Chenmo. Each year I have distributed Dharma texts and sacred art to the participants, and in my own small way I have encouraged the other schools of Tibetan Buddhism and other traditions to hold similar ceremonies. The obstacles I encountered early on are now only a memory, and today many lamas share responsibility for the ceremonies, which are attended by thousands. Now I encourage others to find their own way to support the Monlam. Nothing can have more value, for participating in these prayers for peace means sharing in all the merit generated by the great assembly that gathers here. Pooling your efforts and energy produces far more powerful results than acting alone. You share in a fortune beyond price, an inexhaustible fortune that brings wealth and joy to all beings.

Tarthang Tulku
October 20, 1998

A Letter from Nepal December 2004

Though part of Nepal, the Dolpo area has been Buddhist for at least eight hundred years. The people are dedicated practitioners of Tibetan Buddhism. They live at a subsistence level, farming barley and raising animals. The barley harvest is in September and October and provides food for the long cold winters.

Reading Buddhist teachings in homes is an important personal and cultural activity. Traditionally many families would come together and invite monks and nuns to do readings, which would last four to five days. For monks and nuns, the texts serve a different purpose. With little access to texts or to hard currency to buy texts, the books they receive are critical to their education and progress toward enlightened understanding.

There are about fifty villages in this area. The books are so desired that each village aims to send one hundred people to Bodh Gaya to bring back the books distributed at the World Peace Ceremony. So, as many as five thousand people are now undertaking the thirty-day walk (!) to Kathmandu. Travel in winter can be dangerous, but they cannot leave earlier because they have to help bring in the barley harvest. They have no money to pay for hotel or other accommodations even if they do arrive early in Bodh Gaya.

As they set out from their homes, they feel a mixture of happiness and concern for the difficult journey ahead. Walking in shoes with leather soles and wool uppers, they are always at risk of frostbite. Sleeping in outdoor shelters, they can never really escape from the cold. When they finally arrive in Kathmandu, they have to deal with language barriers and culture shock. The two-day bus ride through the Kathmandu valley to the Nepalese border that follows is a welcome relief from the cold; now all they have to deal with is motion sickness.

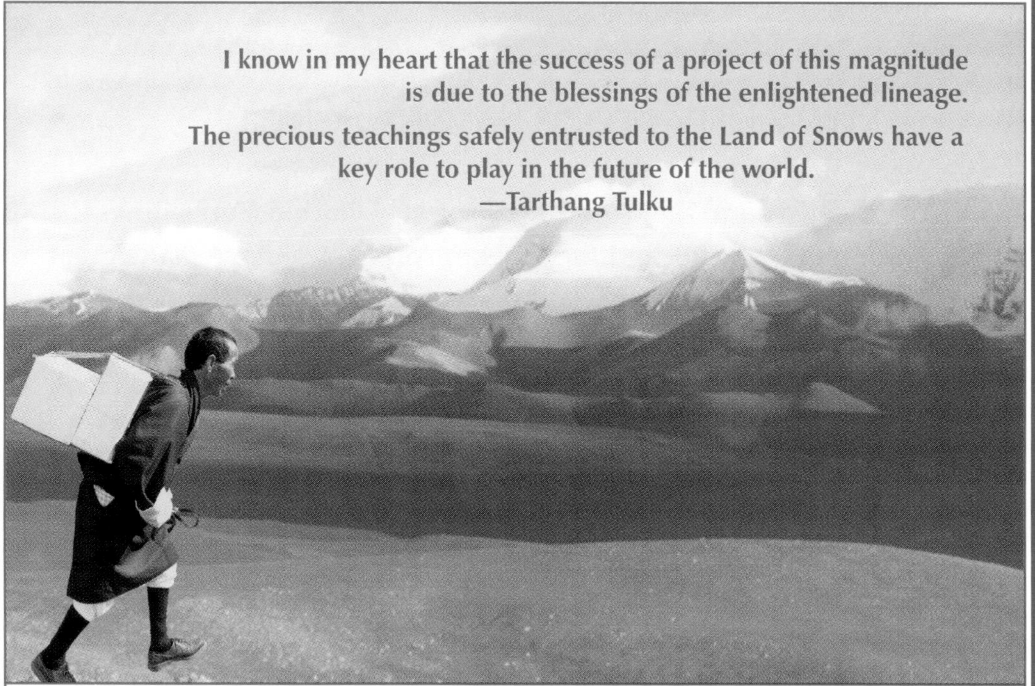

I know in my heart that the success of a project of this magnitude
is due to the blessings of the enlightened lineage.
The precious teachings safely entrusted to the Land of Snows have a
key role to play in the future of the world.
—Tarthang Tulku

When they finally receive the books in Bodh Gaya, they are amazingly happy. The texts are of such high quality, and the recipients share in the joy of everyone around them who is also receiving this tremendous gift. No one is turned away, whether a monk or the most humble lay person.

Strapping the books to their backs, they begin the long journey home. Help is sometimes available, and a few have the resources to hire animals to help lighten the load. Even though the homeward journey brings more hardship, the great happiness and joy in the village when they return makes it all worthwhile.

Though the villages have no power for lights, in more and more homes the altars shine with the presence of these precious books and the devotion and appreciation of their new owners.

—Amdo Lama

A Garland of Jewels
New Libraries of Sacred Scriptures

For fifteen years, the Yeshe De Project, Dharma Publishing, the Nyingma Institute, and the Tibetan Aid Project have made great efforts to realize Tarthang Tulku's vision of libraries filled with sacred scriptures arrayed along the Himalayas like garlands of precious jewels. This vision had its origins in 1990, when the Head Lama of TNMC founded the World Peace Ceremony and distributed 800 books to Tibetan refugees. Quantities increased through the years. In 2004, we crossed the millionth-book milestone and arrived at 1.5 million volumes in 2005. Throughout 2005, we have redoubled our efforts. We now expect to distribute 500,000 volumes in 2006, bringing the total of books produced to two million. When this phase of our work is complete we will have distributed nearly 6,000 sets of 330 traditional Tibetan-style volumes to institutions, families, and individuals in India, Tibet, Nepal, and Bhutan. These are the texts that have shaped the form of Tibetan civilization.

Changing the Landscape of Rural Education

In recent years, we have been able to extend our distribution of texts into the remote Himalayan regions of Ladakh, Dolpo, and Mustang. For the first time, deeply dedicated practitioners in these regions have access to materials they need to preserve the wisdom tradition of Tibet. Now we are hearing that these books are changing the landscape of rural education. Inspired by the free gift of beautifully designed collections of traditional texts, communities across the Himalayas—some very poor—are finding innovative ways to create the institutions of advanced study and practice that can transform their present condition and reshape their future possibilities.

In our travels in the Himalayas, we heard again and again that what is needed in rural regions is libraries stocked with the range of Sutras and commentaries found in the Tibetan Buddhist Canon. TAP has made the creation of such libraries a priority, and for this ***we need your help.***

TAP is Prepared to Act

The Yeshe De Project has already produced ***more than one million books*** under the direction of Tarthang Tulku, and TAP's staff has participated in distributing them to individuals and monasteries in India, Tibet, Bhutan, Sikkim, and Nepal. Within the next few years, we hope to complete distribution of nearly six thousand sets of the bKa'-'gyur, the words of the Buddha, and the commentaries that systematize their teachings, to institutions and families located in lands throughout the Himalayan region.

At this point, we can fully stock a small 500-book library for $2,500. A medium-sized library of about 1,000 volumes would support in-depth study at a cost of $5,000, and a large library that could serve as a regional center of study and practice would house 1,500 books at a cost of $7,500. The support that TAP's donors provide now will strengthen this powerful momentum and create a sound foundation for the future of the Dharma and the Tibetan lineages.

There is no greater gift than the gift of knowledge. We ask for your help at this critical point.

Contact:
Tsering Gellek
2425 Hillside Avenue
Berkeley, California 94704

Sacred Texts Across the Himalayas

Texts have been distributed to:

Bhutan: 34 areas
Bumthang, Choskorling, Chukha, Chirang, Gelegphug, Gurtod, Haa, Khulung, Lhuntshi, Mangal, Mungar, Pari, Paro, Pena Gatsel, Punakha, Phuentsoling, Samchi, Samdrup Jongkhar, Samitang, Shedrup Ling, Shengang, Shingkar, Sorpang, Takazong, Tashigang, Tashiling, Tashi Yangtse, Thangang, Thimphu, Tongsa, Tsa Ling, Wangdi Phodrang, Zhemgang.

Sikkim: 14 areas
Darjeeling, Gangtok, Jangkar, Kalimpong, Lhachen, Lhachong, Lhakang, Lhasang, Malak, Mangalay, Mangam, Miri, Samten Ling, Tashi Yangtze.

India: 21 Areas
Bir, Chamba, Chandragiti, Dehradun, Dharamsala, Kalish, Kumrao, Kunu, Ladakh, Manipat, Manali, Mandi, Mongot, Mundgod, Mysore, New Delhi, Rajpur, Siliguri, Simla, Sonada, Spiti

Nepal: 30 areas
Bagmati, Bangaraya, Bharagila, Chimala, Dolpo, Gorkali, Janatpur, Kangsar, Kanpur, Karnali, Karre, Kathmandu and surrounding areas, Khorka, Korag Kosh, Lo, Lumbini, Mechi, Mugum, Mustang, Narayana, Nawoche, Nubri, Parang Bang, Pokhara, Shagaramatha, Sibi, Sagaramatha, Solukhumbu, Yolmo, Zanakpur.

Tibet: 26 areas
Amdo, Batang, Changtang, Conjo, Derge, Dzachukha, Golok, Gyaron, Khangsar, Kongpo, Lhasa, Ling, Mt. Kailash, Nagchuku, Nangchen, Ngari, Nyarong, Puram, Riwoche, Sakya, Samye, Shigatse, Tehor, Tingri, Tsurpu, U-Tsang

Since the largest Tibetan monasteries and communities are located in India, the greatest number of Yeshe De texts are distributed to Tibetans living in India.

Yeshe De Book Distribution

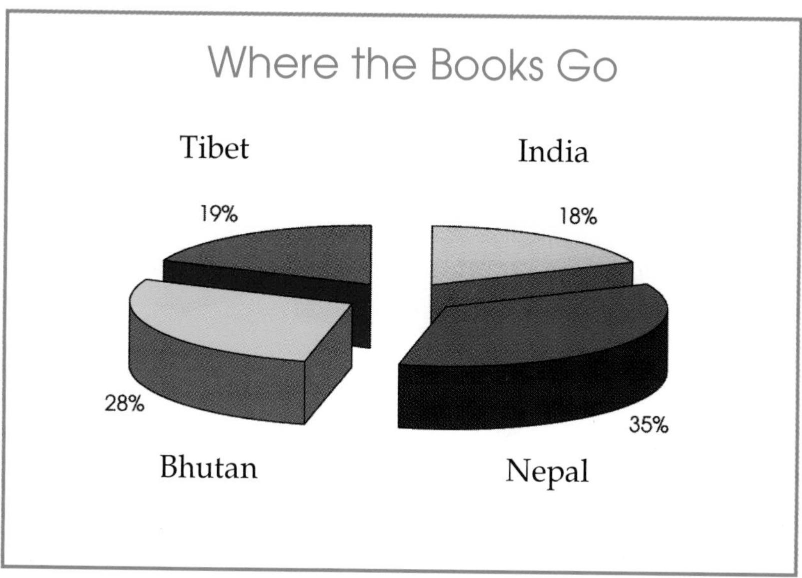

Country	Monasteries Receiving Books
India	612
Nepal	1,184
Bhutan	937
Tibet	636
Total Monasteries Receiving Books	3,369

Members of 1,036 monasteries have attended the World Peace Ceremony over the last fifteen years and have received books distributed by TNMC and TAP representatives. 2,333 unregistered monasteries not officially attending the ceremony send representatives to receive their books.

Who Contributes to Book Production?

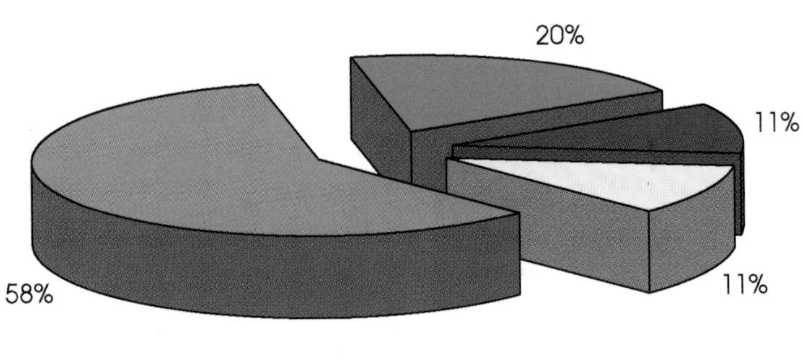

■1 □2 ■3 ■4

1. Dharma Publishing 2. Tibetan Aid Project 3. TNMC 4. Donations

Sponsors Welcome

$150 provides red dye for 8,000 copies of one 1,200-page volume.
$500 provides red dye for 8,000 copies of one 1,600-page volume.
$1,500 provides boxes for 8,000 copies of two 1,600-page volumes.
$2,500 covers cost of stamping covers for 8,000 books.
$3,000 covers cost of fabric wrappers for 8,000 books.
$4,000 ships one 40′ container of books from California to India.
$25,000 provides paper for 8,000 copies of one 1,200-pagevolume.
$32,000 covers cost of printing and binding 8,000 copies of one 1,200-page commentary printed in black ink with red artwork.
$40,000 covers cost of printing and binding 8,000 copies of one 1,600-page Sutra volume printed with artwork in full color.

To sponsor or donate to this worthy effort, contact the
Tibetan Aid Project, 1-800-33-Tibet

Sixteen Years of World Peace Ceremonies
1989–2005

Sangha Assembly	over 90,000
Lay Pilgrima	about 160,000
Days of Puja	175
Butterlamps	14,816,000
Books Offered	1,286,205
Thankas Offered	1,023,848
Prayer Wheels	104,400
Shipment weight	3,303,927 lbs.**
Offerings to the Sangha	$1,158,213
Butterlamps and Lights	$347,474
Puja Offerings	$48,238
Food and Tents	$54,154**
Offerings to the Less Fortunate	$38,204
Sangha Travel	$90,239
Theravadin Monks	$5,873
Other Offerings	$26,691
Miscellaneous Expenses	$28,291
1989 and 1991	$212,398

*Ceremony expenses for the first two years (1989 and 1991) were not categorized.

**Figures for 2005 not included

Dharma Books, Art, and Prayer Wheels Offered at the World Peace Ceremonies 1989–2005

Year	Volumes	Books	Thankas	Prayer Wheels
1989/90	1	800		
1991	1	1,770	1,944	
1992	7	11,600	25,000	
1993	6	8,000	12,100	
1994	3	3,000	28,230	9,000
1995	24	31,268	15,995	
1996	7	17,663	24,283	10,504
1998	3	23,920	121,393	
1999	18	55,032	152,461	
2000	19	113,448	98,398	10,042
2001	21	125,336	267,349	15,000
2002	30	175,665	181,095	20,000
2003	18	96,723	2,000	10,000
2004	42	205,000	73,600	9,828
2005	62	418,000	20,000	10,000
Totals	262	1,286,205	1,023,848	94,374

Summary of Book Distribution 1989–2005

Total participants in the Nyingma Monlam Chenmo, the World Peace Ceremonies at Bodh Gaya, 1989–2005: 237,000 monks, lamas, and nuns

Over 150 Tulkus (reincarnate lamas) and Khenpos (abbots) have received copies of every book each year.

Ten to thirty thousand laypeople are now joining the ceremonies each year.

Members of more than 3,300 Nyingma monasteries in India, Nepal, Sikkim, Ladakh, Bhutan, and Tibet have received individual books.

Beginning in 2000, major Sakya, Kagyu, and Gelug monasteries have received books each year to distribute to their numerous branches.

A complete set of Monlam Dharma books distributed from 1989 to 2005 contains 1,382 unique titles by 180 authors.

A total of over 140,000 folios ornamented with more than 3,000 images, collated into 262 volumes

Total books distributed free of charge as of 2005:

Over 1.2 million

Offerings at Bodh Gaya 1989–2004

Bodh Gaya Offerings	
Bodh Gaya Ceremony	$2,007,378
Longchenpa Ceremony	$395,502
Dharma Bell	$152,916
Bell House	$20,363
Butterlamp House	$127,138
Butterlamp Manufacture	$10,202
300,000 Butterlamps 2003	$15,600
Butterlamp Offerings 2003–2004	$106,790
Ceremony Banners	$5,599
Shelves for the Nyingma Edition	$60,556
Total	$2,757,182

Additional Gifts to the Sangha	
Katags (offering scarves)	$4,435
Thanka Production 1989–2004	$84,661
Prayer Wheels 1989–2004	$166,709
Total	$255,805

Summary of Expenses	
Book Manufacturing 1989–2006	$15,183,192
Offerings at Bodh Gaya 1989–2004	$2,757,182
Additional Gifts to Sangha 1989–2004	$255,805

The Yeshe De staff consists of fifteen committed Dharma students who use this work as a way of practice. All books are given free of charge, and no individual makes any profit whatsoever. If we were operating as a commercial business, the retail price of each book would be at least $15.00.

Book Manufacturing Expenses 1989–2005

Total Materials, Books for 1989–2006	$8,658,098
Press Building and Equipment 1989–2004	
Photo Reproduction Systems	$15,047
Typesetting	17,064
Computer Systems	36,659
Plating	292,894
Printing	379,287
Binding	219,152
Scanning	81,680
Press Building Construction	$645,061
Total	$1,686,844
Yeshe De Staff Expenses 1989–2005	
Direct Support, 15 Dharma students	
$185/month food, insurance, savings	$3,106,014
Community Operating Expenses	$187,200
Utilities, Fuel, Building Maintenance	$160,200
Property & Liability Insurance	$344,450
Total	$3,797,864
Travel and Shipping Expenses 1989–2005	
International Shipping 1989–2005	$543,365
Staff Travel for Distribution 1989–2004	$446,711
Proofreading Travel, Honorariums -2005	$50,310
Total	$1,040,386
Total Book Costs	$15,183,192

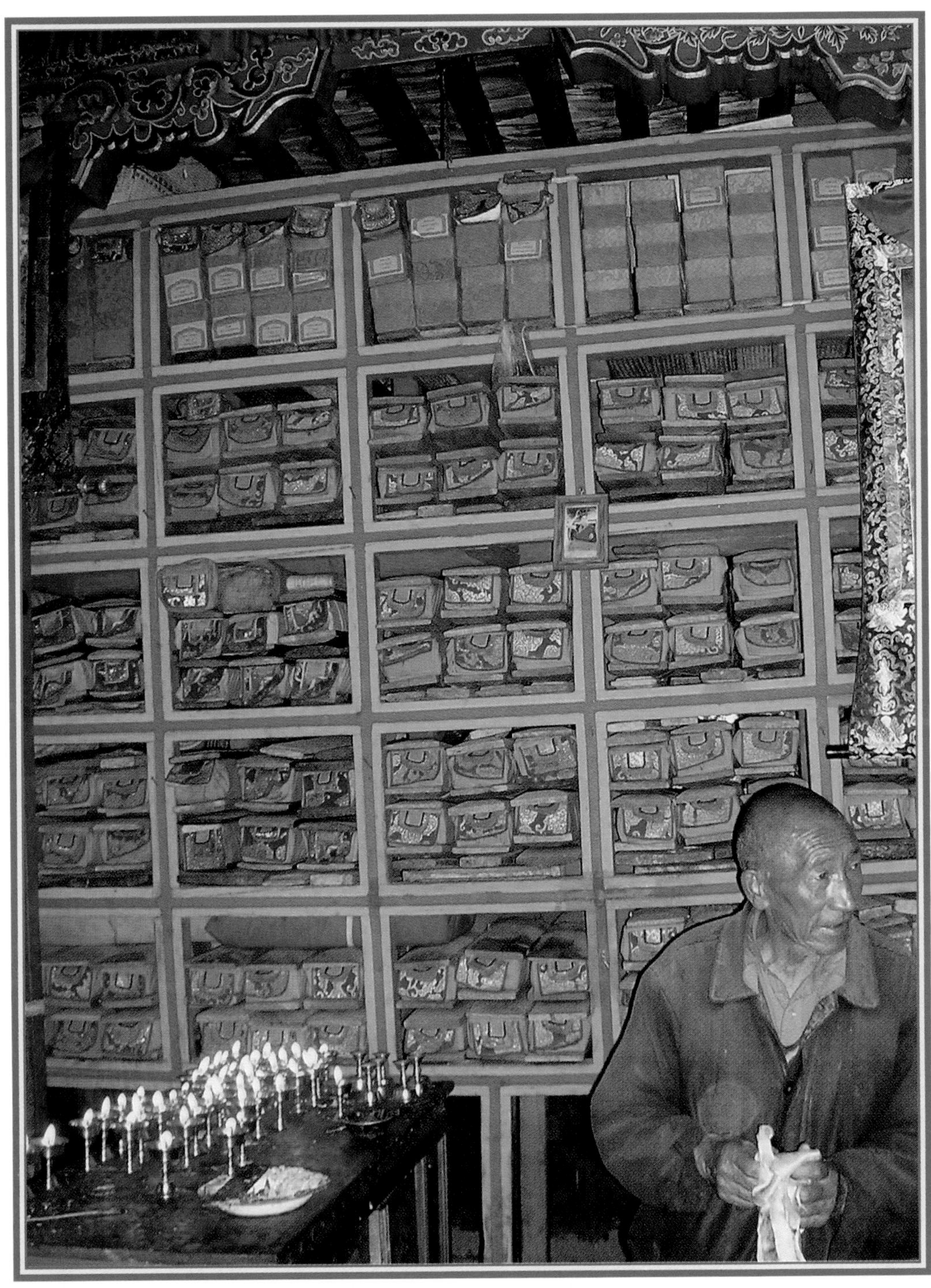

Books produced by the Yeshe De Project, wrapped in red cloth, have made their way to the library of bSam-yas Monastery in Central Tibet. They are placed on the top shelves, a sign of respect.

Chapter Ten

Offerings to the Holy Places of Nepal, Tibet, and Bhutan

In 1983, by the time my work on *The Nyingma Edition* was completed, conditions in Tibet had become less restrictive. Now, after twenty-five years of separation from the land of my birth, I was able to return to my home monastery. But the joy of seeing my family again contrasted painfully with the grief I felt in seeing my monastery completely destroyed. For centuries, Tarthang Monastery (dPal-yul Dar-thang), one of the largest and most beautiful Nyingma monasteries in eastern Tibet, had been a vital complex housing more than five hundred lamas. Now there were only piles of rubble where the temple and buildings once stood.

Some lamas in the area were following the traditions as best they could, but since most of them had been born during the years that Dharma study was impossible, they had little education. Still, their faith in their culture was strong and they were eager to rebuild the monastery. I felt a stirring of hope that this kind of dedication and devotion might keep the spirit of the Dharma alive in Tibet. If so, the Dharma might yet shine forth again in new shapes and forms, and potentially benefit many more people. I resolved to do all I could to support them in rebuilding Tarthang Monastery.

Rebuilding Tarthang Monastery

Through the blessings of my Gurus and the generosity of supporters who understood the significance of this undertaking, TNMC was able to send more than $108,000 between 1983 and 1985 to support reconstruction and reestablish religious practices at Tarthang Monastery. While construction was underway, I learned that the burial place of my teacher, Dar-thang mChog-sprul Rinpoche, had been located. To honor this great master, TNMC sponsored the building of a thirty-three foot relic stupa and provided jewels, silver, and gold-leaf to ornament it. This stupa is now housed in the monastery's temple.

By 1985, a temple and a retreat center with twenty-five residents' rooms had been completed under the direction of my brother, Pega Tulku, and rituals and practices, including the traditional forty-day summertime retreat, had been reinstated. To ensure that these practices continue, TNMC continues to sponsor the traditional rituals, ceremonies, prayers, and retreats undertaken by resident monks.

On my second visit in 1986, I was able to stay for ten weeks to review progress on rebuilding the monastery and present additional funds of $137,417 toward construction of a shedra (bshad-grwa, school for the study of philosophy), one hundred prayer wheels, paintings and sculptures for the main temple, and ceremonies at Tarthang and other monasteries. The shedra, completed a few years later, has 108 rooms, a courtyard, library, and temples. It was possible also to offer funding for monthly ceremonies and support for abbots, supervisors, and staff, as well as funds for ritual implements and living essentials.

During my visit, I was also able to commission the sDe-dge printing house to produce, for the first time since 1936, a complete block-printed edition of the rNying-ma'i rGyud-'bum. These precious texts arrived safely in Berkeley several months later. Together with the Rin-chen gTer-mdzod, the bKa'-'ma, and three additional editions of the rGyud-'bum, the sDe-dge rNying-ma'i rGyud-'bum became the foundation of *Great Treasures of Ancient Teachings,* a massive text preservation project that still awaits completion.

The restored temple of Tarthang Monastery, in 'Gu-log, eastern Tibet

While visiting a third time, in the summer of 1988, I gave funds for constructing a gSer-khang (Golden Temple), designed with 140 pillars and large enough for 1,000 monks. Upon its completion in 1993, TNMC offered additional funds for retreats, ceremonies, and staff expenses and established a fund to enable five hundred monks to participate in the Varṣika, the annual forty-day retreat traditionally observed during the rainy season. To support continued study and practice, TNMC and Dharma Publishing donated two sets of *The Nyingma Edition of the bKa'-'gyur and bsTan-'gyur* together with thankas and Dharma Publishing books.

Prayer Wheel for Healing and Peace

TNMC continues to strengthen the connection of the Nyingma organizations in the West with Tarthang Monastery in Tibet. In 2005, a million-mantra prayer wheel is being constructed for Tarthang Monastery at Odiyan, TNMC's country center in northern California. Planned to be even larger than the massive ten-ton wheel that now turns at the heart of the Odiyan stupa, the new Tarthang

Tarthang Monastery, rebuilt with funds offered by TNMC

Monastery wheel is a gesture of healing to my troubled land. May the mantras it contains calm the agitations of mind and nature, restoring balance to the roof of the world and opening heart and mind to the blessings of peace, wisdom, and compassion, for the benefit of the world and all beings.

Offerings to Neighboring Monasteries in Eastern Tibet

In the late 1980s and early 1990s, we also had the opportunity to make offerings to other local monasteries struggling to continue important lineages and traditions:

Khra-gling-dgon-pa, a branch of Kaḥ-thog bsTan-po-dgon-pa, itself a branch of dPal-yul Dar-thang. Khra-gling also received a set of *The Nyingma Edition of the bKa'-'gyur and bsTan-'gyur.*

Se-dgon-pa, a Jo-nang-pa monastery in 'Gu-log, also received gifts of Dharma books gTun-po-dgon-pa, a monastery specializing in dPal-yul and sNying-thig lineages

g.Yag-mgo-dgon-pa, another branch of dPal-yul Dar-thang

gDong-rdzong-dgon-pa, the hermitage of mDo-mkhyen-brtse

mDo-mkhyen-brtse'i-dgon-pa, a monastery specializing in sNying-thig teachings

Timeline for Reconstruction

1983–1984

Retreat center, temple, and twenty-five residents' rooms for three-year retreats

Stupa dedicated to mChog-sprul Rinpoche

Creation of ten thankas

Forty-nine day summer ceremony

Tara and Heart Sutra pujas

Offerings to ten past teachers and lamas

Separate offering to Khra-gling Monastery

1986

Completion of main temple, paintings, statues, and ceremonies

Shedra construction: eighty-three rooms, temples, and library

One hundred prayer wheels

1988

Initiation of construction of the gSer-khang with facilities for more than one thousand lamas

Endowment fund

First-year expenses

Completion of the shedra

1991

Completion of the gSer-khang

Rainy season retreats for 400-500 lamas

Two years of support for monks, including medical and pilgrimage expenses, ceremonies four times monthly, and daily Dharmapala ceremonies

Sponsorship for copying fifteen volumes of Garlong Terton's teachings for the Yeshe De text preservation project

Donations: two sets of *The Nyingma Edition of the bKa'-'gyur and bsTan-'gyur;* books, thankas, and statues

2005

TNMC donates a million-mantra prayer wheel

Cost summary

1983–1984	$108,000
1986	137,417
1988	290,000
1991	41,248
2005	est. 10,000
Total Cost 1983–2005	**$586,665**

Support for Higher Education in Nepal

Although Tibetans had been extraordinarily successful in recreating the foundations of their culture, in the 1980s, it was becoming clear that there were other factors at work that were eroding their ancient way of life. Nepal and India alike are strongly influenced by materialism and Western views of economic growth, and many young Tibetans are attracted to follow in this direction. Lacking the resources and community support they had in Tibet, monasteries were likely to continue struggling to survive, and the abbots and abbesses might experience greater difficulties helping young Tibetans sustain their dedication to a Dharma education and a religious way of life.

Tarthang Rinpoche (center) with Chokyi Nyima Rinpoche and his brother Chokling Rinpoche on his left, Sai Yung Sang Dechen on his right. Behind her are Tarthang Rinpoche's daughters. *(1988)*

The traditional philosophical education of the Tibetan Buddhist monk takes place in the philosophy college or shedra. An intensive study of Sutras and shastras, combined with performance of ritual and ceremonies, is essential for the preservation and transmission of the tradition. As lamas trained by the great masters in Tibet continued to pass away, there was a growing need to protect the teaching lineages by supporting education for Tibetans in exile.

While traveling in Nepal, I had the opportunity to experience this need directly, and considered how best to respond. Kathmandu, a place of pilgrimage for Tibetans since the time of Guru Padmasambhava and home to thousands of refugees, seemed a promising site for an educational center. Boudha, in particular, had a strong association with the transmission of Buddhism to Tibet. At its center was the renowned Bodhnath stupa, a major attraction for pilgrims and tourists alike, and monasteries and temples had been built there by masters of the four schools of Tibetan Buddhism.

Tibetan Aid Project

Support a Tradition of Compassion, Wisdom, and Peace

Tibetan Aid Project: Two Goals for 1990

Tibetan Penfriend Program Offers Monthly Support

Goal: 150 Western penfriends sending $20/month to:

- **an aged monk or nun continuing studies**
- **a lay Tibetan dedicated to the tradition**
- **a young student receiving teachings**

Ceremonies for World Peace at Bodh Gaya

Goal: Support 1500 monks and nuns for 15 days of prayer:

- **$100 provides all expenses for one person**
- **$50 provides travel for one person**
- **$30 provides food for one person**

Compassion

The Tibetan Aid Project (TAP) Needs Your Help

For over 20 years the Tibetan Aid Project has been dedicated to preserving the Tibetan tradition of compassion, wisdom and peace. TAP's 1990 goals renew its commitment to the Tibetan people by aiding 150 additional monks, nuns and lay people through its penfriend program and by sponsoring 1500 participants for the 1990 Ceremonies for World Peace at the site of Buddha's enlightenment.

* * *

Protected behind the Himalayas for centuries, the Tibetan people developed a culture deeply compassionate and attuned harmoniously to all living things.

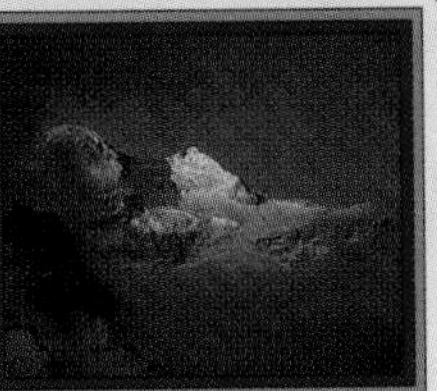

Out of reverence towards higher learning, thousands of Buddhist monasteries became scholastic centers devoted to exploring human awareness, developing wisdom, and creating richly inspiring art.

Though uprooted from their homeland by recent historical events, many Tibetans have set aside personal concerns to rebuild their culture. New monasteries in India, Nepal, Bhutan and Sikkim testify to the strength of their efforts. With your help they can accomplish far more.

We are fortunate that Tibetans have come into the modern world. With them they bring a living wisdom tradition that offers ways to penetrate the root causes of human difficulties.

Wisdom

People-to-People Support Since 1969

The Tibetan Aid Project has tried to aid Tibetans' efforts to rebuild their culture by linking over 2000 Westerners and Tibetans as penfriends, by providing medical assistance, food and clothing, and by sending educational materials to centers preserving Tibet's major lineages and schools of thought.

With assistance this people-to-people friendship program can continue. Your donations can enable a young student to receive teachings, an aged lama or nun to continue their studies, or a lay Tibetan to remain dedicated to the tradition.

By supporting Tibetan culture, we can safeguard a treasury of teachings in a world groping for values and overshadowed by the rush of technology. The contemplative yet practical tradition of Tibet provides a deeply-needed counterbalance to the pressures of our modern world.

Many Westerners have begun to appreciate the capacity of Buddhist thought to open new dimensions of inquiry. Inspiring a comprehensive investigation of human consciousness, the Tibetan tradition brings with it a wealth of knowledge.

In 1988, after meeting with lamas who lived in Nepal, I decided to work with them to establish a shedra in Kathmandu for the education and training of 108 young lamas from Tibet, Nepal, Bhutan, Sikkim, and India. I purchased land where I hoped we could soon build a permanent shedra and leased temporary quarters until that could be accomplished.

Substantial efforts and resources were invested in the new institution, named the Nyingma Institute of Nepal. The Institute followed a traditional program of philosophical studies that included Sanskrit and Tibetan grammar, poetry, composition, logic, history, and philosophical studies in Madhyamaka and Prajnaparamita. Room and board and other necessities for the students were sponsored at first by TNMC, then supplemented a little later with contributions from TAP, as detailed below.

TAP developed and administered a new Pen Friend Program for supporting the 108 monks enrolled at the shedra, and matched each of them with Western sponsors. For each student, TNMC contributed $18.38 per month and TAP offered $14.20, amounting to a total of $32.58 a month over a period of six years.

1989

Pen Friends	$5,880
Other payments	241
Total	6,121

1990

Payment for rent	$3,960
Pen Friends	7,794
Total	11,754

1991

Opposite: TAP's 1990 brochure focused on Pen Friend support for education of monks and nuns and the role of ceremonies in preserving the spiritual strength of the Tibetan Dharma traditions.

Payment for rent	$6,783
Pen Friends	10,484
Total	17,267

1992

Payment for rent	$2,000
Food Offering	1,000
Other payments	1,000
Pen Friends	16,800
Medical	600
Total	21,400

1993

Payment for rent	$5,567
Pen Friends	6,280
Food Offering	1,000
Total	12,847

1994

Payment for rent	$9000
Pen Friends	20,400
Medical	1,300
Other Payments	2,000
Total	32,700

1995

Nepal Shedra Rent	$5000
Pen Friends	5074
Total	10,074

Total TAP's contributions 1989 to 1995:	$112,163
Total TAP/TNMC contributions	$469,446*

* Not including the costs of purchasing and preparing the land intended for the shedra's permanent home.

Despite good intentions on all sides, the connection between the Nyingma Institute of Nepal and the Nyingma organizations in America did not continue. In 1995, the Nepal institute relocated, and since then it has operated independently.

TAP Pen Friend Shedra Support 1988–1993	
Sikkim Shedra	$6,020
Ka-Nying Shedrup Ling	1,920
Nagi Gompa	1,200
Rigo Tulku, Bir	8,500
Khochen Tulku, Dehra Dun	6,800
Taklung Tsetrul, Simla	3,620
Nyingma Institute of Nepal	47,237
Independents	7,800
Mindroling, Tibet	1,400
Other monasteries in Tibet	1,200
TOTAL	$85,697

Expanding Support for Education

TNMC and TAP's support for students attending the Nyingma Institute of Nepal became the model for broader efforts. TNMC has sought to encourage and protect traditional forms of higher education by creating salaries for qualified staff, supporting serious students with scholarships, and providing funds for necessities, books, and supplies.

At the same time, TAP's Pen Friend Program began to sponsor the education of students in other shedras as well as in nunneries. From 1988 to 1993, funds from 425 individual donors from eight countries—the United States, Brazil, Holland, Germany, Japan, Austria, Switzerland, and Hong Kong—were distributed to more than four hundred students and nuns.

In 1994, building on the success of the Pen Friend Program, TAP initiated a new sponsorship program in which donors pledged $30 each month to support the education of a monk or nun. Starting

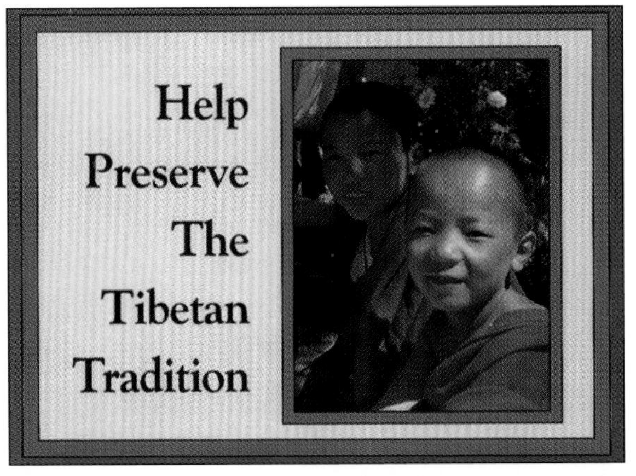

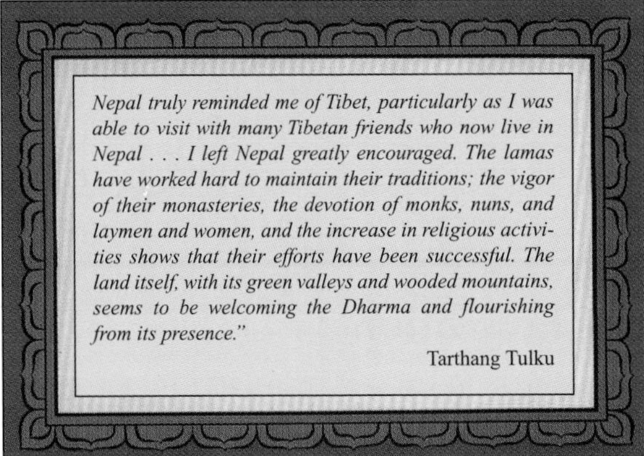

Nepal truly reminded me of Tibet, particularly as I was able to visit with many Tibetan friends who now live in Nepal . . . I left Nepal greatly encouraged. The lamas have worked hard to maintain their traditions; the vigor of their monasteries, the devotion of monks, nuns, and laymen and women, and the increase in religious activities shows that their efforts have been successful. The land itself, with its green valleys and wooded mountains, seems to be welcoming the Dharma and flourishing from its presence."
Tarthang Tulku

TAP's mailing in 1993 encouraged donors to become pen friends and sponsor the education of students in the shedras of Nepal and India.

with this program, funds have generally been sent directly to monasteries rather than to individuals

Offerings to the Sangha in Nepal

In January, 1993, after the World Peace Ceremony at Bodh Gaya, I went to Nepal to visit my lama friends and pay respects to the masters of the lineages. On behalf of TNMC, I offered one year of support for sixty students at the shedra associated with Ka-Nying Shedrup Ling, Chokyi Nyima Rinpoche's monastery in Kathmandu, and donated a set of *The Nyingma Edition of the bKa'-'gyur and bsTan-'gyur* to the monastery of Urgyen Tulku. Offerings were made to support practice at retreat centers near the Asura and

Maratika caves, ancient sites empowered by Guru Padmasambhava. TNMC sponsored retreatants at Asura caves under the guidance of Urgyen Tulku for a year, and a director of TAP gave funds for rebuilding the retreat center at Maratika caves, located high in the mountains of Nepal, several days' journey from Kathmandu. As of 2005, Maratika houses a small temple and shelters for practitioners under the direction of Trulzhig Rinpoche. Fifteen lamas practice here, praying that the teachings introduced into Tibet by Padmasambhava will endure for centuries to come. TAP has continued to contribute funds for basic necessities and repairs so that practice at the Caves can continue.

TNMC also contributed funds for rebuilding Shar Khumbu, a monastery under the direction of Trulzhig Rinpoche, and sponsored ceremonies at the Bodhnath Stupa in 1992 and 1993, including New Year's celebrations for the community from 'Gu-log and the mDo-smad community in Nepal.

Visit to Central Tibet

While in Nepal, I had the opportunity to visit central Tibet, and set out in company with several of my friends on a journey that lasted for forty-five days. It had been thirty-five years since I had last seen this part of Tibet, so rich in history and sacred sites.

What we saw was deeply disturbing. At each of the major Nyingma sites I visited—bSam-yas, sMin-grol-gling, rDo-rje Brag, Shug-gseb, Tshe-ring-ljong, and dPal-ri—the story was the same: almost total destruction, and amidst the ruins a small community of impoverished monks or nuns struggling to survive and to reestablish their tradition. It was very saddening to reflect that some of the greatest achievements of world civilization had been destroyed or had utterly vanished. Only at the most remote sites, including Shug-gseb and a few others, did there seem to be real vitality and a strong sense of devotion to the Dharma.

Everywhere I went, I heard stories of the suffering of the people in the years after the Chinese invasion. The authorities insist that these days are gone and that nowadays the people are benefiting from new policies, but I saw few signs of activity directed at the welfare of the Tibetans: Most new construction seems intended to benefit the Chinese or attract tourists. There were few material advances, and countless reminders of loss and destruction, from the ever-present ruins to the stretches of barren desert that had replaced prosperous farmland and the hard lines that poverty had etched into the faces of the people.

Most of all, I was saddened by what I sensed in the hearts of the Tibetan people. On my travels people were always gracious and respectful, and offered what little hospitality they had available. But underneath, they had lost their spirit. They were dull and subdued, and suffered from paranoia and apathy. Something inside them was damaged, perhaps even dying. Grimly concerned with survival, they simply did not care.

Possibly this can change. Within the limits of our resources, I tried to offer material support at each of the centers I visited, providing stipends for the sanghas there over the next few years, sponsoring ceremonies, arranging for repairs or rebuilding. But this is surely not enough. The Chinese authorities have done their work well, and I do not know whether the heart of Tibetan civilization will be able to survive.

Despite our efforts to support the Dharma and to preserve the art, literature, and cultural heritage of Tibet as a living tradition, time is clearly running out. Young Tibetans are deeply patriotic, but their interest in the old traditions is waning. They see their future in learning about material things and the culture of the West. The irreversible momentum of these fundamental changes leaves me with a real question in mind: Can the rich heritage of the Tibet I was fortunate enough to know survive into the next millennium?

Overlooking bSam-yas, Tarthang Tulku performs a ceremony at the hermitage on the three-peaked mountain of lHas-po-ri, where the Great Guru Padmasambhava subdued the demons that were disrupting the construction of Tibet's first monastery. (1993)

Visiting temples in central Tibet, Rinpoche dialogues with the monks, asks about their work, purposes, and needs, gives blessings, and encourages them in their practice. (1993)

Top, Rūpas of Buddhas of the past, present and future; lower, images of Srong-btsan sGam-po and Padmasambhava. TNMC sponsored the restoration of these precious images at dPal-ri.

Tarthang Tulku offers the King of Bhutan a set of The Nyingma Edition, *its* Guide, *and other Dharma Publishing books.*

Visit to Bhutan

Soon after returning to Nepal from Tibet, I had the chance to visit Bhutan. My first impressions were of a healthy environment: steep mountains and rocky canyons with abundant wildlife, a vigorous agricultural economy that produces a surplus for export, and luxuriant growth everywhere, including lush jungles and miles of colorful rhododendrons.

The health of the Dharma in Bhutan stands in sharp contrast to Tibet. Firmly rooted in the Tibetan Buddhist tradition, the Bhutanese mainly follow the 'Brug-pa bKa'-brgyud (Drukpa Kagyu) school, but there is a strong Nyingma presence as well, and people everywhere have great reverence for Guru Padmasambhava. They also follow the lho-gter (southern gTer-ma) teachings recovered by the great fifteenth-century master Padma Gling-pa, who came from near this region. The principal monasteries in Bhutan have up to five hundred lamas; they are well-maintained and there seems to be a strong tradition of yogic practices.

Revitalizing the Holy Places of Bhutan

In an audience with His Royal Majesty, the King of Bhutan, I offered *The Nyingma Edition of the bKa'-'gyur and bsTan-'gyur* to be housed in the Center of Buddhist Studies in Donkhar. During my visits to the thirty-two monasteries and holy places listed below, I made offerings to high lamas and gave funds for ceremonies and retreats.

mKhyen-brtse Rinpoche's monastery
sPa-gro-sku-gdung mChod-rten, the stupa of Thang-stong-rgyal-po
Nam-mkha'i dGon-pa, the major bKa'-brgyud monastery
Thimphu Thar-pa-gling, the main monastery of Klong-chen-pa
mTha'-'dul-gyi lHa-khang at sPa-gro sKyer-chu
Sras-mkar-dgu-thog
Mes-mes-bla-mes dGon-pa
Grub-thob-rin-po-che'i dGon-pa
sGeng-steng dGon-pa
Pu-rna-sa-po-brang
Nyi-ma-lung dGon-pa
sKu-rje lHa-khang, Bum-thang
Byams-chen lHa-khang
Me-'bar-mtsho
Lha-lcam Padma-gsar-'khrung-khyim
'Jam-dpal lHa-khang
lHa-lung dGon-pa
sPa-gro sTag-tshang
Thim-phu bDud-'dul mChod-rten

In recent years, Her Majesty the Queen Mother Kelsang Wangchuk has sponsored the restoration of holy places in Bhutan and supported traditional practices, particularly at the four sites especially sacred to Guru Padmasambhava: Bum-thang sKu-rje lHa-khang, sPa-gro sTag-tshang, sKyer-chu Jo-bo lHa-khang, and Seng-ge rDzong. TNMC has also encouraged Bhutanese lamas and the Queen Mother to support the rebuilding of Thar-pa-gling, the main monastery of Klong-chen-pa, as well as other retreat sites associated with this great Nyingma master.

In 1995, TNMC offered $18,000 in support for practices at six holy sites, as well as $2,000 toward construction of a retreat center at Seng-ge rDzong, located near the cave of Ye-shes mTsho-rgyal. Built by Lama Serpo, holder of the sNying-thig lineage transmitted by A-dzom 'Brug-pa, the retreat center at Seng-ge rDzong housed nine lamas during its first year, all of whom were engaged in the traditional three-year retreat. Practice at these sacred sites helps the light of the Dharma continue to shine in the world, for the benefit of all living beings. Additional sites supported include:

sPa-gro sTag-tshang   Practices include recitation of prayers relating to rDo-rje sGro-lod, Padmasambhava, Vajrakīla, and Tara.

sKyer-chu Jo-bo lHa-khang   Practices include recitations of the Manjushri-namasamgiti, and prayers relating to Tara, Guru Padmasambhava, and Dharmapalas.

Guru lHa-khang   Practices include recitations of the Manjushri-namasamgiti and prayers relating to Tara, Guru Padmasambhava, and Dharmapalas.

Bum-thang sKu-rje lHa-khang   Practices include prayers relating to Guru Padmasambhava and Tara.

Overleaf: A brief overview of the Dharma in Bhutan, home of sacred sites important to the Nyingma and Kagyud lineages. The Buddhist traditions have been part of Bhutanese culture since ancient times.

The Buddhist Traditions of Bhutan

Bhutan has been associated with the Tibetan Dharma traditions since the seventh century, when Srongsen Gampo, king of Tibet, built two border-subjugating temples here, Kyichu in the Paro Valley in western Bhutan and Jampa in the central region of Bumthang. A century later, during the reign of Trisong Detsen in Tibet, Padmasambhava came to Bhutan, meditated in various locations, and concealed Terma, treasure texts for later recovery.

As Buddhism became established in Bhutan, monasteries were built at places blessed by the presence of the Great Guru which are revered as holy to this day. Taksang Monastery clings to a mountain ledge in Paro at the site of one of Padmasambhava's meditation caves, and the temples of Gom Kora near Tashigang and Kuje in Bumthang stand at other sites empowered by the actions of the Great Guru. Devotion to Padmasambhava, venerated as a second Buddha and spiritual son of the Buddha Amitabha, is reflected throughout Bhutan in accounts of the oral tradition and in statues and paintings of the Great Guru's eight major manifestations. Holy places dedicated to Padmasambhava include the three temples at Taksang and the Taksang Zangdog Palri, named after the Great Guru's Copper Mountain paradise.

The Nyingma and Kagyu schools were the earliest Tibetan traditions established in Bhutan, and they are still the most influential. Gyalwa Lhanangpa in the late twelfth century, founder of the Lhapa Kagyu, built his center in the Paro Valley of western Bhutan, and Phajo Drugom Shigpo in the thirteenth century established the Drukpa Kagyud in the Thimphu region, also in western Bhutan. In the fourteenth century, the renowned Nyingma master Longchenpa founded Tharpaling, Samtenling, Shinkar, and Orgyen Choling monasteries in Bumthang, where he wrote some of his works. In all, Longchenpa is associated with eight Dharma centers in Bhutan, six of which are known today.

The Nyingma tradition in Bhutan was strengthened by the work of the great tertons, reincarnations of Guru Padmasambhava and his disciples, who recovered texts concealed by the Great Guru at the time of Trisong Detsen. Among the greatest of these tertons were Dorje Lingpa (1346–1405) and Padma Lingpa (1450–1521), both of whom are associated with Bhutan. Dorje Lingpa, an emanation of the eighth-century master Vairotsana, established his center at Glingmoka and guided the monastery of Padro. His lineage continues to the present day at Orgyen Choling.

Padma Lingpa, reincarnation of both Padma Sal, daughter of Trisong Detsen, and the great master Longchenpa, was born in Bumthang. He discovered the hidden temple of Lhokyerchu in Bhutan, one of about fifty locations from which he recovered more than seven hundred concealed teachings. The terma he discovered were propagated by outstanding masters in Bhutan and Tibet, and his lineage is still vital today. In Bumthang, Padma Lingpa established the Petsheling, Tamshing, and Kunzangdrak monasteries in Bumthang. Extending from here, his lineage strengthened the influence of the Nyingma tradition throughout eastern Bhutan. The Bhutanese royal family traces its lineage to this great master.

The Drukpa Kagyu tradition continued to flourish, playing a major role in Bhutan's unification in the seventeenth century and giving rise to the early rulers of Bhutan. Among the many prominent masters of this tradition, the most popular throughout Bhutan is Drukpa Kunley (1455–1529), a great siddha and tantric master whose accounts have a prominent place in Bhutan's folk literature. Another fifteenth-century Tibetan siddha, Tangton Gyalpo (1385–1510), was also a skilled engineer, renowned as the builder of iron bridges, eight of which he built in Bhutan.

—Excerpted from *The Stupa: Sacred Symbol of Enlightenment:*

Support for Ceremonies in Tibet, Nepal, and Bhutan, 1988–1996

This summary does not include offerings made to monasteries at the World Peace Ceremony, Bodh Gaya since 1989.

1988: $75,446 for ceremonies: recitations of 100,000 Tara prayers at monasteries in Nepal

Taru Monastery
Zhechen Tennyi Dargye Ling
Dapzang Monastery
Thrangu Tashi Choling
Maitreya Mandir
Shelkar Chosde Gaden Lepshad Ling
Nyingmapa Wishfulfilling Center for Study and Practice
Nenam Pao Rinpoche Monastery
Samtenling Tibetan Monastery
Urgyen Tulku's monastery (500,000 recitations)

The amount above includes funds for additional ceremonies at Palo, Tuthop, and Baro Kagyu Foundation monasteries, donations of prayer flags, travel, and miscellaneous donations and expenses.

1990 Ceremonies **$26,086**

Tamang Buddhist Association, Darjeeling
Zhechen Tennyi Dargye Ling, Nepal
Ka-Nying Shedrup Ling, Nepal
Asura Caves, Nepal
Nyingma Institute of Nepal; others

1990 Monastery endowments **$118,195**

1991 **$28,034**

Support for eight monasteries, nunneries, shedras, and retreat centers in east Tibet for the preservation of Nyingma lineages and philosophical studies:
Khra-gling dGon-pa (branch of Kaḥ-thog)

bsTan-po dGon-pa (branch of Tarthang Monastery)
Se dGon-pa (Jonangpa)
Lung-dkar dGon-pa (Gelugpa)
gYag-mgo dGon-pa (branch of Dar-thang)
gDong-rdzong dGon-pa (hermitage of mDo mKhyen-brtse)
gTum-po dGon-pa, specializing in sPal-yul
and sNying-thig traditions
mDo dGon-pa, specializing in sNying-thig.

1993 Reconstruction support and ceremonies in Central Tibet $121,689

bSam-yas Funds for monthly ceremonies, a total of 248 days of pujas attended by fifty to one hundred lamas; funds for reconstruction of the Pe-har temple.

rDo-rje-brag Three years of support for eighty-two days of ceremonies per year; support for maintenance of forty monks for three years.

sMin-grol-gling Funds for repairing the roof; support for monks, ceremonies, and offerings for three years. Gold for statues of Padmasambhava, King Khri-srong lDe'u-btsan, and Abbot Shantarakshita.

Tshe-ring-ljong Support for the nuns for three years; funds for monthly ceremony offerings; funds to repair the temple roof; shelves for the bKa'-'gyur.

Shug-gseb nunnery Support for ceremonies and living expenses for three years.

dPal-ri Offerings and three years' support for monthly ceremonies.

Nye-phu Shug-gseb Support for ceremonies and living expenses for three years; sponsorship of paintings of the rDzogs-chen lineage.

1993 Nepal

Support to sixty students at the shedra.

Asura and Maratika Caves (Powerful sacred sites renowned as practice places of the Great Guru Padmasambhava). One year of support for retreatants at Asura Caves; funds for rebuilding the retreat center at Maratika Caves.

1995 Nepal and Tibet **$123,190**

NEPAL

Pharping Monastery
Nagi Gompa Nunnery
Trulzhig Monastery
Pharping Stupa Foundation (Sakya)
Losar Ceremony, Ka-Nying Shedrup Ling
Nyingma Institute of Nepal
Maratika Caves

TIBET

Tsongsen Gompa Pagse
rDo-rje-brag Monastery
Shug-gseb Nunnery
Deldre Monastery
Dregong Shedra
Dergun Wenre Monastery
Lhasa Jokhang
sMin-grol-gling Monastery
bSam-yas Monastery
Uru Shaye Lhakhang
Tarthang Monastery Shedra

1996 India, Nepal, and Tibet **$106,753**

NORTHERN INDIA

sMin-gro-gling Monastery
Sakya College
Sakya Monastery
Pema Ewam Choegar Geumay Ling
Ngagyur Samten Choekhor Ling
Rigo Tulku's Monastery
Urgyen Thundup Monastery
Dzongsar Khyentse Shedra
Nyingma Monastery
Kang Thrul Kagyud Monastery
others

NEPAL

Choling Rinpoche
Tenga Rinpoche
Yantse Rinpoche
Dechen Rinpoche
Chokyi Nyima
Urgyen Tulku Memorial
Rabjam Tulku
Taru Rinpoche
Ka-Nying Monastery, retreat support for 10 monks for three years at Pharping

TIBET

Offerings for rDo-rje-brag, given at Bodh Gaya

Chapter Eleven

To Restore the Light: Practices and Holy Places in Tibet

Looking back on the months that I spent in Asia in 1993, I see it as a time of sharp contrasts. The joy of being part of ceremonies at Bodh Gaya was tempered by my experience in Tibet, a land whose tradition and spirit have been broken. Among the Tibetan Buddhist communities in exile and in the Himalayas, there is a sense of vigor and vitality, but here too an uncertain future awaits. Today someone who was sixteen when the Chinese took over Tibet is fifty years old, and the next generation of Tibetans was educated either under communism or in exile. Soon there will be none left who remembers Tibet as it was.

Despite our efforts to support the Dharma and to preserve the art, literature, and cultural heritage of Tibet as a living tradition, time is clearly running out. Young Tibetans are deeply patriotic, but their interest in the old traditions is waning. They tend to see their future in learning about material things and the culture of the West. The irreversible momentum of these fundamental changes raises a serious concern: Can the rich heritage of the Tibet I was fortunate enough to know survive into the next millennium?

Knowing that the continuation of the practice lineages is crucial for the future of the Dharma, I established the Ka-Ter Foundation in 1994. Ka-Ter refers to bKa'-'ma and gTer-ma, the two types of transmission lineages preserved within the Nyingma tradition. It was my thought to extend the efforts begun in Bodh Gaya, Lumbini, and Sarnath to reestablish the holy places as vital centers of inspiration.

The purpose of the Ka-Ter Foundation was to promote and spread the teachings of the Nyingma lineages in Tibet, India, Bhutan, and Nepal; to support the bKa'-dgongs-phur practices and mDo-sgyu-sems-gsum teachings; to restore practices at the now neglected and forgotten ancient holy places; to support the rebuilding of retreat centers, and monasteries, and sponsor ceremonies and prayers as symbolic gestures of our work to preserve and revitalize our Dharma heritage. This focus included the three aspects of kaya, vaca, citta (body, speech, and mind): sku (images), gsung (teachings), and thugs (enlightened mind, stupas).

Special Practices of the Nyingma Tradition

The special teachings of the Nyingma tradition, which were transmitted directly from the Dharmakaya to human Vidyadharas, flowed through two streams: the bKa'-ma and gTer-ma lineages. The bKa'-ma, or continuous transmission, was the Maha, Anu, and Ati teachings, passed from master to disciple in unbroken succession. The gTer-ma or treasure transmission emphasizes practices known as bKa'-dgongs-phur-gsum: the bKa'-brgyad, or Eight Heruka Sadhanas; the Bla-ma-dgongs-'dus, the heart of all Buddhas; and the Phur-pa, or Vajrakila practices. These powerful teachings were brought to Tibet by Guru Padmsambhava and translated in the eighth century at bSam-yas monastery. The Great Guru concealed most of them as gTer-ma, to protect their potency until they were most needed. Through the centuries, they have been brought forth when they will have the greatest benefit and when people are ready to receive their blessing.

From the eighth and ninth centuries until very recent times, the bKa'-dgongs-phur-gsum practices were followed by the entire Nyingma tradition. At the six main Nyingma monasteries (rDo-rje-brag and sMin-grol-gling in central Tibet, and Kah-thog, rDzogs-chen, Zhe-chen, and dPal-yul in eastern Tibet) and at hundreds of monasteries and retreat sites across Tibet, these practices were refined into an inner science for transforming human consciousness. Over time, some of these centers fell into disrepair or were victims of various unfortunate conflicts. With the destruction that followed the Chinese invasion of 1959, the damage was nearly complete, and the lineages were seriously disrupted. The few remaining individuals who still possess the knowledge required for the bKa'-dgongs-phur-gsum sadhanas have been unable to rebuild centers for their study because of lack of funds, unfamiliarity with construction, and inadequate support. Thus, the bKa'-dgongs-phur-gsum practices have been rarely performed in recent years, and the texts for the Bla-ma-dgongs-'dus have not even been available. TNMC seeks to help the monasteries revitalize their traditions by providing the necessary texts, funds, and knowledge. If this can be done, there is hope that the realizations transmitted through these sadhanas can continue to benefit humanity far into the future.

TNMC has also sought to support the bKa'-dgongs-phur-gsum practices in other ways. In 1994, we sponsored a sadhana at H. H. Penor Rinpoche's monastery. In 1995, TNMC distributed the major commentaries on the Bla-ma-dgongs-'dus, prepared and printed by the Yeshe De Project, at the World Peace Ceremony at Bodh Gaya. In 1996, TNMC was able to obtain, print, and distribute 'Jam-mgon Kong-sprul's one-volume version of the sadhanas themselves, together with the two-volume sadhana of the dPal-yul tradition. In addition, the royal family of Bhutan kindly granted permission to reproduce a rare set of the cycle of the thirteen thankas required for practice of the great sadhana. These precious images were also distributed to the Sangha at the 1996 Monlam Chenmo.

Ka-Ter Foundation: The First Effort

The founding document of the Ka-Ter Foundation was published in *Gesar Magazine* 12:2, 12-14 (Spring 1994). In summary, it provided that under the direction of Tarthang Rinpoche, four chief directors would ascertain where support was most needed in India, Nepal, Bhutan, and Tibet. In each land, the directors were to have two assistants and the assistants would have several staff, making a total of twenty individuals.

The founding principles emphasized the preservation and promotion of the three types of bKa'-brgyad practice, derived from the gTer-ma of Nyang-ral Nyi-ma 'Od-zer, Guru Chos-dbang, and Rig-'dzin-rgod-ldem; the Bla-ma dgongs-'dus of Sangs-rgyas-gling-pa; and the Phur-pa practices of the bKa'-ma and gTer-ma. Where these traditional Nyingma practices are being undertaken under the direction of a qualified Vajra master (rdo-rje-slob-dpon), with the participation of monks holding the Vinaya lineage and the appropriate initiations, the Foundation was to offer support. It was thought that three sadhanas of each kind (bKa'-brgyad, dGongs-'dus, and phur-pa) could be supported in India, Nepal, and Bhutan annually. The appropriate places and numbers of sadhanas in Tibet were to be determined on the basis of ongoing support.

Holy Places in Tibet The Ka-Ter Foundation was also established to support important holy places in the central Tibetan regions of dBus and gTsang in five principal ways:

1. support for sgrub-grwa (retreat centers)
2. support for bshad-grwa (shedra, schools for philosophy)
3. support for creating statues
4. offerings for performing pujas
5. funds for rebuilding

The founding document further provided that the Ka-Ter Foundation would gradually support those wishing to perform the sadhanas. It was to focus on shedra support, including the practices of Vajrasattva sadhanas and ten-day periods of study of the Mahayoga gSang-ba'i-snying-po texts and commentaries. Additional activities provided for included the restoration and reconstruction of ancient monasteries as well as the restoration of statues and attention to special needs of the shedras, including the publishing and distribution of rare texts.

Nyingma Buddhist Trust

A second organization, the Nyingma Buddhist Religious Trust, was established in America to support the Ka-Ter Foundation. The Nyingma Buddhist Religious Trust was founded as a non-profit church auxiliary, exempt under the Internal Revenue Code Section 501(c)(3) and 170(b)(1)(A)(ii) and under California Revenue and Taxation Code Section 23701(d). It was funded on April 30, 1994 and granted tax-exempt status on May 19, 1997.

The Six Major Nyingma Monasteries

Central to the Nyingma tradition are six major monasteries: rDo-rje-brag and sMin-grol-gling in central Tibet, and Kah-thog, Zhe-chen, dPal-yul, and rDzogs-chen in eastern Tibet. All six monasteries maintained the bKa'-'ma teachings. Each is associated with specific gTer-ma lineages which became the specialty of that monastery and its branches. These six centers were the parent monasteries of complex networks of subsidiary monasteries, some of which became larger than their parent monastery and developed extensive monastic complexes of their own. Since the early 1980s, when travel in Tibet became possible, TNMC has made efforts to assist these central pillars of the Nyingma tradition in revitalizing their practices. It is hoped that the Ka-Ter foundation can find ways to continue supporting ceremonies and retreats at these important sites and do everything possible to revitalize the lineages here.

Kah-thog Kah-thog rDo-rje-ldan Monastery was founded in Khams in 1159 by Kah-thog Dam-pa-bde-gshegs Shes-rab-seng-ge, a master in the lineage of Zur. Kah-thog was guided by a succession

sMin-grol-gling monastery, one of the six major Nyingma monasteries, is associated with the Upper and Lower Treasures, the gTer-ma teachings recovered by Nyang-ral Nyi-ma 'Od-zer and Chos-kyi dbang-phyug. (2005)

of thirteen great masters, emanations of Manjushri, Avalokiteshvara, and Vajrapani, who continued the bKa'-'ma lineages transmitted through Zur-po-che, Zur-'chung-pa, and sGro-sbug-pa. During this time, more than 180,000 monks passed through Kah-thog as students, practitioners, or temporary residents. Even when knowledge of the Inner Tantras declined in central Tibet, study and practice of these esoteric teachings continued to flourish at Kah-thog Monastery. Kah-thog specialized in the gTer-ma of bDud-'dul rDo-rje (1615–1672) and his disciple Klong-gsal sNying-po, the practices of Maha, Anu, and Atiyoga, the sNying-thig Atiyoga teachings, and the dGongs-pa-zang-thal.

The photographs in this section were taken by participants in the pilgrimage to Central Tibet led by TAP representatives in spring, 2005.

rDo-rje-brag in Central Tibet, home of the Byang-gter, the Northern Treasure-texts, and one of the six major Nyingma monasteries. The ancient retreat caves in these hills are powerful places for practice. *(2005)*

rDo-rje-brag rDo-rje-brag, "Vajra Rock," takes its name from the ridge shaped like a vajra that rises above it. The caves, caverns, and tunnels here established this area as a favored retreat site for Guru Padmasambhava and his disciples. rDo-rje-brag was founded to shelter and protect the Northern Treasures, a gTer-ma collection transmitted to the present day. Originally the residence of two hundred monks and three incarnate lamas, rDo-rje-brag was destroyed by the Mongolian army in 1718, but was soon rebuilt. As recently as 1958, rDo-rje-brag was an active monastery with multiple temples, but these were seriously damaged in the 1960s during the Cultural Revolution. At the time of Tarthang Tulku's visit in 1993, the temples were decimated, the monastery ravaged, and only a few dozen monks and three older lamas remained. TNMC has funded structural repairs and statues as well as three years of support for eighty-

sGrags Yongs-rdzong, near rDo-rje-brag in central Tibet, is the site of a meditation cave used by Guru Padmasambhava. Khri-srong lDe'u-btsan spent time here and established a retreat center. *(2005)*

two days of ceremonies per year. TAP continues to provide for the fifty monks who now live and study at the site.

sMin-grol-gling Established in 1676 by the great Dharma king Chos-rgyal gTer-bdag Gling-pa and his brother, Lo-chen Dharmashri, sMin-grol-gling regularly housed four hundred monks and had three incarnate lineages. Although it was badly damaged by the Mongols in 1718, it soon recovered from the invasion. Its lineages nurtured a long line of accomplished siddhas and scholars.

Teachings preserved here include the bKa'-'ma and gTer-ma lineages of O-rgyan gTer-bdag-gling-pa and a special Atiyoga lineage transmitted through his daughter Mi-'gyur-dpal-sgron. From here, the bKa'-'ma lineages protected and transmitted by O-rgyan gTer-bdag-gling-pa flowed to the major Nyingma monasteries of Khams:

Shug-gseb Ani Gompa (Shugseb nunnery) became renowned as the place where the great Nyingma master Klong-chen-pa (1308–1363) received the text of the mKha'-'gro sNying-thig. The nuns of Shugs-gseb maintain a strong practice.

Kah-thog, rDzogs-chen, Zhe-chen, and dPal-yul, and from there to rGya-mo-rong and 'Gu-log.

sMin-grol-gling maintained a strong connection with the Upper and Lower Treasures, major gTer-mas discovered by Nyang-ral Nyi-ma 'Od-zer and Chos-kyi dBang-phyug, the 'sun' and 'moon' of the great gTer-stons, in the twelfth and thirteenth centuries. Before 1959, sMin-grol-gling was renowned for its beautiful temples and for the frescoes that breathed life into their walls, a statue of Padmasambhava three stories in height, and a large stupa that enshrined the relics of gTer-bdag-gling-pa.

sMin-drol-gling was completely destroyed during the Cultural Revolution of the 1960s. Everything in its spacious central temple was removed. A large hole was cut in its roof so that the temple could serve as a granery for the surrounding area. Wheat filled the

Images of mkhan-slob-chos-gsum: Shantarakshita, Guru Padmasambhava, and the Dharma king Khri-srong lDe'u-btsan, the founding fathers of bSam-yas monastery and the Great Beings who established the foundation for the Dharma in Tibet.

temple for decades; when it was finally removed, what was left of the roof collapsed, and the frescoes inside, formerly protected from the elements by the stored grain, began to deteriorate. To rebuild the roof, preserve the priceless frescoes, and restore the golden image of the mKhan-slob-chos-gsum (Shantarakshita, Padmasambhava, and Khri-srong lDe-btsan), TNMC donated $18,000. In 2005, TNMC sponsored statues of O-rgyan gTer-bdag Gling-pa, his brother, Lochen Dharmashri, and his father, gSang-bdak Phrin-las Lhun-grub.

dPal-yul dPal-yul Monastery was founded in Khams in 1665 by Rig-'dzin Kun-bzang-shes-rab (1636–1699). Rig-'dzin Kun-bzang Shes-rab established here the doctrinal school of Byang-chub rNam-rgyal Chos-gling, which continues today under the guidance of his disciples and incarnations. dPal-yul was known for the strength of its meditation practice. Its special teachings include the gTer-ma

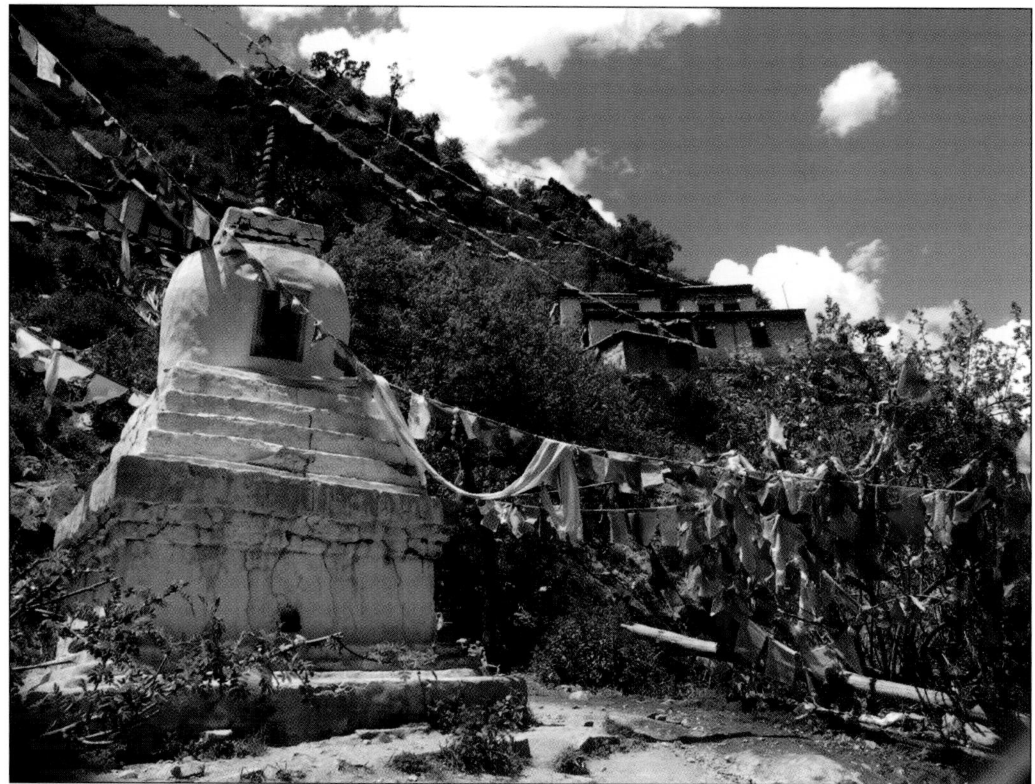

This stupa beside gYa-ma-lung hermitage, located near bSam-yas, is where Padmasambhava created a spring flowing with the water of life and concealed longevity practices as gTer-mas for later recovery.

teachings of Ratna Gling-pa, gNam-chos Mi-'gyur rDo-rje, and 'Ja'-tshon-snying-po. At its height, dPal-yul housed over six hundred monks and had seven incarnate lamas. It was also the center of many branch monasteries, the largest being Dar-thang (Tarthang) Monastery in 'Gu-log, founded in 1882.

rDzogs-chen rDzogs-chen O-rgyan bSam-gtan-chos-gling was founded in Khams in 1685 by Padma Rig-'dzin, disciple of Karma Chags-med, Rig-'dzin bDud-'dul rDo-rje, and gNam-chos Mi-'gyur rDo-rje. An emanation of the siddha Kukkuraja and the Kashmiri Mahapandita Vimalamitra, the great master Padma Rig-'dzin was renowned for his learning and accomplishments. His work for the Dharma at rDzogs-chen was continued by his reincarnations and his many disciples, including the great gTer-ston Nyi-ma-grags-pa. rDzogs-chen specialized in Mahayoga and Atiyoga teachings; its

The monastery of Tshe-ring-ljong, restored in the 18th century by the gTer-ston 'Jigs-med Gling-pa, looks out over a valley near 'Phyongs-rgyas. It was completely destroyed during the Cultural Revoluntion, but has recently been rebuilt.

masters transmitted the thirteen bKa'-'ma lineages as well as important gTer-ma teachings.

Among the largest of Nyingma monasteries in Tibet, rDzogs-chen housed 850 monks and maintained thirteen separate retreat centers prior to 1959. Eleven incarnate lineages maintained rDzogs-chen's strong program of study and practice. rGyal-sras gZhan-phan mTha'-yas established the Shri Simha College here in the mid-nineteenth century.

Zhe-chen Zhe-chen was founded in 1735 by the second Rab-'byams, 'Gyur-med Kun-bzang Nam-rgyal (1713–1769), at Zhe-chen O-rgyan-Chos-rdzong, a Dharma hermitage in Khams. The natural beauty and splendor of the setting made it an inspiring place for study and practice. Zhe-chen bsTan-gnyis Dar-gyas-gling was

Vista from Brag-dmar mGrin-bzang, birthplace of the Dharma King Khri-srong lDe'u-btsan, a powerful site, important historically and a place of pilgrimage since ancient times.

founded nearby in 1665 by the second Zhe-chen Rab-'byams, 'Gyur-med Kun-bzang rNam-gyal. Perched high above a river valley, Zhe-chen housed over two hundred monks and had nine incarnate lineages. It was known for the profoundness of its doctrines and its strict monastic discipline. Following the program of training established at sMin-grol-gling, Zhe-chen supported a long lineage of outstanding masters.

bSam-yas Established in the eighth century by Shantarakshita, Padmasambhava, and the Dharma king Khri-srong lDe'u-btsan. bSam-yas was Tibet's first monastery and the original home of the Tibetan Sangha. Here the Abbot Shantarakshita ordained the first Tibetan monks, and Kashmiri and Indian panditas and Tibetan lotsawas worked together to translate the sacred texts from Sanskrit into Tibetan.

gYa-ma-lung, one of the eight chief hermitages of Guru Rinpoche, Padmasambhava, where the Guru instructed Ye-shes mTsho-rgyal. Vairotsana spent three years here on retreat. The area is largely abandoned, but hermits still meditate here.

Built as a mandala with a three-storied golden temple in its center and white, red, green, and black stupas placed in the four directions, bSam-yas occupies a unique place in Tibetan history and is an integral aspect of Tibetan identity. Yet bSam-yas was seriously damaged and its stupas destroyed during the Cultural Revolution.

The central temple and its four stupas have been rebuilt, but much remains to be done to activate this spiritual center of Tibetan Buddhism. Although its history is closely intertwined with the early transmission of the Dharma to Tibet and the Nyingma tradition, its significance transcends sectarian distinctions. Since the Dharma was restored to Central Tibet in the eleventh to twelfth centuries, bSam-yas has been watched over more strongly by the Sarma traditions. Although it is not one of the six major Nyingma monasteries, TNMC plans to restore at least one of its historic temples.

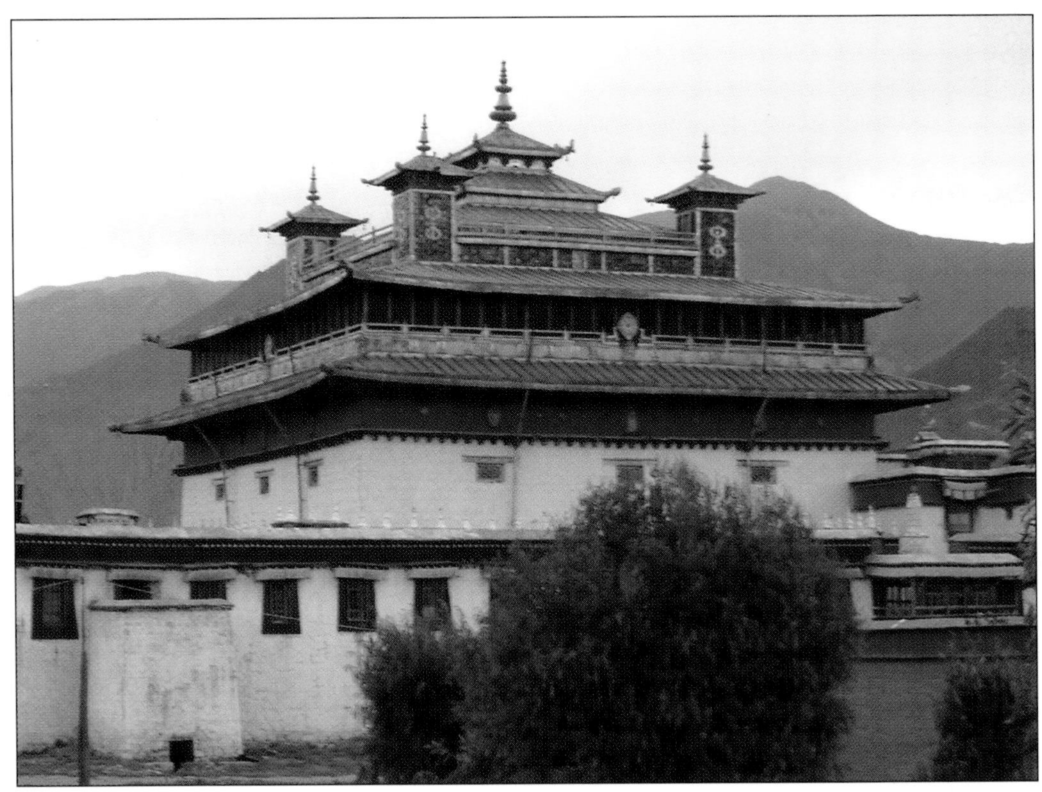

The three-storied golden temple of bSam-yas. An account of its construction and symbolism is given in The Legend of the Great Stupa, *an ancient gTer-ma text.*

Activities of the Ka-Ter Foundation, 1994

In 1994, officers of the Ka-Ter Foundation led by Tulku Sangngak were able to travel to Tibet to visit Nyingma monasteries and retreat centers to distribute funds and determine needs and priorities. Funds were made available for the following purposes:

To the monastery of sMin-grol-gling in Central Tibet, funds were offered for the creation of beautiful statues of the three founders of Buddhism, Guru Padmasambhava, the Abbot Shantarakshita, and King Khri-srong lDe'u-btsan.

At Shug-gseb nunnery, where more than three hundred nuns were given support in 1993, the Foundation offered additional support for twenty nuns to undertake an intensive retreat. Shug-gseb, located high in the mountains overlooking the Nyepu Valley, was founded in the twelfth century. Here the great Nyingma master

The historically important Red and Black Stupas of bSam-yas, destroyed during the Cultural Revolution and since rebuilt. *(2005)*

Klong-chen-pa received transmission of the mKha'-'gro sNying-thig and established lineage of this teaching. It is the home of a small community of nuns following the Nyingma tradition and Tibet's principal center for women practitioners of rDzogs-chen.

At rDo-rje-brag, home of the Byang-gter (Northern Treasures) discovered by Rig-'dzin rGod-ldem, the Foundation provided funds for very large thankas and fabric appliqué hangings in honor of Padmasambhava, as well as support for fifty monks in residence.

At Tshe-ring-ljongs, the monastery where the great master and gTer-ston 'Jigs-med-gling-pa lived, the Foundation contributed funds to rebuild the temple, set up a retreat center and provided support for twenty-five nuns for three years.

At 'Phyongs-rgyas dPal-ri, the most important rNying-ma monastery before the seventeenth century, the Foundation contributed funds to rebuild the temple and restore the statues.

Buddha-image in one of the many caves at Brag Yer-pa, renowned as meditation retreat places of King Srong-btsan sGam-po and Guru Padmasambhava. (2005)

Recent Revitalization Activities of TNMC

Since 1994, the Ka-Ter Foundation has been largely inactive, but TNMC has continued to support reconstruction and remodeling of monasteries, retreat centers, and schools; to replenish libraries by providing books and thankas; and to revitalize the pujas traditionally observed on the tenth and twenty-fifth days of the months of the lunar calendar. TAP, TNMC, and the Yeshe De Project's book production efforts have powered a flow of offerings of funds and books that have reached over three thousand centers in India, Nepal, Tibet, and Bhutan. In the spring of 2005, participants on TAP's pilgrimage to central Tibet carried offerings from TNMC and TAP for the monasteries they visited, adding to the symbolic gestures of renewal and revitalization TNMC has made to Tibetan centers through the years.

An important cave sanctuary at mChims-phu, associated with Padmasambhava, Ye-shes Tsho-rgyal, and other disciples of the Great Guru. (2005)

A Gesture of Healing: Rebuilding the Roof of sMin-grol-gling It is our dream to do everything possible to bring back the blessings of Dharma, to help the lineages survive and provide them what they need to continue to keep the light of the Dharma shining in its traditional homelands. In recent years, TNMC contributed $18,000 to rebuild the roof of sMin-grol-gling Monastery and supported projects and practices at rDo-rje-brag. Now we would like to restore the historic Manjushri Temple at bSam-yas.

The Manjushri Temple, constructed in the eighth century and extensively remodeled by Sakya Pandita in the thirteenth century, is venerated by practitioners of all Tibetan traditions. Like so many others, this temple was stripped of its sacred images and altars during the Cultural Revolution and transformed into a stable for livestock. Left open to the elements for years, the temple was

Renovations are underway at mChims-phu Monastery in Central Tibet, which was badly damaged during the Cultural Revolution. (2005)

deteriorating rapidly; the roof and doors were gone, the floors crusted with debris, and the precious frescoes on its walls were blackened, almost invisible under layers of soot. In 2005, TNMC provided $20,000 to start work on the temple, which is now in the process of being cleaned.

Dharma Peace Bell for bSam-yas A special effort is being made to provide bSam-yas with a Dharma Peace Bell. Cast in Germany with sacred texts and symbols inside and out, this bell is identical to the bells recently offered and installed at the four major Buddhist holy places in India: Bodh Gaya, Sarnath, Lumbini, and Kushinagara. These Dharma bells are potent symbols of Vaca, the sound of enlightenment that resounds in all directions and awakens Bodhicitta, the aspiration to attain enlightenment for the sake of helping others find the way to liberation. May its sound awaken the memories of the people of Tibet and empower their prayers on behalf of all beings.

A view from mChims-phu, a meditation cave of Padmasambhava and his 25 disciples and the site of the transmission of the Heruka sadhanas. *(2005)*

Holy Places of the Nyingma Tradition

In their journey to Tibet in 1994, the four lamas representing the Ka-Ter Foundation evaluated the condition and needs of holy places, centers, and monasteries and compiled a list of the following 205 Nyingma holy places. Among them are well-known historical monasteries and places of retreat. But many more fell into disuse and have been long abandoned. A long-range goal for the new foundations established by TNMC is to locate them all and make offerings at these sacred sites, to rekindle the light of the Dharma and brighten the land of snows. (See "Foundations for the Future," described in chapter thirteen.)

1. lHa-sa Brag-ra-klu-phug Grub-thob lHa-khang, "Lhasa Dragra Lupug." The place where Nyang Ting-'dzin bZang-po, the eighth century disciple of Padmasambhava, achieved the Rainbow Body.

Brag-yer-pa, 'Yerpa Rock', is renowned as caves where Padmasambhava, Vairotsana, and the eighty siddhas of Yer-pa meditated in the eighth century. It is also associated with the seventh-century Dharma King Srong-btsan sGam-po. (2005)

2. Brag-yer-pa Zla-ba-phug, "Drag Yerpa." Practice caves where Guru Rinpoche, the Dharma king Srong-btsan sgam-po, Vairotsana, and the eighty siddhas of Yer-pa meditated. King Khri-srong lDe'u-btsan established a tantric retreat center here.

3. 'O-brgyal-thang Tshe-bcu lHa-khang bShad-grwa-gsar-pa, "Ogyal Tang." A new Shedra located in lHa-sa.

4. dBu-ru Ka-tshal mTha'-'dul gTsug lag-khang, "Katsal." Built by King Srong-btsan sGam-po in the 7th century.

5. dBu-ru Zhwa-yi gTsug-lag-khang, "Zhwa Lakang." Founded by Nyang Ting-'dzin bZang-po. Klong-chen-pa received a vision instructing him to repair this holy place.

6. Chos-lung-btsun Monastery, "Cholung Tsun." Residence of Ra-hor Chos-grags.

Frescoes at bSam-yas have for centuries been a valued part of Tibet's priceless artistic and religious heritage. Destroyed or seriously damaged in the 1960s, some have recently been restored. TNMC seeks to continue this work. (2005)

7. dKar-chung rDo-rje-dbyings, "Karchung." A place connected with King Khri-srong lDe'u-btsan's son, rGyal-sras Mu-khri.

8. 'Bri-gung gZho-stod Ti-sgro, "Tidro." Site of practice caves of Padmasambhava and Ye-shes mTsho-rgyal.

9. 'Bri-gung mThil, "Drigung Til." 'Bri-gung sKyobs-pa Rinpoche's (1143–1217) residence.

10. 'Bri-gung bShad-grwa, "Drigung Shedra." 'Bri-gung sKyobs-pa Rinpoche worked here.

11. Gangs-ri Thod-dkar, "Gangri Tokar." The White Skull Mountain, the site of sacred caves where Kun-mkhyen Klong-chen-pa (1308–1363) perfected realization, redacted the Ya-bzhi, composed the Seven Treasures, and passed into nirvana.

12. Shug-gseb Monastery, "Shug Seb." Associated with Rig-'dzin Chos-nyid bZang-mo.

13. Shug-gseb sGrub-sde, "Shug Seb." Practice center guided by sPrul-sku 'Jigs-med rDo-rje .

14. lCags-zam Chu-bo-ri O-rgyan Nam-mkha'-rdzong, "Chubo Ri." Retreat founded by the great siddha Thang-stong rGyal-po (1385–1510) at dPal Chu-bo-ri, site where 108 great meditators achieved realization in the days of the Dharma Kings and 108 springs arose from the blessings of Padmasambhava.

15. rDo-rje-brag E-wam-Cog-sgar, "Dorje Drag." A major Nyingma monastery founded by Ngag-gi dBang-po, master of the Byang-gter (Northern Treasures) in 1632. E-wam Cog-sgar was the name of the first monastery established earlier at that site by bKra-shis sTob-rgyal.

16. sGrags Yang-rdzong, "Drag Yang Zong." Holy place associated with the Enlightened Body of Guru Padmsambhava and the birthplace of gNubs-chen Sangs-rgyas Ye-shes.

17. mTsho-rgyal Bla-mtsho, "Tsogyal Latso." Small lake at the birthplace of Ye-shes mTsho-rgyal.

18. sGrags-mda' gNubs-chen 'Khrung-khang, "Drag Da." Temple at the birthplace of gNubs-chen Sangs-rgyas Ye-shes, disciple of Padmasambhava.

19. Ngar-phug Tsha-gser bTsun-dgon, "Ngar Pug." Cave in Grags associated with the great siddha Me-long rDo-rje (1243–1303).

20. lHo-brag mKhar-chu, "Lodrag Karchu." Holy place associated with the Enlightened Mind of Padmasambhava and the birthplace of Nam-mkha'i sNying-po, a disciple of the Great Guru.

21. Gra-nang bKra-shis Chos-gling, "Dranang Tashi Choling." The birthplace of Klong-chen-pa.

22. Gra-nang, "Dranang." The original temple built by Klu-mes in the tenth or eleventh century.

23. Gra-phyi O-rgyan sMin-grol-gling, "Mindroling." One of the six major Nyingma monasteries, it was founded by O-rgyan gTer-bdag Gling-pa in 1676. Located south of the gTsang-po river in the valley of Gra-phyi, it preserved the bKa'-'ma lineages, the rNying-ma rGyud-'bum transmission, and the gTer-ma traditions of the great gTer-ston gTer-bdag Gling-pa.

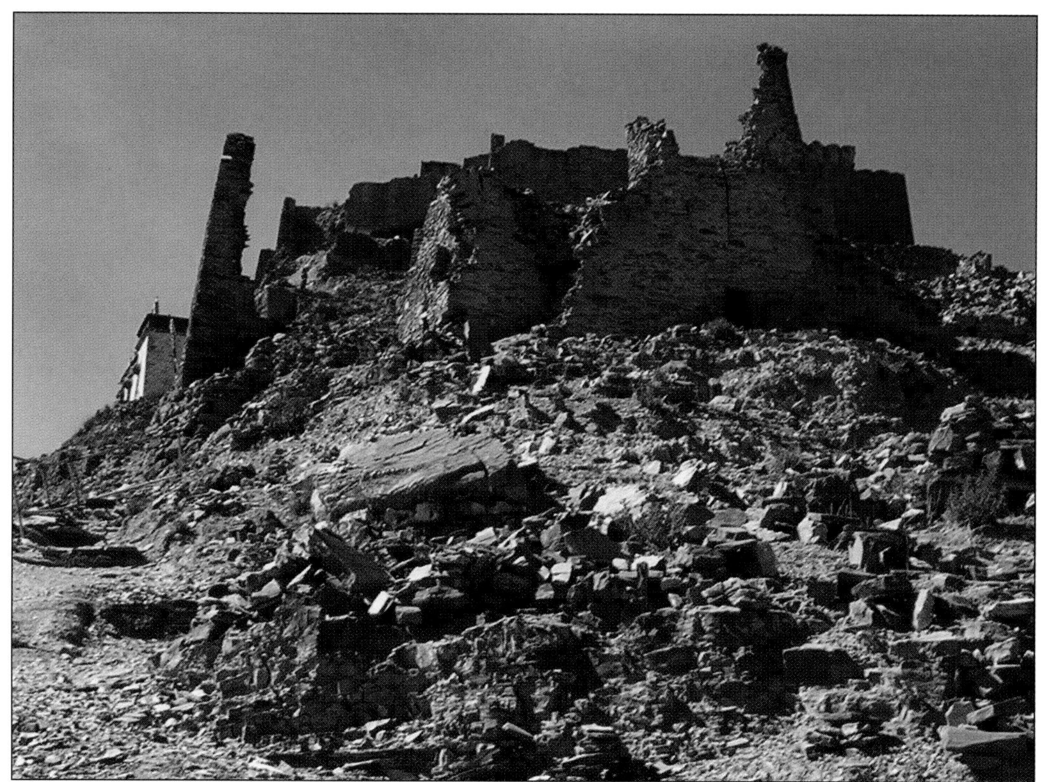

Ruins of a monastic building in Central Tibet are sad reminders of the disruption of Tibet's cultural heritage. *(2005)*

24. bSam-yas gTsug-lag-khang, "Samye Tsugla Khang." Tibet's first monastery, founded on the north bank of the gTsang-po river by mKhan-po Shantarakshita, Slob-dpon Guru Padmasambhava, and Chos-rgyal Khri-srong lDe'u-btsan in the eighth century .

25. bSam-yas mChims-phu Brag-dmar Ke'u-tshang, "Dragmar Keu Tsang." A holy place associated with the Enlightened Speech of the Great Guru Padmasambhava; a meditation cave of the Great Guru and his twenty-five disciples, and the site of the transmission of the Heruka sadhanas.

26. bSam-yas gYa'-ma-lung, "Samye Yamalung." Hermitage behind bSam-yas where Padmasambhava created a spring flowing with the water of life and concealed longevity practices.

27. rTse-thang sNe'u-gdong Ban-tshang, "Neu-dong." Residence of gTer-ma master O-rgyan Gling pa (b. 1323).

28. Yar-lung Shel-brag, "Yarlung Sheldrag." Holy place associated with the Enlightened Qualities of Guru Padmasambhava. Fifty-five

great realized ones attained understanding here in the days of the Dharma kings.

29. Srong-btsan dBang-so dMar-po, "Srongtsen Wangso Marpo." Tomb of the first Dharma King.

30. Tshe-ring-ljongs bTsun-dgon, "Tsering Jong." A nunnery at 'Jigs-med Gling-pa's residence, located on a mountainside near 'Phyongs-rgyas (Chongye) overlooking a valley.

31. Tshe-ring-ljongs sGrub-sde, "Tsering Jong." Retreat center at Tshe-ring-ljongs.

32. dPal-ri Theg-mchog-gling, "Pari Theg Choling." Monastery founded by gTer-chen Shes-rab 'Od-zer (1518–1584).

33. dPal-ri sGrub-sde Rig-'dzin Grub-pa'i dGa'-tshal, "Pari Drup De." Retreat center at dPal-ri.

34. bSam-yas dBen-rtsar lHa-khang, "Samye Wentser Lakang." Temple below mChims-phu .

35. lHo-brag sMra-bo-cog, "Lodrag Mawa Chog." Birthplace and residence of the great gTer-ma master Nyang-ral Nyi-ma 'Od-zer (1124–1192), his sons, and the descendents of Guru Chos-dbang.

36. lHo-brag gNas-zhi bKa'-brgyad lHa- khang, "Lodrag Neshi." Associated with the great gTer-ma Master Gu-ru Chos-dbang (1212–1270).

37. lHo-brag Them-pa Phyag-rdor, "Lodrag Tempa Chagdor." Associated with the gTer-ma master Lho-brag Grub-chen Las-kyi rDo-rje (14th century).

38. Yar-'brog, "Yadrog" Monastery of sTag-lung rTse-sprul.

39. lHo-brag lHa-lung, "Lodrag Lalung" Residence of gTer-ma Master Padma Gling-pa.

40. sNye-mo, "Nyemo." Nunnery on the site where the eighth century master Vairotsana practiced.

41. sNye-mo-rdo, "Nyemo Do." Monastery associated with gTer-ma Master Padma Gling-pa.

42. Zang-zang lHa-brag, "Zangzang Ladrag." The place where the gTer-ma master Rig-'dzin rGod-ldem (1337–1408) discovered the Northern Treasures.

43. Cung Ri-bo-che Residence of the great Siddha Thang-stong rGyal-po (1385–1510).

44. gNas-phu Padma-nyin-dgon, "Nepu Pema Nyin Gon." Monastery associated with gTer-ston Byang-chub Gling-pa.

45. lCags-phug dGon-pa, "Chag Pug Gonpa." Monastery associated with Rig-'dzin rGod-ldem (1337–1408).

46. Nya-mo-hor bSam-gtan Chos-gling, "Nyamohor Samten Choling." Monastery associated with the Northern Treasures.

47. lHun-grub 'Od-gsal-gling, "Lundrup Osel Ling." Monastery north of lHa-sa.

48. dPal-ldan gNas-dga'-dgon, "Pelden Nega Gon."

49. sBra-gur Dza-phug dGon, "Dragur Dapug Gon."

50. Gling-bu dGon, "Lingbu Gon." The residence of Zur-po-che (b. 954).

51. sNye-mo, "Nyemo." Residence of the eighth century master Vairotsana, disciple of Padmasambhava and the first Tibetan siddha.

52. Dwags-lha sGam-po, "Dagla Gampo." Monastery founded by Mi-la-ras-pa's great disciple sGam-po-pa (1079–1153).

53. rTse-le dGon, "Tsele Gon." Monastery associated with Dwags-ston dBang-phyug rDo-rje.

54. Khra-mo-brag, "Tramo Drag." Location where the precious teachings of the mKha'-'gro-snying thig were discovered by Padma Las-'brel-rtsal; also a site where Ratna Gling-pa discovered treasures.

55. Dwags-po Byang-phyogs Ri-khrod bTsun-dgon, "Dagpo Shangsho Ritro." Nunnery and retreat place of the father of Bod-pa sPrul-sku (1907–1959).

56. Kong-po Bang-ri-dgon, "Kongpo Wangri." Residence of gTer-ma master 'Ja'-tshon sNying-po (1585–1656).

57. Kong-po Brag-gsum mTsho-snying-dgon, "Kongpo Drasum Tsonying." Monastery associated with sKyabs-rje bDud-'joms Rinpoche.

58. Kong-po Bu-chu gTer-gyi lHa-khang, "Kongpo Buchu." Built by King Srong-btsan sGam-po in the 7th century.

59. Kong-po Zangs-mdog dPal-ri, "Kong Zangdog Palri." Residence of bDud-'joms Rinpoche.

60. sPu-bo dGa'-ba-lung, "Puwo Gawa Lung." Associated with gTerma master sTag-sham Nus-ldan rDo-rje (1655).

61. dPal-kha gSang-sngags Chos-gling, "Palka Sang Ngag Choling." Associated with Rig-'dzin Chos-kyi rGya-mtsho .

62. sPu-bo Yid-'ong Khrims-gzigs-dgon, "Puwo Yiong Trimzig." Monastery associated with gTer-ma master rTsa-gsum gTer-bdag Gling-pa gNam-lcags rDo-rje (17th century).

63. Byang Nag-chu-khul Dol-skya, "Nagchukul Dolkya." Monastery associated with Dol-sprul.

64. rTa-rna gSang-sngags-gling, "Tana Sang Nga Ling." Monastery associated with 'Ja'-lus rDo-rje.

65. Nag-chu 'Brong-ngur-dgon, "Nagchu Drongur." Residence of So Ye-shes dBang-phyug, the ninth century disciple of gNubs-chen, an essential link in the transmission of Nyingma teachings; Cho-kyi Nyi-ma Rinpoche's monastery.

66. 'Cha'-ru Nyi-grags-dgon, "Charu Nyidrag." Monastery associated with the 17th-century gTer-ma master Nyi-ma-grags.

67. lHo-ba-dan-dgon, "Lowaden." Monastery associated with Nag-po Legs-ldan.

68. Khyung-po Pa-tam-dgon, "Kyungpo Patam." Residence of Khyung-sprul Rinpoche, the disciple of 'Jam-dbyangs mKhyen-brtse and Kong-sprul Blo-gros mTha'-yas.

69. dPal-'bar Thugs-sras-dgon, "Palwar Tuksey." Monastery associated with Drag-sngags Gling-pa.

70. Rom-thang sGom-pa Grwa-tshang, "Romtang." Monastery associated with rGyal-dbang bDe-chen rDo-rje.

71. gSer-pa Ri-khrod, "Serpa Ritro." Hermitage of the Gold Seekers.

72. Ngang-zo-dgon, "Ngang Zo." Monastery associated with Sangs-rgyas-dbon (1251–1296), the nephew of sGam-po-pa and a sTag-lung bKa'-brgyud master.

73. Ne-khrab dGon-pa, "Netrab."

74. gSang-sngags Chos-gling, "Sang Ngag Choling." Monastery associated with gTer-ma master rTsa-gsum Gling-pa (17th century) and residence of the descendents of Se-ston Nyi-ma bZang-po.

75. sGo-chen-dgon pa, "Gochen." Monastery associated with rGyal-ba rGya-mtsho.

76. Gangs-ri-khrod, "Gang Ritro." A mountain hermitage associated with sMan-bla Kun-dga'.

77. Ga-grwa Ri-khrod, "Gadra." Hermitage associated with Karma O-rgyan.

78. sDon-ne bKra-shis Chos-gling, "Doney Tashi Choling." Center associated with dKon-mchog Seng-ge Pandita, a disciple of rTsa-gsum gTer-bdag Gling-pa (17th century).

79. rGyang-rgyad-dgon, "Gyang Gyad." Monastery associated with Ngag-dbang Phrin-las.

80. 'Gam-phu-dgon, "Gampu" Monastery associated with Chos-sku Sangs rgyas.

81. Ta-ka-dgon-pa, "Taka." Monastery.

82. 'Brog-mo-dgon, "Drogmo." Monastery; a branch of rDo-rje-brag.

83. lHun-po Ri-khrod, "Lhunpo Ritro." Hermitage associated with the successive incarnations of gTer-ma master sTag-sham Nus-ldan rDo-rje (1655).

84. Ri-pha bKra-shis-gling, "Ripa Tashi Ling." Center associated with Ri-pa Bla-ma.

85. Khams Ri-bo-che gTsug-lag-khang, "Riboche." Large monastery in Khams founded by bKa'-brgyud master Sangs-rgyas-dbon (1251-1296).

86. Nyingma Grwa-tshang, "Nyingma Gratsang." Nyingma center associated with rJe-drung Rinpoche.

87. Ri-phug-dgon, "Ripug." Monastery associated with Ri-phug Bla-ma.

88. Khyu-mo Ri-khrod, "Kyumo." Hermitage.

89. Chab-mdo Karma-dgon, "Chamdo." Monastery of the Karmapa.

90. gNas-mdo-dgon, "Nedo." Monastery associated with the gTer-ston Karma Chags-med (1613–1678).

91. Khra-chog-ting, "Trachok Ting."

92. mThong-ti Ri-khrod, "Tongti." Hermitage.

93. sMar-khams rGyal-sras-dgon, "Markam Gyalsey." Monastery in southern Khams.

94. Brag-g.yab Bu-dgon, "Draya Bu-gon." Monastery in western Khams.

95. 'Jo-mda' lHa-brang-dgon" Jomda." Monastery in Khams.

96. Sib-mda'-dgon, "Sipda." Monastery associated with the great Nyingma center of Zhe-chen bsTan-gnyis Dar-rgyas-gling in Khams.

97. Khams-pa-sgar, "Kampagar." Monastery associated with Kun-dga' bsTan-'dzin dBu-med.

98. Nang-chen Tshes-bcu-khang, "Nangchen Tsechu Kang." Associated with A-sde Rinpoche.

99. Nang-chen Gad-chag-dgon, "Nang-chen Gadcha." Monastery associated with Tshogs-gnyis Padma Dri-med 'Od-zer (b. 1828).

100. Gad-chag dGon-lag, "Gadcha" Branch monastery.

101. Re-ya-dgon, "Reya."

102. bDe-chen-gling, "Dechen Gling."

103. gSang-chen dGe-dgon, "Sangchen Ge Gon."

104. Cog-rtse Bar-'gag, "Chogtse Bargak."

105. Chos-gling-dgon, "Choling Gon."

106. Chu-brgyad-dgon, "Chugye Gon."

107. Se-rug-dgon, "Serug Gon."

108. mDo-shing-dgon, "Doshing Gon."

109. Chos-'khor-dgon, "Chokor Gon."

110. dGon-nyin-dgon, "Gonyin Gon."

111. rTogs-phud-dgon, "Togpu Gon."

112. rNga-sgang-dgon, "Nga Gang Gon."

113. Nang-chen mGar-dgon, "Nangchen Gar Gon." Monastery associated with mGar-chen Rinpoche

114. lHo-me yel-dgon, "Lomey Yel Gon."

115. Zam-me-dgon, "Zamey Gon." Monastery associated with Chos-kyi Seng-ge.

116. Tshab-sgar sKed-dgon, "Tsapgar Ked Gon." Monastery associated with sKe-sprul Rinpoche.

117. rGyang-yag-dgon, "Gyang Yag Gon" Monastery associated with Khe-skar Bla-ma.

118. mKhar-chen-dgon, "Karchen Gon." Monastery associated with Bla-ma Thar-pa.

119. rNga-sgang-dgon, "Nga Gang Gon." Monastery associated with Nyi-ma sPrul-sku.

120. sTag-khyams Ri-khrod, "Takyam." Hermitage.

121. 'Brong-pa Bar-ma-dgon, "Drongpa Barma Gon." Monastery associated with mTsho-rgyal sPrul-sku .

122. rJa-spar Me-dgon, "Japar Mey Gon." Monastery associated with mTsho-rgyal sPrul-sku.

123. Ri-pa Pad-rnams-dgon, "Ripa Panam Gon." Monastery connected to dGongsar Monastery.

124. rGya-can-dgon, "Gyachen Gon." Monastery associated with rGyal-chen sPrul-sku.

125. gNas-rten-dgon, "Neten Gon." Monastery associated with the great gTer-ma master mChog-gyur Gling-pa (1829–1870).

126. rTa-rna-dgon, "Tanag Gon." Monastery associated with Sangs-rgyas Yer-pa.

127. rDzogs-lcam-dgon, "Dzogchen Gon."

128. Brag-nag-dgon, "Drag Nag Gon." Monastery associated with Brag-nag sPrul-sku.

129. Go-'jo Ra-khrid-dgon, "Gojo Ratri Gon." Monastery associated with Nyag-bla Byang-chub rDo-rje.

130. sTag-mo-dgon, "Tagmo Gon." Monastery associated with Bla-ma Blo-gros.

131. Ra-mgo-dgon, "Rago Gon." Monastery associated with Ra-mgo sPrul-sku.

dPal-yul rNam-rgyal Byang-chub-gling, a major Nyingma monastery founded in 1665 by Kun-bzang Shes-rab. Located in eastern Tibet, dPal-yul housed six hundred monks and maintained seven incarnate lineages, and had numerous branch monasteries.

Its branches include:

132. Ta-la-dgon, "Tala Gon."

133. Thob-ra-dgon, "Tobra Gon."

134. Bang-khang-dgon, "Bangkang Gon."

135. Kha-legs-dgon, "Kaleg Gon."

136. dmar-po-dgon, "Marpo Gon."

137. 'Bo-lo-dgon, "Bolo Gon."

138. bShad-sgrub dGe-'phel-gling, "Shedrup Gepel Ling."

(end of branches of dPal-yul)

139. dKor-khung-dgon, "Korkung Gon" Monastery associated with sPrul-sku O-rgyan.

140. sBa-bang Jo-dgon, "Babang Jo Gon."

141. dGon-gsar-dgon, "Gonsar Gon."

142. rGya-ra-dgon-pa, "Gyara Gonpa."

143. sPyang-khang dGon-pa, "Sheng Kang Gonpa."

144. Rang-gzhon dGon-pa, "Rangzhon Gonpa."

145. dNgul-ra dGon-pa, "Ngulra Gon-pa."

146. Tsha-ru dGon-pa, "Tsara Gon-pa."

147. De-mtha' dGon-pa, "Demta Gonpa."

148. Klu-chung dGon-pa, "Luchung Gon-pa."

149. Sogs-lung dGon-pa, "Soglung Gonpa."

150. Klu-sug dGon-pa, "Lusug Gonpa."

151. Kah-thog rDo-rje-gdan, "Kathog Dorjeden" One of the six major Nyingma monasteries, founded in 1159 by Kah Dam-pa bDe-gshegs (1122–1192). In early times, thirteen generations of masters here maintained the lineages of Maha, Anu, and Atiyoga, the three Inner Tantras. Kah-thog was revitalized and expanded in

1656, and its bKa'-ma lineages were restored by rGyal-sras bSod-nams lDe-btsan (1679-1723).

152. dPal-yul rNam-rgyal Byang-chub-gling, "Palyul Changchub Ling." One of the six major Nyingma monasteries, founded in 1665 by Rig-'dzin Kun-bzang Shes-rab (1636–1699).

153. rDzogs-chen O-rgyan bSam-gtan Chos-gling, "Dzogchen Orgyan Samten Choling." One of the six major Nyingma monasteries, it was founded in the province of Khams in 1685 by rDzogs-chen Padma Rig-'dzin with the encouragement of the Fifth Dalai Lama. rDzogs-chen housed eight hundred and fifty monks and maintained eleven incarnate lineages. It was associated with thirteen retreat centers.

154. Zhe-chen bsTan-gnyis Dar-rgyas-gling, "Zhechen Tennyi Dargye Ling." One of the six major Nyingma monasteries, it was founded in Khams in 1735 by the second Zhe-chen Rab-'byams (1713–1769). Zhe-chen housed two hundred monks and nine incarnate lamas, and was well known for its strict monastic discipline.

155. rDzogs-chen Shri Singha, College at rDzogs-chen Monastery founded by rGyal-sras gZhan-phan mTha'-yas (1800).

156. Zhe-chen bShad-grwa, "Zhechen shedra." College associated with Zhe-chen Monastery.

157. Zhe-chen sGrub-sde, "Zhe-chen Grupde." Practice center associated with Zhe-chen Monastery.

158. dGe-mang-dgon, "Gemang Gon." Monastery under the care of Zhe-chen rGyal-tshab.

159. lCang-ma Ri-khrod, "Changma Ritro." Willow Hermitage where mKhan-po Thub-dga' (20th century) resided.

160. 'Ju-nyung dgon, "Junyung Gon."

161. mKhan-chen 'Jigs-med Phun-tshogs Chos-sgar, "Kenchen Jigme Phuntso Chogar."

162. mKhan-chen Mun-sel Chos-sgar, "Kenchen Munsel Chogar."

163. mKhan-chen Chos-khyab Chos-sgar, "Kenchen Chokyab Chogar."

164. rDo-grub-dgon, "Dodrup Gon." Founded by rDo-grub-chen Rinpoche.

165. dPal-yul Dar-thang-dgon, "Palyul Dartang Gon." Located in 'Gu-log, dPal-yul Dar-thang was the largest branch of dPal-yul Monastery. It was the residence of Dar-thang mChog-sprul Rinpoche and the home monastery of Tarthang Tulku Rinpoche.

166. mDo-mang-dgon, "Domang Gon."

167. A-bse-dgon, "Abse Gon."

168. Dza-ka-dgon, "Dzaka Gon."

169. Ewam-dgon, "Ewam Gon."

170. Cag-bu-dgon, "Chagbu Gon."

171. Yid-lhung-dgon, "Yilung Gon."

172. Nor-lung-dgon, "Norlung Gon."

173. Brag-lhar-dgon, "Drag-lar Gon."

174. Gyang-kar-dgon, "Gyangkar Gon."

175. bKra-shis-dgon, "Tashi Gon."

176. bKod-sde-dgon, "Kodey Gon."

177. dByar-dgon, "Yar Gon."

178. Nyag-be-dgon, "Nyag Bey Gon."

179. A-nges-dgon, "Angey Gon."

180. sMyo-shul-dgon, "Nyoshul Gon."

181. Nyag lCags-mdud-dgon, "Chagdu Gon."

182. gNam-brag-dgon, "Namdrag Gon."

183. 'Byung-khung-dgon, "Jungkung Gon." Follows the Kah-thog tradition.

184. Rang-shar-dgon, "Rangshar Gon" Follows the rDzogs-chen tradition.

185. Jo-mo Khri-dgon, "Jomo Tri Gon" Follows the rDzogs-chen tradition.

186. rTa'u bKra-shis Chos-gling, "Tau Tashi Choling." Follows the rDzogs-chen tradition.

187. A-se-dgon, "Asey Gon." Follows the sMin-grol-gling tradition.

188. Ke-ra-dgon, "Kera Gon." Follows the sMin-grol-gling tradition.
189. Klu-mo Rang-phul-tshogs-dgon, "Lumo Rangpul Tsog Gon." Follows the sMin-grol-gling tradition.
190. Chos-grags-dgon, "Chodrag Gon" Follows the sMin-grol-gling tradition.
192. Dril-dkar-dgon, "Drilkar Gon." Follows the rDzogs-chen tradition

Monasteries in Nyag-rong:
193. lHa-ru-dgon, "Laru Gon." Follows the Kah-thog tradition.
194. Gu-ru-dgon, "Guru Gon." Follows the rDzogs-chen tradition.
195. rTsa-ra-dgon, "Tsara Gon." Follows the Kah-thog tradition.
196. rMe-ba Chos-'grub dGon, "Mewa Chodrup Gon." Follows the rDzog-chen tradition.
197. Phyag-phud-dgon, "Chagpud Gon" Follows the sMin-grol-gling tradition.
198. Ye-le-dgon, "Yeley Gon." Follows the Kah-thog tradition.
199. Gra-lag-dgon, "Dralga Gon." Follows the Kah-thog tradition.
200. Wam-war-dgon, "Wamwar Gon" Follows the dPal-yul tradition.
201. g.Yag-'dra-dgon, "Yagdra Gon." Follows the dPal-yul tradition.
202. A-'dzom-dgon, "Adzom Gon." Residence of 'Brug-pa Rinpoche.
203. Khang-dmar-dgon, "Kangmar Gon." Follows the rDzogs-chen tradition.
204. Ru-ru-dgon, "Ruru Gon."
205. Ka-ra-dgon, "Kara Gon."

Part Five

Extending the Blessings

Chapter Twelve

Expanding Activities

From its inception, TAP has followed specific guidelines to ensure that administrative costs are kept at a minimum so that donations can go directly to program services that benefit Tibetan refugees. While TAP's focus has adjusted from time to time in accord with the changing needs of the Tibetan communities in exile, the emphasis has always been on preserving Tibet's cultural and religious heritage and supporting the education that enables these traditions to continue.

Funds are distributed on a non-sectarian basis. TAP's overhead is extraordinarily low, currently about 10%, with an additional 15% expended for mailings and incidental fundraising expenses. A full 76% of funds goes to program services. TAP's ability to disburse funds efficiently is fostered through TAP's volunteer staff, simple administrative structure, and the barest essential equipment needs. TAP's directors, administrators, and staff do not receive salaries or other forms of compensation from TAP. They live within the Nyingma organizations and receive support for living expenses through Nyingma Centers. Nyingma Centers' work/study program, established to encourage volunteer participation and education, enables full-time volunteers to take classes and live at the Nyingma Institute.

In its earliest years, TAP occupied a small office in a warehouse rented by Dharma Publishing, where a few TNMC students organized rummage sales and other kinds of fundraising efforts. From the

Members of the TAP pilgrimage tour mount the rocky slopes of Yamalung to visit caves associated with Guru Padmasambhava and his disciples.

later 1970s until 1992, TAP's office was a desk in an office that TAP shared with the staff of other Nyingma organizations. During those years, TAP was staffed by a single half-time student and had no dedicated equipment beyond an electric typewriter. Operating with this minimal structure, TAP was able to transfer up to 98% of all donations directly to Tibetans and to services benefiting Tibetans.

As Tibetan refugees founded educational centers and revived traditional Buddhist ceremonies, it became necessary for TAP to increase fundraising efforts to support more ceremonies, fund the shipment of sacred texts and art, and increase disbursements for education. In the years that followed, TAP underwent major changes to accommodate these goals. In 1993, TAP established three offices in Berkeley, one in Los Angeles, and one in each of the Nyingma international centers in Brazil, Holland, and Germeny. Two full-time and two-half-time workers were added to TAP's central office at Dharma House in Berkeley, where the staff could interact with the public and volunteers could work on mailings, sew prayer flags, and help with brochures, coordination for benefit dinners, and other TAP projects.

Direct Mail Campaigns

Working from its office in Dharma House, TAP initiated direct mail campaigns to expand the donor base and began to make large mailings central to its fundraising efforts. The staff began to gather published information and photographs relating to the situation in Tibet and set out to create films, lectures, newsletters, and brochures. When Dharma Publishing set up a showroom at Dharma House in Berkeley, TAP began to offer a small selection of gift items there.

TAP's 20th anniversary brochure (right), published in 1994, was mailed to many thousands of prospective new donors. It clarified the expanded scope of TAP's mission and set the tone for TAP's future activities.

"Beyond the beliefs of any one religion, there is the truth of the human spirit.

Beyond the power of nations, there is the power of the human heart.

Beyond the ordinary mind, the power of wisdom, love, and healing energy are at work in the universe.

When we can find peace within our hearts, we contact these universal powers. This is our only hope."

--Tarthang Tulku, Founder Tibetan Aid Project

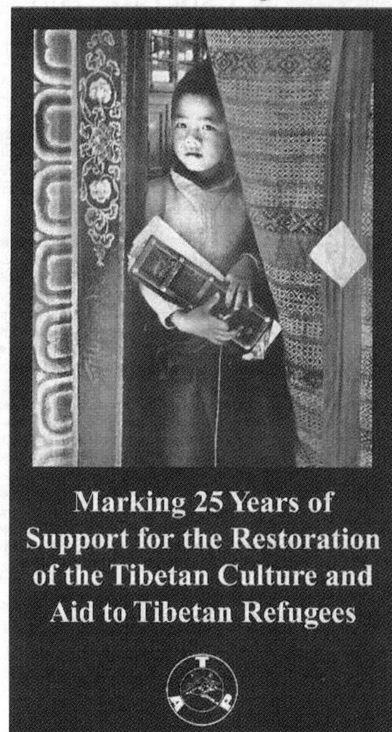

Marking 25 Years of Support for the Restoration of the Tibetan Culture and Aid to Tibetan Refugees

What Does the Tibetan Aid Project Do?

The Tibetan Aid Project (TAP) was founded to provide emergency relief to Tibetan refugees exiled in India and Nepal. However, in recent years our efforts have focused on the long term job of rebuilding and preserving Tibetan cultural and religious traditions.

General Assistance

While only the Tibetan people can provide the impetus to rebuild what they have lost, those of us with material wealth have the opportunity to see that they have what they need to preserve a way of living that is of benefit to us all. Over the years, TAP's general assistance funds have gone to the restoration of monasteries, nunneries, and schools, to provide for the needs of individual Tibetans outside the monasteries, and to sponsor a variety of community, medical, and educational projects.

Preserving Art, Literature, and Ritual Objects

Thousands of hours of volunteer help have allowed the Tibetan Aid Project, in conjunction with the Yeshe De Project and Dharma Publishing, to produce and ship over 60,000 traditional Buddhist texts, over 100,000 art reproductions and 10,000 hand-held prayer wheels to Tibetans. Without these traditional tools, a vital link to transmit the wisdom of the Tibetan tradition would be missing.

Support for Monks and Nuns

In the early days, TAP focused on providing monks and nuns with support for food, housing, and a basic education. Over the years, however, the monastics have become stronger and our funds have gone more towards advanced education. The centers where we now offer the most support have philsophy colleges with eight or nine-year advanced programs that provide a rigorous education in the cultural and religious Tibetan traditions. This training will ensure that the knowledge of an ancient tradition does not die out.

World Peace Ceremony

Held annually since 1989, the World Peace Ceremony provides Tibetan and Westerners alike a unique opportunity to pray for world peace in the most sacred of all Buddhist pilgrimage places—Bodh Gaya, India, site of the Buddha's enlightenment. This year, over 7,000 Tibetans attended, many traveling long distances to participate in this cherished occasion.

In 1994, as TAP added staff and established a presence in Dharma House, it relied more strongly on newsletters, appeals for support, videos, and publications to communicate to potential donors the value of Tibetan culture and the plight of the Tibetan Buddhist tradition. As the scope of activity increased, it became necessary to spend a greater percentage of revenues on fundraising and disseminating information, which included the cost of renting mailing lists. For a time, when TAP was seeking to expand its donor base, this increase was deemed acceptable. It accorded with TAP's mission to raise awareness of the value of Tibetan culture to the West and communicate how TAP's donors are helping to preserve it.

How TAP Communicates: Newsletters and Brochures

The new emphasis on direct mail resulted in a dramatic increase in TAP's fundraising capacity. By the end of 1994, TAP's mailing list had almost tripled in size, to approximately 4,500 names, and mailings had generated over $300,000 in income. This increase was assisted by the purchase of a production-quality printer that enabled TAP volunteers to design and produce more professional fundraising materials. As a result, TAP was able to save substantially on the cost of mailing its first annual campaign letter. A holiday letter, initiated in 1994, also became an annual mailing, and informal newsletters and announcements were prepared as necessary to keep donors and supporters informed of new projects and initiatives. At times TAP also sent out complimentary copies of *Gesar Magazine*, giving donors opportunities to see how TAP's projects fit into the larger picture of Nyingma activities. In 2004, TAP initiated its semi-annual newsletter, "News from TAP." Featuring information on monasteries and nunneries, special projects and events, and plans for pilgrimages, News from TAP invites participation, and introduces members of TAP's staff.

Prayers For Peace

Dear Friend,

We are writing to you on this special holiday occasion to invite you to participate in the making of an historical event, the Bodh Gaya World Peace Ceremony. This sacred ceremony, which Tibetans call Monlam Chenmo or "Wishing Prayers," was founded by Tarthang Tulku Rinpoche under the auspices of the Tibetan Nyingma Meditation Center in 1989. The ceremony, which today includes all four schools of Tibetan Buddhism, lasts for ten days each year. Each day, from sunrise to sunset, the pilgrims united their voices to become a singular and powerful sound on behalf of peace. Although the Tibetan people have suffered unimaginable losses under Chinese occupation, they have not lost either faith and dedication to their religious heritage, nor their belief in prayer. The first year brought together 500 monks and nuns. Every year since 1989, the event has grown and has included visitors from around the world. This year as many as 10,000 participants are expected.

Tibetan monks and nuns need your help.

To a Tibetan monk or nun who practices devotedly, the Peace Ceremony is a precious opportunity to share his or her training with fellow human beings. To pray for compassion and the relief of suffering of all beings at Bodh Gaya is a life's dream. They cherish this privilege as a way of sharing their practice to benefit the world as a whole.

But to attend, these Tibetans must endure a long and arduous trip on foot or horseback from inside Tibet, or on a difficult bus ride from remote parts of Nepal and India. Many of them literally have nothing and need help to pay for even basic transportation, modest accommodations and simple food. Our goal is to raise $25,000, which will go directly to the Tibetan monks, nuns, and teachers at the ceremony. We would be honored if you would join with us in meeting this pledge.

—Wangmo Gellek, TAP's holiday letter, 1994

Thanks to your generous contributions, this letter helped hundreds make the arduous trip to Bodh Gaya from Bhutan, India, Nepal, and Tibet.
—TAP letter, July 1995.

Tibetan Aid Project

"Prayer awakens aspiration for beauty and truth, and opens inner pathways through which knowledge can manifest in our lives."

Tarthang Tulku
Founder, Tibetan Aid Project

August 1997

Dear Friend,

This spring, in over thirty Tibetan monasteries throughout India and Nepal, monks and nuns have been performing special ceremonies, saying prayers for the well-being of all peoples. The wonderful blessings of these ceremonies are possible because of the donations which the Tibetan Aid Project (TAP) receives and then distributes to these centers in Asia. Your support provides direct sponsorship of vital aspects of Tibetan culture.

The sacred texts and art prints that TAP ships to India each year, along with the modest funds we are able to give each center, provide essential support to the Tibetan men and women who are establishing their religious traditions in exile. The centers TAP supports represent all four schools of the Tibetan Dharma tradition and many of the ancient lineages that have endeavored over centuries to develop and pass on specialized aspects of the Tibetan wisdom tradition.

A Tibetan monk prays in order to develop to the stage of a Bodhisattva—a universally compassionate being completely dedicated to the welfare of all sentient beings. By wholeheartedly practicing oral and written teachings within a contemplative environment, it is believed that a monk or nun can lay the foundation for this kind of transformation within one lifetime.

How TAP communicates: Newsletters, brochures, announcements of special events, and holiday cards keep TAP's donor base informed about TAP activities and current priorities for support.

Tibetan Aid Project

Tibetan Buddhist Pilgrims Lighting Butter Lamps and Candles

Prayers for Universal Peace

December 1997

Dear Friend,

In January 1998, over 6000 Tibetan lamas, monks, nuns and laypeople will gather in Bodh Gaya, India for the 9th annual *World Peace Ceremonies.* Over three hundred groups representing more than two hundred Tibetan centers and communities throughout Asia will make the long and arduous journey to Bodh Gaya to participate in the Monlam Chenmo—the Wishing Prayers for World Peace. Over the course of ten days, monks will offer 100,000 recitations of the Manjushri-Namasamgiti, a traditional Buddhist sutra evoking the blessings of wisdom and compassion for all living beings. Each day of the ceremonies, more than 100,000 butter lamps will be lit to demonstrate the Tibetans' wish—and ours—that peace may come to the world.

As you read this letter, four 20 foot containers of Tibetan sacred texts and art prints are making their way by boat from Dharma Publishing's facilities in Berkeley, California to Calcutta, India and then on to Bodh Gaya for the Prayer Ceremonies. The containers hold new typeset editions of traditional Tibetan Buddhist works by learned masters—works no longer generally available to the average Tibetan religious practitioner. It is heart-warming to see Buddhist texts once lost to both India and Tibet on their way to the original home of the Buddha Dharma, where they will be restored to the Tibetan people.

TAP's 1997 annual holiday letter describes the extent of the Yeshe De text project and TAP's role in funding the shipping and transportation costs involved in getting sacred texts to India.

Tibetan Aid Project

Sacred Texts Produced by Dharma Publishing are shipped to India for distribution to Tibetans

December 1998

Dear Friends,

As the holiday season approaches, I am once again pleased to call on you, our base of loyal friends and supporters, to act on your caring and support the Tibetan Aid Project's vital work. Due to the unusually large scope of our work this year, your help is especially important to us during this holiday season. This support can come in many forms: by making a financial contribution, by volunteering your time and expertise, or even just by telling others about your interest and involvement in our project.

TAP's Mission

The Tibetan Aid Project's mission is twofold:

- To enable the preservation and restoration of Tibet's cultural and religious heritage in exile and within Tibet, and
- To promote global awareness of the Tibetan people's plight through events and activities in the Americas and Europe that encourage people around the world to support the Tibetan people's cause.

These two goals are complementary. On the one hand, for those who value the universal wisdom of Tibet's knowledge tradition, TAP's projects are an invitation to participate in preserving an invaluable legacy to the world. On the other hand, through TAP's publications, special events, direct mail campaigns, and website (www.nyingma.org), each year thousands of people learn about the Tibetans' 40 year struggle to salvage their own culture from almost complete destruction—an essential step in expanding TAP's base of support.

TAP's newsletters mailed in the late 1990s indicate TAP's growing involvement with ceremonies and sacred text distribution.

Minimizing Expenses, Maximizing Merit

In 1995, when Dharma Publishing leased additional space in a building adjoining Dharma House, TAP consolidated its Berkeley offices and moved into its present location on the mezzanine of that building, just opposite the offices of Dharma Publishing. The staff was expanded to its present size of three full-time workers and a varying number of part-time volunteers, and computers and other equipment were acquired. With TAP established in its own offices and more new staff involved in day-to-day decisions and activities, the original guidelines were reviewed and revised to accord with TAP's expanded mission.

Special attention was given to minimizing overhead expenses, which had increased as TAP depended more strongly on mailings. Now that TAP's donor base had increased to nearly ten thousand, purchasing lists was no longer seen as essential. Volunteers from Alpha Phi Omega, a local service fraternity, and members of the Cerebral Palsy Foundation helped with the mailings, making it possible to continue mailings while still reducing overhead expenses to their present level of fifteen to sixteen percent of income. Although these limits would be impossible for almost any other non-profit organization with a similar mission, TAP has worked hard to meet these goals, while steadily expanding the range of its financial commitments. Additional guidelines were set in place when a new board of directors was installed in 1997.

Administrative Guidelines

Vision for TAP Keep TAP's structure very simple: one central office in one location. Increase income as possible, while maximizing funds available for program services by keeping overhead as low as possible. Do not spend money on anything unnecessary—such as additional computers, vehicles, or equipment.

Board of Directors The Board of Directors meets twice a year. Board members maintain contact with the TAP office and stay informed as to TAP operations and activities.

Salaries TAP is a humble organization with a small staff. No funds are disbursed for staff salaries. For printing services and other functions, TAP relies on the cooperation of Dharma Publishing and other organizations.

TAP Staff TAP's ideal staff size is three to four people, including an office manager and promotions director.

Office Manager The office manager handles deposits and prepares quarterly and semi-annual financial statements as well as progress reports. The manager obtains receipts for every expense, no matter how insignificant, records them and keeps them on file for directors to review as necessary, and maintains records. The manager reports regularly on activities to TAP's board of directors.

Promotions Director The promotions director handles advertising, fundraising, and outreach correspondence, making certain that brochures, newsletters, and other kinds of public presentations are submitted for editorial and artistic review by TNMC and Dharma Publishing staff.

Guidelines for Office Staff Set daily and weekly goals. Exercise self-discipline and work the same hours every day. Focus on creating a product, such as doing mailings or making prayer flags; take care of administrative details, but do not spend large amounts of time writing letters or doing office work.

Vehicles: Liability insurance Make certain any vehicles owned by TAP or operated by TAP staff have adequate liability coverage. Make certain all TAP staff have sufficient vehicle liability insurance and are qualified to operate any equipment they use.

Prayer flags: Use of Funds Funds generated from flags must only be used to print and ship books and art, or for other activities that directly support the Dharma. Flag materials may be sent to the international Nyingma centers to sew and use for fundraising for TAP program services. Funds generated from flags produced and sold by the international centers are disbursed through TAP's central office in Berkeley.

Prayer Flags Provide recipients of flags with written information on the meaning and importance of prayer flags and how to display them correctly. Include descriptions of the images and texts.

Disseminate Information TAP is authorized to distribute the World Peace Ceremony books and From the Roof of the World to the international Nyingma centers for educational and fundraising purposes.

Focus TAP is non-political and its focus is strictly humanitarian: TAP supports lamas, monks, and nuns who are continuing religious practice and shedras and shedra students training in cultural preservation and philosophical studies. TAP also provides assistance to individual families and supports children's education.

Program Services

When the new board of directors took office in 1997, TAP's program services expanded and volunteer activities were added to help with new preservation projects envisioned by TNMC and implemented by the directors. Today, TAP provides general assistance to monastic centers, monks, and nuns, support for monasteries, and funds for shipping Tibetan texts and reproductions of sacred art to Tibetan practitioners and laypersons. TAP also sponsors traditional ceremonies and promotes awareness of Tibetan civilization worldwide. TAP's board and staff have worked with great care to ensure the sustainability of programs, address new areas of need, and sustain TAP's integrity and vision as an organization dedicated to humanitarian, non-political goals.

Support for monks and nuns TAP has continued to support TNMC and Yeshe De's cultural and religious preservation efforts by offering humanitarian assistance and funds for food, clothing, and education to lamas and monasteries of all Tibetan Buddhist schools, inside and outside of Tibet. TAP receives numerous requests from individuals in need of support and makes every effort to respond to each one. In cooperation with TNMC, TAP supports the development of educational facilities and the restoration of monasteries, nunneries, and schools. Since 1989, it has also provided travel expenses for monks and nuns attending the annual World Peace Ceremony. To generate funds to expand these activities, TAP has increased its mailings of newsletters and encouraged donors to pledge monthly contributions.

The international Nyingma centers in Amsterdam, Holland, and Münster, Germany, which had supported TAP's efforts since 1990, established TAP offices to disseminate information and encourage donations more actively in their own countries. Each year, the names of TAP's donors of all nationalities are read aloud at the Mahabodhi Temple near the conclusion of the World Peace Ceremony.

Monastery support Traditionally the source of education and the arts, monastic centers are the keys to preserving Tibetan culture. The Tibetan Aid Project offers assistance to monasteries and nunneries in India, Nepal, and Bhutan engaged in worthy educational, cultural, and religious projects. TAP also donates funds for maintenance and restoration of monastic centers now being rebuilt in Tibet on a limited scale, and in 2001, TAP helped fund restoration of Baldan Baraivan Monastery, signaling a revitalization of Buddhism in formerly Communist Mongolia. Overall, TAP donors have helped as many as 675 monasteries, nunneries, schools, and retreat centers of all major lineages.

"To the extent that we can, the Tibetan Aid Project helps the Tibetans in their own efforts. The Tibetans going into exile knew the value of their heritage and they sacrificed health and even their lives to protect what they could of it. Beginning with nothing, they have made incredible progress toward re-establishing not only their way of life, but also towards preserving the knowledge that gave meaning and dignity to human life. Their courage and resilience in the face of great hardship testifies that we have much to learn from this unique culture."

—TAP brochure 1998

Each year TAP provides support to more than thirty centers belonging to the four major traditions of Tibetan Buddhism. These funds often support such ceremonies as Tara prayers, bKa'-'gyur readings, and other ceremonies according to the tradition of each monastery, making it possible for lamas and monks to gather together for sustained periods of prayer and meditation. Other examples of support include funds offered to Ka-Nying monastery in Kathmandu to support three years of offerings, tea, and butter for ceremonies to be attended by 250 monks. And funds contributed to a monastery in Pharping to sponsor fifteen monks for a year. Between 1999, when a new Board came into office, and 2004, TAP also contributed to seven Hundred-million Mantra Vajra Guru ceremonies sponsored by TNMC and led by eminent lamas.

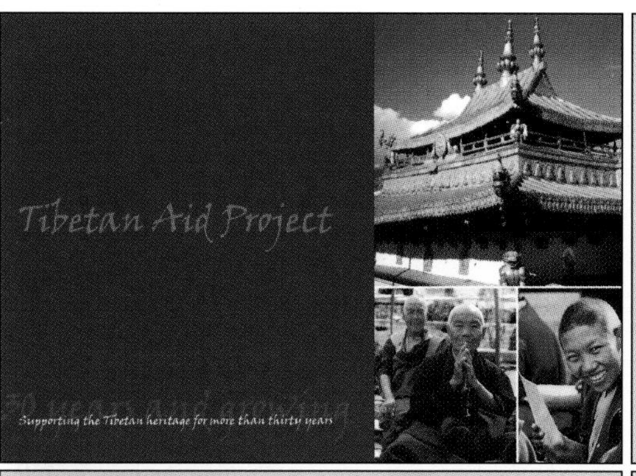
Tibetan Aid Project
Supporting the Tibetan heritage for more than thirty years

Mission Statement

The Tibetan Aid Project (TAP) helps rebuild, preserve, strengthen, and perpetuate Tibet's cultural and spiritual heritage for the benefit of the Tibetan people and all humanity.

***To achieve its mission*, TAP**

Provides financial support for monastic centers, lamas, monks, nuns, and lay people.

Sponsors ceremonies important to sustaining the lineages of all Tibetan Buddhist schools.

Funds production, shipping and distribution of sacred texts, art, and prayer wheels for donation to institutions and individuals.

Promotes awareness of Tibet's heritage through publications, presentations, exhibits, and the production and sale of culturally significant items.

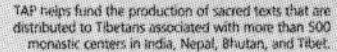

TAP helps fund the production of sacred texts that are distributed to Tibetans associated with more than 500 monastic centers in India, Nepal, Bhutan, and Tibet.

Guiding Principles

We value Tibet's ancient tradition of meditative insight into the potential of human consciousness, passed down from teacher to student as a living lineage for more than twelve centuries.

We respect the knowledge that Tibet can offer the world as a means to secure peace on Earth and honor the worth of all beings.

We apply in our work the practice of skillful means, making selfless action the basis of satisfaction and inner growth.

We strive to practice generosity, ethical conduct, patience, intensity of effort, focus, and wisdom in our work and in our interactions.

We focus to meet the most urgent needs of the Tibetan people and maximize the value of each donor's contribution.

We support the education of young Tibetans, mindful that the next generation will determine the future of this great civilization.

We collaborate with a network of nonprofit Buddhist organizations, each working in its own way to preserve the heritage of Tibet.

We donate our services as individuals, so that funds can go directly to programs that benefit Tibetans and enable them to share their wisdom and compassion with people everywhere.

Tibetan Buddhist stupas, empowered by sacred relics, symbolize the potential for enlightenment that is the heritage of every human being.

Our History

TAP was founded in 1969 by Tarthang Tulku, a leading Tibetan master and teacher, to support the courageous efforts of Tibetans to survive in exile and re-establish their rich cultural heritage. In its first decade, TAP worked to help refugees in need of food, clothing, medicine, and supplies. The Pen Friend Program initiated in 1969 enabled Americans to send funds directly to thousands of Tibetans. Many of the friendships established in the 1970s and 80s through this program continue to the present day.

As needs for basic necessities became less urgent, TAP intensified efforts to support restoration and construction of monasteries and schools of higher learning for Tibetans in exile and also in Tibet. Although the Project continues to provide assistance for monastic centers and monks, nuns, and lay people, its scope has steadily expanded. Current activities include efforts to preserve the wisdom tradition that is Tibet's unique heritage and promote the vitality of its living lineage.

In the early years of exile, Tibetans seeking to rebuild their culture persevered in difficult conditions, using available materials and sites to educate the next generation.

Tibetan Aid Project Today

Guided by the vision of Tarthang Tulku, the Tibetan Aid Project, now in its fourth decade, has steadily expanded its capacity to aid Tibetans dispersed throughout Asia as well as those remaining in Tibet. Significant progress has been made toward preserving Tibet's heritage and communicating its value for all humanity.

Today, TAP helps produce and distribute precious Tibetan texts and reproductions of sacred art, sponsors traditional ceremonies, provides general assistance to monastic centers, monks, and nuns, and promotes awareness of Tibetan civilization worldwide. TAP's board and staff have worked with great care to ensure the sustainability of programs, address new areas of need, and sustain TAP's integrity and vision as an organization dedicated to humanitarian, non-political ends.

The Project is now a global organization. Its nationwide support base, over ten thousand strong, is augmented by affiliates in Amsterdam, Holland; Köln, Germany; and São Paulo and Rio de Janeiro, Brazil. Working in the spirit of community, TAP continues to offer donors new opportunities to participate in preserving the wisdom tradition of Tibet. Help us ensure that this precious resource for all humanity continues to flourish now and far into the future.

Offering blessings and compassion to all beings, Tibetans fly hundreds of prayer flags over the valley of Samye, site of Tibet's first monastery.

Board of Directors

Tarthang Tulku
Wangmo Dixey
Pema Gellek
Tsering Gellek
Jack Petranker
Rosalyn White
Ann Bergfors
Ellen Rockwell

Distributing Sacred Books and Art

Sacred texts, the lifeblood of the Tibetan people, are readied for distribution in Bodh Gaya, India.

To the Tibetan people, nothing is more valuable than books or images that reveal the capacities of the human mind and show the way to enlightened states of being. Since the seventh century, when Tibetan rulers established a written language to preserve and transmit this priceless knowledge, Buddhist texts have been held in the highest esteem, revered by all Tibetans as the foundation of their culture.

Through the centuries, the collections of sacred texts, translated primarily from Sanskrit and enriched by the contributions of Tibet's greatest masters, have been a vital resource. Today these teachings can open new pathways to peace in our troubled times. Tibetan art gives fuller access to the sacred texts. The beauty of its images opens heart and mind to meaning that words cannot adequately express.

Since 1989, under the direction of Tarthang Tulku, some 780,000 texts, 74,000 prayer wheels, and nearly a million sacred images have been produced for free distribution to Tibetan monks, nuns, and lay people. TAP supports this effort by contributing funds toward production and covering all distribution and shipping expenses.

Sponsoring Ceremonies

Ceremonies carried out by large assemblies of accomplished practitioners generate a powerful momentum that deepens the experience of teachings too subtle and profound to be communicated in any other way. For Tibetans living in exile, separated from family and familiar sources of support, ceremonies strengthen the sense of community essential for continuing their traditions.

Together, the Tibetan Nyingma Meditation Center and TAP have sponsored over 1,500 ceremonies at more than a hundred monastic centers. Support for major ceremonies that bring together hundreds of practitioners is offered to centers of all four major Tibetan Buddhist traditions.

Ceremonies can reawaken the sleeping energy of enlightenment and evoke its blessings for the welfare of us all. Out of the pain of unbearable loss, a new vision is emerging, opening a path of positive action and revitalizing the human spirit.
—Tarthang Tulku

The penetrating sounds of Tibetan horns and the rhythmic chanting of prayers focus the mind and awaken deeper dimensions of consciousness.

Promoting Awareness in the West

The Tibetan Aid Project is fully committed to educating people around the world about the heritage of Tibet and the courageous struggles of Tibetans to survive in the face of severe hardships. The Project's central office in Berkeley, California shares resources with TAP offices located in Europe and Brazil. Working internationally, TAP offers educational programs and exhibits on the history and cultural traditions of Tibet.

Supported by its sister organizations, Dharma Publishing and the Yeshe De Project, TAP makes available books, videos, sacred art, and prayer flags that heighten awareness of the vast depths of knowledge cultivated and preserved in Tibet.

As more people explore the riches of Tibetan culture, the importance of preserving it has become increasingly clear. To a world in constant turmoil, the Tibetan heritage opens new avenues to peace, constructive action, and compassionate understanding.

Activated by the motion of the wind, Tibetan prayer flags release a continual stream of blessings, healing disturbances in the environment and promoting harmony in the cosmos and among all beings.

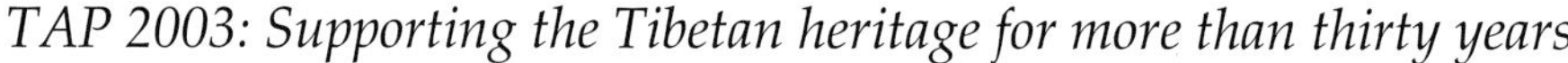

TAP 2003: Supporting the Tibetan heritage for more than thirty years

In all, between 1969 and 2005, over more than three decades of efforts on behalf of Tibetan refugees, TAP has donated about a million dollars worth of direct aid, sponsored ceremonies that preserve the Tibetan tradition, and supported TNMC's efforts to restore books and art to Tibetan individuals and monasteries in Asia.

Shipping art, books, and prayer wheels In support of TNMC and Yeshe De's projects, TAP has funded and facilitated the shipment of large quantities of sacred texts and art reproductions to monasteries in India, Nepal, Tibet, and Bhutan. TAP's staff often took an active role in these shipments, traveling to India to ensure that the offerings arrived safely and on schedule. In 1993 and 1994, and thereafter as necessary, TAP has recruited volunteers to assemble prayer wheels in time to meet shipping deadlines.

In the past five years, the Yeshe De Project has expanded its production of sacred texts, and the quantities of books and art shipped to India has increased greatly each year. Each year, TAP has managed to keep pace with the increase in shipping expenses involved. In 1998, TAP funded shipping costs for 23,920 books and 121,393 thankas; in 1999, it covered expenses for 82,208 books and 152,461 thankas. The shipment in 2000 was the largest up to that time: 166,000 books, nearly a hundred thousand art reproductions, and ten thousand prayer wheels for distribution to lay people, monks, and nuns. This shipment alone filled fifteen twenty-foot containers.

Recent shipments have remained large: 132,500 books, 267,349 thankas, and 15,000 prayer wheels for the ceremony in 2001, 164,000 books, thankas, and 20,000 prayer wheels for the ceremony in 2002, and 128,000 books and 10,000 prayer wheels for the ceremony in 2003. As Yeshe De began to greatly increase production, the number

Opposite: Restating TAP's mission for the 21st century, TAP's compact brochure published in 2003, sets forth the Project's guiding principles and current focus, answering the question, "How do sponsoring ceremonies and shipping books preserve Tibetan culture?"

1 Good Wishes Flag for Success of All Virtuous Actions
Gesar, the great epic hero of Tibet (shown here), embodies all three great Bodhisativas: Manjushri, Avalokiteshvara, and Vajrapani. Heroically working for the benefit of all, his wisdom, compassion, and power never fail. Gesar is surrounded by the four Guardian Kings, who protect the four directions of the cosmos against negative forces. Prayers of blessing surround the figures.
2 Virtuous Compassion Flag
Mantras and prayers invoke the blessings of the Enlightened Ones. Lord Buddha (pictured) is encircled by the Bodhisattvas: Avalokiteshvara, Heart of Compassion,whose hands are joined in prayer; Manjushri, Perfect Wisdom, whose sword cuts through confusion; Vajrapani, Wielder of the Vajra, who manifests the transforming power of truth; and also by Guru Padmasambhava, who brought Buddhism to Tibet.
3 Prajnaparamita Wisdom Flag for Transformation
The foundation for Bodhisattva practice, the Perfection of Wisdom teachings, including the Heart Sutra, show the way to transcending self-centeredness and suffering. Guru Padmasambhava (seen above), at center, is surrounded by Prajnaparamita and three other female wisdom-beings whose compassion and power cut through obstacles to inner freedom.
4 Eight Bodhisattvas Flag for Compassion and Wisdom
The Eight Great Bodhisattvas (example shown) manifest joy, compassion, loving kindness, and equanimity, the four immeasurables of spiritual practice. Mantras and prayers to the Eight Bodhisattvas activate these blessings for the benefit of all beings.
5 Protection Flag for the Transformation of All Obstacles
Five female Bodhisattvas offer protection from emotional distress and bodily harm, enabling the teachings of Perfect Wisdom to support the wish for enlightenment. Surrounded by the text of the Heart Sutra, Sitatapatra (shown above) holds the white umbrella. Images of Tara, Prajnaparamita, Purnashabari, and Marici frame the text.
6 Enlightenment Flag of the Thirty-Five Buddhas
Thirty-five Buddhas of Forgiveness are grouped in four large circles around the four-armed Avalokiteshvara, Bodhisattva of Compassion (pictured). By acknowledging our shortcomings through mantras and prayers to these great beings, we help clear away confusion that perpetuates suffering, strengthen our resolve to do better, and open pathways for new beginnings.
7 Goodness and Success in All Actions Flag
Eight goddesses of good fortune, each holding one of the eight auspicious symbols (example shown), stimulate positive thoughts and creative energy that invoke the blessings of the Buddhas and Bodhisattvas. The blessings of the Enlightened Ones dispel all feelings of loss and confusion, awakening great joy and supporting the growth of wisdom and compassion.
8 Samantabhadra's Prayer for Enlightened Practice Banner
This prayer, the Pranidhana Raja, presents Bodhisattva Samantabhadra's deep aspiration to attain enlightenment to benefit all living beings. The message of this revered text, taught by the Buddha and recited for thousands of years, will be borne on the wind wherever the flag is flown. Banner measures 64 x 52 inches.
All the prayer flags contain a rich array of sacred images and texts. The images shown here illustrate the beauty of the art.

Prayer flags created by Tarthang Tulku, Head Lama of TNMC, are printed on sun resistant sailcloth with sacred images and texts. They are sewn by TAP volunteers and made available through TAP's website.

of books distributed increased still further, to 205,000 books in 2004 and 418,000 books in 2005, with even larger shipments projected for 2006 and 2007. ***Shipments to Tibetans now total more than 1,500,000 books, more than a million art reproductions, and 94,374 handheld Dharma wheels.*** All are crucial in sustaining the ability of Tibetans to continue transmitting their traditions.

Outreach education The Tibetan Aid Project is committed to educating people around the world about the heritage of Tibet and the courageous struggles of Tibetans to survive in the face of severe hardships. The Project's central office in Berkeley, California, shares resources with TAP offices located in Europe and Brazil. Working internationally, TAP offers educational programs and exhibits on the history and cultural traditions of Tibet. Supported by its sister organizations, Dharma Publishing and the Yeshe De Project, TAP makes available books, videos, sacred art, and prayer flags that heighten awareness of the vast depths of knowledge cultivated and preserved in Tibet.

Prayer flags Tibetans have known for centuries that prayer flags imprinted with sacred images and mantras transmit blessings and healing energy into the world through the power of the wind. Prayer flags empowered by mantras affect natural, elemental forces on a subtle level beyond ordinary human perception. As they fly in the wind, the flags exert a protective, balancing influence on the environment and generate benefits for all sentient beings. For many years, TAP volunteers have participated when possible in the final preparation of sacred texts, prayer wheels, and prayer flags. In mid-year several members of TAP's staff went to Odiyan to silkscreen five thousand prayer flags as a Dharma offering. Since that time, TAP has been authorized to distribute eight different prayer flags to donors and its staff has continued to participate in major prayer flag printings at Odiyan. Skilled volunteers sew the printed cloth into 42″ x 56″ prayer flags, with borders and chevrons in five colors. In recent years, TAP has also offered prayer flags on its website.

Fostering Understanding: Pilgrimages to Holy Places

The World Peace Ceremonies have given TAP's friends and supporters welcome opportunities to connect more deeply with the Tibetan people and the meaning of their traditions. In 1995 and again in 1999 and 2001, TAP organized pilgrimages to the four most holy places of Buddhism. The focal event for these pilgrimages was a journey to Bodh Gaya to participate in the World Peace Ceremony. At Bodh Gaya and also at the Longchen Varna Sadhana at Sarnath, the pilgrims were able to help with the distribution of texts and the organization of the ceremonies. Traveling with experienced guides,

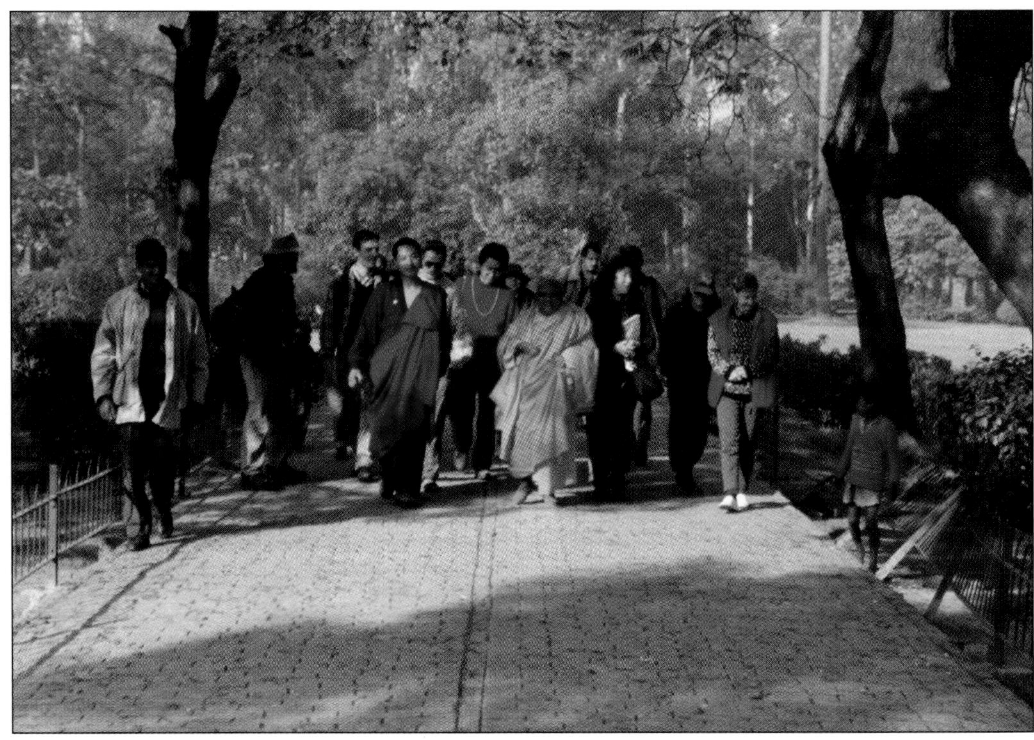

Approaching Kushinagara, site of the Buddha's Parinirvana.

the pilgrims also visited Lumbini, where the Buddha was born; Kushinagara, where the Blessed One passed from life; and Sarnath, where the Buddha first taught the Dharma. Thirty pilgrims took part in the first pilgrimage, and fifteen joined in the second.

The experience gained in 1995 led TAP to structure the 1999 and 2001 pilgrimages along the lines of a retreat. Each day began with a one-hour group meditation, at which traditional prayers were chanted. Meals were generally taken together. Mornings were devoted to visiting pilgrimage sites, sitting at the ceremonies (in Bodh Gaya and Sarnath), or working on projects related to book and thanka distribution or offerings.

Each evening throughout the course of the pilgrimage there were readings from relevant texts. In Bodh Gaya, for example, readings from *The Voice of the Buddha*, the life story of the Buddha Shakyamuni, helped bring to life the significance of the Vajrasana, site of

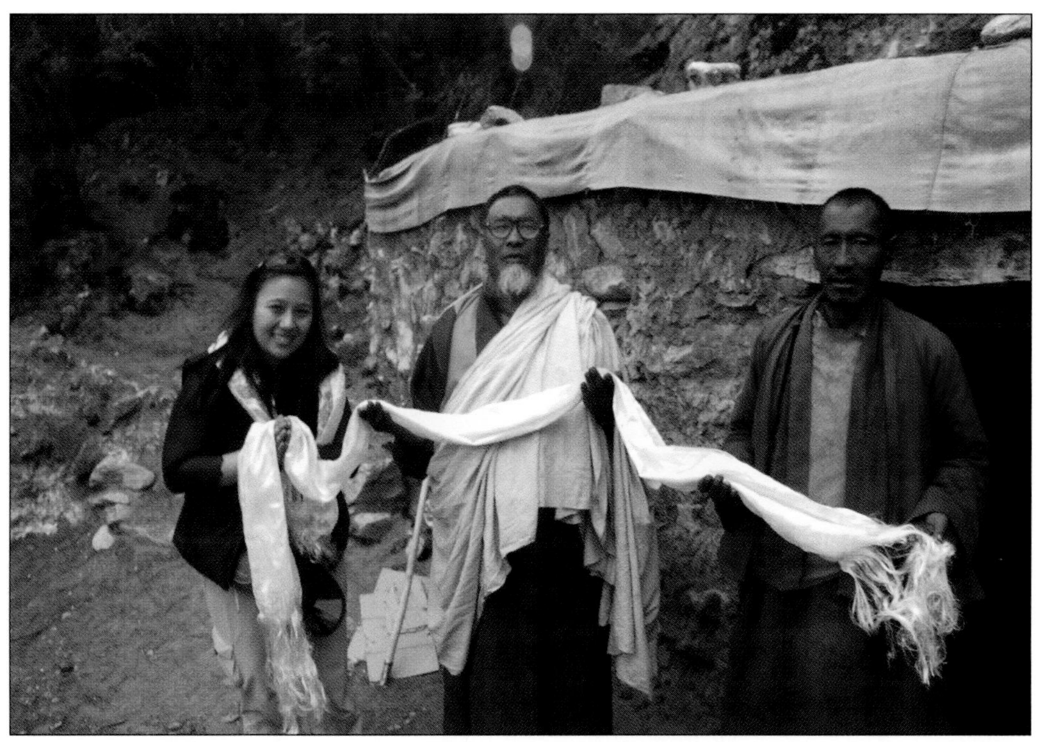

Offering katogs to the lama at Drag Yongzong, central Tibet.

the Buddha's enlightenment. Readings from a text on the meaning of refuge by the great fourteenth-century master Klong-chen-pa helped clarify the opportunity that the Monlam Chenmo offered.

To prepare for their sunrise visit to Vulture Peak near Rajgir, pilgrims memorized the Heart Sutra, given by the Buddha at that very place. Together they recited the text, then sat for a time in silent meditation. In Kushinagara, where the Buddha passed away, a two-hour reading of the Mahaparinibbana Sutta encouraged pilgrims to reflect deeply on the significance of impermanence. At the Longchen Varna in Sarnath, the pilgrims read and reflected on the teachings of Klong-chen-pa.

In the Kathmandu Valley of Nepal, the pilgrims visited the Asura caves at Pharping and the Svayambhu and Bodhnath stupas, as well as Nagi Gompa Nunnery, Ka-Nying Monastery, and other active centers of Dharma practice. At Ka-Nying, the pilgrims had

Tibet pilgrimage, 2005: Top: Approaching Dorje Drag by boat. Center: The vistas of Gangri Tokar. Below: Lama dances at Mindroling.

the good fortune to hear a Dharma discourse by Ven. Chokyi Nyima Rinpoche, a highly respected lama whose own studies as a young man were assisted by donations made through the TAP Pen Friend Program. Fluent in English, the lama spoke eloquently about the value of Yeshe De, TAP, and TNMC's efforts to restore to the Tibetan exile community the texts and art of their tradition.

Pilgrimage to Tibet

Pilgrimage was as much a part of ancient Tibetan lifestyle as a summer vacation is in the West today. Pilgrims would travel from power-place to power-place, paying homage as they advanced on their spiritual journey. In Tibet, the most powerful places of pilgrimage are cave-sites at the upper reaches of prominent valleys, giving the pilgrim a sense of being at the center of a mandala. Cave-hermitages of Padmasambhava, Tibet's Great Guru, are renowned as power-places of geomantic perfection.

In June, 2005, TAP organized and led a three-week pilgrimage to major holy places of central Tibet. TAP's representatives Lama Palzang, Pema Gellek, Sandra Olney, and Richard Dixey, accompanied by fourteen other participants from the United States, Europe, and South America, visited monasteries, nunneries, and retreat centers as well as historic sites related to the transmission of Buddhism to Tibet in the eighth century.

While in Lhasa, the pilgrims were able to visit the monastery of Mindroling, a major center of the Nyingma tradition. From Lhasa, they traveled west to the valley of Samye, home of the famous monastery and translation center where Tibetan lo-tsa-bas worked with the great abbot Shantarakshita and panditas from India and Kashmir to translate nearly a thousand Buddhist texts from Sanskrit into Tibetan. In the surrounding hills are the remote retreat centers where the great guru Padmasambhava meditated together with his disciples in the eighth century. Pilgrims followed the ancient trails

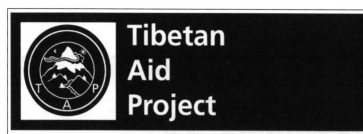

Tibetan Aid Project

News from TAP Issue 2 Spring 2005

INSIDE THIS ISSUE:

Greetings from the TAP Office

We are happy to offer you a variety of ways to support TAP's program service initiatives.

Thanks to many of you for your survey responses which helped guide us in developing articles for this newsletter.

We enjoyed your comments and look forward to receiving your ideas and opinions once again.

In our next issue you will hear all about TAP's pilgrimage to Tibet.

In the meantime, may the unfolding of spring tickle your heart.

The Yoga of Pilgrimage

The Potala Palace in Lhasa, the former seat of the Tibetan government.

Pilgrimage was as much a part of ancient Tibetan lifestyle as summer vacation is in the West today. Pilgrims would travel from power-place to power-place paying homage on their journey toward attaining enlightenment.

The physical exertion and stimulation of all the senses are integral to the pilgrimage experience in Tibet. As Keith Dowman says in his book *The Power-Places of Cental Tibet: A Pilgrim's Guide,* the body and mind are transformed and cleansed through "the rarity of the Tibetan atmosphere stretching the lungs to their limit; the sense of immense space and isolation; the unpolluted purity of the environment; and the unfiltered rays of the sun."

The most powerful places of pilgrimage are cave-sites at the upper reaches of prominent valleys, giving the pilgrim a sense of being at the center of a mandala. Cave-hermitages of Padmasambhava, Tibet's Great Guru, are characterized as power-places of geomantic perfection.

The Tibetan Aid Project's pilgrimage to Tibet this June will offer a rare first-hand experience of the spiritual legacy and rich cultural history deeply rooted in this land. Both Shugseb nunnery and Mindroling monastery, described in this newsletter, will be on the pilgrims' three week itinerary.

Bodh Gaya 2005: Cherished Moments

While in Bodh Gaya this past January, I went to dinner at a Tibetan restaurant, off the usual tourist track. Once my eyes adjusted to the darkness (a typical power outage) and clouds of incense smoke, I saw that the restaurant was filled with Bhutanese men, wearing their distinctive knee-length tunics. The pilgrims were lounging in chairs and on platforms, waving incense around, fingering their malas, and reading aloud from their prayer books.

Some of them were turning the prayer wheels they had received that very day from our distribution team. One man was slowly and gently running his hand over his prayer wheel, eyes awash with joy; another was rubbing his prayer book on different parts of his head, quietly saying, "Ahhhhhhh," over and over.

I have never before seen such appreciation. Although I was part of the team "offering" texts to Tibetans, I felt as though I was "offered" a great deal more just by being there. What a joy to witness such clear-eyed and open-hearted gratitude.

--Megan Wainman,
Tibetan Aid Project Staff

TAP's newsletters feature information on current activities, items such as pilgrimage and sacred sites of interest to its friends and supporters, and personal accounts by TAP staff members of their experiences with distributing sacred texts and art.

mostly on foot to make offerings at Chimphu, Yamalung, Sheldrak, Drag Yongzong, Gangri Tokhar, and Tandrik. They were also able to visit Dorje Drag, historically one of the six major Nyingma monasteries, the nunneries of Tsering Jong and Shugseb, and the tomb of Srong-btsan sGam-po in Yarlung, the Valley of the Kings. To each sacred site, they carried donations from TAP and were able to offer them directly to monks and nuns responsible for religious observances and upkeep.

The leaders' knowledge of these sacred sites and their significance within the Nyingma tradition made this pilgrimage an extraordinary experience. All income from this journey, as well as offerings from individual pilgrims, went directly to the monasteries and nunneries visited, to encourage their renewal and revitalization. If interest persists, TAP may continue to offer pilgrimage tours to central Tibet and possibly also to other regions. Additional information is given in "Foundations for the Future," page 290.

The Dharma Text Inputting Project

At the end of 2000, TAP was asked to take financial responsibility for the Dharma Text Inputting Project (DTIP). This project supports the training of monks and nuns to input texts using methods developed by the Yeshe De Project over the past fifteen years. This system, which produces texts in Tibetan script from romanized Tibetan transliterated using the Wylie system, relies on custom-designed software that reproduces the elegant typeface designed for the sacred texts.

The DTIP initiative came at a particularly appropriate moment. While the Yeshe De Project has worked wonders in preparing more than five hundred volumes of texts for distribution to the Tibetan community, DTIP holds out the possibility of being able to do far more extensive work. Equally important, by training Tibetan monks in the Yeshe De Project's exacting standards, DTIP looks ahead to a

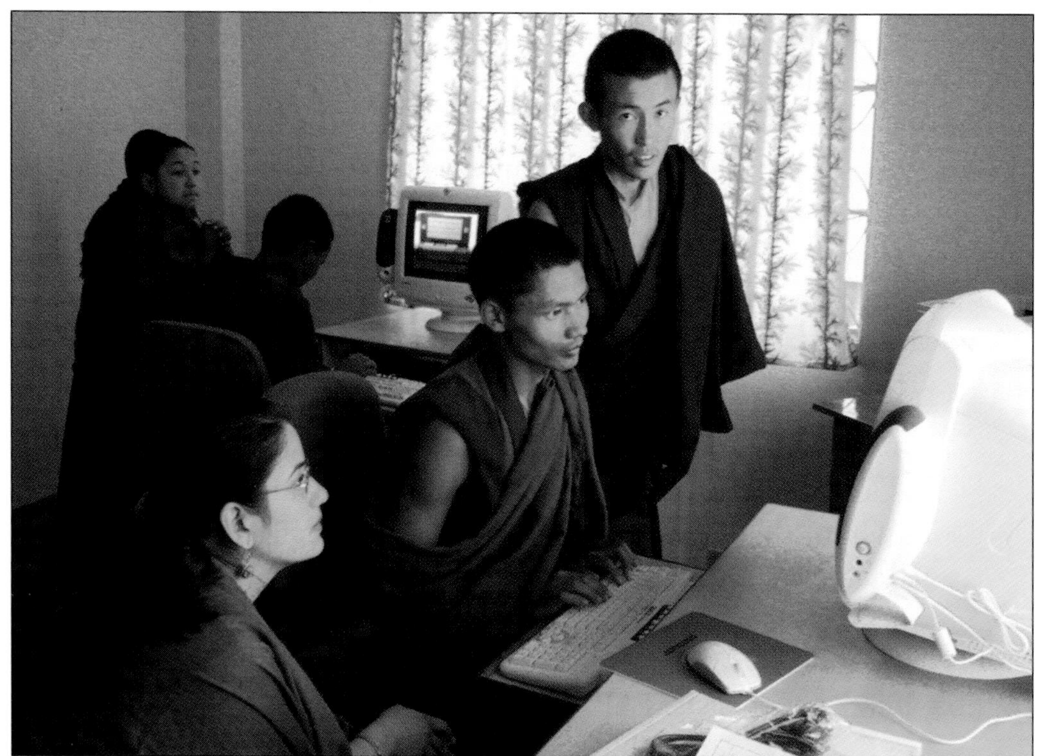

Monks in Nepal receive instruction in operating Yeshe De typesetting programs from Tsering Gellek of the Dharma Text Inputting Project. This project is meant to enable Tibetan monks and nuns to take an active role in preserving the sacred texts of their tradition.

time when the Tibetan exile community will be able to take full responsibility for restoring their heritage.

A generous donation from a TAP supporter enabled DTIP to begin operations in December 2000. One of TAP's board members received intensive training in the methods used by the Yeshe De Project, then traveled to Asia to communicate this knowledge to Tibetan monks in India and Nepal. While preliminary training was underway, the Yeshe De staff evaluated its procedures and programs in terms of their use by native speakers of Tibetan. They also considered inputting procedures used by other centers in India and Nepal. Based on this research, the decision was made to continue using Yeshe De's procedures and software. Inputting projects were initiated at Ka-Nying Shedrup Ling Monastery in Nepal, Pangaon

Caves in Manali, India, and the monastery of H.E. Taklung Tsetrul in Simla, India. The initial show of interest was encouraging, but some technical difficulties persist, and progress has been slow. As a result, the Yeshe De staff continues to do the inputting for the Tibetan texts prepared for offering at Bodh Gaya. Lamas in India and Nepal have graciously helped with the final proofreading.

The Community of a Thousand Blessings

> *The teachings we are preserving are the vibrant heart of knowledge—the wish-fulfilling gem that brings into being all the qualities that the world most needs.*
>
> —Tarthang Tulku

In 2002, while helping to fund the Yeshe De Project's production of the Ratnakuta Sutra (Treasury of Jewels), a collection of forty-nine treasured texts, TAP began expanding its support for sacred text preservation. Eight thousand copies of each of the six volumes in this collection were prepared by the Yeshe De Project, printed at Odiyan by Dharmacakra Press, and shipped to India in December for distribution to Tibetan lamas, monks, and nuns at the 2003 World Peace Ceremony in Bodh Gaya.

This opportunity to encourage the education of a new generation of scholars and practitioners inspired TAP to create the Light of Wisdom Fund in January, 2003. To support it, TAP initiated a new project named the Light of Wisdom Campaign. The campaign's goal was to raise $600,000 over three years, enough to cover the expenses of producing about a hundred thousand books containing more than three hundred Sutras.

The Sutras, the authentic words of the Buddha, are a treasury of knowledge and inspiration, the foundation of all traditions of Tibetan Buddhism. The Yeshe De Project is producing this precious collection in two formats: a large format in the traditional loose-leaf

style, with full-color illustrations of Buddhas and Bodhisattvas on each title page; and a western-bound format, also with beautiful illustrations. The traditional loose-leaf volumes are well-suited for temples and libraries, while the bound format is ideal for students and educational institutions. Prepared with respect and care by TNMC and the Yeshe De staff, these volumes will inspire Tibetans' efforts to embody the wisdom and compassion of their heritage.

Through the Light of Wisdom Campaign, TAP invited donors to pledge $3,000 a year for three years. A second level of participation, created to enable many more people to participate in the Community of a Thousand Blessings, was offered for those able to pledge $30 a month for three years.

TAP's brochure notes that the great heritage of Tibetan civilization is at risk of extinction. "The last masters trained in Tibet are passing away, leaving the young with few sources or guidance and inspiration. Without intensive educational efforts, Tibetan culture may not survive into the next generation."

"*THE LIGHT OF WISDOM CAMPAIGN* helps support the production and distribution of treasured Tibetan texts. These beautiful books preserve the heart and soul of a great wisdom tradition, rooted in the values of ethics, integrity, compassion, and untiring effort. They are a vital resource for the Tibetan people, cut off from their own culture and living in exile. Produced and distributed without charge, they provide the basis for a curriculum that can guide study and practice for generations.

"Recognizing the importance of this project, the Tibetan Aid Project has made a commitment to raise $600,000 over three years toward producing these texts. Since this means doubling our total income, we are relying on major donors. At the same time, we want everyone to have a chance to participate in this project. That is why we have created the Community of a Thousand Blessings.

A Simple Daily Practice
A Major Long-Term Contribution

"To deepen the meaning of your gift, we encourage you to bring it into your daily life. When you join, you will receive a brass butter lamp and a starting supply of candles. Each day you can light a candle, either as part of your daily practice or at any other special time. As you do, you may want to dedicate your act of giving to bringing the benefits of wisdom and compassion—the heart of the Tibetan tradition—to all beings. Dozens of community members will be making the same wish that day, contributing toward the same goal.

"Renew your pledge each day, rededicate your good wishes each time you light the lamp, and you will be part of a project of tremendous significance for our times. As they flow from heart to heart, the blessings of this action will multiply.

A simple daily practice, and lo and behold! A thousand blessings have come your way."

International fundraising efforts for this worthy project included establishing TAP in the United Kingdom, personal contacts, grant applications, and increased participation by the international Nyingma centers. As a result of these efforts, mid-way through 2005, the Light of Wisdom campaign is very near to realizing its goal.

Since the Ratnakuta Sutras were distributed at the World Peace Ceremony in 2003, the Yeshe De Project has printed two additional collections—the Avatamsaka Sutra and the Prajnaparamita Sutras. The Sutras that remain are being prepared for distribution in early 2006. These volumes will be presented to schools, monasteries, nunneries, and individuals as a religious, linguistic, and cultural resource for the preservation and continuation of Tibetan culture.

Masters of the Tibetan tradition know well that the wisdom expressed in the Sutras has the power to transform our understanding of the capacities and range of human consciousness. Although most of the students who prepare and print these volumes may lack experience with the depth of the wisdom these texts contain, they have faith in their value and work diligently for long hours to produce them. Placed in the hands of Tibetan masters, this vital knowledge will remain active in the world, a priceless treasure for lives growing increasingly pressured and insecure. Efforts to tap this treasure will continue, and the blessings of the wisdom they embody will flow ever more directly into human lives.

Income-Generating Activities

TAP's sources of income include donations, bequests, and income from sales of specific Dharma Publishing books: *From the Roof of the World, Your Friends the Tibetan Refugees,* all the children's books in the Jataka Tales Series, four volumes documenting the World Peace

Ceremony, and *Ancient Tibet*, a history of the land and people of Tibet to the end of the eighth century. TAP has also received income from sales generated by a gift catalog featuring books and other items related to its primary aims. Since 2003, TAP's gift catalog has been posted online as part of TAP's new web presentation.

As part of TAP's efforts to educate the public about Tibetan culture, TAP has made available to its friends and supporters such items as videos and books on the Bodh Gaya 1994 World Peace Ceremony, the Tibetan Aid Project, and pilgrimage sites in Kathmandu; Tibetan cards and calendars; and tapes of Tibetans chanting mantras and prayers. TAP's staff also participates in printing and sewing prayer flags, offered to donors as a gesture of appreciation.

Benefit Dinners Since 1996, TAP has held a series of benefit dinners that have helped extend the circle of regular donors. Several well-known chefs have donated their services, often working in improvised quarters to produce gourmet meals. Starting in May 1998, TAP has hosted annual gourmet dinners in the Brazilian Room at Tilden Park, located high in the Berkeley hills. Food and wine merchants have contributed generously in support of these evenings, attended by about a hundred people each year.

The success of the annual spring dinners inspired similar events in Los Angeles and Marin County. In 2001, TAP took this program a step further by hosting an elegant dinner at San Francisco's City Club, an historic site in San Francisco's financial district. Organized through the generosity of a leading San Francisco chef, this dinner, named "Taste and Tribute," featured vegetarian food donated and prepared by seven renowned culinary masters, as well as silent and live auctions. The first Taste and Tribute dinner, held on September 20, 2001, was attended by more than 150 people and generated over $33,000 in income for TAP's projects. This includes $12,000 from auction items donated by local merchants and supporters.

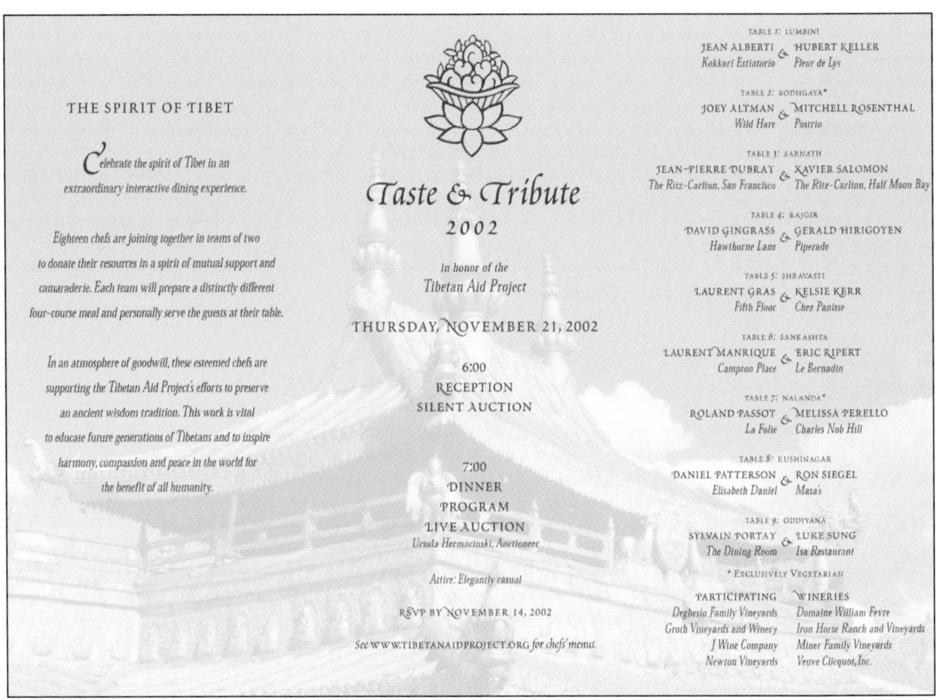

THE SPIRIT OF TIBET

Celebrate the spirit of Tibet in an extraordinary interactive dining experience.

Eighteen chefs are joining together in teams of two to donate their resources in a spirit of mutual support and camaraderie. Each team will prepare a distinctly different four-course meal and personally serve the guests at their table.

In an atmosphere of goodwill, these esteemed chefs are supporting the Tibetan Aid Project's efforts to preserve an ancient wisdom tradition. This work is vital to educate future generations of Tibetans and to inspire harmony, compassion and peace in the world for the benefit of all humanity.

Taste & Tribute

2002

In honor of the
Tibetan Aid Project

THURSDAY, NOVEMBER 21, 2002

6:00
RECEPTION
SILENT AUCTION

7:00
DINNER
PROGRAM
LIVE AUCTION
Ursula Hermacinski, Auctioneer

Attire: Elegantly casual

RSVP BY NOVEMBER 14, 2002

See WWW.TIBETANAIDPROJECT.ORG *for chefs' menus.*

TABLE 1: LUMBINI
JEAN ALBERTI & HUBERT KELLER
Kokkari Estiatorio — *Fleur de Lys*

TABLE 2: BODHGAYA*
JOEY ALTMAN & MITCHELL ROSENTHAL
Wild Hare — *Postrio*

TABLE 3: SARNATH
JEAN-PIERRE DUBRAY & XAVIER SALOMON
The Ritz-Carlton, San Francisco — *The Ritz-Carlton, Half Moon Bay*

TABLE 4: RAJGIR
DAVID GINGRASS & GERALD HIRIGOYEN
Hawthorne Lane — *Piperade*

TABLE 5: SHRAVASTI
LAURENT GRAS & KELSIE KERR
Fifth Floor — *Chez Panisse*

TABLE 6: SANKASHYA
LAURENT MANRIQUE & ERIC RIPERT
Campton Place — *Le Bernadin*

TABLE 7: NALANDA*
ROLAND PASSOT & MELISSA PERELLO
La Folie — *Charles Nob Hill*

TABLE 8: KUSHINAGAR
DANIEL PATTERSON & RON SIEGEL
Elisabeth Daniel — *Masa's*

TABLE 9: ODDIYANA
SYLVAIN PORTAY & LUKE SUNG
The Dining Room — *Isa Restaurant*

* EXCLUSIVELY VEGETARIAN

PARTICIPATING WINERIES
Deghesio Family Vineyards — *Domaine William Fevre*
Groth Vineyards and Winery — *Iron Horse Ranch and Vineyards*
J Wine Company — *Miner Family Vineyards*
Newton Vineyards — *Veuve Clicquot, Inc.*

In November 2002, eighteen celebrated chefs recruited by the same chef as for the previous event created a unique dining experience at the Ritz-Carlton San Francisco for the second Taste and Tribute dinner. At each of nine tables named after Buddhist holy places, two chefs worked together to prepare a dinner specifically for that table. No two dinners were alike.

The spring and fall benefit dinners provide opportunities to present Tibetan culture and TAP's program services. Guests have been inspired by videos of the World Peace Ceremony and the work of the Yeshe De Text Preservation Project shown at the dinners. In 2004, when TAP was seeking contributions for preserving ancient murals at Samye Monastery, guests at the Taste and Tribute dinner responded generously, contributing a total of $14,000 for this meritorious project alone. Additional funds were raised through the auction of donated goods and services.

Planning events of this quality is a specialized skill. TAP's staff benefited from advice by well-wishers, but struggled to cope with the many details necessary for making the dinners successful. As in

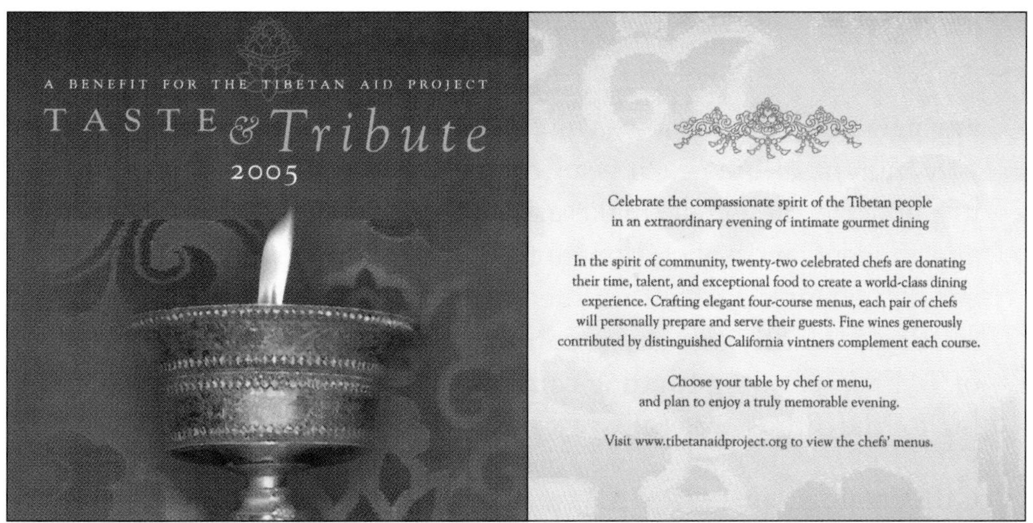

Above, TAP's 2005 Taste and Tribute announcement: "Celebrate the compassionate spirit of the Tibetan people in an extraordinary evening of intimate gourmet dining. In the spirit of community, twenty-two celebrated chefs are donating their time, talent, and exceptional food to create a world-class dining experience."

Held annually since 2001, the Taste & Tribute dinner, now the highlight of TAP's fundraising effort, offers Bay Area society an opportunity to learn more of Tibet's heritage and the ways individuals and groups can help preserve Tibetan culture.

Right: "Save the Date" cards announce the dinners well in advance.

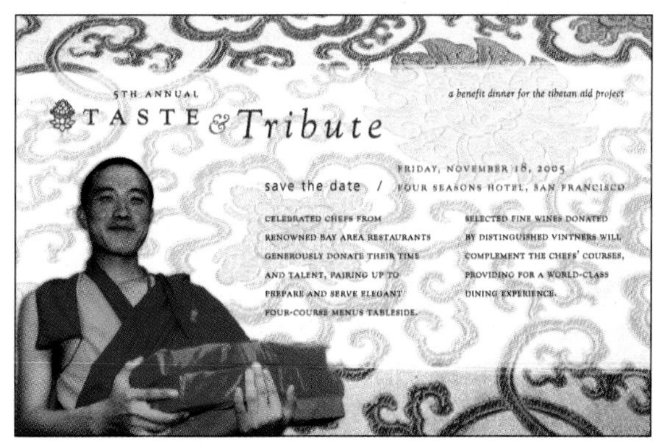

Graphic artists help TAP by volunteering time and skills to create tasteful, eye-catching designs.

any new undertaking, it was important to build momentum and devote months of time each year, contacting hundreds of individuals to publicize the event, make arrangements for donations of food and flowers, and solicit donations of auction items. By 2004, these efforts had proved fruitful: the Taste and Tribute dinner was attracting a steadily increasing patronage, especially welcome in light of TAP's expanding funding commitments. In 2005, the entire seating for the dinner was fully reserved weeks in advance of the event.

Gift Catalog In 1995, TAP created its first gift catalog. The two-page flyer let donors and supporters know that it was possible to obtain videos of the World Peace Ceremony as well as books relating to the Ceremonies and to the history and culture of Tibet. Encouraged by the positive response, TAP has continued to prepare and mail a gift catalog each year until 2003, when the gift catalog became part of TAP's website. TAP's website also offers prayer flags, prayer wheels, books for adults and children, CDs, meditation cushions (zafus), malas, incense, t-shirts imprinted with auspicious emblems, cards, calendars, and jewelry.

Community Involvement TAP continues to develop projects and events that reach out to the larger community of supporters in the Bay Area and encourage participation in fundraising activities. These events enable TAP to convey information on the unique qualities of Tibetan culture, the historical significance of Tibet's religious and cultural traditions, and the value of preserving the knowledge these traditions have transmitted to modern times.

Grant proposals TAP received several small grants prior to 1995. In 1996 TAP renewed efforts to obtain funding from grants and submitted two applications. When these efforts proved unsuccessful, the staff sought the assistance of a professional consultant and in 1997 created a grant-writing library. In 1997 TAP prepared a proposal in conjunction with the Yeshe De Project, also unsuccessful, and continued grant research through 1998. In the fall of 1998,

TAP's executive director participated in a grantwriting internship with the Catholic Charities of the Archdiocese of San Francisco, which donated several books to TAP's grantwriting library. The staff continues to pursue possibilities for grants that will extend the scope of TAP's activities and strengthen the long-range benefits of TAP's work for Tibetans and Tibetan culture.

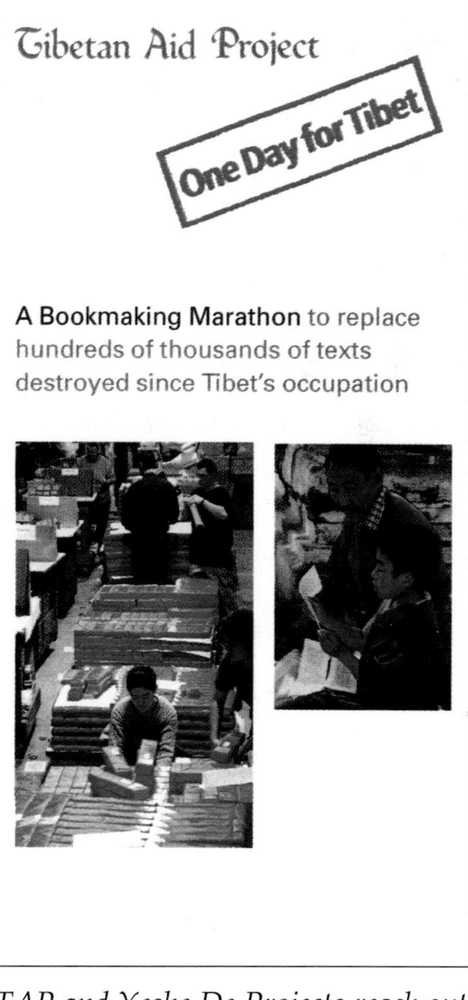

Tibetan Aid Project
One Day for Tibet
A Bookmaking Marathon to replace hundreds of thousands of texts destroyed since Tibet's occupation

TAP and Yeshe De Projects reach out to the larger community of well-wishers and supporters. Here TAP seeks sponsors for volunteers assembling books for shipment to Bodh Gaya.

Special Events In January 1996, TAP participated in a World Peace Day Celebration in Berkeley held during the World Peace Ceremony in Bodh Gaya. During Odiyan's Open House that same summer, TAP joined in greeting more than nine thousand visitors, providing information on its activities and making available prayer flags, books, and art. In 1996 and again in 1997, TAP gave guided tours of Dharma Publishing's exhibitions of sacred texts and art. Among TAP's other activities are receptions and showings of videos that portray the situation of the Tibetan people, the work of the Yeshe De Project, and the serene and inspiring beauty of the World Peace Ceremonies.

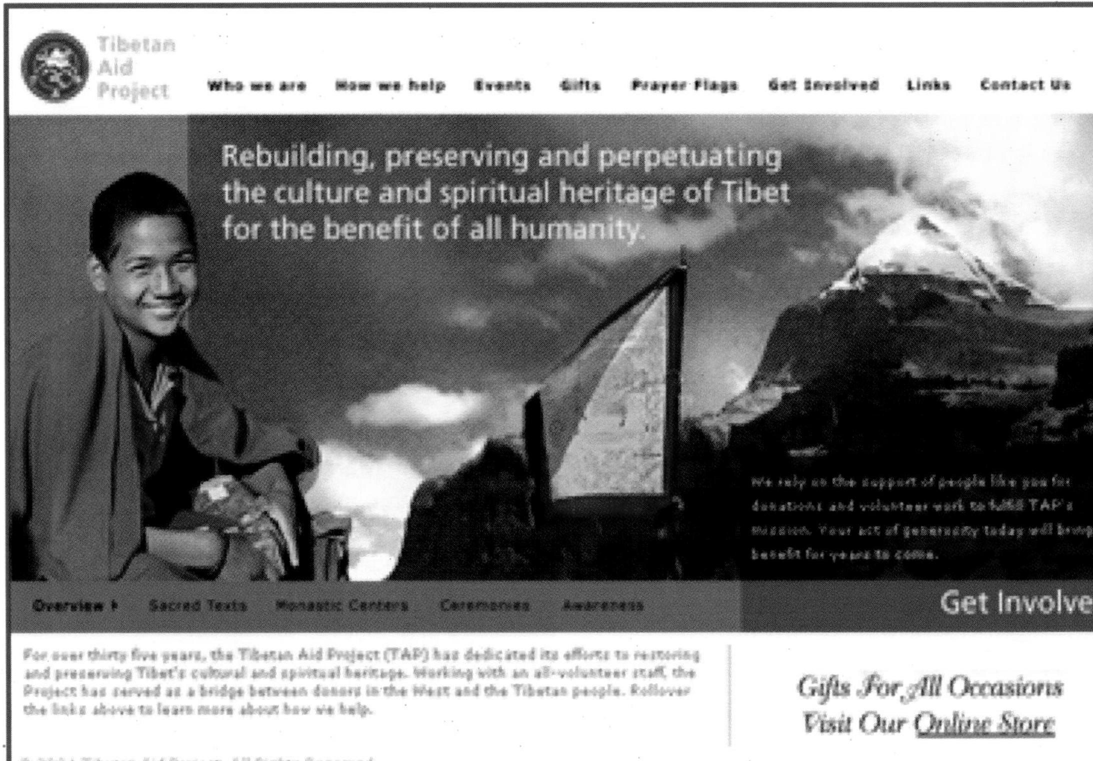

How TAP Communicates: New Web Page

To communicate the vision and purpose of TAP to a wider audience and clarify its role within the mandala of Nyingma organizations, TAP created web pages linked to the Nyingma Centers website. In summer 2002, to increase awareness of TAP, its identity, its mission, and its projects, TAP set up its own website, accessible at www.tibetanaidproject.org. Developed over the following year, this site makes it easy for people to get involved and become a part of TAP's network of support, which now reaches around the world. Supporters can now connect directly with TAP through making donations, volunteering, or purchasing prayer flags, prayer wheels, CD's, jewelry, books, zafus, and other gifts online.

Above, TAP's new web page invites participation with pages on Who We Are, How We Help, Events, Gifts, Prayer Flags, and Get Involved.

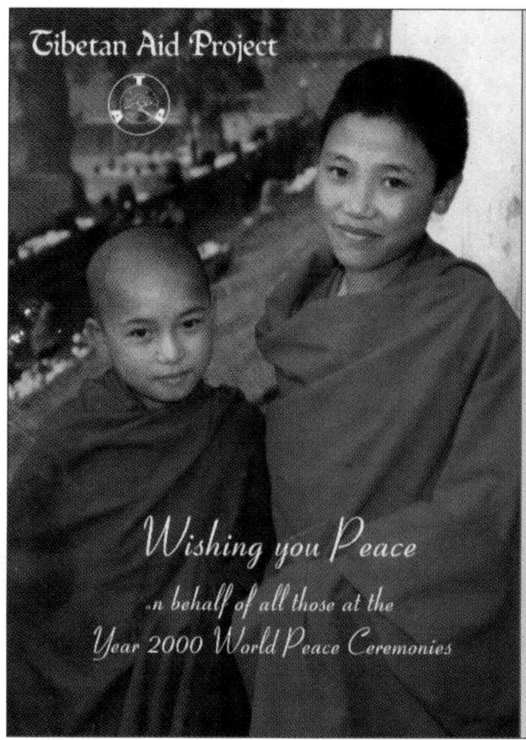

Would you like your friends or family to receive this Holiday Card?

Simply make a donation of $25 or more in their name, and the volunteers at TAP will mail this inspiring image of Tibetan nuns at the World Peace Ceremonies with a notification of your gift on the back.

For the past ten years, thousands of exiled Tibetan monks and nuns have gathered each January at the World Peace Ceremony in Bodh Gaya, India. There they offer prayers that the world find peace and all beings be free from suffering. Sponsored by the Tibetan Nyingma Meditation Center and the Nyingma Monlam Chenmo Foundation, these ceremonies bring together thousands of lamas, monks, and nuns. Donations made now to the Tibetan Aid Project (TAP) help deliver over 100,000 volumes of traditional texts to the Tibetans participating in the first World Peace Ceremony of the new millennium.

The Tibetan Aid Project's major services are

- Financial support to Tibetan monasteries and nunneries
- Shipping sacred texts and art to the World Peace Ceremonies
- Sponsoring prayer ceremonies
- Increasing Western awareness of the endangered Tibetan culture

TAP is a project of the Tibetan Nyingma Relief Foundation, a registered 501 (c) (3) corporation. U.S. non-profit tax I.D. #23-7433901

2910 San Pablo Avenue
Berkeley, CA 94702
1-800-33-TIBET or (510) 848-4238
tap@nyingma.org

Fundraising items offered through TAP's web site include several kinds of prayer wheels and cards with Tibetan images.

Documenting the Tibetan Refugee Experience

In 1991, TAP sponsored the publication of a book of photographs received from supporters and donors over the years. Dharma Publishing editors prepared the text, then worked with Tarthang Tulku to design and produce the book. As completed in 1992, *From the Roof of the World* is a unique historical document, a reminder to Tibetans of a critical time in their history and their courageous struggle to preserve their heritage.

Additional photographs, together with an account of TAP's activities, were published in 2001 in a second book, *Your Friends the Tibetan Refugees.* This volume blends historical photographs with an illustrated overview of the Tibetan Aid Project, providing updated information on the situation of the Tibetan refugees and TAP's continuing response. This present volume, the third in this series, includes the foundations established to preserve and revitalize the sacred sites throughout the Himalayas. Proceeds from sales of these books support TAP's refugee assistance programs

TAP International

The Tibetan Aid Project is now a global organization. Its nationwide support base, over ten thousand strong, is augmented by affiliates in Amsterdam, Holland; Köln, Germany, and São Paulo and Rio de Janeiro, Brazil. TAP volunteers in these countries educate the public and raise funds by organizing benefit dinners, making visual presentations and exhibits, and disseminating information on Tibetan culture and TAP. Like volunteers in Berkeley, they also produce prayer flags and engage in other projects that have a worthy purpose and convey the importance of preserving Tibetan culture. Many members responsible for TAP's international activities have developed a strong connection with the value of TAP's work through participation in the World Peace Ceremonies in India and by working with Yeshe De's production staff in Berkeley.

Investment in the Future

As the year 2005 comes to a close, TAP, about to begin its thirty-sixth year of continuous operation, is supported by 3,500 currently active donors. This support has enabled TAP to continue its work in distributing sacred texts and art, providing aid for monastic centers and individual monks and nuns, sponsoring traditional ceremonies, and facilitating the disbursement of funds offered by TNMC to monasteries in Tibet. In 2002, TNMC offered funds to restore statues of the Abbot Shantarakshita, King Trisong Detsen, and Guru Padmasambhava to Mindroling, Dorje Drag, and Samye, Tibet's first monastery, as well as funds for restoration projects, support for retreats for monks and nuns, and other worthy projects.

In TNMC initiated research into the cost of repairing the damaged walls and roof of Jampel Ling, the Manjushri Temple of Samye, and restoring its water-damaged frescoes and murals, the finest in Samye. The site was examined in 2005 during the pilgrimage to Tibet, and a program for reconstruction has been drafted and agreed upon. As a first step, TNMC offered $10,000 to repair the roof and protect the frescos from further damage. Offerings have also been made to sponsor ceremonies at Mindroling, Dorje Drag, Shugseb, and other monasteries and retreats, and also to sponsor the restoration of additional statues to Mindroling and Dorje Drag. A report of offerings are given on page 370.

TAP's newsletter has reached out to 60,000 new homes across the country, promoting awareness of Tibet's situation and the progress of Tibetan refugees in rebuilding their culture in exile. New streams of revenue opened this year have the potential of extending further the vision of a revitalized heritage of knowledge that can benefit humanity far into the future.

Combined, the generosity of TAP's donors and the efforts of TAP's volunteer staff have enabled TAP to carry out more work than might seem possible for such a small organization. Working within the mandala of the Nyingma organizations, TAP's staff benefits from the expertise of senior students who serve as advisers, from the skills of Dharma Publishing editors and sales representatives, from the production capacities of Dharma Press, and from the generosity of the Nyingma Institute in offering accommodations and educational programs for TAP's staff. In turn, the staff have been challenged to develop and extend their skills. In doing so, they have encouraged the work of the Yeshe De Project, strengthened connections with the Nyingma lineage, supported the vision of the Head Lama, and benefited the mandala as a whole.

"All of TAP's activities support the vision of the Head Lama of TNMC, who continues to guide TAP and shape its mission. TAP is deeply privileged for this opportunity to help forge the links between Tibet's past glories, the present struggles of its people, and a future open to all possibilities. As more Westerners come to appreciate the value and beauty of Tibetan culture, they may understand the vision that has sustained TAP for more than three decades. If even a few people can glimpse the potential of the knowledge transmitted within the Tibetan tradition, TAP's years of dedicated service will have been well spent, an offering to the Dharma and to the whole human race."

—*Your Friends the Tibetan Refugees*, p. 229

May no people on this earth ever again live as refugees.
May all dwell in harmony in their own homelands,
free to fulfill their own destinies.

Tarthang Tulku

Past Administrations

1974–75
Tarthang Tulku, President
Nazli Gellek*
Jane Wilhelms
Karen Mendelsohn*
Joel Lipman
Annette Beven
Grania Davis*

1975–76
Tarthang Tulku, President
Steven Beven
Marjorie Kimball
Jane Wilhelms
Pauli Woodbury*
Donna Egge*

1976–79
Tarthang Tulku, President
Steven Beven
Judy Rasmussen*
Donna Egge*

1979–80
Tarthang Tulku, President
Judy Rasmussen*
Donna Egge*

1980–88
Tarthang Tulku, President
Judy Rasmussen*

1988–89
Tarthang Tulku, President
Judy Rasmussen*
Judy Roberts
Ann Bergfors

1989–92
Tarthang Tulku, President
Judy Rasmussen*
Victoria Riskin*
Ann Bergfors*

1992–94
Tarthang Tulku, President
Judy Rasmussen*
Victoria Riskin*
Wangmo Gellek

1994–96
Tarthang Tulku, President
Judy Rasmussen*
Victoria Riskin*
Wangmo Gellek*
Javier Rockwell*

1996–97
Tarthang Tulku, President
Wangmo Gellek
Pema Gellek
Tsering Gellek

* = major participants in daily operations

Past Administrations

1997–99

Tarthang Tulku, President

Wangmo Gellek, Vice-President

Javier Rockwell,
General Secretary

Pema Gellek, Officer for
Foreign Communications
and Education Assistance

Tsering Gellek, Treasurer;
Officer for Health Development

Advisory Committee

Arnaud Maitland

James McNulty

Robert Byrne

Padma Maitland

Nelson Chamma Filho

Paulina Rabinovich

Bob Dozor (1998-99)

Richard Kingsland (1998-99)

Full Time Staff

Javier Rockwell,
General Manager

Ingrid Tan, Office
Manager/Secretary1999

1999 to 2000

Board of Directors

Tarthang Tulku, President

Wangmo Gellek

Pema Gellek

Tsering Gellek

Ellen Rockwell

Rosalyn White

Jack Petranker

Ann Bergfors

Full-time Staff

Erin Clark, Coordinator

2000–04

Board of Directors

Tarthang Tulku, President

Ellen Rockwell,
Financial Advisor

Ann Bergfors, Financial Officer

Wangmo Gellek, Vice President

Pema Gellek, Secretary

Tsering Gellek

Jack Petranker, Legal Advisor

Rosalyn White, Public Relations

Leigh Deering,
April 2001–2004

Coordinating Secretary

Sandra Olney

Consultants

Barbara Gortikov

Victoria Riskin

Kristine Winber

Current Administration and Major Donors

Board of Directors
Jack Petranker
Wangmo Gellek
Pema Gellek
Tsering Gellek
Rosalyn White

Staff
Sandra Olney, Coord. Secretary
Megan Wainman
Airi Kandel
Rachel Rozado
Duncan Bronston

Volunteers
Lu and Richard Carter
Hugh Joswick
Eric Needham
Susan Newman
Ron Rice
Geraldine Tablit
Richard Wales and Lorell Long

Light of Wisdom Advisors
Renie Byrne
Kathleen Daly
Tsering Gellek
Mark Henderson
Sandy Olney
Jack Petranker
Rosalyn White

Light of Wisdom Donors
Anonymous, Netherlands, UK, US
Hal Arbit and Carrie Kramlich
Mary Brumder
Nelson Chamma
Kuan-Hui Chiang
Magda Costa
Harriet Dopkin
Bob Dozor and Ellen Barnett
Annie Fuller
Ed Hannibal
Mike Hansen
Camie and Mark Howard
Olivia and Thacher Hurd
Piet Hut
Emily Lewis
Nancy Martin
Margaret Mitchell
Sandy McMahon
Jack Petranker
Kenneth and Frances Reid
Vicki Riskin
Paul Smith
Endy Stark
Holley Childhouse Stevens
Don and Leslie Tinker
Bep van Hezendonk
Yoke Lian Wong
Susan Zimmerman

Pledge Donors
Phoenix Bao
Laurence Berarducci
Cynthia A. Birch-Walker
Marcia L. Bradwick
Joyce L. Bruget
Carl and Susan Brungardt
Betty Jo Byrne
Faith A. Campbell
Irene Cannon-Geary
Lin Chang Ching
Sylvia E. Devoss
Charlyne J. Eshleman
Gary Fogg
Elisabeth Garst
Judith Irwin
Narayanan and Veena Kallingal
Allen R. LeCours
Peng Liew
Steven and Pia J. Logan
Sally M. Martin
Susan, Paul, and Leala Means
Margaret Mitchell

Neal J. Pollock
Javier Rockwell
Rick Sibley
David Song
Holly Childhouse Stevens
Katie and Trond Storli
Yolanda M. Vazquez
Harriet L. Warkentine
Leni and Alan Windle

Major Donors
Terry Adams and Carey Sakai
Garu Ashley
Peter and Alice Broner
Donna Carlson
Robin and Curtis Caton
Sigrid Christensen
James Craft
Kathleen M. Daly
Lawson and Leslie Day
Arjun and Diana Divecha
Wangmo and Richard Dixey
D. Michael and Cathy Enfield
Andrew Fitts
Allan C. Fix
Barbara Gabel and Robert Zachowski
Elisa Gerarden and Gregory Hale
Barbara Goodbody
Barbara Gortikov
Brenda Griswold
Larry and Carie Haimovitch
Helen and R. Allen Hermes
Richard Howard
Ted and Janet Kelter
Richard C. Kingsland
and Alice N. Lemon
Timothy Kochis
R. Scott Leebrick
Pirkko Liikanen
Jim and Bev Losi
Pui-Chong Lund
Laurent and Cathinka Manrique
Dr. Marijah McCain
and Stephen McCain
Mary Ann McGuire
Sandy and Ellen McMahon
Thomas and Lenore Mead
Carol Mendelsohn
Diane Denman Moxness
Sharon Muneno and Ray Johnston
Michelle Odom
Leanne Palmer
Andrew S. Paul
Eric Ripert
Scott and Carol B. Ritchie
Lou Scharpf
Allen W. Shelton
Tanya Slesnick
Janet Smith

Donors
David Ayster
Deborah Black
Virginia Bronson
Aimee Carroll
Patricia Clemens
Linda and Keith Copenhagen
Perry Dexter
Bob and Dori Grant
Skip Jirrels and Pam Koppel
Jon Klein
Angela Lackey and Alan Olson
James Lamb
Scott and Marie Leary
Tony Leto and Aelita Putnina
Elaine Levine and Rhoberta Hirter
Eva Lindholm
Nicklaus Lorenzen
Peter Macherner
Eileen McEntyre
Jim and Anita McNulty
Connie Meaney
Brian Mills
Donna Morton
Claudio Naranjo
Elizabeth Nguyen
Doug and Toni Nurnberg
Robyn Brode Orsini
Santosh Philip
Paula Rozin
Terry Ryder
Lori Lee Sernisch
Saurin Sunny Shine
Colleen Gilmore Stone
Chau and Jim Yoder
Paola Zamperini

Chapter Thirteen

Reuniting the Threads of Buddhadharma

In the holy places, where the momentum for enlightenment took birth, where it shone forth in the form of a Buddha, where it entered the hearts of the Sangha, and where its physical form passed away, the Lord Buddha left behind symbols that point the way to enlightenment. Like a wish-fulfilling gem, these symbols need to be activated through appreciation, polished with care and respect for their power, and placed high on the altar of our consciousness, where their blessings can be invoked through prayer. When we approach the holy places with humility and respect, set aside self-centered concerns, and pray to the enlightened ones with full-hearted devotion, blessings fall like rain, transforming the karma of those who suffer.

—Tarthang Tulku

For thirty-five years, I have sought ways to revitalize the holy places of the Buddha by sponsoring ceremonies that encourage the Sangha to congregate at these sacred sites. In support of these ceremonies, we have established foundations for each of the four major Tibetan schools in the hope that they will observe these Monlam Chenmos in perpetuity. Our Nyingma organizations have made offerings of sacred texts, art, banners, plaques, and prayer wheels. We have also produced books in English and distributed them widely, wishing to share with others a sense of the beauty that the holy places can awaken in the human heart and mind.

In the late 1990s, inspired by the World Peace Ceremony and the long association of bells with vaca, the Buddha's speech, I envisioned the possibility of providing a Dharma bell for the Vajrasana at Bodh Gaya, so that the sound of enlightenment could radiate from here into the ten directions—bearing prayers for peace and cutting through the confusion of samsara.

The World Peace Bells

In November, 1998, I initiated the World Peace Bell project. The bell was to be dedicated to the memory of the Tibetans who had perished as a result of the disturbances in Tibet over the past fifty years. It was important that the bell be cast with raised letters on the inside as well as on the outside, which is rarely done in the West. The Sanskrit mantras and prayers were to be in ornate Lantsa script and the texts in Tibetan, all framed in ornamental borders. Preparing the design was made far more complex by the need to shape the texts to both the convex and concave curves of the bell.

The first casting of the bell, made in Austria in 1999, was installed at Odiyan, where it served as the model for the Peace Bell, intended to be offered to the Mahabodhi Temple in Bodh Gaya. This new bell was to be cast in Germany, where the preparation of church bells is a highly developed art. Members of Nyingma Zentrum, TNMC's German affiliate, put great efforts into fundraising and preparing wax models for casting. Their involvement was auspicious, for the merit of sponsoring such a meritorious offering would help heal the karma that still lingers in their country in the wake of World War II.

Late in 2001, after years of planning and development, the first Peace Bell, five feet in diameter and five feet high, weighing more than two tons, was successfully cast. A few months later, when its ornamental arch was cast and finished, the bell and its arch were shipped to India in August, 2002. A representatives from TNMC familiar with heavy construction went to Bodh Gaya to oversee

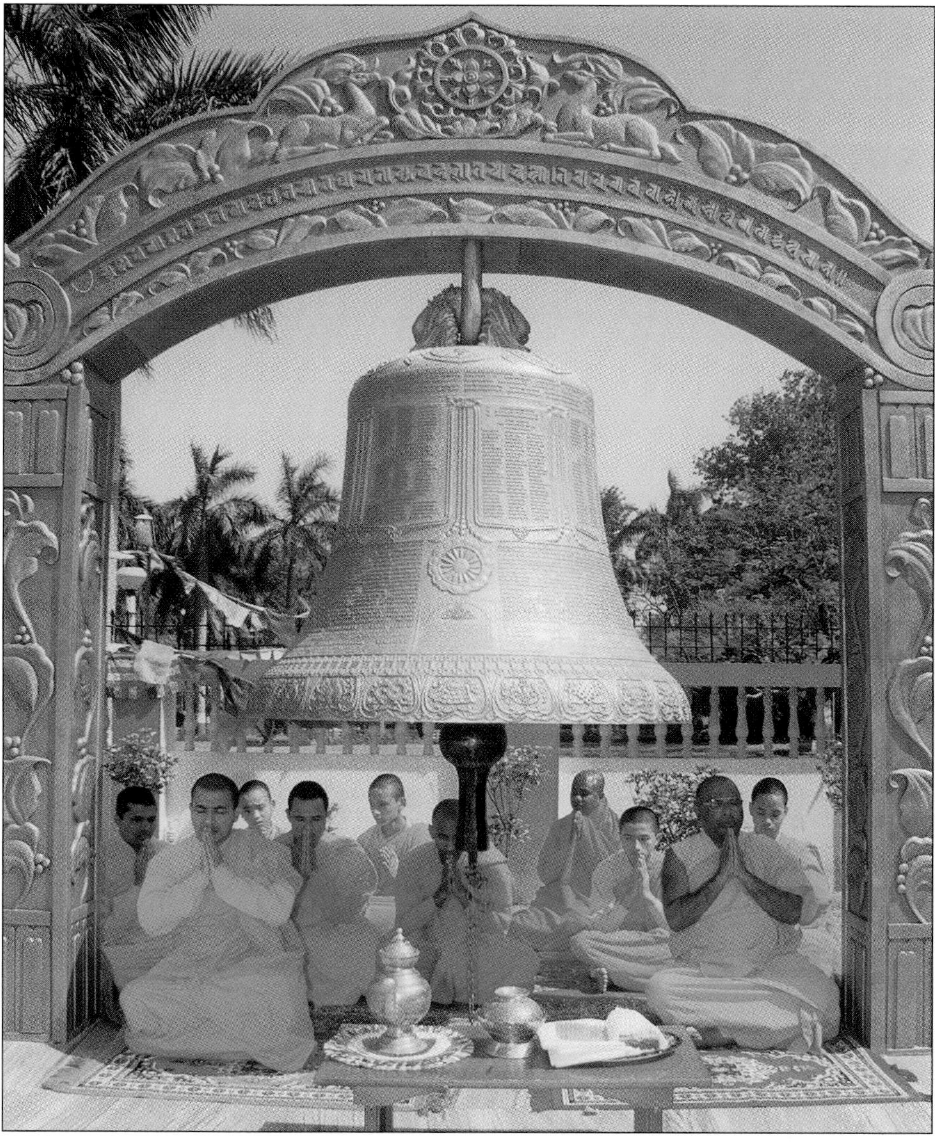

The Peace Bell is a powerful sacred symbol, a support for kaya in its beauty and a support for vaca in its sound, rich in overtones that disseminate the teachings throughout time and space. Consecrated at Sarnath, 2005.

the installation in the meditation garden next to the Mahabodhi compound. On December 13, the Peace Bell sounded for the first time, announcing that day's opening of the Mahabodhi Temple. Since then, the Mahabodhi Peace Bell has rung each morning and during ceremonies. For some, these bell ringings evoke the celebra-

Consecrating the World Peace Bell in Kushinagara, 2005

Symbolism of the Bell

In the Buddhist tradition, a bell symbolizes wisdom. The hollow of the bell symbolizes the wisdom of cognizing emptiness, while the clapper represents the skillful means that causes this wisdom to resound in the mind and in the wider world. Looking upon the four holy places with eyes of reverence, we open our hearts to the aspects of wisdom the Buddha displayed in each of these sacred sites. In offering bells to each one, we indicate our wish to hear and comprehend the profound teachings of the Buddha. At Lumbini, we may understand the wisdom of birth, creation, or appearance as expressed in the manifestation of the Buddha's life. At Bodh Gaya, we may experience a glimmer of the wisdom of enlightenment; at Sarnath we may contemplate the wisdom of the Dharma, and in Kushinagara we may find peace in the wisdom of impermanence, as expressed in the Buddha's Parinirvana.

शाक्यवंशका राजा शुद्धोदन तथा रानी मायादेवीको कोखबाट भद्रकल्पका चौथो शाक्यमुनि बुद्ध दिव्य उद्यान लुम्बिनीमा जन्मिनुभएको हो। बुद्धवचनकै रूपमा चिनिने यो महान धर्मघण्ट बज्दाखेरी भित्रि हृदयदेखि निस्किएको सुत्र, मन्त्र तथा प्रार्थनाले भरिपूर्ण शब्दहरूको आवाज अनायासै गुञ्जिन थाल्छ। यस धर्म घण्टबाट प्रतिध्वनित भएको मंगल ध्वनिले सुन्ने सबैको भित्रि मन नै छुनपुग्छ। फलस्वरुप उसले सुख तथा शान्तिको अनुभव गर्न थाल्छ।

नेपाल अधिराज्यको सम्मानमा,जम्बुद्विपमा विराजमान तथा संरक्षकको रूपमा रहनुभएका सबै बुद्धहरूको सम्मानमा, यशस्वी शाक्यवंशको सम्मानमा तथा नेपालको धर्म, संस्कृति र इतिहासप्रति ठूलो आदर व्यक्त गर्दै संद्धर्भम। ठूलो श्रद्धा राख्ने सबै तिब्बतवासीहरूको तर्फबाट शान्तिको प्रतिकको रूपमा सदाको लागि यो धर्मघण्ट समर्पण गरिएको छ।

मोन्लाम छेमो का संस्थापक श्री तारथाङ टुल्कु - कुनगा गेलेग येशे दोर्जे आनन्द स्वस्ताम ज्ञामवज्र
मिति २३ मई, २००५

Homage to Buddha, Dharma, and Sangha

Here in the celestial garden of Lumbini, the fourth Buddha in the Bhadrakalpa was born the son of King Shuddhodana and Queen Mayadevi of the Shakya clan. Each time this great bell symbolizing the Buddhavacana rings out, sound flows from its open heart through the sutras, mantras, and prayers upon its surface, and fills the mind of all who hear its melody with the blessings and peace of Dharma.

In honor of the Kingdom of Nepal, the patron of all the Buddhas who have reigned in Jambudvipa, and in honor of the illustrious Clan of the Shakyas, with great respect for the history, culture, and religion of Nepal, and on behalf of the Tibetans full of faith in Dharma, this bell is dedicated as a symbol of peace for all time.

By the Founder of the Monlam Chenmo
Tarthang Tulku Kun-dga' dGe-legs Ye-shes rDo-rje Ananda Swastam Jnana Vajra

To commemorate the installation of the Peace Bell at the Buddha's birthplace in the garden of Lumbini, the Head Lama of TNMC had this dedication etched on bronze and gold-plated for mounting on the bell's ornamental arched frame. The finished size of the plaque is 17"x 21."

tions of past times, when monks and nuns assembled here in large gatherings and drums and horns resounded to mark the end of the rainy season retreat.

Encouraged by the success of this project, I initiated the casting of three more bells and arches to be placed at the Buddha's birthplace in Lumbini, the site of the first teaching in Sarnath, and the place of the Buddha's Parinirvana, at Kushinagara. The casting of the bells proceeded smoothly, an auspicious sign; the bells arrived safely in India, and I asked Tsering Gellek and Amdo Lama to see them through customs and arrange for their installation at each of the three sites. This assignment met with unforeseen difficulties and took much longer than expected, but our representatives were able to persevere. Somehow, they were sustained by the merit of this project, by the power of prayer, or perhaps by the blessings still vibrant at these sacred sites. At each site in turn, even when failure seemed immanent, the obstacles melted way, one by one. As the bells finally rang out, sending the Buddha's teachings reverberating through each site, everyone present—from townspeople to government officials and archaeologists—felt the joy of obstacles overcome. Many expressed their appreciation for this symbol of spiritual power and the awakening of human potential.

Foundations for the Future

I feel it is important to continue to do all we can to bring the Dharma back to all the places where it once thrived, and to strengthen its practices wherever they have weakened. In 2005, to work toward restoring and revitalizing the Dharma traditions in India, Tibet, Nepal, Bhutan, and Ladakh, I established five foundations: Shiksha Light, Vajra Light, Ananda Light, Buddhadharma Light, and Mangalam Light. For each foundation, two governing directors and two assisting officers are responsible for ensuring its integrity and carrying out its specific purpose, guidelines, and directives. From their articles of incorporation:

Shiksha Light Foundation Governing Directors, Pema Gellek and Lama Palzang. Assisting Officers, June Rosenberg and Elizabeth Cook. The purpose of the Shiksha Light Foundation is to strengthen the Dharma and encourage study and practice by Dharma students. The goal is to restore the strength of Dharma practice to the times more than a century ago when the teachings flourished in Tibet. The Shiksha Light Foundation will make scholarship grants to qualified bshad-grwa (shedra) students and sgrub-grwa (drup-dra practitioners, and will also provide support for qualified long-term students and practitioners engaged in full-time study or practice, whether on solitary retreat or in groups.

Vajra Light Foundation Governing Directors, Pema Yangchen and Lama Pega. Assisting Officers, Sylvia Gretchen and Leslie Bradburn. The specific purpose of the Vajra Light Foundation is to ensure that the traditions of bKa'-ma and gTer-ma and of all schools of Tibetan Buddhism survive for future generations. To achieve this purpose, the Vajra Light Foundation will give highest priority to supporting the practice of any sadhana directed to Guru Rinpoche at any monastery, nunnery, or Dharma center belonging to any school in Greater Tibet. If funds permit, the Foundation can also support practice in India, Bhutan, Nepal, and throughout the Himalayas, and support the practice of sadhanas and similar practices common to all schools of Tibetan Buddhism. Grants can be made for short-term ceremonies (such as three-day, one-week, or ten-day ceremonies) or for long-term ceremonies (such as those that continue for one year or more).

Ananda Light Foundation Governing Directors, Tsering Gellek and Amdo Lama. Assisting Officers, Rosalyn White and Sally Sorenson. The purpose of the Ananda Light Foundation is to ensure that the traditions of the Nyingma school can be preserved and restored throughout Greater Tibet, including dBu and gTsang, Khams, A-mdo, rGyal-rong, and 'Gu-log. To accomplish this goal, the Ananda Light Foundation is authorized to make grants for the following purposes:

To support the practice of sadhanas and pujas
To provide tea, gtor-ma, tshogs, or butter lamps at sadhanas
To support lamas, monks, and nuns during the summer retreat
To create or restore stupas, statues, thankas, or prayer wheels
To build or restore living quarters

To support Dharma publications
For medical facilities or to help sustain the health of lamas
To support the creation or embellishment of Dharma symbols
To restore a tradition associated with a particular monastery or center
To support traditional annual and monthly practices
To support virtuous Dharma activity.

The Light of Buddhadharma Foundation Governing Directors, Wangmo and Richard Dixey. Assisting Officers, Jack Petranker and Nelson Chamma. The inspiration for the Light of Buddhadharma Foundation International is the compassion and wisdom of the Buddha, as expressed in the Buddhadharma and brought forward through the living tradition of the Sangha. The vision and aspiration of the Foundation is to apply the principles of loving compassion to achieve peace and harmony for all humanity. Extending Ven. Tarthang Tulku's work for world peace and the Buddhist heritage, the Foundation's mission is to support preservation and restoration of the shrines and cultural artifacts of the Aryadesha (India); to support pilgrimages and religious ceremonies at the holy places for practitioners of all Buddhist schools and denominations; to support research into and understanding of the texts, practices, and symbols of Buddhism, especially by sponsoring educational events at the holy places; and to promote non-violence and mutual respect among all beings through the worldwide cooperation of men and women of good will.

Mangalam Light Foundation The purpose of the Mangalam Light Foundation is to provide fundraising support for the four grant-making foundations named above.

Inquiries about these foundations or related volunteer possibilities can be directed to Cooordinator, Light Foundations, 2425 Hillside Avenue, Berkeley, CA 94704, or e-mail: bettyc@nyingma.org.

Activities of the Light Foundations

The Light Foundations began operations in 2005. Plans are in progress to encourage Theravadin ceremonies and support the four major Tibetan Buddhist schools. At present, Bodh Gaya will continue to be a major focus of our efforts. The Light of Buddhadharma Foundation plans to contribute to the Buddha Jayanti observance in Bodh Gaya in 2006 by sponsoring fifty Theravadin monks from Sri Lanka, Thailand, India, and elsewhere to assemble under the Bodhi Tree and recite the entire Tipitaka, the sacred texts preserved in Pali. The ceremony will begin after the World Peace Ceremony, about the same time as the Longchen Varna Sadhana. It is possible that monks can stay on longer, giving lectures for a month or so. We would like to support these practices as an annual observance, one that joins Theravadin and Mahayana traditions in a shared purpose: to bring back the unparalleled blessings of this holy place, for the sake of the world and the thousand Buddhas yet to appear.

Lost to the Buddhist world for nine hundred years, Bodh Gaya is once again a living spiritual center, not only for Tibetans in exile, but for all who cherish the thought of freedom and enlightened action in the world. Now that people of many lands come to study and practice at Bodh Gaya, we hope to encourage the return of the two brothers—the Theravada and Mahayana traditions—to other sacred sites also blessed by the presence of the Buddha. Projects intended to revitalize the four major holy places and encourage activities at Nalanda, Rajgir, Samkasya, Shravasti, and other historically important sites include building shrines, organizing pilgrimages, and improving road access.

It is my dream that places sacred to all Buddhists can become a meeting ground for Theravadin and Mahayana practitioners of both East and West. The Light of Buddhadharma Foundation will work to encourage monks of the Theravadin Bharati Sangha to practice at these sites, guide vipassana and samatha meditation, and give seminars and lectures for Westerners who come to India on pilgrimage. Eventually the Foundation may be able to support educational programs at these sacred sites for all Buddhist traditions, in the spirit of the original monastery of Nalanda. Eventually, centers of learning and transmission may take form, as did Nalanda in centuries past, to nourish the vitality of all Buddhist traditions.

The Light of Buddhadharma Foundation is interested in supporting these kinds of activities. TAP will continue to operate in all areas of Buddhadharma service, furthering the Dharma activities of the Theravada and Bodhicitta traditions, the replenishment of libraries throughout Himalayan lands, and the activities of the five Light foundations. If you would like to help or participate in projects related to our purpose, please communicate your interest to TAP.

Opportunities to Rediscover the Holy Places of Tibet

The success of the Tibet pilgrimage tour in 2005 encourages us to plan more pilgrimages to the Land of the Snow Lion. The logistics take at least six months of planning and preparation, and additional on-site research would be very helpful. Tibet is rich in historic sites dating to the sixth and seventh centuries, as well as spiritually powerful meditation retreats abandoned centuries ago and now largely forgotten. Some are mentioned in guides composed by Khyentse Rinpoche, Kathog Siddha, and other Tibetan masters—texts that can guide us today in our efforts to rekindle the light of the Dharma in Tibet.

For modern pilgrims, it is important to get a feeling for the land and culture, to understand what the traditions embody and appreciate what they can give to the world today. Both central and eastern Tibet have beautiful mountains, where caves open to stunning vistas that bring rapture to the heart and clear the mind of confusion. Although the environment has suffered in recent years, the mountains remain—gigantic, snow-capped, and majestic, serene and eternal, rising like Mount Meru far above samsaric concerns. For those seriously involved in the spiritual path, the isolation of these remote retreats accommodates the ripening of virtue, clarity, and insight in ways that cannot easily be duplicated elsewhere today. While other lands may have some quiet places of retreat, the valleys and mountain caves blessed by the meditations of Padmasambhava have a special power that is tangible and unique.

The sacred places allow us to glimpse how Bodhisattvas lived and worked for the Dharma in ancient times. The passage of time has not completely erased the positive energy generated through their practice. Although Tibet—and the world—has changed much in recent years, these sites can still inspire us today with a higher vision of human potential and purpose.

Benefits of Pilgrimage

I hope that Westerners will continue to participate in pilgrimages to the holy places of India and Tibet. These pilgrimages enable TAP to help Tibetan practitioners, and they benefit Westerners as well. Nearly everywhere, life is speeding up more each year; problems erupt ever more forcefully in the environment and amongst people. Hate, anger, and sensual emotions range out of control, creating a difficult and unhealthy atmosphere for humans and non-humans alike. In the world outside, in the internal workings of individuals, beings and nature alike are confused and out of balance, while peace and happiness are nearly impossible to sustain for long.

Buddhism is a symbol of peace and harmony—qualities that are largely lacking today. The prayers of the Sangha, supported by the blessings of the lineage and our own efforts to understand, may be the only way left to invoke the qualities of peace and joy, to generate harmony and compassion, and make the world a stable place for ourselves and future generations. For those who wish to share in these experiences, pilgrimage is an excellent way to begin. TAP and its sister Nyingma organizations can accommodate this interest and recommend how best to proceed.

This book indicates what we have accomplished up to this point in working for the Dharma. If our work can further the Dharma and open opportunities for others to benefit, we are grateful. If it inspires others to carry it further and fill the world with the light of wisdom and compassion, our lives and our work will have been blessed with meaning and value far beyond our aspirations.

Beyond the beliefs of any one religion,
there is the truth of the human spirit.
Beyond the power of nations,
there is the power of the human heart.

Beyond the ordinary mind,
the power of wisdom, love, and healing energy
are at work in the universe.
When we can find peace within our hearts,
we contact these universal powers.
This is our only hope.

Tarthang Tulku

Part Six

My Time is Gone

1959

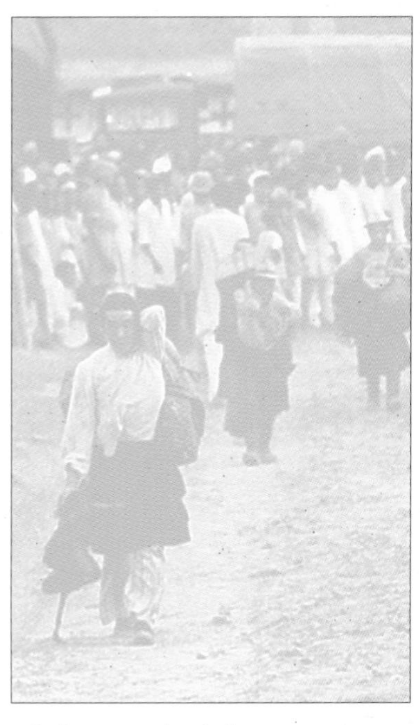

Refugees make their way to camps set up by the government of India.

In March, the Dalai Lama and his close supporters leave Lhasa and make their way to India. Thousands more soon follow. By year's end, around 60,000 Tibetans have sought refuge in Himalayan countries and in India.

Refugee camps are set up in India at Missamari and Buxa Duar, a former British prisoner-of-war facility; refugees are processed, then routed to Ladakh and other camps in northern India, where they are assigned to government-sponsored road construction projects. Overcrowding, exhaustion, heat, diet change, and disease take a heavy toll.

1960

Refugees entering northern India face a profoundly changed way of life.

Buxa Duar transit camp is closed. An educational center established there continues, but problems with disease and sanitary conditions persist. The Indian government establishes the first permanent refugee settlement at Bylakuppe in southern India. The first refugees arrive there in December.

A 70-member drama troupe founded in Dehra Dun begins to tour India to raise funds for refugee settlement in Clement Town.

Rudimentary attempts at education begin within the early transit camps. A residental school for young men opens in Musoorie with 50 students, followed by schools in Simla and Darjeeling.

The Sangha returns to the seat of enlightenment. Tibetan lamas, monks, and nuns gather at the Bodhi Tree to pray for world peace and harmony among all beings.

Refugees move into bamboo shacks in the camp set up at Missamari.

The first Tibetan nursery school, founded in Dharamsala, soon develops into the Tibetan Children's Village.

1961

500 refugees settle in a second Tibetan settlement, founded in January at Kailaspura in Kalimpong.

The Tibetan Medical Center is founded in Dharamsala.

1962

Settlements take form at Tezu in Arunchal Pradesh and at Mundgod and Phuntsokling in remote tribal areas of Orissa, and Tibetan refugees complete the first permanent residences at Bylakuppe. The refugees focus on agriculture and begin to develop cottage industries and market their products in both India and Nepal. In Nepal, Tibetans begin to produce and market rugs, and European relief agencies offer technical assistance.

Refugees begin printing texts using woodblock-based technology.

A small printing press is established in lower Dharamsala to print textbooks in Tibetan. A few lamas begin to set up small presses for printing sacred texts.

At the request of Dudjom Rinpoche, Tarthang Tulku accepts a fellowship at Sanskrit University in Varanasi, where he rents a garage and founds Dharma Mudranalaya. He acquires a small hand-press, creates a Tibetan typeface, and works to learn the basics of printing.

1963

Refugee lamas continue to work to re-establish their culture. The Buddhist School of Dialectics is established.

Progress on starting up Dharma Mudranalaya is slowed by lack of funds. Tarthang Tulku sends out an appeal:

"With good fortune and your help many wonderful ideas could be realized. The press could become a center for study and scholarship. English and Hindi language translations, as well as the Tibetan texts, could be published and the light of Dharma circulated around the world."

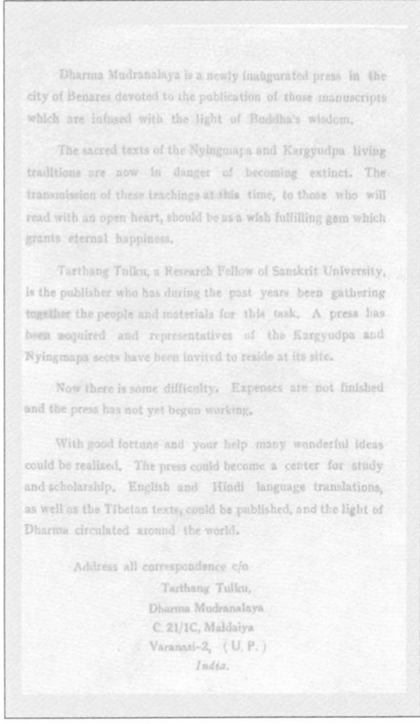

Dharma Mudranalaya is a newly inaugurated press in the city of Benares devoted to the publication of those manuscripts which are infused with the light of Buddha's wisdom.

The sacred texts of the Nyingmapa and Kargyudpa living traditions are now in danger of becoming extinct. The transmission of these teachings at this time, to those who will read with an open heart, should be as a wish fulfilling gem which grants eternal happiness.

Tarthang Tulku, a Research Fellow of Sanskrit University, is the publisher who has during the past years been gathering together the people and materials for this task. A press has been acquired and representatives of the Kargyudpa and Nyingmapa sects have been invited to reside at its site.

Now there is some difficulty. Expenses are not finished and the press has not yet begun working.

With good fortune and your help many wonderful ideas could be realized. The press could become a center for study and scholarship. English and Hindi language translations, as well as the Tibetan texts, could be published, and the light of Dharma circulated around the world.

Address all correspondence c/o
Tarthang Tulku,
Dharma Mudranalaya
C.21/1C, Maldaiya
Varanasi-2, (U. P.)
India.

Announcing the formation of Dharma Mudranalaya, Sarnath.

1964–1965

After several years of learning and preparation, Dharma Mudranalaya readies and prints its first typeset books: works by Klong-chen-pa, Lama Mi-pham, and dPal-sprul Rinpoche.

Tibetans establish cottage industries in exile. Rug weaving thrives in Nepal.

1967

A Tibetan monastery is founded at Clement Town.

The center for scholarly studies established at Buxa Duar in 1960 is closed and a new center is planned for Sarnath. 60 lamas from the four major schools are sent to Mussoorie for training in operating the new center: 56 are Gelugpa, 4 are Sakya, 2 are Kagyu, and 2 are Nyingma.

Many refugees become laborers on road crews in northern India.

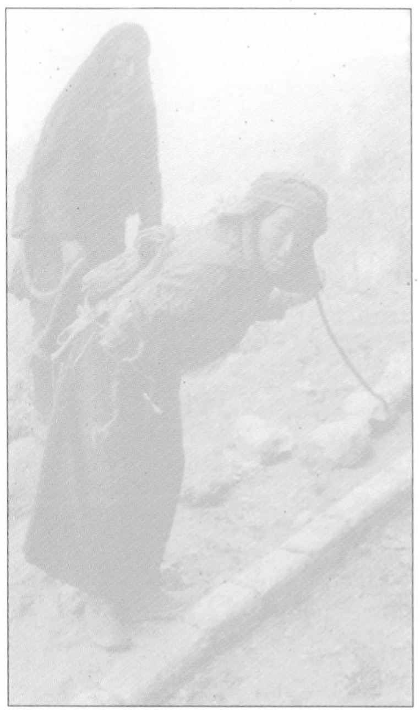

Men and women alike work hard, doing heavy labor to survive.

1968

The Central Institute of Higher Tibetan Studies is founded in Sarnath; affiliated with Sanskrit University until 1977, it is staffed by the monks and lamas trained in Mussoorie.

After publishing twenty major texts he had brought with him to India, Tarthang Tulku leaves India with his family; traveling first to France, he continues on to America and arrives in New York.

1969

Thirty thousand refugees are now resettled into permanent sites in India, Nepal, and Bhutan. Many thousands more continue to work on road gangs and move from place to place as the work requires.

TNMC Tarthang Tulku arrives in Berkeley and establishes the Tibetan Nyingma Meditation Center (TNMC). As Head Lama of TNMC, he communicates the urgency of the plight of Tibetan refugees to students, who assist in collecting clothing, vitamins, medicines, and other useful items to send to Tibetan refugees. Wishing to assist Tibetan refugees seeking to survive in new lands, he works to find ways of providing basic humanitarian aid such as food, clothing, and supplies.

"After I came to America and opened the Tibetan Nyingma Meditation Center in 1969, my students and I did whatever we could to help the Tibetan refugees. We collected old clothes, shoes, and vitamins and sent them to

India. At one point we even shipped tons of survival biscuits from Civil Defense bomb shelters in Los Angeles. This project presented a tremendous task of coordination and communication for our small group, but the benefit to the refugees was less than we had hoped, because the food did not keep well in the Indian heat. Our later efforts were more successful.

—Tarthang Tulku

Children also work hard gathering wood for cooking and heating.

Pen Friend Program The Head Lama initiates a pen friend program, asking students to send ten dollars each month to a refugee in need of assistance. He establishes the Tibetan Aid Project to facilitate the program and assigns a student to help with communication and correspondence.

Head Lama of TNMC Receives letters from Tibetan refugees; responds to all correspondence written in Tibetan; continues to encourage participation in the Pen Friend Program and trains a few students to keep records of correspondence and connect Tibetans with American pen friends.

Storytellers play an important role in sustaining cultural traditions.

1970

Support for Refugees The Head Lama receives and responds to an increasing flow of letters from Tibetan refugees. TAP works to obtain pictures of refugees and their living situations in India to compile information for pen friends and communicate to the West the refugees' desperate need for humanitarian aid.

Tarthang Tulku arrives in Berkeley in 1969 and begins relief efforts.

This 1970 brochure announces the purpose and vision of TNMC.

Pen Friend Program The Head Lama continues to encourage participation in the Pen Friend Program and urges students to ask friends traveling to India to hand-carry medical supplies, funds, vitamins, and other essentials.

Transmitting Funds Various methods for transferring funds to Tibetans are implemented over the years, but problems remain. The number of pen friends continues to grow as more people learn of the efforts Tibetans are making to survive and reestablish their culture.

Head Lama of TNMC Continues to address issues related to the difficulties and sufferings of the refugees. Through TNMC, contributes funds regularly to leaders of the traditions.

Fundraising TAP, which is not set up to receive and distribute funds directly, holds rummage and flea market sales to raise funds for the construction of Zangs-mdog dPal-ri, a Nyingma monastery in India. Volunteers raise funds through crafts fairs, rummage sales, auctions, concerts, film benefits, and seminars.

1971

Developments in India The Tibetan Library of Works and Archives is founded in Dharamsala. A major cultural center, its library and museum house over 20,000 manuscripts and a permanent photographic exhibit.

Pen Friend Program Continues to gather information on the problems of the refugees; responds to problems reported by pen friends with transmitting funds. About two hundred

Westerners are now participating in the Pen Friend Program.

Supporting Relocation Efforts The Head Lama initiates research on the legal requirements for bringing lamas to America to prepare for teaching students interested in traditional studies and translation.

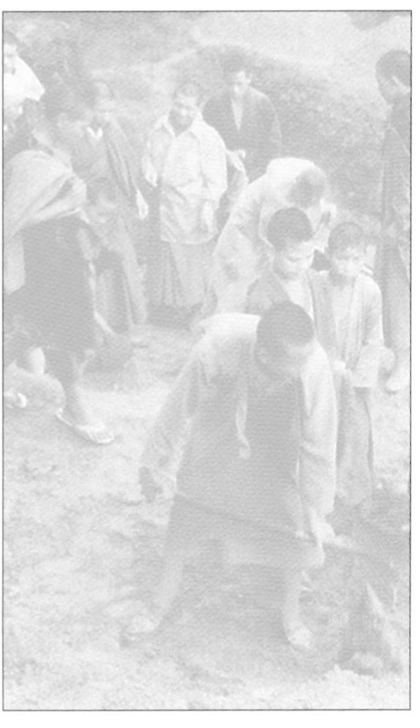

Lamas begin work on rebuilding the monastery of Zangs-mdog dPal-ri.

1972

Fundraising An office for the Tibetan Aid Project is established at Padma Ling, the headquarters of TNMC in Berkeley. TAP volunteers prepare bulk mailings in an effort to reach out to a wider public.

Supporting Relocation Efforts TNMC directs research into immigration procedures and ways to bring Tibetan lamas to the U.S. Initiates applications for seed-money grants for the creation of a self-supporting country center for Tibetan refugees and Western Dharma students.

Teachers make do with improvised blackboards in open-air courtyards.

Sponsoring Ceremonies Working through TAP, TNMC begins to sponsor ceremonies for the four Tibetan Buddhist schools: repetitions of the rGyal-wa bKa'-'gyur Rinpoche ceremony involving a recitation of the 108 volume bKa'-'gyur, the word of the Buddha; readings of the Heart Sutra, Bhaishajyaguru (Healing Buddha) Prayers, Sitatapatra (White Umbrella) Prayers, the Ye Dharma mantra, bSam-pa lhun-'grub ceremonies, recitations of the Manjushri-namasamgiti, and sadhanas for specific realizations. More than 1,000 ceremonies have been sponsored, not including the World Peace Ceremony.

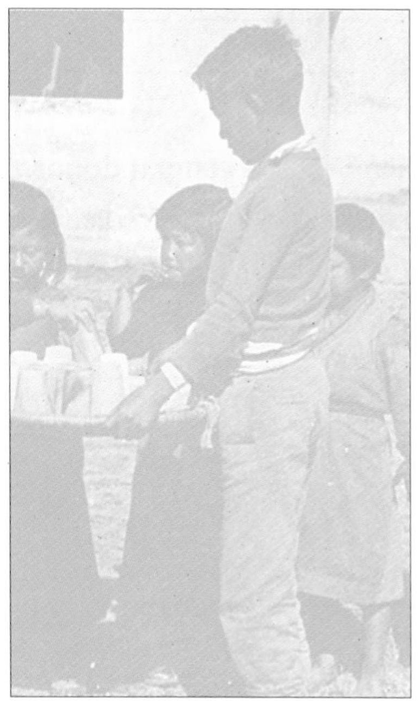

The older children help the younger, sustaining the spirit of community.

Supporting Relocation Efforts TNMC continues to research immigration procedures and apply for foundation grants to secure a country center and bring Tibetan lamas to the U.S.

Connecting to the Lineage TNMC/TAP host the visit of H.H. Dudjom Rinpoche and Lama Gyaltrul Domang. His Holiness blesses the opening of TNMC's second art exhibit and gives initiations to TNMC students.

1973

Pen Friend Program Estimated aid given to refugees through the Pen Friend Program from 1969 through 1973 averages $36,000 each year.

Supporting Relocation Efforts Efforts are mounted to establish immigration procedures for Tibetans. TNMC seeks support from the federal government for bringing sixty Nyingma lamas and their families to the United States to teach and translate. These efforts extend over many years and eventually reach to Washington, where friends seek information and advice. But they are ultimately unsuccessful.

Gesar News becomes TNMC's "wind horse," a vehicle for communication.

Distributing Information TNMC publishes the first issue of *Gesar News,* a magazine established to inform TNMC members and provide a forum for them to share their experiences. *Gesar News* encourages travelers to carry medicines and supplies to the refugees in India and reports on their efforts. It provides a vehicle for informing supporters how the Tibetan schools are surviving in India and how individuals are working to reestablish their culture.

1974

Administration An office for TAP is established at Dharma Press' facilities on Doyle Street in Emeryville, which is staffed by a group of five volunteers.

Administrative Developments *Gesar News*, expanded and renamed *Gesar Magazine*, reports that responses from supporters indicate that pen friends are experiencing continuing difficulties in sending funds to India. The Head Lama decides to create a corporation empowered to receive and distribute funds directly.

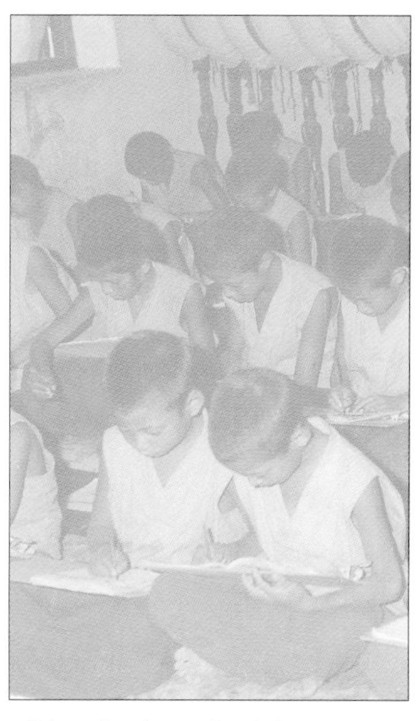

Education immediately becomes a high priority for young Tibetans.

Incorporation On November 8. after several years of assisting Western pen friends with the complexities of sending funds to India, TAP is incorporated as the Tibetan Nyingma Relief Foundation (TNRF), a California non-profit public benefit corporation, corporate registration number 725771. Corporation later receives tax-exempt status as a religious and charitable organization under California Revenue and Taxation Code section 23701(d) and the Internal Revenue Code sections 501(c)(3), 170(b)(1)(A)(ii).

Fundraising The board of directors. composed of TNMC and Nyingma Institute staff, immediately establishes a fundraising program, hosting benefit dinners, talks, and slide shows. From October to December, TAP/TNRF raises almost $10,000.

Continuing their traditions in exile: scenes from the refugee camps.

Pen Friend Program TAP reports show that as of November, 1974, six hundred Tibetan

H. H. Gyalwa Karmapa addresses students at the Nyingma Institute.

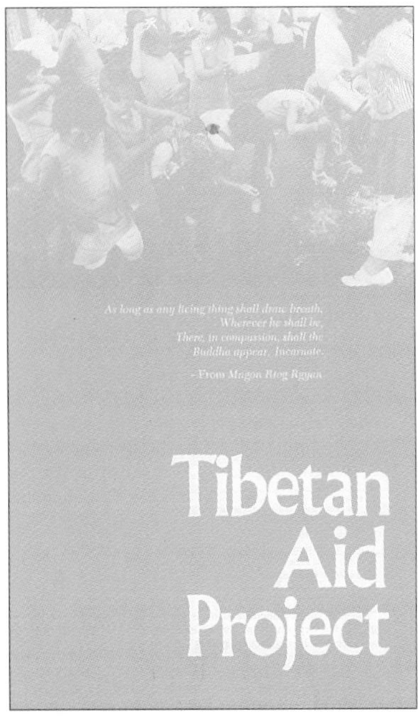

TAP begins to invite participation in its programs and benefits.

lamas and students have received ongoing support through the Pen Friend Program.

"Through the Pen Friend Program, hundreds of Americans were able to help Tibetan refugees in India, Nepal, and Bhutan. Encouraged by TAP and its activities, many Americans also gave direct aid independently. In 1974, when TAP was reorganized under the Tibetan Nyingma Relief Foundation, the Pen Friend Program continued and later became active in Europe and South America as well. Through TAP and TNRF, many people have been able to help support the new refugee monasteries."

—Tarthang Tulku

Lama Visits Sponsored H. H. Sakya Trizin, spiritual leader of the Sakya school, visits the Nyingma centers in late August and gives blessings to the Nyingma community.

H. H. Gyalwa Karmapa, head of the Karma Kagyud school, visits the Nyingma centers, presides over the Black Hat ceremony at Padma Ling, and gives blessings to TNMC students in October.

Support for Monastery Construction TNMC initiates an effort to raise funds for Ven. Penor Rinpoche's Nyingma Monastery in Bylakuppe, South India, which is under construction but badly in need of assistance. In December, TAP sends an emergency contribution for the monastery's 250 lamas. Through an announcement in *Gesar Magazine,* TAP invites readers to donate directly to the monastery.

1975

Expanding Services TAP begins to supplement the Pen Friend program by sending books and thanka reproductions, supporting ceremonies, and hosting visits of high lamas to the United States.

Direct Aid: Food In a time of food shortages in India, TAP organizes a large food shipment to Tibetan refugees, which the Catholic Relief Service agrees to match and raises funds for shipping.

Fundraising TAP sponsors six benefits in the second quarter of 1975, including piano concerts and an all-day crafts fair in San Mateo. The first benefit concert is held in October.

A two-day benefit seminar titled "The Tibetan Approach to Emotional Balance," held at the University of Southern California in Los Angeles, is attended by more than two hundred mental and physical health professionals. TAP distributes tapes of this program as part of its fundraising efforts.

Humanitarian Aid TAP supports a medical program in progress and needs to find reliable sources for delivering aid, but difficulties in transmitting funds to India continue.

Receipts & Disbursements In January and February, 1975 TAP raises $3,400 in funds and distributes $1,400 in direct relief; $2,000 is saved for shipping a massive donation of food to India, and additional fundraising is undertaken to raise the balance of the shipping costs.

H.H. Sakya Trizin visits Padma Ling and the Nyingma Institute, 1974.

Dances performed by lamas convey central aspects of ceremonies.

H. H. Dilgo Rinpoche performs ceremonies at Padma Ling and Odiyan.

TAP raises and disburses $18,407 to monasteries and refugees in India, Nepal, and Sikkim during TNRF's first fiscal year.

1976

Lama Visits Sponsored H. H. Dudjom Rinpoche, head of the Nyingma school, and the distinguished Nyingma masters H. H. Dilgo Khyentse visit the Nyingma centers and give talks and blessings to numerous guests. H. H. Dilgo Khyentse, accompanied by Zhechen Rabjam, performs ceremonies at Padma Ling and at Odiyan.

Fundraising TAP invests $4,226 in production of the Jataka Tales, a series of children's books based on the previous lives of the Buddha. By arrangement with Dharma Publishing, TAP receives half of profit from sales.

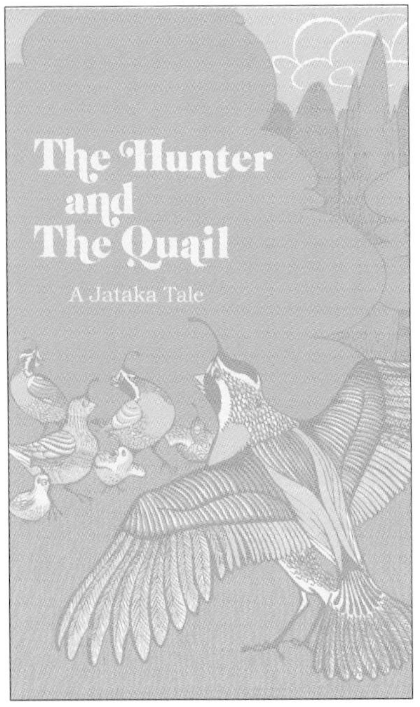

Jatakas adapted for children support relief efforts for children of refugees.

A second benefit concert is held in San Francisco in February and a third on May 16 at Stanford University.

Receipts & Disbursements From November 1, 1975 to October 31, 1976, TNRF's second full fiscal year: Receipts: $34,947 in donations, sales of the Jataka Tales and fund-raising events, and savings account interest. Disbursements: $35,975; $17,970 in relief funds to refugees living in India and Nepal; $9,201 for visiting lamas and immigration expenses; $2,014 for office expenses; the remainder for costs of fundraising amd producing Jataka Tales. TAP also distributes $3,151 from Americans to their Tibetan pen friends. Overhead is kept to the barest minimum and no salaries are paid, enabling nearly all funds raised to be sent to Tibetans.

1977

Ceremony Sponsorship To maintain and sponsor traditional Buddhist ceremonies in all four schools in Nepal, India, and Sikkim, donates more than $25,000 between 1974 and June 1977. These funds also provide general assistance to the Dharamsala Clinic and other worthy efforts, and support the visits of H. H. Dudjom Rinpoche, H. H. Dilgo Khyentse Rinpoche, H. H. Karmapa, Dodrup Chen Rinpoche, Lama Gyaltrul, Lama Jigtse, Thinley Norbu, and Tulku Thondup (who visits in 1978).

H.H. Dudjom Rinpoche (left) visits Odiyan and blesses the land, 1976.

Monastery Support TNMC directs fundraising and disbursement of $25,000 to monasteries and lamas in India, Nepal, and Sikkim during TNRF's third fiscal year.

Pen Friend Program TNMC works out problems with banking procedures encountered by pen friends in sending funds to India. More than one thousand pen friends are now sending monthly assistance to Tibetans.

Fundraising TAP mounts a spring mailing of 25,000 brochures to increase resources for ceremony support. Income generated: $5,000 in donations and pledges for further donations. Total receipts, 1974–June 30, 1977: $78,000.

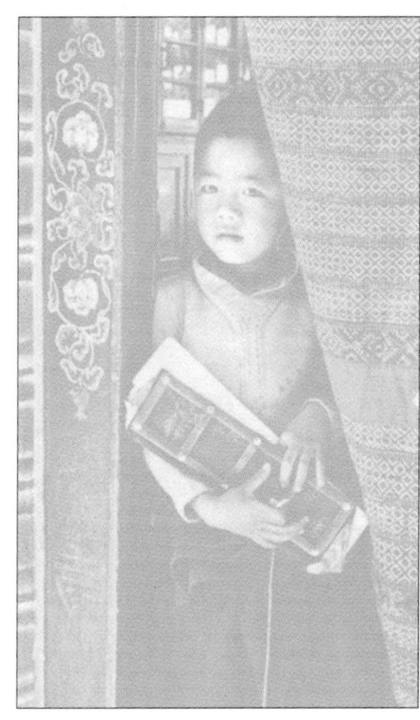

This young monk came to symbolize TAP's wish to support education.

Receipts & Disbursements Total receipts, 1974–June 30, 1977: $78,300. This represents $50,770 in donations; $19,727 from Pen Friends; $5,473 from Special Projects; $1,418 in Jataka

Tales royalties; and $1,910 in interest. Total disbursements, $84,081: relief support, $51,530; Pen Friend distribution, $20,122; and the rest for office, promotion, and food transportation costs. Jointly, TNMC and TAP disburse over $100,000 between 1974 and 1977 on behalf of Tibetan refugees.

H.H. the Dalai Lama addresses the public at the Nyingma Institute.

1978

Sponsoring Ceremonies TNMC requests H.H. Dilgo Khyentse to preside over 100,000 recitations of the Bhadracarya-pranidhana-raja at Bodh Gaya in 1978 and arranges funding.

Receipts & Disbursements Between November 1977 and September 1978, TAP receives $11,520 in donations, $6,970 to distribute for pen friends, $5,119 as income from special projects, $2,359 as income from Jataka Tales, and $199 in interest. Total receipts: $26,170. TAP disburses $16,068, including $8,178 for direct relief and $5,206 for pen friends (the remainder is distributed after the close of the present fiscal year).

A poster produced by TAP to encourage pen friend participation.

1979

Lama Visits In October, H. H. Tenzin Gyatso, the 14th Dalai Lama, addresses a public assembly at the Nyingma Institute and blesses *The Nyingma Edition of the bKa'-'gyur and bsTan-'gyur,* which is being prepared for production at Padma Ling, headquarters of TNMC.

Pen Friend Program TAP continues its longstanding Pen Friend Program and increases donations for the building of monasteries, stupas, the restoration of statues, and the creation of paintings and other ritual materials.

Sponsoring Ceremonies TNMC generates a stronger focus on ceremonies and support for educational facilities to train a new generation of Tibetan teachers and support long-range cultural preservation.

Preserving Sacred Texts The Head Lama initiates and directs the preparation, design, and production of *The Nyingma Edition of the bKa'-'gyur and bsTan-'gyur.*

Receipts & Disbursements Between November 1978 and October 1979, TAP receives $7,952 in donations, $2,734 to distribute for pen friends, $916 in royalties from Jataka Tales, and $126 from interest and miscellaneous sources, for a total income of $11,729. Disbursements include $6,986 in direct relief and $4,894 distributed on behalf of pen friends. Total disbursements: $13,283.

Presiding lamas during a ceremony at Tashi Jong, near Dharamsala.

1980

Pen Friend Program As of March, TAP has received 2,000 requests for pen friends from Westerners. Estimating that a minimum of 200 people send $15 per month to their Tibetan pen friends, total support from 1969 through March 1980 comes to $405,000. Since 1974, when TNRF became able to distribute funds directly, TAP has disbursed an additional $33,073 to Tibetan pen friends on behalf of Western sponsors, as well as $25,901 in direct relief. The combined total of TNMC and TAP disbursements for

Lamas rehearse dance movements for a ceremony at Tashi Jong.

Monks and nuns of Golok welcome Tarthang Tulku home in 1983.

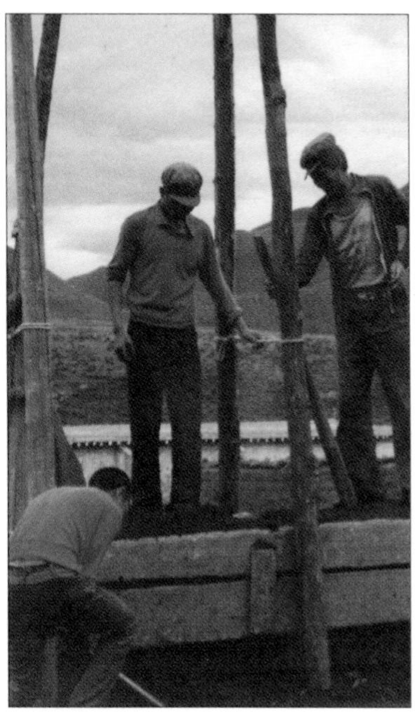
The monastery and its temple are rebuilt from the ground up.

support to refugees from 1969 to March, 1980 reaches $577,905.

Ceremony sponsorship and travel support Between 1976 and March, 1980, TNMC disbursed $66,717 to sponsor ceremonies in India and Nepal and $47,214 to sponsor immigration and visits by high lamas of all Tibetan schools.

Preserving Sacred Texts TNMC and Dharma Publishing combine resources to begin production of *The Nyingma Edition of the bKa'-'gyur and bsTan-'gyur.*

1981–1988

Re-orienting Priorities Major humanitarian aims have been met; the Pen Friend Program continues, and TAP operates on a smaller scale. TNMC steps up support for ceremonies, reconstruction of Tarthang Monastery in Tibet, education, and donations of sacred texts and art to Tibetans in Tibet and in exile.

1981

Sponsoring Ceremonies TNMC sponsors prayer ceremonies in India, Nepal, Sikkim, and Bhutan, including 100,000 recitations of the Manjushri-namasamgiti at Bodh Gaya. When H. H. Dilgo Khyentse is unable to attend the ceremony in Bodh Gaya, the ceremony is carried out by the Rinpoches Dodrup Chen and Dechen Dorje. Total disbursed for ceremonies in 1981: $20,701.

Preserving Sacred Texts *The Nyingma Edition of the bKa'-'gyur and bsTan-'gyur* is published, and distribution to research institutions begins. Plans are made to continue this work.

1983–1984

Support for the Sangha in Tibet The Head Lama visits his homeland in 'Gu-log, eastern Tibet, for the first time in thirty years and finds Tarthang Monastery monastery completely destroyed. Determines to support local efforts to rebuild the monastery and sponsor those wishing to continue lead a religious life. To honor his teacher, Dar-thang mChog-sprul Rinpoche, he offers funds for a stupa to be placed in the monastery's temple.

The 33′ golden stupa built in honor of Dar-thang mChog-sprul Rinpoche.

Reconstruction of Tarthang Monastery The Head Lama initiates the construction of a temple for the thirty lamas living in temporary quarters and provides an endowment of $50,000 for rebuilding: $58,000 is added to this amount in 1984.

During construction, the burial place of Dar-thang mChog-sprul Rinpoche, Tarthang Tulku's teacher, is located. TNMC sponsors a 33′ relic stupa and provides jewels, silver, and gold-leaf for ornamentation. The stupa is housed in the monastery's temple.

Lamas review progress in rebuilding Tarthang Monastery in Tibet.

1985

Sponsoring Ceremonies Funds contributed to sponsor ceremonies in all four major schools of Tibetan Buddhism between January 1976 and March 1985 total $128,327.

Ven. Dzongsar Khyentse Rinpoche visits TNMC, 1986.

1986

Lama Visits Sponsored Dzongsar Khyentse Rinpoche, the reincarnation of 'Jam-dbyangs mKhyen-brtse Chos-kyi-blo-gros, greets TNMC students at Padma Ling and gives a talk at the Nyingma Institute.

Support for Reconstruction The Head Lama visits eastern Tibet for the second time, for a period of ten weeks. Reviews progress on rebuilding Tarthang Monastery and offers additional funds of $137,417 towards construction of an eighty-three room philosophical school, one hundred prayer wheels, paintings and sculptures for the main temple, and ceremonies at Tarthang and other monasteries.

TNMC guides this overview of the origins of Tibetan land and culture.

1987

Support for Education To support educational programs, TNMC donates to Tibetan monasteries in Asia three sets of *The Nyingma Edition of the sDe-dge bKa'-'gyur and bsTan-'gyur*, thirty-four copies of the *Guide to the Nyingma Edition*, thirty-three sets of *The Fortunate Aeon* (Bhadrakalpika Sutra), eighteen copies of *Ancient Tibet*, twenty copies of the *Dhammapada*, and 1,225 thanka reproductions.

Sponsoring Ceremonies Sponsors ceremonies at thirty-one centers, including memorial prayers for H. H. Dudjom Rinpoche; Tara Prayers and recitations of the Heart Sutra and bSam-pa Lhun-grub; and twenty-one recitations of the bKa'-'gyur Rinpoche, the words of the Buddha in 108 Tibetan volumes. Provides funds for construction and publishing projects at three monasteries. TAP/TNMC sponsorship of ceremonies for the four Tibetan Buddhist schools since 1976 totals $227,733.

1988

Sponsoring Ceremonies As monasteries are established in the Tibetan refugee communities, TNMC focuses on support for traditional practices, ceremonies, and education. The Head Lama visits Nepal, offers funds for a hundred thousand recitations of Tara prayers and other traditional ceremonies.

Completed, the temple of Tarthang Monastery opens for practice.

Support for Schools and Education Noting a great need for building up the intellectual side of a traditional Dharma education, the Head Lama explores with Tarthang Chogtrul Rinpoche the possibility of establishing a philosophical school in Kathmandu, which leads to the founding of the Nyingma Institute of Nepal. TNMC provides financial support for the housing and educational program for 108 monks and engages Khenpo Rigzin to guide the Institute's programs.

Support for Reconstruction in Tibet The Head Lama visits Tarthang Monastery in 'Gulog, eastern Tibet, for the third time to review the progress of its shedra's educational programs and donates one million yüan for construction of the new temple for a thousand lamas. Gives 1,020,000 yüan (about $290,000) for completion of the Tarthang shedra.

Monks of Tarthang Monastery bring the Nyingma Edition to the temple.

Support for Education in Tibet The Head Lama donates two copies of The *Nyingma Edition* and a set of the bKa'-ma, texts especially

Tarthang Tulku hosts the visit of Khyentse Sangyum-ma at Odiyan.

Yeshe De staff hand-binds volumes of *Great Treasures of Ancient Teachings*.

important to the Nyingma tradition, to support the monks' education and practice.

Sacred Art Shipping and Distribution TAP offers more than $1,000 for shipping thankas directly to Tibetan monasteries in India and Nepal.

Fundraising To support the Head Lama's efforts, TAP begins to expand its donor base and develop its fundraising capacities.

Sponsoring Lama Visits TAP sponsors the visit of Khyentse Sangyum-ma, widow of 'Jam-dbyangs mKhyen-brtse Chos-kyi-blo-gros, to Odiyan and the Nyingma centers in Berkeley.

1989

Mission Expands TAP's priorities expand to include revitalization of Tibet's religious and cultural heritage: building monasteries and nunneries, supporting monks and nuns through the Pen Friend Program, contributing funds to the World Peace Ceremony in India and Nepal, and transporting sacred texts and sacred art to replenish monasteries and nunneries. In December, 1989, TAP contributes $7,077 toward the cost of transporting texts and art to be distributed at the first World Peace Ceremony.

Sponsoring Ceremonies TNMC sponsors 100,000 recitations of the Manjushri-nama-samgiti and offerings of butterlamps and other traditional substances at five Gelugpa temples including Sera and Drepung. These recitations are performed during 1989 and 1990.

TNRF and TNMC's combined contributions to ceremonies conducted within the four major schools of Tibetan Buddhism total $247,233 from 1976–April 1989, in addition to direct aid and donations of sacred texts and art.

The Mahabodhi Temple, Bodh Gaya, site of the World Peace Ceremony.

Re-establishing a Tradition: The World Peace Ceremony TNMC sponsors and organizes the 25-day first World Peace Ceremony at Bodh Gaya and provides for repair and ornamentation of the Mahabodhi temple. The Head Lama personally establishes the program of recitations for the ceremony, which centers on a hundred thousand repetitions of the Manjushri-nama-samgiti, said by dGa'-rab rDo-rje, Vimalamitra, Padmasambhava, and Rong-zom Mahapandita to embody the highest Nyingma teachings. Total expenses for this ceremony, including travel and donations to lamas and monasteries, come to $248,748.

Donating Sacred Texts The Head Lama distributes to ceremony participants 800 copies of Tibetan texts prepared in Berkeley.

1990

TAP International TAP establishes offices in TNMC-affiliated Nyingma centers in Holland, Germany, and Brazil. All centers generate support for the Pen Friend Program and sponsor special events to raise funds for TAP projects.

Monks circumambulate the Temple daily to open and close the ceremony.

Support for Education and Ceremonies TNMC offers $26,086 to support educational programs and ceremonies at the Tamang Buddhist Association, Darjeeling; Shechen Dargye Ling, Kathmandu, Nepal; Ka-Nying Shedrup

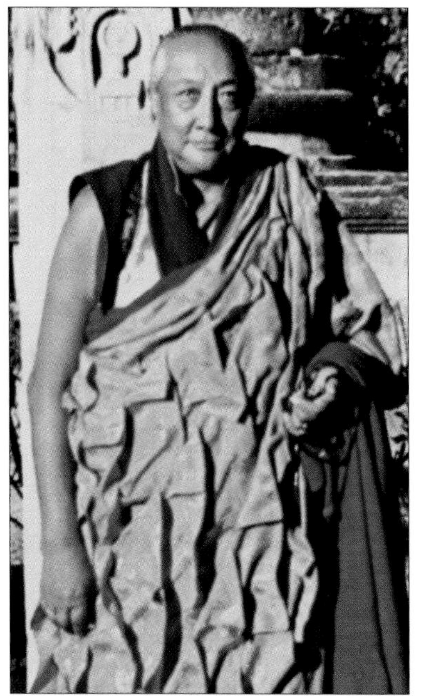

Dilgo Khyentse Rinpoche supports the ceremony in January 1991.

Ling, Nepal; Asura Caves, Nepal; and the Nyingma Institute of Nepal. The Head Lama donates additional funds to establish endowments for Tarthang Monastery and Se dGon-pa in Tibet.

Sends funds to Bodh Gaya, requesting prayers in which all donors' names are read to the assembly of two thousand monks beside the Mahabodhi Temple.

1991

Sponsoring Ceremonies TNMC sponsors the second World Peace Ceremony. H. H. Dilgo Khyentse presides during the opening days but withdraws due to illness and passes away later in 1991. Prayers are offered in commemoration.

TAP sponsors publication of an historic account of Tibetan refugees.

Support for Education and Preservation TAP ships 82 boxes containing 1,760 sacred texts and 1,944 thankas by air freight to the second World Peace Ceremony in January at a cost of $11,200. Later in 1991, TAP pledges to continue supporting the shipping of books and art to the World Peace Ceremonies.

Information and Documentation TAP and Dharma Publishing cooperate in producing *From the Roof of the World,* an account of the Tibetan refugees compiled to preserve an accurate historical record for future generations. The volume draws heavily upon twenty years of concerted efforts by TNMC and TAP to support the refugees and presents pictures and news received from the refugee centers:

"Our primary purpose in preparing this book is to offer these images to the refugees themselves, that they may more fully understand and appreciate the value of the experiences recorded here. In keeping with the policies TAP and TNMC have followed since their earliest days, TAP will use all proceeds from the sale of the book to benefit the Tibetan refugees." —Tarthang Tulku

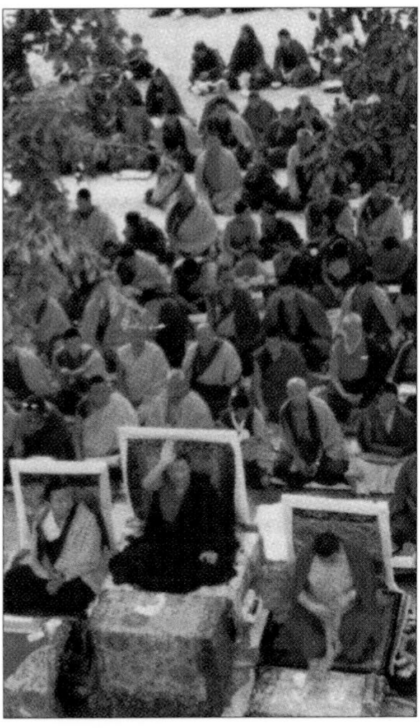

Minling Trichen and his disciples at the World Peace Ceremony 1992.

Shipping of Sacred Texts and Art For distribution at the third World Peace Ceremony at Bodh Gaya in 1992, TAP ships 14,000 books and 25,000 sacred art prints to India by ocean freight at a cost of $12,500. Filling three containers, this shipment is the largest quantity of books brought into India up to that time.

1992

Documentation and Information *From the Roof of the World: Refugees of Tibet,* is distributed to participants in the World Peace Ceremony.

Monks participating in the ceremony continue their practice of prostrations.

Sponsoring Ceremonies The Head Lama sponsors and participates in the third World Peace Ceremony at Bodh Gaya, where he offers a fresh coating of white lime for the ancient Animeshcalocana Stupa, directs the distribution of books and thankas and holds planning sessions with the leaders of the six major monastic traditions of the Nyingma school. He continues to work with high lamas of the Gelug, Kagyu, and Sakya traditions to establish World Peace ceremonies in Sarnath, Kushinagara, and Lumbinī.

The Head Lama visits sMin-grol-gling, offers support for statues and repairs.

Tarthang Tulku visits the Asura Caves in Nepal with Chokyi Nyima.

In Nepal, TNMC sponsors New Year celebrations for the communities from the Tibetan provinces of 'Gu-log and mDo-smad.

Shipping of Sacred Texts and Art For distribution at the fourth World Peace Ceremony at Bodh Gaya in 1993, TAP raises funds for shipping 8,000 books and 12,100 thanka prints, The cost comes to $17,260.

1993

Support for Monks and Nuns In Nepal, TNMC offers support for sixty students for one year at Ka-Nying Shedrup Ling, headed by Chokyi Nyima; offers one year of support for retreatants guided by Urgyen Tulku at Asura Caves.

TNMC sponsors three hundred nuns for one year at Shug-gseb gompa.

Support for Reconstruction in Tibet The Head Lama enters Tibet on March 22 in company with Khochen Tulku to visit holy places in central Tibet. In Tibet, he offers support for reconstruction, repair of statues, ceremonies, and staff expenses to bSam-yas, gYa'-ma-lung, mChims-phu, rDo-rje-brag, sMin-grol-gling, Shug-gseb, 'Phyongs-rgyas dPal-ri, and Tshe-ring-ljongs. Later offers support also to Gangs-ri Thod-dkar, mKhar-chu, Yar-lung Shel-brag, Ti-gro, Brag Yang-rdzong, Seng-ge-rdzong, Khra-brug, Yer-pa, 'U-yug, and other places in the central regions of dBus and gTsang.

To revitalize the bKa'-dgongs- phur-gsum, special practices of the bKa'-'ma and gTer-ma lineages in Tibet, India, Bhutan, and Nepal, the Head Lama establishes the Ka-Ter Foundation. The Foundation is to promote and spread the teachings of the sNga-'gyur-rnying-ma lineages in Tibet, India, Bhutan, and Nepal.

Offerings for Ceremonies TAP sponsors the printing of 50,000 images of Padmasambhava for distribution to lay people in India and Tibet, and offers a symbolic donation of $108 for thread for World Peace Ceremony banners.

Sponsoring Ceremonies The Head Lama sponsors and participates in the 1993 World Peace Ceremony, where he distributes sacred texts and thanka prints, makes offerings to the lineages, and offers gold leaf for the statue of the Buddha.

Tarthang Rinpoche visits monasteries in central Tibet.

TNMC sponsors World Peace Ceremonies in Lumbini (Sakya and Kagyu) and in Sarnath (Gelug) in January and February, 1993.

Establishing Foundations for the Future In concert with Penor Rinpoche and other prominent Nyingma lamas, the Head Lama founds the Nyingma International Monlam Chenmo Foundation in India to continue the World Peace Ceremony in perpetuity. Seven Nyingma lamas agree to serve as its directors. Beginning in 1994, Nyingma organizations in Asia assume responsibility for administering and coordinating the annual ceremony.

Disseminating Information TAP establishes an information archive to assemble published information and photographs relating to the situation in Tibet. Projects are initiated to develop information about Tibetan history and

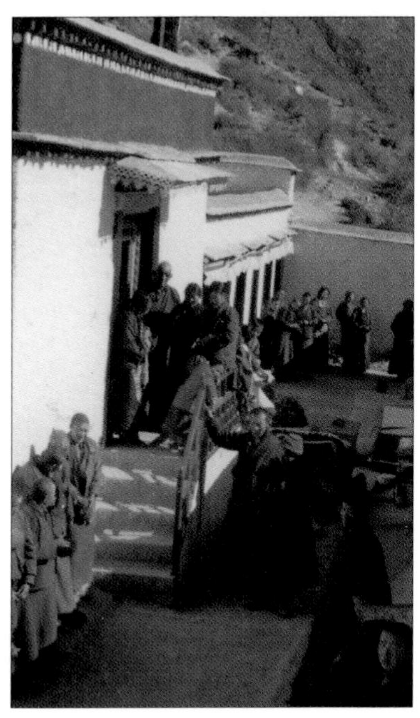

TNMC sponsors 300 nuns for a year at Shugs-gseb gompa.

Visit to rDo-rje-brag, one of the six major Nyingma monasteries.

Monument to enlightenment: the Mahabodhi temple and stupa, 1993.

civilization through films, lectures, brochures, and larger publications.

Administration TAP's donor base expands from 86 in 1988 to 441 and annual income increases to $113,580. The staff increases from two part-time directors and one part-time staff member to two part-time directors and four staff (two full-time, two part-time).

Expanding Outreach TAP increases activities and establishes two offices in Berkeley and one in Los Angeles.

Support for Traditional Practice The Head Lama initiates the preparation of banners and prayer wheels. He designs four 10′ x 33′ appliqué hangings for ornamenting the sides of the Mahabodhi Temple at Bodh Gaya during the next World Peace Ceremony. He also selects forty-two texts and prayers from the bKa'-'gyur, including the Eight Thousand-line Prajnaparamita, to create the "Dharma Wheel Cutting Karma," a new hand-turned prayer wheel to be offered to participants in the 1994 World Peace Ceremony.

Information and Publications TAP sponsors publication of *World Peace Ceremony, Bodh Gaya,* a history of Bodh Gaya and a photographic documentary of the ceremonies from 1989–93. This book is prepared for distribution to TAP donors and participants at the fifth World Peace Ceremony in 1994.

Shipping of Sacred Texts and Art In December, for distribution at the fifth World Peace Ceremony at Bodh Gaya in 1994, TAP ships

2,000 books, 28,230 thanka prints, and 9,000 prayer wheels to India.

1994

Expansion of World Peace Ceremonies TNMC sponsors World Peace Ceremonies for all four schools: Nyingma in Bodh Gaya, Gelug in Sarnath, Kagyu in Lumbini, and Sakya in Boudha, Nepal. Participates in the Nyingma Monlam in Bodh Gaya; distributes two thousand books and three thousand thanka reproductions. After the ceremony, the Head Lama leads TNMC representatives on pilgrimage to Shravasti, Kushinagara, Rajagriha, Sarnath, and Kathmandu, then sponsors and participates in a one-day Four Schools Monlam held at the Great Stupa of Boudha, near Kathmandu.

The Head Lama arranges funding of the 1994 World Peace Ceremony. Costs come to $317,916.

Support for the Four Schools TNMC offers seed money for three new foundations to provide support for continuing the Monlam Chenmo ceremonies of the Sarma schools. These foundations are established to guarantee that at least one thousand practitioners of each tradition can come together for annual observances dedicated to world peace. The Sakya Foundation is headed by H. H. Sakya Trizin, the Kagyu Foundation by Ven. Chokyi Nyima Rinpoche, and the Gelugpa Foundation by Ven. Samdong Rinpoche.

The Head Lama formulates plans for a second Nyingma ceremony to be held at Sarnath after

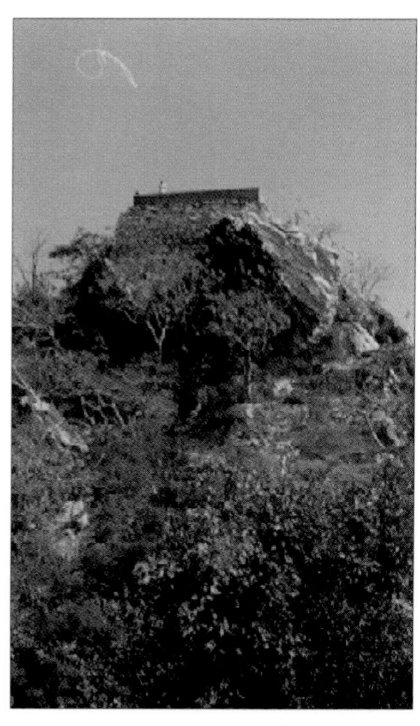

Vulture Peak, Rajgir, where the Buddha taught the Prajnaparamita.

Tibetan Aid Project
"Beyond the beliefs of any one religion, there is the truth of the human spirit.
Beyond the power of nations, there is the power of the human heart.
Beyond the ordinary mind, the power of wisdom, love, and healing energy are at work in the universe.
When we can find peace within our hearts, we contact these universal powers. This is our only hope."
–Tarthang Tulku, Founder Tibetan Aid Project
Marking 25 Years of Support for the Restoration of the Tibetan Culture and Aid to Tibetan Refugees

The scope of TAP's program services greatly expands.

TAP initiates major fundraising campaign in 1994 to meet new goals.

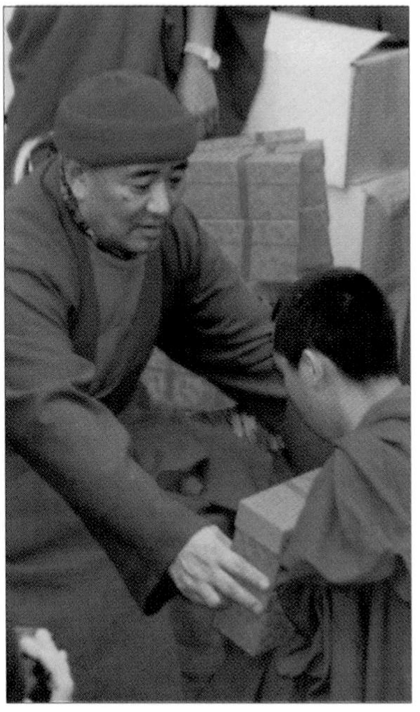

Tarthang Tulku distributes sacred texts at the World Peace Ceremony.

Stupa at Boudha, Nepal, site of the Four Schools Monlam, 1994.

the World Peace Ceremony, on the anniversary of Klong-chen-pa's parinirvana.

Support for Monks and Nuns TAP transforms the Pen Friend program into a monk/nun sponsorship program in which donors give $30 monthly. All funds donated are now forwarded to monasteries rather than to individuals.

Pilgrimage to Holy Places TAP organizes a forty-five person pilgrimage to the major Buddhist sites in Nepal and India.

Fundraising Inspired by the Head Lama, TAP increases efforts to generate funds to support monastic communities in Asia, help the Yeshe De Project ship sacred texts to the Bodh Gaya World Peace Ceremony, sponsor the education of monks and nuns, and provide for the basic needs of Tibetan refugees living in India. TAP reaches out to 200,000 Americans through a direct mail campaign, with excellent results.

Disseminating Information TAP creates an information archive to assemble all published information and photographs relating to the situation in Tibet and begins projects to develop information about Tibetan history and civilization in films, lectures, brochures, and larger publications.

Information and Publications TAP sponsors publication of *World Peace Ceremony, Bodh Gaya 1994* and *Prayers at Holy Places* (historic information on the Tibetan Buddhist traditions and photographic documentaries of the ceremonies), prepared for distribution to TAP donors and participants at the sixth Nyingma

World Peace Ceremony and the ceremonies of the Sarma schools in 1995.

Sacred Text Shipping and Distribution TAP funds the shipping of 31,250 books and 15,995 thanka reproductions to India and assists with their distribution at the 5th World Peace Ceremony in Bodh Gaya and the Longchen Varna Sadhana in Sarnath, 1995.

Ritual Arts Projects TAP helps assemble thousands of sheets of mantras for the Dharma Wheel Cutting Karma hand prayer wheels to be offered to participants in the World Peace Ceremony.

Sponsors Ka-Ter Emissaries in Tibet In 1994, officers of the Ka-Ter Foundation led by Tulku Sangngak were able to travel to Tibet to visit Nyingma monasteries and retreat centers to distribute funds and determine needs and priorities. Funds were made available for the following purposes:

At sMin-grol-gling monastery in central Tibet, funds were provided for the repair of statues of the three founders of Buddhism in Tibet: Guru Padmasambhava, the Abbot Shantarakshita, and King Khri-srong lDe'u-btsan.

At Shug-gseb nunnery, where more than three hundred nuns received support in 1993, the Foundation offered additional support for twenty nuns to undertake an intensive retreat.

At rDo-rje Brag, the Foundation provided funds for giant thankas and fabric appliqué hangings in honor of Padmasambhava, as well as support for fifty monks in residence.

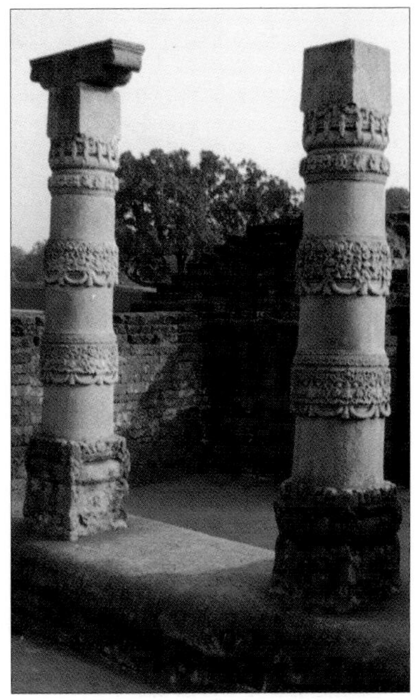

Ancient pillars at Sarnath, visited during the pilgrimage tour, 1993.

Books commemorate the World Peace Ceremony assemblies.

On behalf of the Ka-Ter Foundation, lamas trek to monasteries in Tibet.

Support for Reconstruction TAP provides $50,794 for monastery and retreat reconstruction in Tibet.

Long-range Support for the Nyingma Sangha The Head Lama founds the Bodhgaya Religious Trust and the Nyingma Buddhist Trust.

Support for Ceremonies in Perpetuity The Bodh Gaya Religious Trust is created to support the annual observance of the World Peace Ceremony in 1994; receives tax-exempt staus on August 14, 1997 under the Internal Revenue Code sections 501(c)(3), 170(b)(1) (A)(ii).

Leaders of the Nyingma Sangha in Asia, working through the Monlam Chenmo Foundation, assume responsibility for administration and coordination of the annual ceremony.

The Nyingma Buddhist Trust is created to support the reconstruction of monasteries in Tibet and the restoration of important Nyingma practices. Receives tax-exempt status on May 19, 1997 under Internal Revenue Code section 501(c)(3), 170(b)(1)(A)(ii).

Ka-Ter emmisaries raise a TNMC prayer flag at mChims-phu.

Support for Traditional Practices The Head Lama creates a btags-grol containing twenty-seven sacred texts selected from the Ya-bzhi and gTer-ma collections. Folded accordion-style, btags-grols can be placed in a pouch and worn on a cord around the neck. Five hundred are produced for distribution to lamas attending the 1995 World Peace Ceremonies at Bodh Gaya. Several thousand more are prepared for later distribution.

Guru Rinpoche, one of the sacred images at dPal-ri restored by TNMC.

Fundraising and Program Support TAP increases its capacity to generate and mail letters and brochures. Initiating annual campaign and holiday letters, it expands its donor base to 1,800 names, and produces and mails nearly 200,000 brochures, generating income of over $300,000 in its most extensive fundraising campaign to date. Funds raised are distributed to support monastic communities in Asia, defray shipping costs of books and art contributed by TNMC and Dharma Publishing, sponsor the education of hundreds of monks and nuns, and provide for the basic needs of Tibetan refugees living in India.

Grant Proposals TAP mounts a major effort to create a grant proposal for funding the shipping of multiple sets of *Great Treasures of Ancient Teachings* to Tibetan monasteries in Asia, a project intended to restore the teachings that form the foundation of Dharma transmission to masters of the lineage.

1995

Nunnery of Tshe-ring-ljongs, associated with 'Jigs-med Gling-pa.

Support for Education The Head Lama attends the 6th World Peace Ceremony in Bodh Gaya, where he distributes sacred texts and thanka reproductions to individuals and monasteries. Among them are the essential commentaries of the Mahayoga and Anuyoga Tantras. The essential texts of all three Inner Tantras are now restored to masters of the Nyingma lineages.

Sponsoring Ceremonies TNMC sponsors the first Longchen Varna Sadhana at Sarnath on

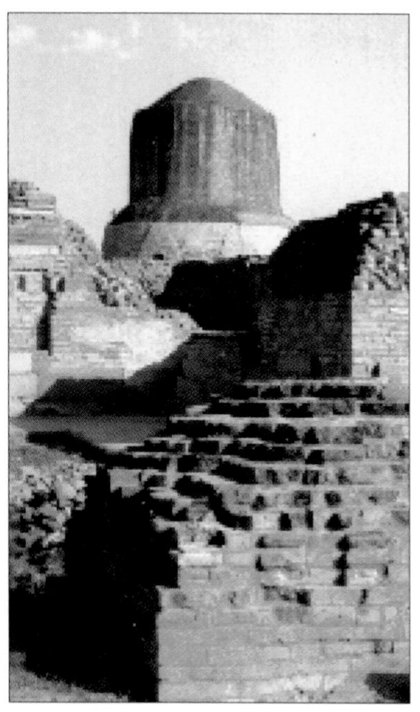

The Dhamekh Stupa in Sarnath, site of the 1995 Klong-chen-pa ceremony.

TAP sets up an information table at Dharma House in Berkeley.

February 15–18. After the World Peace Ceremony, fifteen hundred Nyingma lamas and monks assemble at the Dhamekh Stupa to invoke the blessings of the lineage upon all sentient beings.

TAP/TNMC sponsors bKa'-'gyur readings for five Gelug monasteries: Sera, Drepung, Gaden, Gyudmed, and Gyuto. Offers $500 for ceremonies to each of eight Nyingma monasteries, also to Kagyu, Sakya, and Gelug monasteries in India and Nepal.

Foundations for the Future TNMC offers seed funding for the Varna Longchen Foundation, established to support the continuation of the Longchen Varna at Sarnath. Ven. Khenpo Thupten Mewa and Ven Tulku Orgyen Topgyal serve as managers; members include Khenpo Magpo Konchog, Thupten Gyatso, Donag Gyatso, and Tsultrim Angmo.

Disseminating Information TAP begins to develop a web site to disseminate information on TAP activities.

Lama Visits TNMC hosts the visit of Ven. Chokyi Nyima Rinpoche, abbot of Ka-Nying Shedrup Ling in Kathmandu. The Rinpoche gives a talk on the importance of study and practice at the Nyingma Institute in August.

Support for Traditional Practice Directs TNMC students to frame ninety-eight thankas in traditional cloth hangings for offering at Bodh Gaya: Bla-ma-dgongs-'dus (four sets of seventeen thankas) and two sets of fifteen images of Buddhas, Herukas, Guru Rinpoche,

Pehar, Visions of 'Jam-dbyangs mKhyen-brtse, Yamantaka, and Kurukulle.

Support for Ceremonies TNMC obtains 100,000 brass butter lamps in Bhutan and donates them to Bodh Gaya to be used during the World Peace Ceremony beginning in 1996.

Benefit Pilgrimage TAP staff leads a World Peace Pilgrimage in 1995 to coincide with the World Peace Ceremony. Thirty people participate in the twenty-two-day pilgrimage, which begins at Kathmandu, visits Lumbini and Tilaurakot (one of the two sites tentatively identified as Kapilavastu, the Buddha's early home), and continues on to Kushinagara, Varanasi, Sarnath, and Bodh Gaya, where pilgrims make offerings and participate in the World Peace Ceremony. Funds from the pilgrims support continuation of the ceremonies.

Administration TAP creates new office space at Dharma House, where volunteers participate in sewing prayer flags, fundraising, office work, research projects, warehouse work, grant writing, and graphic design.

Fundraising The donor base doubles after 1994 mailing of 150,000 brochures. TAP creates its first gift catalog.

Disseminating Information TAP participates in coordination efforts among Bay Area Tibetan support groups and mounts an effort to locate sympathetic individuals and organizations to help distribute information and brochures.

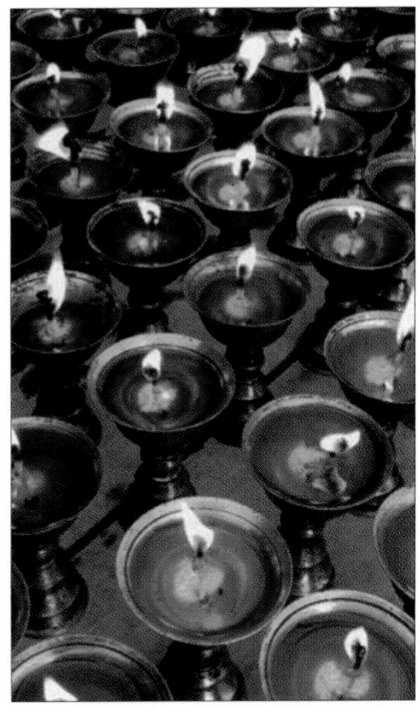

Butter lamps symbolize bodhicitta, mind awakened to enlightenment.

Symbols sculpted into ceremonial tormas become offerings of wisdom.

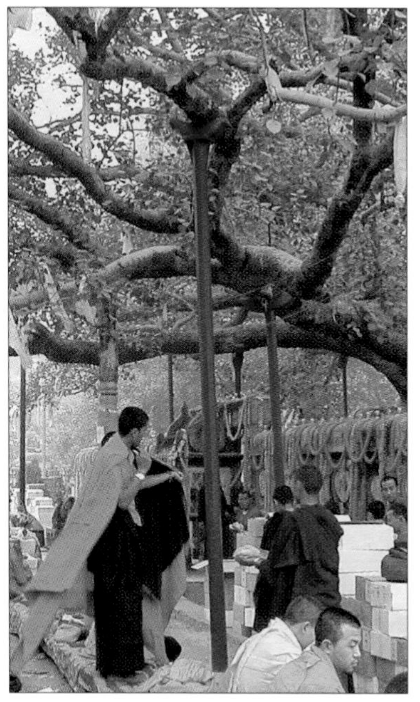

Books shipped by TAP are distributed under the Bodhi Tree.

Information and Publications TAP sponsors publication of *World Peace Ceremony, Bodh Gaya 1995,* a photographic documentary of the Nyingma and Sarma schools' Monlam Chenmos, prepared for distribution to TAP donors and participants at the Nyingma and Sarma ceremonies in 1996.

Sacred Text Shipping and Distribution TAP funds the shipping of 17,663 books, 24,283 thanka reproductions, amd 10,504 prayer wheels to India and assists with their distribution to Tibetans participating in the seventh World Peace Ceremony in Bodh Gaya and the Varna Longchen Sadhana in Sarnath, 1996.

1996

Support for Ceremonies As of 1996, expenditures for supporting ceremonies 1974–96, exclusive of the World Peace ceremonies, total $606,156.

TAP/TNMC sponsors bKa'-'gyur readings for five Gelug monasteries: Sera, Drepung, Gaden, Gyudmed, and Gyuto. Sponsors Vajrakila and Tsog Pujas at Nyingma monasteries in Clement Town, Rewalsar, Bir, Pharping, Kathmandu, Kasumpti, Manali, and other locations. Sponsors Kagyu and Sakya monlams, and others..

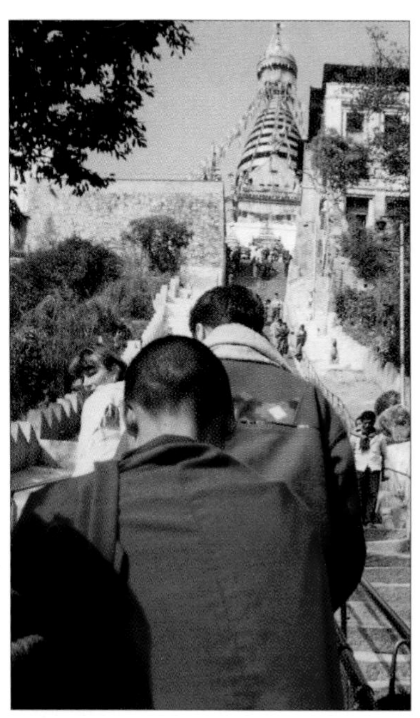

TAP pilgrims ascend the steps to the Svayambhu Stupa in Nepal.

World Peace Ceremony 6,000 lamas, monks, and nuns and many more thousands of laypersons assemble at Bodh Gaya for the seventh observance of the World Peace Ceremony. TAP/TNMC make offerings of $40,000 to Monlam participants.

Support for Monasteries TAP/TNMC offers support for six ancient retreat centers in Bhutan; contributes to the Lama Serpo building fund in Bhutan, the Gesar Drama Troupe, and provides assistance to Tibetan nomads through Doctors Without Borders.

TNMC creates formal letters in Tibetan to send to thirty monasteries requesting specific kinds of ceremonies.

Fundraising TAP/TNRF fundraising dinner at the Nyingma Institute generates donations of $10,000. The staff prepares a video of TAP projects for presentation.

TAP staff assists with preparations for the Odiyan Open House in June, generates more than $25,000 from that event, and distributes three hundred prayer flags to donors.

TAP staff works in conjunction with TNMC to print four thousand prayer flags, 1,500 for gifts to donors and 2,500 to be flown at Odiyan. TAP acquires a commercial Bernina sewing machine to increase flag production.

Disseminating Information TAP launches a web site in conjunction with the other Nyingma centers.

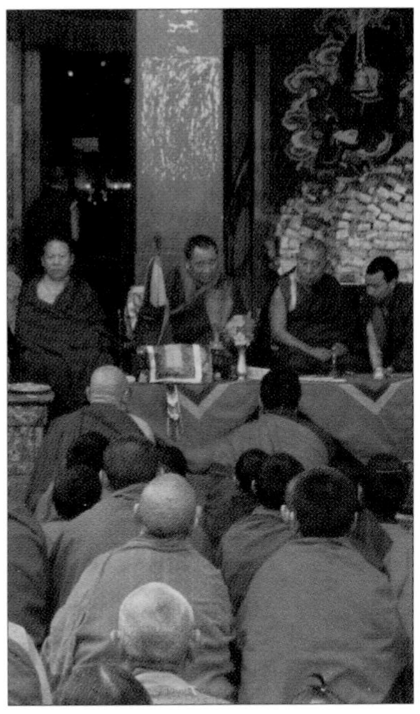

TNMC offers support for ceremonies at Rewalsar. 1996.

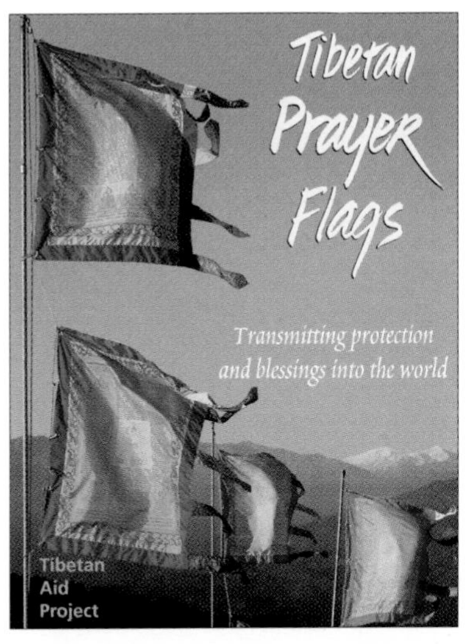

TAP is authorized to sew TNMC's prayer flags and offer them as gifts to donors. Flags printed and sewn by TAP volunteers are later offered to the public through this brochure and on TAP's web site.

1997

Support for Ceremonies TAP/TNMC sponsors bKa'-'gyur readings for five Gelugpa monasteries: Sera, Drepung, Gaden, Gyudmed, and Gyuto. Sponsors the Sakya and Kagyu Monlams and ceremonies commemorating the passing of Tarig Tulku, supports ceremonies at

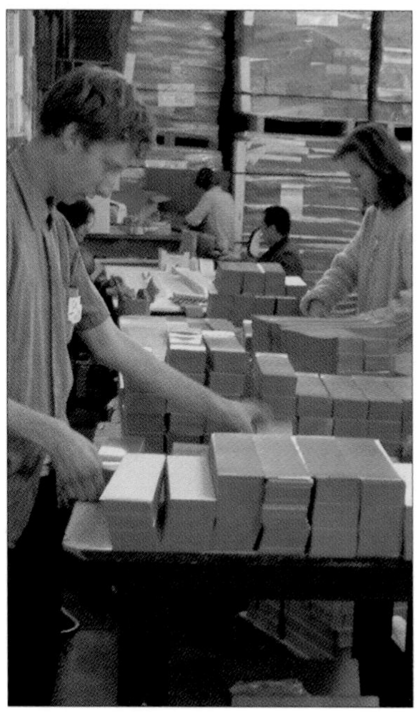

Yeshe De volunteers prepare books for shipment to India.

TAP's holiday card conveys the spirit of the World Peace Ceremony.

Ka-Nying Shedrup Ling, Pharping, and Nagi Gonpa in Nepal and numerous others in India and Tibet. Offerings to monasteries in 1997 total more than $75,000.

Support for Book Production TAP contributes $40,000 toward the cost of producing sacred texts for distribution at the World Peace Ceremony, about 7.5% of the total production cost for that year.

Sacred Text Shipping and Distribution TAP funds the shipping of 23,920 books and 121,393 thanka reproductions for distribution at the ninth World Peace Ceremony in 1998.

The Head Lama participates in the World Peace Ceremony in Bodh Gaya and the Longchen Varna Sadhana in Sarnath, and directs the distribution of books and thankas.

Expansion Abroad TAP is officially registered in Holland as a non-profit foundation for the preservation of Tibetan culture.

1998

Support for Ceremonies TAP/TNMC sponsors bKa'-'gyur readings for five Gelug monasteries: Sera, Drepung, Gaden, Gyudmed, and Gyuto. Sponsors the Sakya and Kagyu Monlams and a Hundred Million Vajra Guru Ceremony by Ven. Trulzhig Rinpoche. TNMC also supports ceremonies by Chokyi Nyima and ceremonies at Nagi Gonpa, monasteries in Bhutan, and a number of smaller monasteries.

Support for Monasteries TAP/TNMC offers $5,050 for the reconstruction of Taksang monastery in Bhutan, $4,500 for Pharping, Nepal, and $3,000 for the Sakya Lamas Center as well as a number of smaller offerings to other centers.

Information and Fundraising TAP hosts a benefit dinner in Berkeley's Tilden Park in May with volunteer chefs contributing their skills. Nearly a hundred people attend. This dinner becomes a model for similar benefit dinners organized in Los Angeles and Marin County.

Sacred Text Shipping and Distribution TAP funds the shipping of 55,032 books and 152,461 thankas to India for distribution at the tenth World Peace Ceremony in 1999.

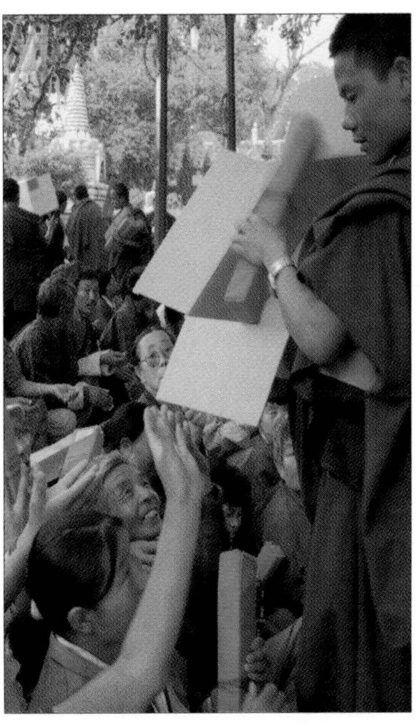

Laypeople as well as monks receive sacred texts with great joy.

1999

Support for Ceremonies TAP/TNMC sponsors bKa'-'gyur readings for five Gelug monasteries. Sponsors the Sakya and Kagyu Monlams, a Hundred Million Vajra Guru Ceremony by Khenpo Thubten Mewa, and the Fish Saving Ceremony by Shaptrul Rinpoche, also supports ceremonies by Khocchen Tulku, Rigo Tulku. Taklung Tsetrul, and Urgyan Tobgyal, as well as ceremonies at Dzongsar Institute, Sakya Lama's College, and Ngor Monastery.

Support for Monasteries TAP/TNMC offers $5,000 to Men Tse Khang monastery in India and Maratika Caves, Nepal.

TNMC prepares a major Deb-ther for the Sangha attending the World Peace Ceremony in 2000. Contents include Klong-che-pa's summary of the twelve acts of the Buddha, names of the thousand Buddhas of the Bhadrakalpika,

TIBETAN AID PROJECT

Tibetan monks receive a valued text to help them continue their tradition.

July 1999

Dear Friend,

As we move towards a new millennium, the survival of Tibetan culture is still in question. For fifty years the Tibetan plateau has been occupied and the people's way of life subject to external regulation. The severe restrictions of the 1960s and 70s were loosened in the 80s but are now being tightened once again. It is uncertain whether Tibetans in Tibet will be able to practice their own religion in a meaningful way. Since the transmission of Tibet's own ancient culture is now impeded, traditional knowledge is in danger of being lost. For the past thirty years, Dharma Publishing and the Yeshe De Project have undertaken major preservation efforts to help guarantee the survival of Tibet's sacred texts and art, vital elements in any culture. More than 150,000 books and 400,000 art prints have already been donated as gifts to Tibetan libraries and individual practitioners over the last two decades. Since the late 1970s, the Tibetan Aid Project has sponsored the shipping of these texts and art to Asia.

Many Thousands of Books are Currently Being Prepared for Tibetan Monasteries of All Schools and will be Offered at the *Monlam Chenmo*.

Your Donation of $150 can Ship 300 Sacred Texts to Asia.

To the Tibetan people, there is nothing more meaningful than a Buddhist book or image, for faith in the Buddha and his teachings is central to their lives. The heart of Tibet's civilization is an ancient wisdom tradition transmitted across the Himalayas from India, the homeland of the Buddha. Translated from Sanskrit into the highly sophisticated sacred language of Tibetan, the Buddha's teachings were preserved in the Land of Snow for thirteen hundred years. The Tibetan Canon is the most comprehensive set of Buddhist teachings remaining in the world, covering subjects ranging from philosophy and metaphysics to healing and medicine. The equally sacred ritual arts present an enormous array of symbols that support the growth of enlightened understanding.

Serious study and meditation using these resources was undertaken in more than 6,000 major monasteries and many thousands of retreat centers, holy places, and hermitages across Tibet. With the interruption of this ancient way of life, the majority of sacred books and art have been destroyed. If the efforts made by all those endeavoring to restore this precious heritage are successful, perhaps 75% can be rescued.

TAP's fundraising letters focus on the importance of sacred texts, 1999.

Offerings of light illumine an ancient stupa at the World Peace Ceremony.

Dharma books help a new generation keep the Dharma teachings alive.

and a puja to the Sixteen Great Arhats. Abundantly illustrated with thankas of Buddhas and Arhats, this volume includes verses composed by the Head lama, a photographic album of the World Peace Ceremony, a list of texts being offered to the Sangha, and names of Buddhas andmasters of the Nyingma lineage.

Sacred Text Shipping and Distribution TAP funds shipping of 113,448 books, 98,398 sacred art prints and 10,042 prayer wheels for distribution at the 11th World Peace Ceremony in 2000.

TAP organizes a pilgrimage to holy places in India and Nepal; the fifteen pilgrims also assist with book distribution and participate in the ceremonies in Bodh Gaya and Sarnath.

2000

Support for Ceremonies TAP/TNMC sponsors bKa'-'gyur readings for Sera, Drepung, Gaden, Gyudmed, and Gyuto. Sponsors the Sakya and Kagyu Monlams, the Hundred Million Vajra Guru Ceremony by Ven. Taklung Tsetrul, and the Fish Saving Ceremony by Shatral Rinpoche.

Support for Monasteries TAP/TNMC offer $1,000 each to Nagi Gonpa in Nepal and Taksang, Kurje Lhakhan, Senge Drak, and Kyerchu monasteries in Bhutan.

Sacred Text Shipping and Distribution TAP raises funds for shipping 125,336 books, 267,349 sacred art prints, and 15,000 prayer wheels to India for distribution at the 12th World Peace Ceremony in 2001. This count represents sets of 21 volumes of typeset texts containing 102 titles by 30 authors.

Offerings to the Four Schools Beginning in 2000, major Sakya, Kagyu, and Gelug monasteries receive books each year to distribute to their many branches.

The Dharma Text Inputting Project TAP was asked to take financial responsibility for the Dharma Text Inputting Project, initiated to support the training of monks and nuns to input texts using methods developed by the Yeshe De Project.

TAP representative works with monks in Nepal for the Inputting Project.

2001

Support for Ceremonies TAP/TNMC sponsors bKa'-'gyur readings for Sera, Drepung, Gaden, Gyudmed, and Gyuto. Sponsors the Sakya and Kagyu Monlams, the Hundred Million Vajra Guru Ceremonies by H. H. Sakya Trizin and Ven. Trulzhig Rinpoche, and the Fish Saving Ceremony by Shatral Rinpoche.

Lamas, monks, and nuns recite and often memorize entire texts.

Documentation and Information TNMC and TAP sponsor publication of *Your Friends The Tibetan Refugees,* documenting their combined efforts on behalf of Tibetan Dharma, people, and culture from 1969 through 2000.

TNMC prepares a Deb-ther containing 'Jigs-med Gling-pa's root text for the Yon-tan-mdzod and numerous thankas and financial reports for distribution to Tibetan participants in the World Peace Ceremony in 2002.

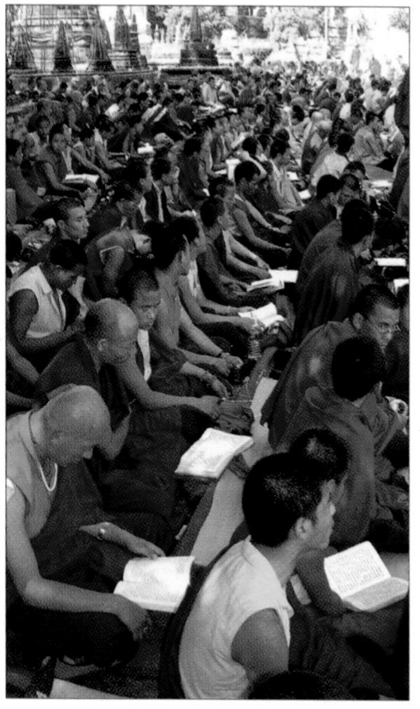

7,000 lamas, monks, and nuns recite prayers at the 2003 ceremony.

TAP's Tsering Gellek distributes prayer wheels to laypersons.

Information and Documentation TAP Netherlands mounts two workshops and a photographic exhibit at the library in The Hague.

Sacred Text Shipping and Distribution TAP funds cost of shipping 175,655 books, 181,095 sacred art prints, and 20,000 prayer wheels for distribution at the 13th World Peace Ceremony in 2002. The shipment fills thirteeen 40′ shipping containers.

Funds for Program Services With the support of a leading San Francisco chef, TAP organizes the first Taste and Tribute Dinner at San Francisco's City Club. The dinner becomes an annual event.

2002

Support for Ceremonies TAP/TNMC sponsors bKa'-'gyur readings for Sera, Drepung, Gaden, Gyudmed, and Gyuto monasteries. Sponsors the Sakya and Kagyu Monlams, the Hundred Million Vajra Guru Ceremony by H. H. Sakya Trizin, and others.

Revitalization of Holy Places TNMC agrees to design and sponsor the construction of butter-lamp houses and work to improve sanitary facilities near the Mahabodhi compound.

TNMC representatives travel to Bodh Gaya to work with the Temple Management Committee on installing the World Peace Bell sponsored by Nyingma Zentrum and cast in Germany. The bell is set in place and rung for the first time on December 13.

Empowerments for Sacred Sites TNMC offers a set of *The Nyingma Edition of the bKa'-'gyur and bsTan-'gyur* and the complete Pali Tipitaka to the Mahabodhi Temple in Bodh Gaya.

Information and Documentation TNMC prepares a Deb-ther containing the complete Tibetan text of the Man-ngag-rin-po-che'i-mdzod, a work revered as one of Longchenpa's seven treasures, to be offered to the Sangha attending the World Peace Ceremony in 2003.

Sacred Text Shipping and Distribution TAP funds cost of shipping 96,723 books, 2,000 thankas, and 1,000 prayer wheels for distribution at the 14th World Peace Ceremony in 2003.

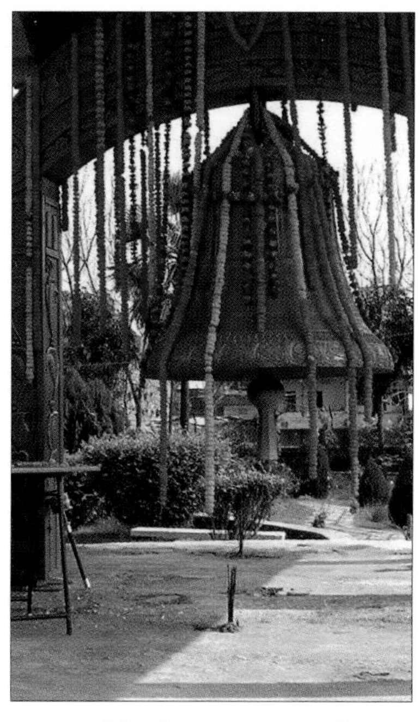

Buddhadharma Peace Bell, Meditation Garden, Bodh Gaya.

2003

Support for Ceremonies TAP/TNMC sponsors bKa'-'gyur readings for Sera, Drepung, Gaden, Gyudmed, and Gyuto monasteries. Sponsors the Sakya Monlam, Tshogs and Guru Rinpoche pujas, and Dorje Phurba ceremonies at Rewalsar Lake.

Support for Production of Sacred Texts The opportunity to fund a new series of sacred texts inspires TAP to initiate the Light of Wisdom campaign for major donors and invites supporters to participate in the Community of a Thousand Blessings. Dedicated to supporting the spiritual heart of traditional Tibetan culture, the campaign extends and further empowers TAP's mission to distribute sacred texts and art, support education of monks and nuns, support schools and monastic centers in Tibet,

Theravadin monks on pilgrimage at the stupa in Kushinagara.

Yeshe De bindery prepares books for shpment in December, 2003.

The Tibetan Aid Project

is pleased to announce a campaign to provide the Tibetan people with priceless resources for preserving their heritage and way of life.

This new initiative will expand our continuing efforts to preserve the Tibetan heritage for the sake of all humanity, by printing a special collection of texts that contain the direct teachings of the Buddha—the heart and soul of Tibetan culture.

Please join us by supporting the LIGHT OF WISDOM CAMPAIGN

Our Goal is to raise $600,000 by December 2005

TAP establishes the Light of Wisdom Campaign in 2003.

and support all Tibetan Dharma traditions by sponsoring traditional ceremonies. The goal is to raise $600,000 by December 2005.

Building Community To create a mutually beneficial network for individuals interested in supporting Tibetan culture and the production of sacred texts, TAP founds the Community of a Thousand Blessings. Members pledge to contribute $35 monthly for three years.

Support for Traditional Practices TNMC sponsors more than 100,000 butter-lamps daily during the World Peace Ceremony in 2003. Following the ceremony, TNMC sponsors a seven-day pilgrimage to holy places for an assembly of 67 Theravadin monks.

Sacred Text Shipping and Distribution TAP funds the cost of shipping 205,000 books, 73,600 sacred art prints and 9,828 prayer wheels for distribution at the 15th World Peace Ceremony in 2004.

Information and Fundraising TAP produces a new brochure, "Tibetan Aid Project: 30 Years and Growing," summarizing TAP's mission, its guiding principles, and the main classes of its program services.

2004

Support for Ceremonies TAP/TNMC sponsors bKa'-'gyur readings for five Gelug monasteries: Drepung, Gaden, Gyudmed, and Gyuto. Funds the Monlam prayer ceremonies of the Kagyu and Sakya schools

Information and Fundraising TAP mails the 2004 Losar letter celebrating the Tibetan Year of the Wood Monkey and announcing its support for the Yeshe De Project's publication of the Avatamsaka Sutra, the most extensive teaching preserved in the Tibetan bKa'-'gyur.

TAP publishes the first issue of "News from TAP," reporting on the distribution of books at the 2004 World Peace Ceremony in Bodh Gaya, and featuring short articles on the monasteries and nunneries TAP is supporting.

Fundraising In December, TAP mails participants in the Light of Wisdom campaign and the Community of 1,000 Blessings a letter describing how joyfully Tibetans received the distribution of this year's shipment of books and the extraordinary efforts they made to carry them to their home monasteries and villages.

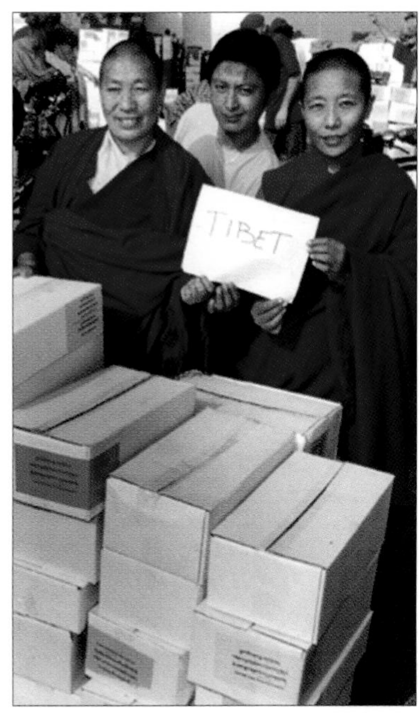

Books ready to be carried from Bodh Gaya to centers in Tibet.

Sacred Text Shipping and Distribution TAP funds cost of shipping 418,000 books, 20,000 sacred art prints and 10,000 prayer wheels for distribution at the 16th World Peace Ceremony in 2005.

2005

In February, TAP greets donors with a Losar letter inviting them to join in the spirit of renewal that Losar kindles in the hearts of Tibetans young and old. TAP's fundraising letter emphasizes the value of preserving the knowledge contained in traditional sacred texts and distributing them to Tibetans gathered for the World Peace Ceremony in Bodh Gaya.

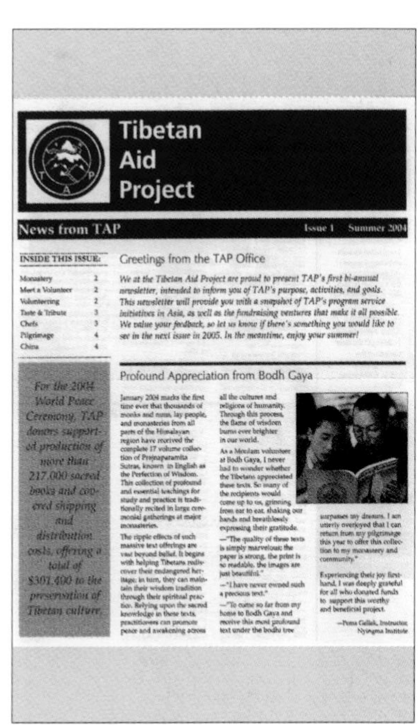

Tibetan Aid Project

News from TAP — Issue 1 Summer 2004

INSIDE THIS ISSUE:

Monastery	2
Meet a Volunteer	2
Volunteering	2
Taste & Tribute	3
Chefs	3
Pilgrimage	4
China	4

For the 2004 World Peace Ceremony, TAP donors supported production of more than 217,000 sacred books and covered shipping and distribution costs, offering a total of $301,400 to the preservation of Tibetan culture.

Greetings from the TAP Office

We at the Tibetan Aid Project are proud to present TAP's first bi-annual newsletter, intended to inform you of TAP's purpose, activities, and goals. This newsletter will provide you with a snapshot of TAP's program service initiatives in Asia, as well as the fundraising ventures that make it all possible. We value your feedback, so let us know if there's something you would like to see in the next issue in 2005. In the meantime, enjoy your summer!

Profound Appreciation from Bodh Gaya

January 2004 marks the first time ever that thousands of monks and nuns, lay people, and monasteries from all parts of the Himalayan region have received the complete 17 volume collection of Prajnaparamita Sutras, known in English as the Perfection of Wisdom. This collection of profound and essential teachings for study and practice is traditionally recited in large ceremonial gatherings at major monasteries.

The ripple effects of such massive text offerings are vast beyond belief. It begins with helping Tibetans rediscover their endangered heritage; in turn, they can maintain their wisdom tradition through their spiritual practice. Relying upon the sacred knowledge in these texts, practitioners can promote peace and awakening across all the cultures and religions of humanity. Through this process, the flame of wisdom burns ever brighter in our world.

As a Monlam volunteer at Bodh Gaya, I never had to wonder whether the Tibetans appreciated these texts. So many of the recipients would come up to us, grinning from ear to eat, shaking our hands and breathlessly expressing their gratitude.

—"The quality of these texts is simply marvelous: the paper is strong, the print is so readable, the images are just beautiful."

—"I have never owned such a precious text."

—"To come so far from my home to Bodh Gaya and receive this most profound text under the bodhi tree surpasses my dreams. I am utterly overjoyed that I can return from my pilgrimage this year to offer this collection to my monastery and community."

Experiencing their joy firsthand, I was deeply grateful for all who donated funds to support this worthy and beneficial project.

—Pema Gellek, Instructor, Nyingma Institute

"News from TAP" communicates the experience of distributing saced texts.

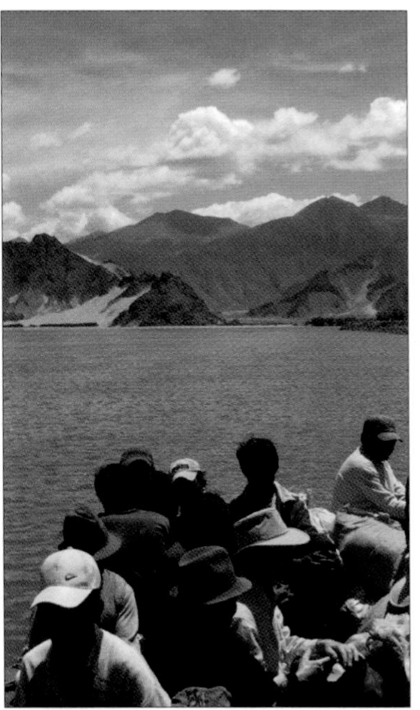
Pilgrims approaching rDo-rje-brag in central Tibet.

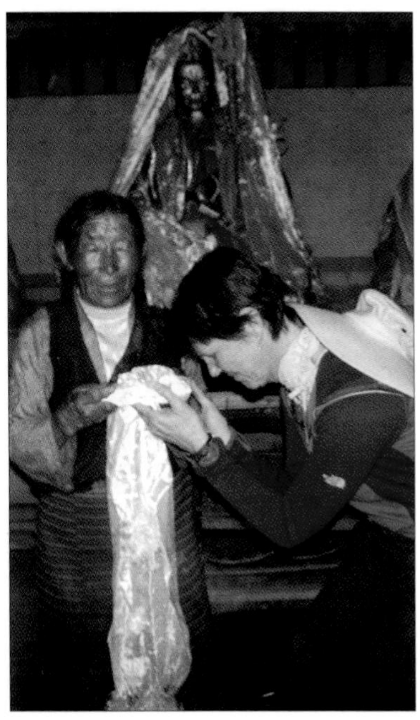
A TAP pilgrim receives a blessing at the ancient retreat at Yamalung.

Support for restoring the Dharma heritage of India and Tibet Head Lama of TNMC establishes five foundations to continue cultural preservation and revitalization projects. These are the Prajna Light, Ananda Light, Vajra Light, Light of Buddhadharma, and Mangalam Light foundations.

TAP sponsors, organizes, and leads a three-week pilgrimage to major holy places in central Tibet, making offerings at bSam-yas, sMin-grol-gling, rDo-rje-brag, and ancient retreat centers where the Great Guru Padmasambhava transmitted the Dharma to his disciples.

TAP raises funds in anticipation of shipping more than 500,000 books, several thousand sacred art prints, and 10,000 prayer wheels to Bodh Gaya for distribution in 2006.

A complete set of sacred texts distributed from 1989 to 2005 consists of 140,000 folios compiled into 262 volumes and ornamented with more than 3,000 images. It preserves 1,382 unique titles by 180 authors.

Members of more than 3,300 Nyingma monasteries in India, Nepal, Sikkim, Ladakh, Bhutan, and Tibet have received individual copies of sacred texts produced by the Yeshe De Project.

The total cost of books produced 1989–2005: $12,760,161. Anticipated cost of books produced for 2006: $2,000,000.

The World Peace Bell Project continues. Three bells are shipped from Germany to India for installation at Lumbini. Following the Buddha's path after enlightenment, the bell team travels to Sarnath to install the first new bell. Permission was granted to place the bell near the Bodhi Tree, in view of the Dhamekh Stupa. The head Bhante of the Mahabodhi Society consecrates the bell and promises to have it rung twice each day. The sound of the bell carries about 7 kilometers.

Consecrating the World Peace Bell, Sarnath, 2005

Continuing their assignment, the bell team continues to Lumbini, the birthplace of the Buddha and one of the most beautiful of the holy places. When the bell arrives in Nepal, the country is in turmoil; to restore order, the king has dissolved thr parliament, shut down communications, and severely restricted travel.

Recognizing the Bell as a valuable public monument, the Minister of Finance approves the bell's passage through customs. The bell is donated to the Lumbini Development Trust, which manages the Sacred Garden.

The bell is taken to Lumbini and installed next to the eternal peace flame, a short distance from the spot where the Buddha was born. It was consecrated at dawn on the day of the Buddha Jayanti (Buddha's birthday) celebration.

The World Peace Bell, consecrated at Lumbini in 2005

Completing their assignment, the bell team proceeds to Kushinagara, site of the Buddha's Parinirvana. Although no new monuments or changes have been permitted for many years near the Kushinagara temple and stupa, now a World Heritage Site, permission is finally granted. The bell is installed near the eastern gate, within the gardens of the Mahaparinirvana temple, on May 29. Locals report the sighting of golden lights above the temple, an auspicious sign of peace and harmony.

Tables and Charts

Tibetan Nyingma Relief Foundation

Year	Revenues	Program Services	% of Revenues*
11/74–10/75	$27,111	$17,936	66%
11/75–10/76	34,947	35,975	103%
11/76–10/77	30,135	30,207	100%
11/77–10/78	26,549	22,405	84%
11/78–10/79	11,729	13,891	118%
11/79–10/80	39,852	30,824	77%
11/80–10/81	26,214	31,881	120%
11/81–10/82	1,623	1,048	65%
11/82–10/83	1,408	502	36%
11/83–10/84	650	7,025	1081%
11/84–10/85	6,515	5,845	90%
11/85–10/86	1,883	1,853	98%
11/86–10/87	2,718	2,751	101%
11/87–10/88	12,428	12,130	98%
11/88–10/89	21,292	10,612	50%
14 year total	**$245,054**	**$224,885**	**92%**
11/89–10/90	66,711	29,990	45%
11/90–10/91	83,363	75,252	90%
11/91–10/92	132,653	67,886	51%
11/92–10/93	113,580	75,818	67%
11/93–10/94	367,233	185,393	50%
11/94–10/95	196,786	108,550	55%
11/95–10/96	294,314	182,592	62%
7 year total	**$1,254,640**	**$725,481**	**58%**
22 YEAR TOTAL	**$1,499,694**	**$950,366**	**63%**

*% of revenues going directly to Tibetan refugees, excluding all overhead

TAP Income and Expenses

1994	
Income	$367,234
Expenses	413,594
Net	-46,360

1995	
Income	$245,537
Expenses	220,230
Net	25,327

1996	
Income	$344,173
Expense	295,000
Net	49,173

1997	
Income	$312,163
Expense	294,903
Net	17,260

1998	
Income	$344,389
Expense	355,300
Net	-10,911

1999	
Income	$293,485
Expense	302,826
Net	-9,347

2000	
Income	$228,987
Expenses	155,977
Net	73,010

2001	
Income	283,822
Expenses	238,964
Net	44,858

2002	
Income	$248,693
Expenses	309,379
Net	-60,687

2003	
Income	$489,356
Expenses	523,181
Net	-39,148

2004	
Income	$596,748
Expenses	478,173
Net	102,975

2005	
Income	$500,000 (est.)
Expenses	500,000 (est)
Net	000

TAP Program Services

1994

Monastery support	$9,000
Offerings to Monlam participants	40,000
Monlam book distribution	5,393
Monlam book production	9,511
Ceremony photography	1,004
Storage and shipping of texts and thankas	33,927
Nyingma Institute Nepal	9,804
Shipping of prayer wheels	506
Refugee relief, laypeople	3,090
Monastery and retreat reconstruction in Tibet	50,794
Support for lamas at Odiyan	927
Unspecified	22,364
TOTAL 1994	$185,393

1995

Monastery support	$12,533
World Peace Ceremonies	
Offerings to participants	10,000
Book distribution	169
Invitations to 1996 ceremonies	350
10,000 prayer wheel kits (TAP's contribution only)	6,415
Monlam book production (TAP's contribution only)	2,070
Shipping of texts and thankas	15,290
Shipping of texts and thankas for 1996	9,003
Storage of texts and thankas	21,200
Refugee relief, laypeople and independents	13,020
Monastery support, Tibet	15,000
Monastery support, Nepal	800
Support for lamas at Odiyan	2,700
TOTAL 1995	$108,550

1996

Monastery support	$76,975
Bhutan: support for six ancient retreat centers	18,000
World Peace Ceremony Bodh Gayā, Offerings	40,000
Bodh Gayā book distribution Committee expenses	3,042
Shipping and book storage	25,200
Kagyu and Sakya Monlams	6,450
Support for individual lamas	2,125
Doctors without Borders, Assistance to Tibetan nomads	3,000
Gesar Drama Troupe	4,000
Lama Serpo Building Fund (Bhutan)	2,000
Support for lamas at Odiyan	1,800
TOTAL 1996	$182,592

TAP Program Services

1997

Monastery support	$300
Shipping of texts and thankas	78,563
Ceremonies	
Five Gelugpa ceremonies	5,000
Tarig Tulku	10,000
Ka-Nying Shedrup Ling	3,000
Nagi Gompa	600
Pharping	6,000
Khocchen Tulku	3,000
Urgyen Tobgyal	3,000
Taklung Tsetrul	3,000
Sakya Trizin	3,000
Thrulzhig Dezhak	3,000
Tashi Jong Monastery	3,000
Nyingma Rewalsar	3,000
Rigo Tulku	3,000
Sakya Lamas College	1,000
Sang Ngak Chokhorling	600
Dzongsar Institute	1,000
Daddul Rabten Ling	600
Ngor Monastery	1,000
Nyima Zangpo	500
Khenpo Thubten Mewa	3,000
Zangdog Palri	1,500
Chogyi Trichen	1,000
Drikung Kyabgon Chetsang	1,000
Passang Dorji	1,920
Other monasteries	5,000
Odiyan Lama support	1,800
Kagyu and Sakya Monlams	10,327
Seva Foundation	50
Tibetan Meditation Center	40
TNMC	7,000
Assistance to individuals	1,896
Scholarships	5,000
TOTAL 1997	$172,696

1998

Monastery and nunnery support	
Sakya Lamas Center	$3,000
Ngor Monastery	250
Taksang reconstruction	5,050
Pharping	4,500
Yeshi Lama	100
Chokyi Nyima	525
Shipping books and thankas	$98,737
Ceremonies	
Nyingma Monlam	$5,000
Sakya and Kagyu Monlams	10,000
Vajra Temple	216
Sakya School	2,750
Nyingma School	1,000
Gelugpa School	5,000
Kagyu School	5,500
Funds to Bhutan	5,000

* Ceremonies sponsored in conjunction with TNMC

** Total disbursed by TAP, not including contribution of TNMC

TAP Program Services

Smaller monasteries	4,750
Chokyi Nyima	24,700
Nagi Gonpa	1,000
Chogye Trichen	250
Sakya Lamas College	250
Sakya Monlam 1999	10,000
Sakya Tharig	118
Namkhai Nyingpo	2,500
Trulshik Rinpoche Hundred Million Vajra Guru	13,201
Lobsang Dorje	10,000
Odiyan	216
Assistance to individuals	1,193
TOTAL 1998	$214,806

1999

Monastery support

Men Tse Khang, India;
Maratika Caves, Nepal $5,000

Shipping books and thankas
$118,280

Ceremonies

Offerings at Nyingma Monlam Chenmo	$2,293
Varna Longchen Monlam	15,000
Khenpo Thubten Mewa Hundred Million Vajra Guru	10,500
Shatral Rinpoche	10,500
Khocchen Tulku	1,500
Rigo Tulku	1,500
Taklung Tsetrul	1,500
Urgyan Tobgyal	1,500
Sera Monastery	1,000
Gaden Monastery	1,000
Gyuto Monastery	6,000
Gyudmed Tantric College	7,000
Drepung Monastery	7,000
Rewalsar Retreat Center	1,500
Sakya Lamas College	1,000
Sakya Center	1,000
Dzongsar Institute	1,000
Ngor Monastery	1,000
Odiyan Projects	1,096
Assistance to individuals	1,045
Other	659
TOTAL 1999	$197,873

2000

Books and thankas

Shipping books and thankas
(paid in January 2001) $77,960

Text storage,
Ka Nying Shedrup Ling $280

Ceremonies

Sakya Monlam Chenmo	$5,000
Kagyu Monlam Chenmo	6,000
Ka Nying Shedrup Ling	500
Nagi Gonpa	1,000
Taksang, Bhutan	1,000
Kurje Lhakhang, Bhutan	1,000

TAP Program Services

Senge Drak, Bhutan	1,000
Kyerchu, Bhutan	1,000
Sera Monastery	1,000
Drepung Monastery	1,000
Gyuto Monastery	1,000
Ganden Monastery	1,000
Gyudmed Tantric College	1,000
Shatral Rinpoche	2,380
Taklung Tsetrul Hundred Million Vajra Guru	12,000
Dharma Text Inputting Project (paid Jan.–Feb 2001)	$21,527
Writing projects	$2,080
Special fund for upcoming projects	$50,202
Miscellaneous expenses	$431
TOTAL 2000	$188,360

2001

Monastic Center Support

Sera Monastic University	$1,000
Drepung Monastery	1,000
Gyuto Tantric University	1,000
Gyudmed Tantric University	1,000
Gaden Mahayana University	1,000
Ngagyur Dubgyud Choepheling	300
Baldan Baraivan Monastery	100
Total Monastic Center Support	$5,400

Shipping books and thankas	$90,320

Ceremony Support

Kagyu Monlam Chenmo	$3,000
Sakya Monlam Chenmo	3,000
Hundred Million Vajra Guru Mantras (Trulzhig Rinpoche)	12,000*
Hundred Million Vajra Guru Mantras (H.H. Sakya Trizin)	12,000*
Fish Saving Ceremony (Shatral Rinpoche)	4,000*
Odiyan Ceremonies for TAP supporters	$216
Support for individual lamas	$2,400
Assistance to individuals/groups	$750
Dharma Text Inputting Project	$20,000
Misc. administrative fees	$523
TOTAL 2001	$140,930**

2002

Monastery Support

Gyudmed Tantric University	$1,000
Drepung Monastery	1,000
Sera Mahayana Monastic University	1,000

TAP Program Services

Gaden Mahayana University	1,000
Gyuto Tantric University	1,000
Dolma Phodrang (H.H. Sakya Trizin)	2,500
Lhalam Monastery	3,000
Tsering Jong Nunnery Retreat	500
Tsering Jong Monastery	500
Pari Taksholang Monastery	500
Mindroling Monastery	1,000
Samye Monastery	1,000
Dorje Drak Monastery	1,000
Shugseb Nunnery	500
Nagi Gonpa	2,200
Total Monastery support	$17,700

Sacred Text Production and Distribution

Sacred Text Production	$90,000
Shipping books and thankas	68,219
Total books and distribution	$159,219

Traditional Ceremony Support

Kagyu Monlam Chenmo	$3,000
Sayka Monlam Chenmo	3,000
Hundred Million Vajra Guru Ceremony (H.H. Sakya Trizin)	2,000
Lhasa Tsog - Jowo	300
Rigdzing Chenmo, Dorje Drak	300
Health and Longevity Prayer at Odiyan for TAP supporter	108
Total ceremony support	$8,708

Support for individual lamas	$1,500
Aid to Individuals/Groups	$300
Dharma Text Inputting Project	528
Misc. administrative expenses (phone, fax, mail, wire transfer fees, recruitment)	$1,045
TOTAL 2002	$189,000

2003

Monastery support

Gaden Mahayana University	$1,000
Gyuto Tantric University	1,000
Sera Mahayana Monastic University	1,000
Drepung Monastery	1,000
Gyudmed Tantric University	1,000

Sacred Text Production and Distribution

Text Production Support	$190,000
Shipping books and thankas for ceremony in 2003	$45,530
Book Unloading Costs	2,000
Food and Lodging	4,650
Airfare	7,113
Shipping books and thankas for ceremony in 2004	$37,050
Insurance	1,014
Text storage	22,136

TAP Program Services

(2003 continued)

Ceremonies

Sakya Monlam	$3,000
Tshogs & Guru Rinpoche pujas (Ngagyur Camten Chockhorling)	1,000
Dorje Phurba Ceremonies (Rewalsar Lake)	500
Vajra Temple ceremony for Gortikovs	108
Grant to TNMC for ceremonies	35,813

Aid to Individuals	$1,408

Other expenses

Maratika Caves, Nepal	$500
Transportation-Volunteers	1,820
Lunches-Volunteers	1,724
Prayer Flag Project	5,799
Photo Archive Project	115
Wire & mail fees, phone	346

TOTAL 2003	$366,626

2004

Monastery support

Drepung Monastery	$1,000
Gaden Mahayana Monastic University	1,000
Gyudmed Tantric University	1,000
Gyuto Tantric University	1,000
Sera Je Monastic University	1,000
Nagi Gompa	150

Sacred Text Production and Distribution

Text production support	$188,000
Shipping books and thankas	52,976
Distribution team expenses	42,998
Boxes	22,258
Yeshe De Project space	19,112
Insurance (shipping)	833

Ceremonies

Sakya prayer ceremony	$3,000
Enlightenment stupa ceremonies for TAP donors	216
Vajra Temple ceremony for TAP donor	108

Aid to Individuals	**$275**

Other expenses

Fees, lunches, transport	$4,572
Photo Archive Project	647
Phone/Fax/Courier	604
Prayer Flag Project	101

TOTAL 2004	$339,892

2005 (*See details on page 371)

Monastery Support

Offerings to places visited during pilgrimage 2005*	$41,200

Sacred Text Production and Distribution

Text production Jan-Nov.	$160,000
Shipping texts & thankas	$108,361
China text printing project:	$13,375
TOTAL to date 2005	$322,936
TOTAL Program Services 1974–2005	**$3,083,485**

Ceremonies and Offerings of Books and Thankas (TAP and TNMC) 1969–1996

Tibetan Lamas	Ceremonies	Thankas to '91*	Books*
H.H. the Dalai Lama	$ 9,514	$ 60,038	$166
H.H. Gyalwa Karmapa	2,181	-	-
H.H. Sakya Trizin	5,035	3,213	19
H.H. Chogye Trichen	500	-	-
H.H. Dudjom Rinpoche	3,689	1,850	50
H.H. Dilgo Khyentse Rinpoche and Rabjam Rinpoche	30,997	28,994	970
H.H. Yongdzin Ling Rinpoche	3,268	796	50
H.H. Penor Rinpoche	20,315	17,949	236
H.H. Gyalwa Drukchen	9,670	13,412	166
Adzom Choktrul Pelo	80	-	-
Jadrel Sangye Dorje	4,069	11,462	-
Dazang Rinpoche	1,736	-	-
Dodrupchen Rinpoche	6,445	8,059	384
Dodzong Rinpoche	5,409	9,532	169
Drigung Bontrul Rinpoche	2,452	50	-
Trulshik Dezhag Rinpoche	18,200	19,064	366
Golok Tulku	2,887	11,561	50
Dzongsar Khyentse Yangtrul	8,150	6,507	627
Gedun Tulku	50	-	-

*Since 1991, books and thankas have been distributed primarily but not exclusively at the World Peace Ceremonies. Data on these ceremonies is included in "Revitalizing Holy Places," Part Four.

Ceremonies and Offerings of Books and Thankas (TAP and TNMC) 1969–1996

Tibetan Lamas	Ceremonies	Thankas to '91	Books
Gongna Rinpoche	$1,475	$1,114	$50
Jedrung Rinpoche	3,588	4,119	50
Tulku Urgyen, Chokyi Nyima Rinpoche, Choling Rinpoche	19,690	7,502	429
Khamtrul Rinpoche	1,850	-	-
Khenpo Aped, Sakya College	4,200	6,845	225
Khenpo Dazer	2,420	537	50
Khenpo Palden Sherab	2,616	2,646	-
Khenpo Sangye Tendzin	1,112	3,383	50
Khenpo Rigdzin Dorje	3,000	-	-
Khenpo Thubten Mewa	10,492	15,283	100
Khenpo Dechen Dorje	10,800	9,472	691
Khyentse Sangyum	7,412	3,044	-
Khetsun Zangpo Rinpoche	2,910	2,527	292
Khocchen Tulku	4,715	-	-
Ringo Tulku	21,197	6,746	461
Ripapa Tulku and Dorje Namgyal	3,981	8,537	100
Jadrel Rinpoche, SNS Monastery	6,500	-	-
Taklung Tsetrul Rinpoche	27,515	6,109	241
Tara Tulku	735	-	-
Tarig Tulku	11,634	497	150
Tarthang Choktrul Rinpoche	4,399	2,855	175
Tishen Rinpoche	678	-	-
Tragu Rinpoche	3,720	965	66
Orgyan Tobgyal Rinpoche	5,215	-	-

Ceremonies and Offerings of Books and Thankas (TAP and TNMC) 1969–1996

Tibetan Center	Ceremonies	Thankas to '91	Books
Bir Sakya Lamas School	$500	$219	-
Bumthang Tharpaling	4,547	1,164	$167
Dapzang Monastery	850	-	-
Drepung Monastery	10,805	23,482	200
Dzongsar Chode Datsang	652	5,970	-
Dzongsar Sakya College	7,323	6,507	-
Drigung Kagyud School	250	-	-
Duddul Rapten Ling	500	-	-
Dzongsar Shedra	500	-	-
Gaden Choepel Ling	9,054	9,054	-
Gaden Jam Ghon	1,062	-	-
Gaden Jantse Datsang	3,950	-	-
Gaden Mahayana University	1,000	-	-
Gaden Shartse Norling	6,905	11,044	150
Gaden Tharpa Choeling	452	5,970	-
Gaden Thubten Choeling	452	5,970	-
Gelugpa Students Welfare Comm.	1,826	6,766	-
Gyudmed Tantric College	10,215	11,104	100
Gyuto Tantric College	8,489	10,945	150
Kagyud Student Committee	873	-	-
Kagyudpa and Sakyapa	6,450	-	-
Nagi Gonpa	600	-	-
Nenang Pawo Rinpoche Monastery	673	-	-
Ngor Monastery	500	-	-
Nyingma Students Welfare Committee, Varanasi	6,412	11,044	271

Ceremonies and Offerings of Books and Thankas (TAP and TNMC) 1969–1996

Tibetan Center	Ceremonies	Thankas to '91*	Books*
Nyingmapa Buddhist Monastery, Rewalsar	$11,825	$8,278	$167
Nyingmapa Mahabuddha Vihara, Dehra Dun	19,181	13,362	329
Orgyen Heru-Kai Phodrang, Rewalsar	1,000	-	-
Padmasambhava Caves, Lama Wangdor	3,536	3,989	-
Phuntso Nya Yab Choling	1,000	-	-
Sakya Monastery Dehra Dun	4,875	3,383	-
Sakya College	1,000	-	-
Sakya Students Union	877	4,358	50
Samten Dechen Choling	300	-	-
Sera Mahayana Monastic and Philosophy University	9,496	18,367	200
Tharpaling Shedra	500	-	-
Shelkar Chosde Gaden Legshad Ling	678	-	-
Tashi Jong	1,000	-	-
Theckling Monastery	752	5,970	-
Ugyen Wangdi, Monastery project	250	-	-
Zangdok Palri Monastery	4,438	5,174	50
Nepal Monasteries: Stupas & Prayer Flags	6,609	-	-
Total All Other Monasteries, All Four Major Schools,	167,168	124,802	-
Totals*	**$606,156**	**$571,590**	**$8,149**

*Totals do not include TNMC donations of the *Nyingma Edition of the Tibetan Buddhist Canon* or offerings, support, and book and thanka distribution at the World Peace Ceremonies.

TAP/TNMC Ceremony Support 1993–2004

Nyingma

Venerable Khocchen Tulku
Nyingmapa Mahabuddha Vihara, Clement Town, India

9/8/94	Ceremonies	$500
7/1/95	Ceremonies	500
4/23/96	Vajrakīla Sadhana	1,000
11/12/96	Tsog Puja	3,715
4/5/97	Lama, Yidam, and Dakini Tsog-bum	3,000
4/24/99	Ceremonies	1,500
2003	Hundred Million Vajra Guru Mantras	12,000

Ven. Mindrolling Trichen
Nyingmapa Mahabuddha Vihara, Clement Town, India

4/4/98	Amitayus Long Life	$300

Ven. Lama Tenzin Namgyal
Nyingma Buddhist Monastery, Rewalsar, India

9/8/94	Ceremonies	$500
7/1/95	Ceremonies	500
4/22/96	Vajrakila Sadhana	1,000
4/5/97	Vajrakila Prayers, Guru Rinpoche Sadhanas, Tara Prayers	3,000
4/24/99	Ceremonies	1,500
2/11/03	Dorje Phurba ceremonies	1,000

Ven. Rigo Tulku, Nyingmapa Monastery, Bir, India

9/8/94	Ceremonies	$500
7/1/95	Ceremonies	500
4/22/96	Vajrakila Sadhana	1,000
11/12/96	Tsog-bum: Lama, Yidam, and Dakini	3,715
4/5/97	Vajrakila Sadhanas	3,000
4/24/99	Ceremonies	1,500

Ven. Rabjam Rinpoche
Zhechen Monastery, Kathmandu, Nepal

9/8/94	Ceremonies	$500

VEN. ROZAR GYATSO

11/18/93	bKa'-'gyur Rinpoche Reading	$5,000

VEN. SHATRAL RINPOCHE
RIGZIN DRUBJE GHATSAL MONASTERY, PHARPING, NEPAL

9/8/94	Ceremonies	$500
7/1/95	Ceremonies	500
4/23/96	Tsog, Vajrakila Mantras, Sampa Lhundrup, Barchad Lamsel	5,000
4/23/96	Barchad Lamsel, Sampa Lhundrup, Vajrakila, and Tara	1,000
9/16/96	Tarthang Tulku Longevity Ceremony, Amitayus Prayers	500
4/5/97	Lama, Yidam, and Dakini (10th, 25th), Tara Prayers	6,500
1/4/99	Ceremonies	4,000
3/1/00	Long Life Prayers	2,380
2001	Fish-saving ceremony (in conjunction with TNMC)	4,000

VEN. TAKLUNG TSETRUL, THUPTEN DORJE DRAK EWAM CHOKGAR NYINGMA MONASTERY, KASUMPTI, INDIA

7/1/95	Ceremonies	$500
4/23/96	Vajrakila Sadhana, Guru Rinpoche Tsog	500
9/16/96	Tarthang Tulku Longevity Ceremony, Amitayus Prayers	500
11/12/96	Tsog-bum: Lama, Yidam, and Dakini	3,715
4/5/97	Phurba Tsog or Vajrakila	3,000
4/24/99	Ceremonies	1,500
7/25/00	Hundred Million Vajra Guru Mantras	12,000
2005	100,000 Tara and 100,000 Tsok Offerings	(est) 1,000

VEN. TRULSHIG DEZHAK RINPOCHE, KATHMANDU, NEPAL

4/23/96	Vajrakila Mantras, 100,000 Taras, Sampa Lhundrup	$1,000
9/16/96	Tarthang Tulku Longevity Ceremony, Amitayus Prayers	500
4/5/97	Vajrakila Prayers	3,000
6/23/98	Hundred Million Vajra Guru Mantras	11,700
7/29/98	Vajrakila Sadhana or Guru Rinpoche Tsog-bum	1,500

2001	Hundred Million Vajra Guru Mantras	12,000
2/11/2003	Ceremonies at Maratika Caves	500
2003	Hundred Million Vajra Guru Mantras	12,000
2004	Hundred Million Vajra Guru Mantras	12,000
2005	100,000 Tara and 100,000 Tsok offerings	(est) 1,000

Ven. Khenpo Thupten Mewa, Ngagyur Samten Chokhorling Institute, Manali, India

9/8/94	Ceremonies	$500
7/1/95	Ceremonies	500
4/22/96	Vajrakila Sadhana	1,000
9/16/96	Tarthang Tulku Longevity Ceremony, Amitayus Prayers	500
11/12/96	Lama, Yidam, and Dakini Tsog-bum	3,715
4/5/97	Lama, Yidam, and Dakini Tsog-bum	3,000
1/6/99	Hundred Million Vajra Guru Mantras	9,000
2/11/2003	Guru Rinpoche Pujas	1,000

Ven. Khenpo Rigzin Dorje

9/8/94	Ceremonies	$500
4/23/96	Vajrakila Sadhana, Tara Prayers, Barchad Lamsel	3,000

Ven. Urgyen Topgyal Rinpoche, Gyurmeling Monastery, Bir, India

7/1/95	Ceremonies	$500
4/22/96	Vajrakila Sadhana	1,000
9/16/96	Tarthang Tulku Longevity Ceremony, Amitayus Prayers	500
11/12/96	Tsog-bum: Lama, Yidam, and Dakini Tsog-bum	3,715
4/5/97	Lama Yidam and Dakini Tsok Bum	3,000
4/24/99	Ceremonies	1,500

Ven. Urgyen Tulku Rinpoche

8/19/95	Offering at Padma Ling	$500

Total Nyingma Donations 1993–2005* (to date) $181,155

KAGYU

Ven. Chokyi Nyima Rinpoche Ka-Nying Shedrup Ling, Kathmandu, Nepal

9/8/94	Ka-Nying: Ceremonies	$500
1/13/95	Nagi Gompa: prayers	490
5/12/95	Three Long Life Ceremonies for Tarthang Tulku	4,200
6/24/95	Additional Long Life Ceremony for Tarthang Tulku	715
8/19/95	Personal offering at Padma Ling	800
8/23/95	General support for monks	2,690
4/22/96	Ceremonies	6,300
4/23/96	Nagi Gompa: Tara Prayers	600
10/28/96	Kagyu/Sakya Monlams: Tsog-bum, 1997 Lumbini	6,450
4/5/97	Pharping: one year of biweekly pujas	6,000
4/5/97	Lama, Yidam, and Dakini Tsog-bum	3,000
4/5/97	Nagi Gompa: Tara Prayers	600
6/12/97	Kagyu/Sakya Monlams, January 1998, Lumbini	10,000
12/12/97	Kagyu/Sakya Monlams, January 1998, Lumbini	10,000
4/13/98	Three-year offering for Daily Tea	24,700
4/22/98	Nagi Gompa: 100,000 Tara Prayers	1,000
5/18/98	Pharping: 10th, 15th, 25th, 30th Tsog	4,500
7/29/98	Kagyu Monlam at Lumbini	10,000
9/4/98	Offerings at Nyingma Institute, Berkeley	525
2/22/00	Special ceremony for a lama's death	500
10/11/00	Kagyu Monlam at Lumbini	6,000
10/23/00	Nagi Gompa: Tara Prayers	1,000
2001	Kagyu Monlam at Lumbini	3,000
2002	Kagyu Monlam	3,000

Ven. Drikung Kyabgon, Phiyang Gonpa, Ladakh, India and Jang Chubling, Dehra Dun, India

4/16/97	Tara Prayers or Tsog-chod	$1,000
4/4/98	bKa'-'gyur Readings, Heart Sutra, Tara Prayers	1,000

Ven. Khamtrul Rinpoche Khampagar Monastery, Tashi Jong, India

4/22/96	Tara Prayers and Sampa Lhundup	$500

4/5/97	Lama, Yidam, and Dakini Tsog-bum	3,000
4/4/98	Guru Rinpoche Tsog-bum	3,000

TOTAL KAGYU DONATIONS 1993–2005 (TO DATE) $114,570

SAKYA

VEN. CHOGYE TRICHEN, JAMCHEN LHAKHANG, KATHMANDU, NEPAL

10/11/94	Ceremonies	$500
4/16/97	Tara Prayers	1,000
4/22/98	bKa'-'gyur Reading,Tara, and Sherab Nyingpo	250
2001	Sakya Monlam	3,000
2001	Hundred Million Vajra Guru Mantras (in conjunction with TNMC)	12,000

VEN. DZONGSAR GONGNA RINPOCHE

4/23/96	Prayers	$300

DZONGSAR INSTITUTE, BIR, INDIA

9/8/94	Ceremonies	500
7/1/95	Ceremonies	500
8/31/95	Ceremonies	500
4/23/96	Tara Prayers and Sampa Lhundrup	500
4/5/97	Tsog-chod	1,000
4/4/98	bKa'-'gyur Reading,Tsog-bum w/Tara, Vajrakila, Guru	1,750
4/24/99	Ceremonies	1,000

NGOR MONASTERY, MANDUWALA, INDIA

4/23/96	Tara Prayers and Sampa Lhundrup	$500
4/ 5/97	bKa'-'gyur Reading	1,000
5/13/98	Tara, bKa'-'gyur Reading, Heart Sutra	250
4/24/99	Ceremonies	1,000

SAKYA LAMAS COLLEGE, RAJPUR, INDIA

9/8/94	Ceremonies	$500
7/1/95	Ceremonies	500

4/23/96	Vajrakila Sadhana	1,000
4/5/97	Chod	1,000
4/22/98	Vajrakila Sadhana	250
4/24/99	Ceremonies	1,000

SAKYA MONASTERY

4/23/96	Vajrakila Sadhana	$1,000

VEN. SAKYA TRIZIN, SAKYA DOLMA PHODRANG, RAJPUR, INDIA

4/5/97	Vajrakilaya Tsog Pujas	$3,000
4/4/98	Vajrakila Sadhana	2,250
5/18/98	Sakya Monlams: Lumbini, 1999	10,000
4/24/99	Ceremonies	1,000
1/10/00	Sakya Monlams	5,000
2001	Sakya Monlam	3,000
2001	Hundred Million Vajra Guru Mantras	12,000
2002	Hundred Million Vajra Guru Mantras	12,000
2002	Sakya Monlam	3,000
11/07/03	Sakya Monlam	3,000
12/24/04	Sakya Monlam	3,000
1/2005	Vajrakila sadhana, 3 days	3,000

VEN. THARIG TULKU (DECEASED)
SAKYA THARIG MONASTERY, KATHMANDU, NEPAL

4/23/96	Stupa	$10,000
4/2/97	Stupa	10,000
6/3/98	Offerings for commemoration of Tharig Tulku's passing	108

TOTAL SAKYA DONATIONS 1993–2005 (TO DATE) $111,158

GELUG

DREPUNG MONASTERY, MUNDGOD, INDIA

11/5/93	Ceremonies	$500
9/8/94	Ceremonies	500
7/1/95	Ceremonies	500
1/2/96	Tara/Sitatapatra Ceremonies	700
11/12/96	bKa'-'gyur/bsTan-'gyur Readings, White Tara, Heart Sutra, Sitatapatra	1,000
3/25/97	bKa'-'gyur Readings	1,000
4/4/98	bKa'-'gyur Reading, White Tara, Heart Sutra	1,000
4/24/99	bKa'-'gyur Readings	1,000
6/23/99	Special ceremony	6,000
4/10/00	bKa'-'gyur Readings	1,000
2001	Ceremonies	1,000
2002	Ceremonies	1,000
3/12/03	rGyal-wa bKa'-'gyur Rinpoche readings	1,000
3/12/04	rGyal-wa bKa'-'gyur Rinpoche readings	1,000

GADEN MAHAYANA UNIVERSITY, MUNDGOD, INDIA

11/5/93	Ceremonies	$500
9/8/94	Ceremonies	500
7/1/95	Ceremonies	500
1/2/96	Tara/Sitatapatra Ceremonies	700
11/12/96	bKa'-'gyur/bsTan-'gyur Reading, White Tara, Heart Sutra, Sitatapatra	1,000
3/25/97	bKa'-'gyur Readings	1,000
4/4/98	bKa'-'gyur Reading, White Tara, Heart Sutra	1,000
4/24/99	bKa'-'gyur Readings	1,000
4/10/00	bKa'-'gyur Readings	1,000
2001	Ceremonies	1,000
2002	Ceremonies	1,000
3/12/03	rGyal-wa bKa'-'gyur Rinpoche readings	1,000
3/12/04	rGyal-wa bKa'-'gyur Rinpoche readings	1,000

Gyudmed Tantric University, Gurupura, India

11/5/93	Ceremonies	$500
9/8/94	Ceremonies	500
7/1/95	Ceremonies	500
1/2/96	Tara/Sitatapatra Ceremonies	700
11/12/96	bKa'-'gyur Reading	1,000
3/25/97	bKa'-'gyur Readings	1,000
4/4/98	bKa'-'gyur Reading, White Tara, Heart Sutra	1,000
4/24/99	bKa'-'gyur Readings	1,000
6/23/99	Special Ceremony	6,000
4/10/00	bKa'-'gyur Readings	1,000
2001	Ceremonies	1,000
2002	Ceremonies	1,000
3/12/03	rGyal-wa bKa'-'gyur Rinpoche readings	1,000
3/12/04	rGyal-wa bKa'-'gyur Rinpoche readings	1,000

Gyuto Tantric University, Bomdila, India

11/5/93	Ceremonies	$500
9/8/94	Ceremonies	500
7/1/95	Ceremonies	500
1/2/96	Tara/Sitatapatra Ceremonies	700
11/12/96	bKa'-'gyur/bsTan-'gyur Reading, White Tara, Heart Sutra, Sitatapatra	1,000
3/25/97	bKa'-'gyur Reading	1,000
4/4/98	bKa'-'gyur Reading, Dugkar, Tara, Heart Sutra	1,000
4/24/99	bKa'-'gyur Readings	1,000
6/23/99	Special Ceremony	5,000
4/10/00	bKa'-'gyur Readings	1,000
2001	Ceremonies	1,000
2002	Ceremonies	1,000
3/12/03	rGyal-wa bKa'-'gyur Rinpoche readings	1,000
3/12/04	rGyal-wa bKa'-'gyur Rinpoche readings	1,000

Sera Mahayana Monastic University, Bylakuppe, India

11/5/93	Ceremonies	$500
9/8/94	Ceremonies	500
7/1/95	Ceremonies	500
1/2/96	Tara/Sitatapatra Ceremonies	700

11/12/96	bKa'-'gyur/bsTan-'gyur Reading, White Tara, Heart Sutra, Sitatapatra	1,000
3/25/97	Sungbum Puja	1,000
4/4/98	bKa'-'gyur Reading, White Tara, Heart Sutra	1,000
4/24/99	bKa'-'gyur Readings	1,000
4/10/00	bKa'-'gyur Readings	1,000
2001	Ceremonies	1,000
2002	Ceremonies	1,000
3/12/03	rGyal-wa bKa'-'gyur Rinpoche readings	1,000
2004	rGyal-wa bKa'-'gyur Rinpoche readings	1,000

TOTAL GELUGPA DONATIONS 1993–2005 (TO DATE) $73,000

BHUTAN

BUMTHANG THARPALING TEMPLE

11/5/93	Ceremonies	$500
9/6/96	Lama Mipham and Longchenpa Anniversary	500
11/18/96	Lama, Yidam, and Dakini Tsog-bum	3,000

JAMPA LHAKHANG

11/18/96	Tsog-bum: Lama, Yidam, and Dakini	$3,000
4/4/98	10th, 15th, 25th, 30th Tara, Vajrakila, Guru Rinpoche Tsog	500

KURJE LHAKHANG

11/18/96	Tsog-bum: Lama, Yidam, and Dakini	$3,000
4/4/98	10th, 15th, 25th, 30th Tara, Vajrakila, Guru Rinpoche Tsog	500
4/13/00	Tsog-bum Ceremonies	1,000

KYERCHU MONASTERY

4/13/00	Tsog-bum Ceremonies	$1,000

VEN. NAMKHAI NYINGPO LHODRAK KHARCHU MONASTERY

6/6/98	Padmasambhava Pujas	$2,500

Nyima Lung Monastery

11/18/96	Tsog-bum: Lama, Yidam, and Dakini	$3,000
4/4/98	10th, 15th, 25th, 30th Tara, Vajrakila, Guru Rinpoche Tsog	500

Paro Monastery

11/18/96	Tsog-bum: Lama, Yidam, and Dakini	$3,000
4/ 4/98	10th, 15th, 25th, 30th Tara, Vajrakila, Guru Rinpoche Tsog	500

Pema Shedrup Choling

6/28/95	Ceremonies	$500

Queen Mother Kesung Choden Wangchuk, Thimphu

10/29/97	Ceremonies at Bhutanese Centers	$5,000
4/4/98	Prayers in the seven holy places of Longchenpa, with torma and tsog	2,500

Senge Dzong Monastery

11/18/96	Lama, Yidam, and Dakini Tsog-bum	$3,000
4/4/98	10th, 15th, 25th, 30th Tara, Vajrakila, Guru Rinpoche Tsog	500
4/13/00	Tsog-bum Ceremonies	1,000

Taksang Monastery

4/13/00	Tsog-bum Ceremonies	$1,000

Total Donations to Bhutan Monasteries 1993–2000 $36,000

BODH GAYA WORLD PEACE CEREMONY EXPENSES*

1989/90	Total Ceremony Expenses	135,593
1991	Total Ceremony Expenses	76,805
1992	Total Ceremony Expenses	146,515
1993	Total Ceremony Expenses	169,603
1994	Total Ceremony Expenses	90,316
1995	Total Ceremony Expenses	115,698
1996	Total Ceremony Expenses	233,920
1997	Total Ceremony Expenses	108,812
1998	Total Ceremony Expenses	94,584

*Funded by TNMC/Bodh Gaya Trust. Does not include cost of book production, shipping, or distribution.

1999	Total Ceremony Expenses	106,461
2000	Total Ceremony Expenses	113,116
2001	Total Ceremony Expenses	103,893
2002	Total Ceremony Expenses	149,372
2003	Total Ceremony Expenses	106,272
2004	Total Ceremony Expenses	111,556
2005	Total Ceremony Expenses	163,157
TOTAL 1989–2005		$2,025,673
TOTAL Longchen Varna Expenses 1995–2005		$423,265

SPECIAL CEREMONIES

Ven. Duddul Rabten Ling Nyingmapa Monastery, Mahandragada, India

4/23/96	Tara and Barchad Lamsel	$500
4/5/97	Lama, Yidam, and Dakini Tsog-bum	600
4/4/98	Vajrakila Tsog-bum	300

Ven. Taklung Nyima Zangpo Ogyan Kunzang Chokhorling Monastery, Darjeeling, India

9/30/95	Ceremonies	$500
4/5/97	Lama, Yidam, and Dakini Tsog-bum	500
4/4/98	Tsog-bum	500

Phuntso Nya Yab Choling Monastery

4/23/96	Vajrakila Sadhana	$1,000
4/4/98	Guru Rinpoche or Tsog-bum	500

Samten Decchen Choling Monastery

9/16/96	Ceremonies	$300

Sang-Ngak Chokhorling Mundgod, India

4/5/97	Tara Prayers and Lama, Yidam, and Dakini Tsog-bum	$600
4/4/98	Tara Prayers and Lama Yidam, and Dakini Tsog-bum	600

Ven. Zangdok Palri, Nyima Dra-Tsang, Darjeeling, India

7/1/95	Ceremonies	$500
4/5/97	Lama, Yidam, and Dakini Tsog-bum	1,500

Baldan Baraivan Monastery, Mongolia

2001	Ceremony	100

Ngagyur Dupgyud Choephel Ling

2001	Ceremony	300

Lhasa Tsog-Jowo

2001	Ceremony	300

Longchenpa Ceremony (Longchen Varna), Sarnath, India

1/1/99	Monlam Ceremony	$15,000

Special/Other Donations 1993-2005 $23,600

TAP DISTRIBUTION OF SACRED TEXTS, THANKAS, & PRAYER WHEELS

1994	Shipping and distribution expenses	$49,337
1995	Shipping and distribution expenses	24,293
1996	Shipping and distribution expenses	28,242
1997	Shipping and distribution expenses	78,563
1998	Shipping and distribution expenses	98,737
1999	Shipping and distribution expenses	118,280
2000	Shipping and distribution expenses	78,240
2001	Shipping and distribution expenses	90,320
2002	Production, shipping, and distribution expenses	159,219
2003	Production, shipping, and distribution expenses	309,492
2004	Production, shipping, and distribution expenses	326,179
2005	Production, shipping, and distribution expenses	281,736

Distribution of Ceremony Offerings to the Four Schools and Monasteries in Bhutan

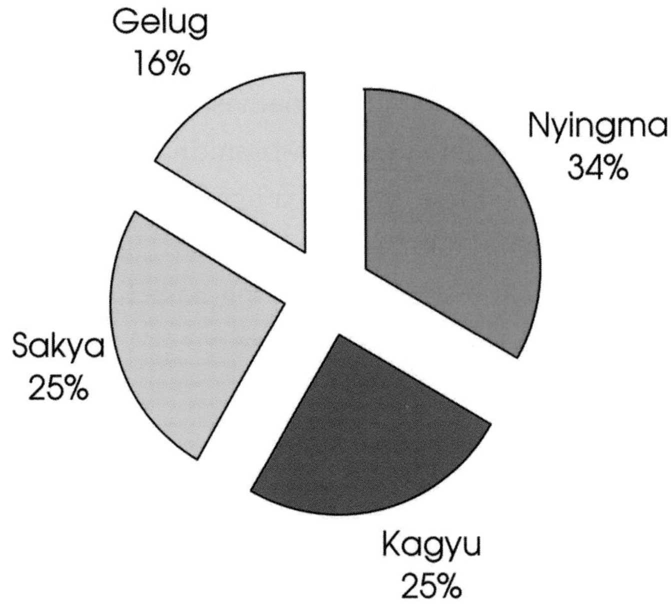

Distribution of World Peace Ceremony Offerings

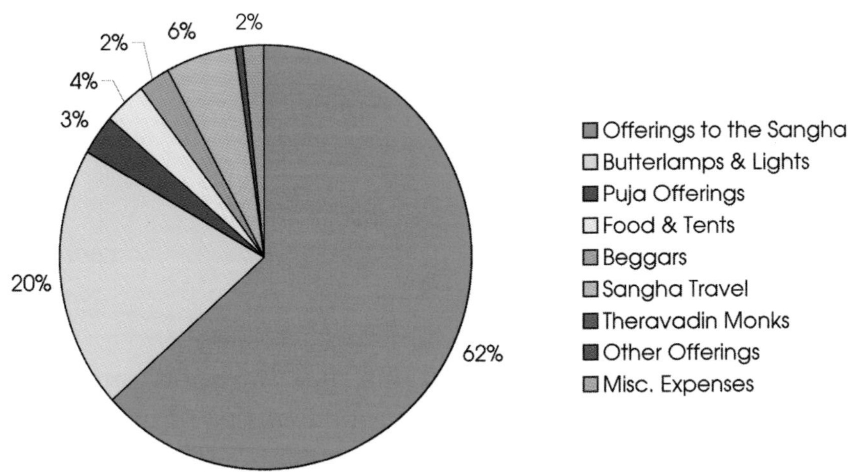

TNMC Dharma World Peace Bells

Texts Cast in Relief on Each Bell

Refuge Prayers
Bodhicitta Prayers
Arya-manjushri-namasamgiti
Samantabhadracarya-pranidhanaraja
bsTan-pa'i-rgyas-pa'i-smon-lam
Prajnaparamita-hridaya (Heart) Sutra
Byang-chub-sems-dpa'i-ltung-ba-bshags-pa
Las-sgrib-rgyu-gcod-gzungs-sngags-brgya-pa
bKra-shis

Locations

1. Vajra Temple Dharma Bell, installed Odiyan, Summer, 1999
2. Bodh Gaya Peace Bell and Arch, installed Bodh Gaya, 12/2002*
3. Cintamani Peace Bell and Arch, installed Odiyan, 12/2004
4. Sarnath Peace Bell and Arch, installed Sarnath 3/2005
5. Lumbini Peace Bell and Arch, installed Lumbini 5/2005
6. Kushinagara Peace Bell and Arch, installed Kushinagara 5/2005
7. World Peace Bell, Kathmandu, 1/2006
8. World Peace Bell, Tibet, 2006

Size: 5′ (150 cm) diameter, 5′ (150 cm) high

Average weight, bells	2.3 tons
Average weight, arches	1.2 tons
Material, bells and arch	cast bronze
Average cost, each bell and arch	$100,000*

*Cost includes international and internal transport, and marble platforms and installation charges for bells installed in India. Land for the bells was donated by the governments of India and Nepal. Cost of the original bell (Bodh Gaya): $152,916; installation and Bell House: $20,393.

Tibet Pilgrimage 2005
Monastery Support**

Offered by TNMC

Dorje Drag, for four statues	$7,000*
Mindroling, for three statues: Orgyen Terdag Lingpa, Lochen Dharma Shri, Sangdak Thinley Lhundrup	$7,000*
Dorje Drag, for Rigzin Chenpo:	$1,000
Shugseb Ani Gompa, funds pledged earlier to sponsor nuns on retreat	about $5,000
Total offered by TNMC	20,000*

*Estimate, depending on actual costs

Offered by Individuals

Samye	$10,000	Wenza Nunnery (Anigonpa Chimpu)	200
Dorje Drag	6,000	Tsongtsen Gonpo's Tomb	100
Mindroling	6,000	Chimpu Temple	97
Tarthang Monastery	5,000	Gangri Tokar	97
Tsering Jong Nunnery	3,000	Tandruk	97
Chimpu Retreatants	1,815	Yumbalagang	97
Yeshe Tsultrim	1,500	Jokhang: gold paint	56
Chimphu Food	1,317	Dorje Drag – Attendant	48
Shugseb Nunnery	1,000	Chimpu Practitioners	42
Misc. Administrative	779	Hepo Ri	30
Tent	707	Amount Later Returned to Berkeley	835
Yamalung	585		
Sheldrak	500		
Drakmar	439		
Drag Yongdzong	353		
Tsogyal Lhatso	300	TOTAL OFFERED BY INDIVIDUALS	$41,200
Ani Gonpa	200		

**Leaders: Richard Dixey, Pema Gellek, Sandy Olney
Participants: Irene Byrne, Robin and Curtis Caton, Nelson Chamma, Magda Costa, Kathleen Daly, Guusje Ebbens, Barbara Gortikov, Nancy Martin, Thomas and Lenore Mead, Victoria Riskin, Linda Welner, Kristine Winber

Yeshe De Book Production at Dharmcakra Press

Dharmacakra Press prepares the Tibetan-style loose-leaf pothi volumes. 1. Typesetting 2. Plating 3. Printing Sutras and shastras on the Heidelberg Presses 4. Printing mantras for prayer wheels on the 65" Harris press, manufactured in 1936.

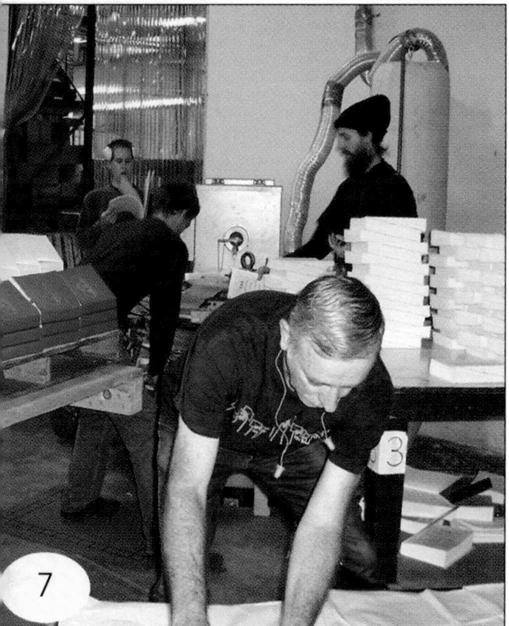

Yeshe De Book Production at Dharma Mangalam Press

Dharma Mangalam Press prints, folds, collates, and binds the gold-stamped soft-cover editions of Sutras and shastras. 5. Collating 6. Book Assembly, Warehouse 7. Perfect Binding 8. Gold Stamping Covers.

The Tibetan Aid Project (TAP) is a 100% volunteer organization. Three full-time staff and a board of eight directors work without salary to extend the benefits of donors' contributions. The support of dedicated volunteers, low overhead costs, and collaborative working relationships with other non-profit organizations enable TAP to make the most out of every dollar received.

TAP is a 501c(3) organization registered under the name Tibetan Nyingma Relief Foundation, federal tax identification number 23-7433901. Contributions are tax deductible. TAP's financial records are carefully maintained and reviewed annually by a Certified Public Accountant. Reports on TAP's activities and financial disbursements are published in each issue of *Gesar Magazine* and included in each edition of the *Annals of the Nyingma Lineage in America*.

Tibetan Aid Project
2910 San Pablo Avenue
Berkeley, CA 94702, USA
800-33-Tibet 510-848-4238
tap@tibetanaidproject.org www.tibetanaidproject.org

Tibetan Aid Project
Instituto do Nyingma Rio
Rua Casuarina 297, Casa 2
Rio de Janeiro RJ
CEP 22261-160, Brazil
Phone: 21-527-9388
nyingma@barralink.com.br

Tibetan Aid Project
Nyingma Zentrum Deutschland
Siebachstrasse 66
Köln
Germany
Phone: 49-221-589-0474
info@nyingmazentrum.de

Tibetan Aid Project
Instituto Nyingma Brasil
Rua Cayowaa 2085, Sumare
CEP 01258-011
Sao Paulo
Brazil
Phone: 11-3864-4785

Tibetan Aid Project
Nyingma Centrum Nederland
Reguliersgracht 25
1017 LJ Amsterdam
The Netherlands
Phone: 20-620-5207
nyingmacentrum@nyingma.nl

HOW TO HELP TAP's active network of supporters extends throughout the United States and abroad. However you choose to help, your caring and participation are deeply appreciated.

DONATIONS by mail, phone, or online are put directly to work. Always refining its focus to meet the most urgent needs, TAP maximizes the value of each contribution. You may donate funds, stocks, or goods, or consider including TAP in your estate planning. The Tibetan Aid Project is a tax-exempt, 501c(3) organization. All contributions are deductible.

Suggested donation levels:

Donor: $50 Supporter: $108 Sponsor: $500 Patron: $1,500

PLANNED GIVING The work of the Tibetan Aid Project builds for the future, maintaining a tradition that can bring benefits for generations to come. You can help by participating in TAP's planned gift program:

- A gift to TAP in your will or trust
- Designate TAP as the beneficiary of a life insurance policy

TAP has consultants available to talk with you and help clarify your planned giving goals. Contact TAP for information.

TELL YOUR FRIENDS In your own area, tell friends, family members, local foundations, universities, and businesses about TAP or have us contact them for you.

VOLUNTEERS mean everything to TAP, for that is who we are. Volunteers and work/study participants are always welcome to come and join us—for a week, a month, six months or longer. For volunteers making a six-month commitment, we provide room, board, and classes on Tibetan Buddhist themes as well as the opportunity to do meaningful work in a special environment.

web and graphic design
event planners
bookkeeping and accounting
office workers
technical consultants
prayer flag sewers

Sign up for:
e-mail newsletter
TAP's mailing list

tap@tibetanaidproject.org
www.tibetanaidproject.org

Further Reading

Books from Dharma Publishing

Ancient Tibet (1986)

From the Roof of the World: Refugees of Tibet (1992)

Holy Places of the Buddha (1994)

Your Friends, the Tibetan Refugees (2001)

Additional Sources

Adhe, Ama. *The Voice that Remembers*. Boston: Wisdom Publications, 1997

Bureau of H.H. the Dalai Lama. *Tibetans in Exile 1959–1969: A Report on Ten Years of Rehabilitation in India*. Dharamasala, 1969.

Dalai Lama, *My Land and My People*. New York: McGraw Hill, 1962.

Grunfeld, A. Tom. *The Making of Modern Tibet*. New York: M.E. Sharpe, 1987.

Karan, Pradyumna. *The Changing Face of Tibet: The Impact of Chinese Communist Ideology on the Landscape*. Lexington, KY: Univ. Press of Kentucky, 1976.

Richardson, Hugh. *Tibet and its History*. London: Oxford Univ. Press, 1962.

Shakya, Tsering. *The Dragon in the Land of Snows: A History of Modern Tibet since 1947*. New York: Penguin Compass, 2000.

Stein, R.A. *Tibetan Civilization*. Stanford, CA: Stanford Univ. Press, 1972.

von Fürer-Haimendorf, Christopher. *The Renaissance of Tibetan Civilization*. Oracle, AZ: Synergetic Press, 1990.

More information on the activities of the Tibetan Aid Project can be found in *Gesar Magazine* and in the five volumes of the *Annals of the Nyingma Lineage in America*. More information on the World Peace Ceremonies and on the traditions of the schools of Tibetan Buddhism is available in the *World Peace Ceremony Series* and the *Crystal Mirror Series*, both from Dharma Publishing.

Gifts Available from the Tibetan Aid Project

www.tibetanaidproject.org

Prayer Flags, large	$108.00
Prayer Flags, small, 10″x12″, set of 15 flags	$23.00
Greeting Cards, Blank, and Losar Cards	$9.50–12.50
Electric Prayer Wheel	$679.00
Handheld Prayer Wheel	$250.00
Malas, Aventurine, Rose Quartz, Carnelian, more	$42–52.00
Book Bags: red/dragon; red/medallion; green/floral	$15.00
Meditation cushions (zafu), red or royal blue	$35.00
Designer T-Shirts with auspicious emblems, short sleeve	$19.95
Designer T-Shirts with auspicious emblems, long sleeve	$24.95
Cashmere scarves, 12″x60″	$85.00
Singing bowls	$64.00
Offering bowls	$32.00
Door Mantra, Avalokiteshvara or Padmasambhava	$9.95

CDs Recent offerings include:

Salva	$16.95
Music as Medicine	$15.95
Seven Metals	$15.95
Rain of Blessings	$15.95
Vajra Chants	$15.95
The Lama's Chants	$17.95
Quiet Mind	$16.95
Musical Journey of a Tibetan Nomad	$16.95

Books

Ancient Tibet	$16.95
From the Roof of the World	$24.95
Your Friends the Tibetan Refugees	$24.95
Gesture of Balance	$14.95
Living Without Regret	$16.95
Tibetan Relaxation	$24.95

Children's Books

Value of Friends	$7.95
Magic of Patience	$7.95
Monster of Lotus Lake	$7.95
Rabbit Who Overcame Fear	$7.95
Jatakas on Audiotape	$6.95